D0071302

Practical IDL Programming

*Creating Effective Data Analysis and
Visualization Applications*

Practical IDL Programming

Creating Effective Data Analysis and Visualization Applications

LIAM E. GUMLEY

Space Science and Engineering Center
University of Wisconsin-Madison

MORGAN KAUFMANN PUBLISHERS

An Imprint of Elsevier

Amsterdam Boston Heidelberg London New York Oxford
Paris San Diego San Francisco Singapore Sydney Tokyo

Senior Editor	Denise E.M. Penrose
Publishing Services Manager	Scott Norton
Assistant Publishing Services Manager	Edward Wade
Associate Production Editor	Marnie Boyd
Editorial Coordinator	Emilia Thiuri
Cover Design	Ross Carron Design
Text Design	Side by Side Studios/Mark Ong
Composition	Side by Side Studios/Susan Riley
Technical Illustration	Side by Side Studios/Susan Riley, Mark Ong
Copyeditor	Ken DellaPenta
Proofreader	Carol Leyba
Indexer	Ty Koontz
Printer	Courier Corporation

Cover credits: René Magritte, *The Human Condition II*, 1935, Private Collection, Photograph Supplied by SuperStock, Inc. © 2001 C. Herscovici, Brussels / Artists Rights Society (ARS), New York

Designations used by companies to distinguish their products are often claimed as trademarks or registered trademarks. In all instances in which Morgan Kaufmann Publishers is aware of a claim, the product names appear in initial capital or all capital letters. Readers, however, should contact the appropriate companies for more complete information regarding trademarks and registration.

Morgan Kaufmann Publishers
An Imprint of Elsevier
340 Pine Street, Sixth Floor, San Francisco, CA 94104-3205, USA
http://www.mkp.com

ACADEMIC PRESS
An Imprint of Elsevier
525 B Street, Suite 1900, San Diego, CA 92101-4495, USA
http://www.academicpress.com

Academic Press
Harcourt Place, 32 Jamestown Road, London, NW1 7BY, United Kingdom
http://www.academicpress.com

© 2002 by Academic Press
All rights reserved
Printed in the United States of America

   09 10 11   9 8 7

No part of this publication may be reproduced, stored in a retrieval system, or transmitted in any form or by any means—electronic, mechanical, photocopying, or otherwise—without the prior written permission of the publisher.

Permissions may be sought directly from Elsevier's Science and Technology Rights Department in Oxford, UK. Phone: (44) 1865 843830, Fax: (44) 1865 853333, e-mail: permissions@elsevier.co.uk. You may also complete your request on-line via the Elsevier homepage: http://www.elsevier.com by selecting "Customer Support" and then "Obtaining Permissions"

Library of Congress Control Number: 2001090637
ISBN-13: 978-1-55860-700-2

ISBN-10: 1-55860-700-5

This book is printed on acid-free paper.

Foreword

David Stern
Founder, Research Systems, Incorporated

My goal in writing IDL has been to create a tool for scientists and engineers that could be used both for ad hoc data analysis and as a programming language for building technical applications. IDL is a specialized fourth-generation language providing a framework that includes functions and components for scientific computing and visualization. It is the ability to quickly and easily investigate data; to rapidly apply various fits, filters, and transformations; and to then immediately see the results that sets IDL users apart from those who run Fortran or C programs. Unlike C, Fortran, or even Java, IDL is an interactive tool that can be programmed or scripted.

I still enjoy using IDL for exploring new data sets and answering new questions. This is a fun and intellectually challenging trial-and-error process, somewhat akin to solving a mystery, which usually concludes with an answer. Once the researcher obtains the answer and learns how to analyze and visualize a given type of data using ad hoc methods, the next step is to automate the process, and then to perhaps embed it in a graphical user interface so that others may benefit from its use.

Many IDL users are comfortable with ad hoc analysis and display but have not yet mastered the language features or skills necessary to build more complex programs or applications, in particular those driven by GUIs. This is not a particularly straightforward process, and this book does a great job in aiding this transition.

Practical IDL Programming begins with a concise presentation of the basics of IDL, its syntax, and data and control structures. It then explains how to access data of various types in files, including the complicated and poorly understood netCDF and HDF formats. Four chapters are devoted to creating graphics, charts, and displaying images, on the screen, the printer, and for publication. The final chapter describes how to build an application with a graphical user interface for a wider range of users.

Liam Gumley is eminently qualified to write a book on IDL. He has been a long-time user of IDL and has created a number of impressive applications used by many scientists. Professionally, he writes software applications for the Cooperative Institute for Meteorological Satellite Studies (CIMSS), at the University of Wisconsin. He posts frequently to the always-active IDL newsgroup, `comp.lang.idl-pvwave`, and is a respected voice there.

Liam distills what he feels is important for an IDL programmer to know, rather than simply presenting a complete reference without editorial comments. In IDL, as in any reasonably complete package, there are usually 10 ways to perform any task. For any particular problem, one method will be the best, and one will be the worst, with the remainder falling somewhere in between. Liam's goal is to impart an understanding of IDL's operation to the reader, so that he or she can select the best method for the problem at hand.

The IDL beginner will welcome this book because, while it starts with the basics, it is nonetheless a comprehensive treatment of the language. There are a multitude of examples, plus code for designing a GUI-based application for interactively viewing images. The experienced user will find the book valuable for its reference sections and discussions on the proper way to program in IDL, which unfortunately is not always obvious.

On behalf of Research Systems Incorporated and the community of IDL users and programmers, I would like to thank Liam Gumley for writing this valuable and long overdue book. *Practical IDL Programming* serves as a useful tutorial, source of examples, and reference for those wishing to learn or to master IDL. It gives me great pleasure to recommend this book to you.

Acknowledgments

This book arose from a desire to share the lessons I have learned from my work with IDL. Naturally, I did not learn about IDL all on my own. Instead, I am fortunate to work in a research environment with experienced and knowledgeable colleagues whose advice helped me to develop the ideas presented in this book. The genesis of this book was the morning discussions over coffee with my good friend Paul van Delst, who challenged and tested my ideas about IDL and programming in general. Paul Menzel provided me with enough data analysis and visualization challenges that I had little choice but to hone my skills as an IDL programmer. And for everyone who stopped by my office to ask a "quick question" about IDL, this book is for you.

Early in the project it was my good fortune to establish a working relationship with Research Systems, Inc., the makers of IDL, and I have benefited greatly from their encouragement and support. In particular I must thank David Stern of RSI for kindly agreeing to write the foreword for this book. The team at Morgan Kaufmann, led by Denise Penrose, made it easier than I had ever hoped to bring the book to fruition, and they deserve credit for turning my manuscript into what I hope will be a pleasing and useful reference for IDL programmers.

I am indebted to the following reviewers who played a large part in the development of the manuscript: Paul van Delst of the University of Wisconsin–Madison, Nick Bower of Curtin University of Technology, Martin Schultz of the Max-Planck-Institut fuer Meteorologie, Molly Houck of

RSI, and Randall Frank from Lawrence Livermore National Laboratory. Their suggestions dramatically improved the content, style, and organization of the book, and any errors that remain are mine alone.

I have also learned a great deal from the contributors to the Usenet newsgroup `comp.lang.idl-pvwave`, whose willingness to discuss the intricacies of IDL often provided the stimulus to investigate a topic further. Some results of exchanges on the newsgroup are to be found in this book.

Finally, I owe the greatest debt to my wife, Janine. If not for her patience and understanding, I would never have completed this book.

Table of Contents

1

Introduction

This book provides a solid foundation in the fundamentals of programming in Interactive Data Language (IDL), an array-oriented data analysis and visualization environment developed and marketed by Research Systems, Incorporated (RSI) of Boulder, Colorado. IDL is available for Windows, MacOS, UNIX (including Linux), and VMS platforms.

The first version of IDL for VAX/VMS was released in 1981 by RSI founder David Stern. Since then, IDL has emerged from its roots in the astronomical and space sciences to become a widely used tool in research, educational, and commercial settings in areas as diverse as the earth sciences, medical physics, and engineering test and analysis. Examples of real-world tasks where IDL is used include analyzing and visualizing images from the Hubble Space Telescope; rendering three-dimensional volumes of the human body from magnetic resonance imaging; and monitoring and controlling the plasma field of a nuclear fusion tokamak.

The long-term success of IDL stems from its flexible modes of operation, which include rapid interactive analysis and visualization; a powerful programming environment; and fully developed cross-platform end-user applications that range from an advanced remote sensing image processing suite (ENVI) to a comprehensive terrain and river network analysis package (RiverTools). In addition, IDL offers a broad range of fundamental data types, making it possible to read almost any input data format. The availability of IDL on all major UNIX platforms (including Linux), Windows, and MacOS facilitates data analysis in multiplatform environments and ensures that applications developed on one platform can be successfully ported to new platforms when hardware changes are necessary. Finally, the worldwide community of IDL users contributes to and maintains a collection of freely available Internet-based libraries, which at the time of writing included over 5,000 separate routines.

1.1   ABOUT THIS BOOK

This book begins by explaining the fundamentals of IDL and then moves on to explain how the fundamentals may be used to develop data analysis and visualization applications. The first chapter begins with a discussion of the philosophy behind the book; explains where the supporting materials for the book may be found; and summarizes the conventions used for IDL code examples. The chapter continues with instructions on how to start an IDL session and how to use the built-in online help. The chapter concludes with an outline of the remaining chapters in the book.

Who Should Read This Book?

Readers of this book will include anyone who wishes to use IDL effectively to analyze and visualize data. Newcomers to IDL will find a thorough description of the basics of the IDL syntax, with special attention paid to the effective use of arrays, as well as the fundamentals of visualization in IDL. Readers with a moderate level of prior exposure to IDL (perhaps only in interactive mode) will learn the mechanics of writing understandable and efficient IDL programs and receive practical advice such as how to create publication-quality PostScript output. Advanced users of IDL will appreciate the many hard-won nuggets of advice about IDL peculiarities, such as a detailed description of the differences between 8-bit and 24-bit graphics modes and the implications for IDL programming. Readers at all levels will appreciate the realization of IDL programming concepts in example programs that can be used immediately for real-world tasks. Prior exposure to a procedural language such as C or Fortran will be helpful, but not essential, for readers of this book.

Why Write This Book?

I wrote this book to help IDL users at all levels advance to the point where writing understandable and efficient IDL programs is second nature. Part of the attraction of IDL is that you can accomplish a great deal with only a few commands in interactive mode. A side effect, however, is that a sizable fraction of IDL users never progress beyond the point of entering individual commands and are never able to fully exploit the capabilities of IDL as a programming language. In my experience, the transition from casual command-line user to effective IDL programmer is often long and frustrating, if the user makes the transition at all. All the necessary information can be found somewhere in the manuals that accompany IDL, but with several thousand pages spread over five or more volumes, it is often difficult to know exactly where to look when you have a question. I felt strongly that there was a place for a book written by an experienced IDL programmer that gathered together essential information about IDL programming, assembled it in a logical sequence, and presented it with practical and illustrative example programs that solve real-world problems.

What about Objects?

A new object data type and an Object Graphics system were introduced in IDL 5.0 in 1996. These new features help to broaden the scope of the language and allow complex graphical displays to be constructed, particularly in the area of three-dimensional visualization. However, effective object-oriented programming in IDL requires a rather different approach when compared to the more commonly used procedural programming paradigm that has existed in IDL since it was first released. In this book, I have chosen to limit the discussion strictly to procedural programming, since I believe a larger audience for this topic exists in the community of IDL users. Likewise, this book only describes the Direct Graphics system in IDL and does not explore the realm of the Object Graphics system. At the time of writing, the Direct Graphics system offered much simpler (i.e., easier to program) ways to create visualizations in IDL. To do justice to objects and the Object Graphics system in IDL, I believe a separate book is required that describes how object-oriented principles are applied in IDL; hopefully such a volume will emerge in the not-too-distant future. In the meantime, the chapters of this book that describe the fundamental syntax of the language should prove useful to those writing object-oriented programs in IDL.

Supporting Materials

The source code for the example procedures and functions shown in this book are available online at the author's website:

```
http://www.gumley.com
```

It is recommended that you download the programs to a directory on your system, and then add the directory to the IDL path by one of the following methods:

- If you are running the IDL Development Environment, select File, Preferences, Path, and add the directory to the default search path.
- On UNIX platforms you may add the directory to the IDL path environment variable IDL_PATH. For example, if you stored the programs in a directory named /home/billg/idl, the syntax would be as follows:

```
% setenv IDL_PATH ${IDL_PATH}:/home/billg/idl     (C shell)
$ export IDL_PATH=${IDL_PATH}:/home/billg/idl     (Korn shell)
```

Typographic Conventions

Throughout this book the following typographic conventions are used. Commands that are intended to be entered at the IDL command line will appear as follows:

```
IDL> tvscl, dist(256)
```

Procedures and functions (i.e., programs) will appear as follows:

```
PRO HELLO

print, 'Hello world'

END
```

The program text may be entered in the IDL Development Environment editor or in any other text editor. The name of the text file should be the same as the procedure or function name (e.g., `hello.pro`), and lowercase file names are recommended.

Special Characters

IDL recognizes a number of special characters within IDL programs or when commands are entered at the command line. The most important special characters are described below.

The semicolon character designates the beginning of a comment. Any text following a semicolon on a given line is ignored. For example:

```
PRO HELLO

; A simple program
print, 'Hello world'    ; This line prints a message

END
```

If the last character on a line is a dollar sign, the current command is continued on the next line. For example:

```
IDL> print, 'The quick brown fox ', $
IDL>    'jumped over the lazy dog'
```

If the first character on the line is a dollar sign, any text that follows is executed as an operating system command. For example, to list the contents of the current directory on a UNIX platform:

```
IDL> $ls -l
```

1.2 ABOUT IDL

One of the strengths of IDL is its support for a variety of hardware and operating system combinations. Whether you are accustomed to a Windows, MacOS, or UNIX (including Linux) environment, a version of IDL is probably available for your system. The platforms supported by IDL 5.4 are shown in Table 1.1. For an up-to-date list of supported platforms and operating system versions, see the RSI website (`http://www.research-systems.com`).

Table 1.1   Platforms supported by IDL 5.4.

Platform	Vendor	Hardware	Operating system
Windows	Microsoft	Intel x86	Windows
Macintosh	Apple	PowerMac, G3, G4, iMac	MacOS
UNIX	Intel	Intel x86	Linux
	SUN	SPARC	Solaris
	SUN	Intel x86	Solaris
	HP	PA-RISC	HP-UX
	IBM	RS/6000	AIX
	SGI	Mips	IRIX
	Compaq	Alpha	Tru64 UNIX
	Compaq	Alpha	Linux
VMS	Compaq	Alpha	VMS

IDL in Perspective

To better understand some of the features offered by IDL, it is useful to compare it to two other languages that are widely used in data analysis: C and Fortran. Some of the features of IDL that distinguish it from these well-known languages are the following:

1. IDL offers interactive and compiled programming modes (C and Fortran offer compiled mode only).
2. IDL is optimized to perform array operations (C and Fortran are optimized to perform scalar operations).
3. IDL variables may be created or redefined with a new type, size, or value at any time (C and Fortran variables may be redefined at run-time with a new size or value only).
4. IDL includes built-in routines for visualization, numerical analysis, and graphical user interface development (C and Fortran require external libraries).

Note   While Fortran-9x includes array operations, many Fortran-9x compilers still implement scalar operations more efficiently.

Obtaining IDL

The IDL software can be obtained via download from the RSI anonymous FTP server, or by contacting RSI via email to request a CD-ROM. The demonstration (unlicensed) version of IDL will run with nearly full functionality for seven minutes, and may be restarted as many times as desired. For a fully functional licensed version of IDL, or if you have any questions about pricing, installation, or technical support, please contact RSI via one of the methods listed below:

Phone:	303-786-9900
Fax:	303-786-9909
Mail:	Research Systems, Inc. 4990 Pearl East Circle Boulder, CO 80301
Web:	`http://www.researchsystems.com`
Anonymous FTP server:	`ftp.researchsystems.com`
Technical support, bug reports:	`support@researchsystems.com`
Product information:	`info@researchsystems.com`
Sales and pricing information:	`sales@researchsystems.com`
Consulting services:	`consulting@researchsystems.com`
Training courses:	`training@researchsystems.com`

1.3   RUNNING IDL

IDL can be started in two different modes. Either mode may be used depending on your own preference.

The first mode is the IDL Development Environment (idlde), which is available on all supported platforms and provides a graphical user interface to IDL, including a built-in editor. On Windows and Macintosh platforms, double-click the IDL icon to start idlde. On UNIX platforms, type idlde at the operating system prompt to start the IDL Development Environment (for VMS, type idl /de). The default layout of idlde in IDL 5.4 for Windows is shown in Figure 1.1 (the layout on other platforms or other IDL versions may appear slightly different).

Commands are entered in the Command Input window, and text output is displayed in the Output Log window. The Variable Watch window allows the name, type, and value of variables to be tracked during a session. The Editor window is where IDL programs are edited. You can select which windows to display via the Window menu. To change the default screen layout, see the Preferences dialog under the File menu.

The second mode is the IDL Command Line, which is only available on UNIX (including Linux) and VMS platforms. To start IDL in this mode,

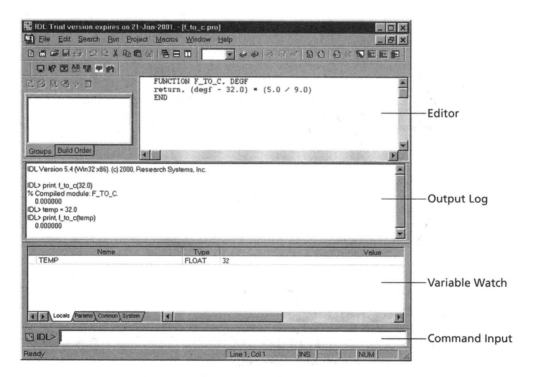

Figure 1.1 Default layout of idlde **in IDL 5.4 for Windows.**

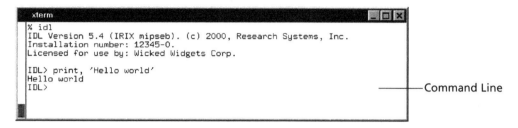

Figure 1.2 Default appearance of the IDL Command Line in IDL 5.4 for IRIX.

type `idl` at the operating system prompt. The default appearance of the IDL Command Line in IDL 5.4 for IRIX is shown in Figure 1.2.

In either mode, interactive commands are entered at the IDL prompt as shown in the following example:

```
IDL> print, 'Hello world'
```

To see a demonstration of the capabilities of IDL, try running the built-in `demo` procedure:

```
IDL> demo
```

To close an IDL session, type `exit` at the IDL prompt:

```
IDL> exit
```

1.4   ONLINE HELP

IDL has an online help system that includes indexed electronic versions of all the IDL manuals. To access the IDL online help from the command line, just type a question mark:

```
IDL> ?
```

The online Help window from IDL 5.4 for Windows is shown in Figure 1.3. It will appear differently on other platforms and in other IDL versions.

The Contents button leads to the online versions of the IDL manuals. The following manuals are of particular interest:

- *Using IDL* covers interactive analysis and visualization in IDL.
- *Building IDL Applications* describes how to construct programs in IDL and serves as a reference for the basic syntax of the language.

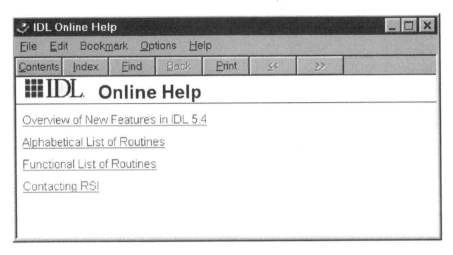

Figure 1.3 Online Help window in IDL 5.4 for Windows.

- *IDL Reference* contains a description of all built-in procedures and functions and serves as a reference for the IDL graphics devices and global system variables.
- *Scientific Data Formats* describes how IDL can read and write common data formats including netCDF, CDF, HDF, and HDF-EOS.

To display Portable Document Format (PDF) versions of all manuals, double-click the IDL Online Manuals icon on Windows and MacOS platforms, or type idlman at the operating system prompt on UNIX or VMS platforms. PDF manuals can also be found on the IDL installation CD-ROM in the info directory.

The Index button in the Online Help window leads to a searchable index of the IDL help system (this is useful when you require help for a particular topic, procedure, or function). In IDL 5.2 and higher versions, you can access the online help for a specific topic by typing a question mark at the command line, followed by a single word. For example, to access the online help for the built-in tvscl image display procedure:

```
IDL> ? tvscl
```

For procedures and functions that are included as source files with the IDL distribution, the doc_library procedure can be used to view the prolog for a particular routine. For example, to view the prolog for the congrid function:

```
IDL> doc_library, 'congrid'
```

To start the online help system independently of IDL, double-click the IDL Help icon on Windows and MacOS platforms, or type idlhelp at the operating system prompt on UNIX or VMS platforms.

1.5 OUTLINE OF THE CHAPTERS

This book begins with the basics of IDL syntax, emphasizing the proper use of arrays. It then moves on to discuss the mechanics of program construction and points out the critical information (e.g., argument checking, parameter-passing mechanisms) that make it possible to write reliable IDL code. Once the foundations of writing IDL programs are established, the book goes on to demonstrate and explain how these concepts are applied to developing IDL applications. One of the major goals of this book is to take the mystery out of IDL programming. Too often I've heard IDL programmers say words to the effect that "I don't understand why it works this way in IDL, but it works." I believe that by exposing the fundamental underpinnings of IDL early on, the reader has a much better chance of being able to tackle problems in IDL related to his or her own area of interest. This book is organized not as a training manual, but as a logically ordered guide to IDL programming. Rather than attempting to give the reader a flavor for every aspect of IDL, I have tried to concentrate on sound principles that users can apply no matter what particular application they wish to develop in IDL.

Chapter 2, "Fundamentals of IDL Syntax," begins with a description of the two programming modes available in IDL, interactive mode and compiled mode, and gives guidance on when each mode is appropriate. It explains the data types supported and the dynamic nature of variable types, and considerable attention is devoted to array creation, indexing, and manipulation—a crucial skill in IDL programming. The chapter describes the arithmetic, Boolean, and relational operators available in IDL, along with their side effects and restrictions. It also covers the use of structures and pointers, with emphasis on avoiding memory leaks.

Chapter 3, "Writing IDL Programs," describes the basic IDL program units (procedures and functions) and explains how they may be compiled manually or automatically. It describes the mechanism for running programs, emphasizing the importance of returning to the main level in the event of a program halt. Next the control statements available in IDL are described, with a functional program demonstrating how each statement is used. The chapter explains the use of parameters and keywords, the parameter-passing mechanisms, and methods for checking input and output parameters. The chapter concludes with the use of scripts and include files, followed by global variables, error-handling mechanisms, and advice on efficient programming.

Chapter 4, "Input and Output," explains the methods available for data input and output in IDL. First, the basics of formatted and unformatted input and output are explained, followed by sample programs that show how to read ASCII and binary input files, including the use of structures to read mixed binary data types, and how to deal with byte-swapping. The chapter also gives an overview of scientific data formats in IDL, followed by detailed examples for reading and writing data in netCDF and HDF files.

Chapter 5, "Direct Graphics," describes the Direct Graphics system in IDL, including information on the available graphics devices and differences between 8-bit and 24-bit graphics mode. It gives detailed instructions on how a specific graphics mode can be selected at startup and explains the concept and workings of graphics windows. It also describes the differences between Indexed Color and Decomposed Color and includes instructions on how colors and the color table are used in each mode. Finally, a section on display mode troubleshooting answers common questions about IDL graphics problems.

Chapter 6, "Plotting Data," covers methods for creating and configuring plots in IDL. It includes examples of how to create and configure line, scatter, polar, bar, and histogram plots. It also explains the fine-tuning of plot properties such as axes, linestyles, symbols, and labels (including mathematical equations). Example programs that extend the functionality of the built-in plotting procedures are also included in this chapter. Contour, surface, and shaded surface plotting is described in detail, along with instructions on how to resample irregularly gridded data. The final section discusses mapping, with instructions on how to configure the various map projections in IDL and how to plot contours and display images on map projections.

Chapter 7, "Displaying Images," explains how images are displayed in IDL. The chapter discusses both types of images supported (PseudoColor and TrueColor) and the built-in procedures for displaying and scaling image data. Scaling of image data is covered in depth (including histogram clipping) followed by a description of how images can be resized and positioned to fit the current display. The display of TrueColor images is discussed next, followed by advice on how to display images on the PostScript and Printer graphics devices. The chapter concludes with a detailed description of an image display program that is device and image independent.

Chapter 8, "Creating Graphical Output," describes how graphical output from IDL may be saved to a file or printed. The chapter begins by describing the differences between raster and vector output in IDL, and then proceeds to methods for saving the contents of a graphics window to a raster image file. Next, the creation of publication-quality PostScript output is covered in depth. The chapter gives detailed instructions on how to configure and use the PostScript graphics device, including font selection and generation of encapsulated PostScript, followed by an example program that automates the selection of PostScript output. The Printer graphics device is covered in similar detail, showing how high-quality output can be produced on local or networked printers, including those that do not support PostScript. The chapter concludes with an example program that automates selection of Printer output.

Chapter 9, "Graphical User Interfaces," gives an introduction to graphical user interface (GUI) programming with the IDL widget toolkit, including recommendations on when a GUI is appropriate, and on GUI design. The chapter describes the basic widget types in IDL and gives examples of how each widget is created and configured. Guidelines for GUI layout are given, along with examples of well designed and poorly designed GUIs. Events and event handling are described, along with example programs that demonstrate how events are managed in single and multiple instances of a GUI. The chapter concludes with the design and implementation of a GUI application for image display, with detailed explanations of how each component functions. The application implements a resizable image display window with an intelligent graphics device and color handling, and built-in output to raster and vector output formats.

2

Fundamentals of IDL Syntax

This chapter covers the basics of IDL programming. If you are acquainted with a high-level procedural language such as C or Fortran, some of the concepts presented will be familiar. However, IDL differs from these languages in significant ways, and it is a mistake to think of IDL as a simple variant of Fortran. You will find that it pays to learn to think in IDL terms rather than C or Fortran terms, particularly when it comes to the dynamic nature of variable types and the efficiency of array processing in IDL.

In this chapter, the two modes of IDL programming are explained: interactive mode and compiled mode. Then IDL variables are introduced, with emphasis placed on the ability of IDL to redefine the type, size, and value of variables at runtime. Array syntax is introduced next, and special attention is given to array creation and indexing. The use of IDL expressions and arithmetic operators is described, including the effects of type conversion in expressions, and the efficiency of array arithmetic. The relational and Boolean operators available are then described, followed by an explanation of structure and pointer usage in IDL. The chapter concludes with techniques for working with arrays, including determining array properties, locating values in arrays, and array reordering and resizing.

2.1 INTERACTIVE AND COMPILED MODES

Commands may be executed in IDL in two different modes. In interactive mode, commands are typed at the IDL prompt and executed when you press the Enter key. This mode is especially appropriate for prototyping and interactive analysis because it provides immediate feedback in numerical and visual form without requiring you to write any code. In compiled mode, programs consisting of sequences of IDL commands are created and executed. IDL supports two kinds of program units known as *procedures* and *functions*, which are described in more detail in Chapter 3. Compiled mode allows you to develop sophisticated data analysis and visualization applications that can be reused by you and your colleagues and that are portable between different IDL platforms.

Interactive Mode

Interactive mode allows you to rapidly analyze and visualize data using concise and efficient single-line commands. In interactive mode, commands typed at the IDL prompt are executed when the Enter key is pressed. For example, to create a sine wave plot:

```
IDL> x = findgen(201) * 0.1
IDL> y = sin(x)
IDL> plot, x, y
```

Here a floating-point array (x) is created with 201 elements, where the first element is equal to 0.0, the last element is equal to 20.0, and the interval between elements is equal to 0.1. Then a second floating-point array (y) is created, where each element is equal to the sine of the corresponding element in the first array. Finally, the two arrays are plotted on a two-dimensional line plot.

Interactive mode allows you to see results quickly without the traditional edit/compile/execute model required by languages such as C or Fortran. One of the best features of interactive mode is that it allows you to immediately visualize the results of your work in the form of a plot, image, contour, or other graphical representation. Many of the examples in this book are presented in interactive mode to allow instant demonstration of IDL programming principles. In general, interactive mode is appropriate when the time taken to complete a task is short, and the task is simple enough to require the use of only a few commands.

Compiled Mode

Compiled mode allows you to create more complex applications for analyzing and visualizing data than can be created in interactive mode. For example, the commercial image-processing application ENVI is coded entirely in IDL. In compiled mode, sequences of IDL statements are formed into programs that are edited, compiled, and executed. For example, try creating the following program in the idlde editor, or any other text editor, and save it in a file named hello.pro:

```
PRO HELLO

print, 'Hello world'
map_set, /continents, /grid

END
```

To compile and run the program, enter the following commands:

```
IDL> .compile hello.pro
IDL> hello
Hello world
```

Compiled mode is used when the program needed to accomplish a task is larger than a handful of interactive mode commands. In addition, compiled mode programming offers all the benefits of programming in languages such as C and Fortran, such as the encapsulation of related tasks into single conceptual units that are well tested and documented. Whenever you find yourself typing more than about 10 different commands in sequence in interactive mode, you should consider using compiled mode to create a program for that task.

2.2   VARIABLES

In high-level languages such as C and Fortran, data-typing statements in the program source code (e.g., C: int, Fortran: integer) instruct the compiler how to define each variable in the program. At runtime, the type of each variable in the program remains fixed. IDL offers more flexibility for variable typing because it must allow new variables to be created in both interactive and compiled modes.

IDL allows you to create new variables at any time and also allows you to redefine existing variables at any time. For example, to create a 32-bit floating-point scalar variable with a value of 1.0, and then verify its type:

```
IDL> var = 1.0
IDL> help, var
VAR             FLOAT     =      1.00000
```

To redefine the variable as a 16-bit signed integer with a value of 1,024, and then verify its type:

```
IDL> var = 1024
IDL> help, var
VAR             INT      =     1024
```

As you can see, the variable retains no memory of its previous type and value. The ability to create new variables dynamically in IDL provides great flexibility in IDL programming. However, it also means that you must diligently keep track of the types of all variables in your IDL programs (the `help` procedure called in the examples above will be explained in more detail later in this section).

Data Types

IDL provides a rich selection of data types, allowing you to work with a wide variety of real-world data sets and applications. The numeric data types available in IDL are described in Table 2.1.

In addition to numeric data types, IDL includes several nonnumeric data types that add programming flexibility. The nonnumeric data types available in IDL are described in Table 2.2.

IDL is an array-oriented language, and any IDL variable type (numeric or nonnumeric) can be used to form a multidimensional array (this will

Table 2.1   Numeric data types.

Data type	Explanation	Bits	Range
byte	Unsigned integer	8	0 to 255
int	Signed integer	16	−32,768 to 32,767
uint	Unsigned integer	16	0 to 65,535
long	Signed integer	32	-2^{31} to $2^{31}-1$
ulong	Unsigned integer	32	0 to $2^{32}-1$
long64	Signed integer	64	-2^{63} to $2^{63}-1$
ulong64	Unsigned integer	64	0 to $2^{64}-1$
float	IEEE floating-point	32	-10^{38} to 10^{38}
double	IEEE floating-point	64	-10^{308} to 10^{308}
complex	Real-imaginary pair	64	(See float)
dcomplex	Real-imaginary pair	128	(See double)

Table 2.2   Nonnumeric data types.

Data type	Explanation
string	Character string (0–32,767 characters)
struct	Container for one or more variables
pointer	Reference to a dynamically allocated variable
objref	Reference to an object structure

be explained in more detail later in this chapter). IDL objects are not described in this book. Object-oriented programming in IDL deserves a book of its own!

Keeping Track of Variable Types

The help procedure is an effective way to keep track of variable types and sizes, whether it is called from the IDL command line, or from within an IDL program. For scalar variables, help prints the name, type, and value of the argument:

```
IDL> value = 3.32
IDL> help, value
VALUE           FLOAT     =        3.32000
```

For array variables, help prints the name, type, and size of the argument:

```
IDL> arr = [2, 3, 4, 5, 6]
IDL> help, arr
ARR             INT       = Array[5]
```

Liberal use of the help procedure is an excellent way to ensure that your IDL variables always have the correct type and size. If you are using the IDL Development Environment, the Variable Watch window can also be used to track the type and value of variables.

Type Conversions

IDL provides functions that convert variables from one type to another, while retaining the value of the variable (except for truncation when converting to integer types). For example, to convert a variable to long type, the long() function is used:

```
IDL> x = 3.14159
IDL> help, x
X               FLOAT     =        3.14159
IDL> x = long(x)
IDL> help, x
X               LONG      =        3
```

The syntax used to create numeric and string data types and the corresponding functions for type conversion are shown in Table 2.3.

When converting between IDL data types, truncation takes place when the output variable type has fewer bytes than the input variable type:

```
IDL> value = 257
IDL> help, value
VALUE           INT       =        257
IDL> value = byte(value)
IDL> help, value
VALUE           BYTE      =        1
```

Table 2.3   Type syntax and conversion functions.

Data type	Syntax example	Conversion function
byte	1B	byte()
int	1	fix()
	1S	
uint	1U	uint()
	1US	
long	1L	long()
ulong	1UL	ulong()
long64	1LL	long64()
ulong64	1ULL	ulong64()
float	1.0	float()
	1.0E+0	
double	1.0D	double()
	1.0D+0	
complex	Use complex()	complex()
dcomplex	Use dcomplex()	dcomplex()
string	'Hello world'	string()

Before the conversion, value is int type (signed 16-bit integer), and after the conversion value is byte type (unsigned 8-bit integer). When value is converted, only the least significant 8 bits are extracted, and the most significant 8 bits are ignored. IDL issues no warning in this case.

Note The default integer data type in IDL is a 16-bit signed integer. That is, when you define an integer in the range −32,767 to 32,767 without appending a type identifier as shown in Table 2.3 (e.g., B, S, L), the type is int by default:

```
IDL> a = -32767
IDL> help, a
A               INT       =    -32767
IDL> a = 1000
IDL> help, a
A               INT       =      1000
```

Converting Floats to Integers

When the fix and long functions are used to convert floating-point variables to integers, truncation takes place:

```
IDL> arr = [4.32, 7.89, -1.25, -2.93]
IDL> print, fix(arr)
      4       7      -1      -2
IDL> print, long(arr)
          4           7          -1          -2
```

The round, floor, and ceil functions allow more control over how floating-point variables are converted to integers. The round function returns the long integer that is nearest to its argument; floor returns the nearest long integer that is less than or equal to its argument; and ceil returns the nearest long integer that is greater than or equal to its argument:

```
IDL> print, round(arr)
          4           8          -1          -3
IDL> print, floor(arr)
          4           7          -2          -3
IDL> print, ceil(arr)
          5           8          -1          -2
```

Converting between String and Numeric Types

String variables can be converted to numeric type:

```
IDL> print, float('3.2'), float('123ABC')
      3.20000      123.000
```

If the string variable does not contain a valid numeric value, a warning message is printed and the output value is zero:

```
IDL> print, float('Hello')
% Type conversion error: Unable to convert given
  STRING to Float.
% Detected at:  $MAIN$
     0.000000
```

When converting from `byte` to `string` type, the result is a scalar variable containing the ASCII characters corresponding to the input `byte` values:

```
IDL> print, string([48B, 49B, 50B, 51B])
0123
```

When converting from `string` to `byte` type, the result is an array containing the ASCII values corresponding to each character in the input `string`:

```
IDL> help, byte('ABCD')
<Expression>    BYTE      = Array[4]
IDL> print, byte('ABCD')
  65  66  67  68
```

Variable Names

A variable name in IDL must begin with a letter and may be up to 128 characters in length. Valid characters for variable names include the letters a-z, the digits 0-9, and the underscore character. Case is ignored, and spaces are not allowed. IDL reserved words cannot be used as variable names. Table 2.4 lists the reserved words in IDL.

You should take care to ensure that built-in IDL function names are not used as variable names. If you use a function name as a variable name, the results can be confusing:

```
IDL> intarr = 123.45
IDL> print, intarr(5)
      0       0       0       0       0
```

Table 2.4   Reserved words in IDL.

and	endfor	gt	or
begin	endif	if	pro
case	endrep	le	repeat
common	endwhile	lt	then
do	eq	mod	until
else	for	ne	while
end	function	not	xor
endcase	ge	of	
endelse	goto	on_ioerror	

In this example, an int variable named intarr is defined with a value of 123.45. However, IDL has a built-in function named intarr (it creates an int array), and in the example intarr is called to create an array with five elements. This is undesirable, as intarr now has two meanings (a scalar variable and a built-in function). Variable names should have only one meaning within the context of a program.

To check whether a built-in function with a particular name already exists, you can use the online help:

```
IDL> ? intarr
```

If intarr is already defined as a function, the entry INTARR function will appear in the list of search matches.

To check whether an add-on function with a particular name already exists, try compiling the function:

```
IDL> .compile getpos
% Compiled module: GETPOS.
IDL> .compile dingbats
% Can't open file for input: dingbats
  No such file or directory
```

In this example, a function named getpos was found in the IDL path and compiled, and thus getpos should not be used as a variable name. However, no function named dingbats was found, and thus dingbats can be safely used as a variable name. This technique only works if the function getpos is contained in a source file named getpos.pro; it will not work if the source file containing the function is named otherwise.

2.3   INTRODUCTION TO ARRAYS

Arrays with one to eight dimensions can be formed from any IDL data type. A compact syntax allows arrays to be processed without the use of loops, which often makes for conceptually simpler coding. In addition to the compact syntax, array operations in IDL are optimized for speed. You will find that processing an entire array with an array operation is much faster than processing each array element in turn.

For example, to find the sum of 1 million uniformly distributed random numbers:

```
IDL> npts = 1000000L
IDL> data = randomu(-1L, npts)
IDL> sum = total(data)
```

On a modest personal computer, the `total` function returns a result in 0.11 seconds. The same task could also be carried out in a loop:

```
IDL> sum = 0.0
IDL> for i = 0L, (npts - 1L) do sum = sum + data[i]
```

On the same computer the loop requires 2.64 seconds to return a result, more than 20 times slower than the array operation. Thus the two most compelling reasons to use arrays in IDL are

1. Array operations are much faster than loops.
2. Array syntax is more compact than a corresponding loop construct.

One of the secrets to becoming an effective IDL programmer is learning how to use arrays effectively. Once you have trained yourself to think and program in terms of IDL array operations rather than loops, you will be well on the way to becoming an effective IDL programmer.

Note   There are cases where the speed of a loop is not important, such as using a loop to read lines of text from an input file (the speed of this operation is governed by the disk I/O speed). But, in general, array operations are preferred over loops.

Creating Arrays

Arrays are created and referenced in IDL by using square bracket characters []. To create a one-dimensional array, the array values are enclosed in square brackets:

```
IDL> x = [0, 1, 2, 3, 4]
IDL> help, x
X               INT       = Array[5]
IDL> print, x
      0       1       2       3       4
```

Note Prior to IDL version 5.0, parentheses ( ) were used to create and reference arrays. However, this allowed for confusion between array names and function names, so in IDL 5.0 the square bracket array syntax was introduced (although parenthesis array syntax was kept for backward compatibility). If you are using IDL 5.0 or higher, the use of square brackets for arrays is recommended. Square bracket array syntax is used throughout this book.

Multidimensional arrays can be created by using nested square brackets:

```
IDL> x = [[0, 1, 2], [3, 4, 5], [6, 7, 8]]
IDL> help, x
X               INT       = Array[3, 3]
IDL> print, x
      0       1       2
      3       4       5
      6       7       8
```

Values can be appended to an existing array:

```
IDL> arr = [0, 1, 2, 3, 4]
IDL> arr = [arr, 5, 6, 7, 8]
IDL> print, arr
      0       1       2       3       4       5       6
      7       8
```

Array Storage Format

Arrays in IDL are stored in column-major format, the same storage format used by the Fortran programming language. Column-major format means that consecutive array elements are stored sequentially in memory, with the first array dimension (the column dimension) varying the fastest. For example, a two-dimensional array in IDL with four columns and two rows that can be written as

$$A_{0,0} \quad A_{1,0} \quad A_{2,0} \quad A_{3,0}$$

$$A_{0,1} \quad A_{1,1} \quad A_{2,1} \quad A_{3,1}$$

is stored sequentially in memory in the following order:

```
A[0, 0], A[1, 0], A[2, 0], A[3, 0], A[0, 1], A[1, 1],
  A[2, 1], A[3, 1]
```

This is worth remembering because in IDL it is natural to read or write entire arrays. For example, say you write an IDL array with dimensions (*ncolumns*, *nrows*) to a file. In a Fortran program to read the file, the array would be dimensioned (*ncolumns*, *nrows*). In the C programming language, which uses row-major format, the last array dimension varies the fastest, so the array would be dimensioned (*nrows*, *ncolumns*).

Functions for Creating Arrays

Built-in functions allow you to create arrays of a given type with every element initialized to zero, or with every element set to its array index value. For example, to create zeroed and index arrays with six elements each:

```
IDL> zeros = intarr(6)
IDL> index = indgen(6)
IDL> print, zeros, index
      0       0       0       0       0       0
      0       1       2       3       4       5
```

In an index array, the array values increase by one for every consecutive array location in memory. For multidimensional index arrays, the index value increases by one along the leftmost array dimension first:

```
IDL> index = indgen(5, 3)
IDL> print, index
```

```
    0      1      2      3      4
    5      6      7      8      9
   10     11     12     13     14
```

The functions available for creating zeroed and index arrays are shown in Table 2.5.

The replicate function creates an array by replicating a scalar value into an array with specified dimensions:

```
IDL> arr = replicate(2.0, 4, 2)
IDL> print, arr
      2.00000      2.00000      2.00000      2.00000
      2.00000      2.00000      2.00000      2.00000
```

Alternatively, the make_array function creates an array with specified dimensions that can either be a zeroed array, an index array, or an array set to a particular value. To create a zeroed array, the dimensions and type of the array must be specified:

```
IDL> zeroed = make_array(3, 2, /byte)
IDL> print, zeroed
   0   0   0
   0   0   0
```

Table 2.5 Zeroed and index array creation functions.

Data type	Zeroed array	Index array
byte	bytarr()	bindgen()
int	intarr()	indgen()
uint	uintarr()	uindgen()
long	lonarr()	lindgen()
ulong	ulonarr()	ulindgen()
long64	lon64arr()	l64indgen()
ulong64	ulon64arr()	ul64indgen()
float	fltarr()	findgen()
double	dblarr()	dindgen()
complex	complexarr()	cindgen()
dcomplex	dcomplexarr()	dcindgen()
string	strarr()	sindgen()

To create an index array, the index keyword must be passed:

```
IDL> index = make_array(4, 3, /float, /index)
IDL> help, index
INDEX           FLOAT     = Array[4, 3]
IDL> print, index
      0.000000      1.00000      2.00000      3.00000
      4.00000      5.00000      6.00000      7.00000
      8.00000      9.00000      10.0000      11.0000
```

To create an array where each element is set to a value, the value keyword must be set to the desired value:

```
IDL> arr = make_array(6, /long, value=32L)
IDL> help, arr
ARR             LONG      = Array[6]
IDL> print, arr
          32            32            32            32            32
          32
```

The make_array function is particularly useful in IDL programs in cases where the size and type of an array are not known until runtime.

Floating-Point Grid Arrays

One-dimensional grid arrays with arbitrary spacing can be created accurately and efficiently in IDL. For example, say a float array is required with evenly spaced values from 1000.0 to 1010.0 in steps of 0.1. First, the endpoints of the array and the step size are defined as float variables:

```
IDL> x1 = 1000.0
IDL> x2 = 1010.0
IDL> dx = 0.1
```

Next, the number of grid array elements is computed via the floor function (round off error is avoided by adding 1.0e-5):

```
IDL> nx = floor((x2 - x1) / dx + 1.0e-5) + 1L
IDL> help, nx
NX              LONG      =             101
```

Then, the grid array values are computed, and the last five values are printed with four decimal places of precision:

```
IDL> arr = lindgen(nx) * dx + x1
IDL> help, arr
ARR             FLOAT     = Array[101]
```

```
IDL> print, arr[96:100], format='(5f11.4)'
  1009.6000  1009.7000  1009.8000  1009.9000  1010.0000
```

Grid arrays should not be created by repeated addition because round-off errors will cause the array values to become increasingly less accurate:

```
IDL> arr = fltarr(nx)
IDL> arr[0] = x1
IDL> for index = 1, (nx - 1) do arr[index] = $
IDL>    arr[index - 1] + dx
IDL> print, arr[96:100], format='(5f11.4)'
  1009.5977  1009.6976  1009.7976  1009.8976  1009.9976
```

In addition to the inaccuracy problem, this method uses an inefficient loop to compute the grid array.

2.4   ARRAY INDEXING

Array indices (also known as *subscripts*) in IDL are zero-based and positive. That is, the first array element is always stored at index zero. This sometimes causes confusion for programmers who are accustomed to Fortran, where array indices are one-based by default. Scalar values or multidimensional arrays of any numeric data type may be used as array indices. Data types that are not long integers are used as though they were converted to long integers when used as array indices.

Array indices can be specified in either of two forms:

```
array[index]
```

or

```
(array_expression)[index]
```

The first form appends the index in square brackets to an array name:

```
IDL> arr = indgen(10) * 3
IDL> print, arr, format='(10i6)'
     0     3     6     9    12    15    18    21    24    27
IDL> index = 5
IDL> print, arr[index]
    15
```

The second form appends the index in square brackets to an array expression in parentheses:

```
IDL> print, (arr * 10)[index]
   150
```

When the array index is a scalar value, out-of-bounds index values cause an error:

```
IDL> index = -1
IDL> print, arr[index]
% Attempt to subscript ARR with INDEX is out of range.
% Execution halted at:  $MAIN$
```

Indices can also be specified in array form:

```
IDL> index = [3, 5, 7, 4, 2]
IDL> print, arr[index]
      9      15      21      12       6
```

Note When indices are specified as an array, index values that are out of bounds are silently clipped to the minimum or maximum permitted index values:

```
IDL> index = [-1, 0, 6, 9, 1000]
IDL> print, arr[index]
      0       0      18      27      27
```

Array Indexing Examples

Examples of array indexing, applied to the following array, are shown below:

```
IDL> arr = indgen(8) * 8
IDL> print, arr
      0       8      16      24      32      40      48      56
```

- Scalar index:
```
IDL> print, arr[6]
     48
```

- Index range:
```
IDL> print, arr[0:3]
      0       8      16      24
```

- All indices:
```
IDL> print, arr[*]
      0       8      16      24      32      40      48      56
```

- All indices from a specified index to the last index:

```
IDL> print, arr[5:*]
      40      48      56
```

- Indices are specified by an array:

```
IDL> index = indgen(3)*2
IDL> print, index
       0       2       4
IDL> print, arr[index]
       0      16      32
```

- Indices are given by a variable expression:

```
IDL> i = 3
IDL> print, arr[i-1:i+1]
      16      24      32
```

Multidimensional Array Indexing Examples

Multidimensional arrays are indexed using a similar syntax. Examples of multidimensional array indexing, applied to the following array, are shown below:

```
IDL> arr = indgen(4, 4) * 4
IDL> print, arr
       0       4       8      12
      16      20      24      28
      32      36      40      44
      48      52      56      60
```

- Scalar index:

```
IDL> print, arr[0, 0]
       0
```

- Indices include all elements in the first row:

```
IDL> print, arr[*, 0]
       0       4       8      12
```

- Indices include all elements in the first column:

```
IDL> print, arr[0, *]
       0
      16
      32
      48
```

- Index range over two dimensions:

```
IDL> print, arr[0:2, 0:2]
      0        4        8
     16       20       24
     32       36       40
```

One-Dimensional Indexing

No matter how many dimensions an array may have, it can always be indexed as though it were a one-dimensional array. That is, you can reference any element in a multidimensional array by specifying an index that represents the zero-based offset of the element from the start of the array in memory. For example, there are two ways to access the 11th element of the following array:

```
IDL> arr = indgen(4, 4) * 4
IDL> print, arr
      0        4        8       12
     16       20       24       28
     32       36       40       44
     48       52       56       60
IDL> print, arr[2, 2]
     40
IDL> print, arr[10]
     40
```

Keep in mind that IDL stores arrays in column-major format, so you must count each column on successive rows until the 11th element is found. Scalar variables can also be referenced using a one-dimensional array index:

```
IDL> var = 273.15
IDL> print, var[0]
     273.150
```

This technique can be used to get the first element of a variable, regardless of whether the variable is a scalar or an array.

Index Sampling

In some situations you may need to sample every *n*th element along an array dimension. In the case of a one-dimensional array, this is a simple task:

```
IDL> n = 10
IDL> arr = indgen(10) * 100
IDL> print, arr, format='(10i6)'
     0   100   200   300   400   500   600   700   800   900
IDL> index = lindgen((n + 1) / 2) * 2
IDL> print, index
           0           2           4           6           8
IDL> print, arr[index], format='(10i6)'
     0   200   400   600   800
```

In this example, an index array was created with half as many elements as the data array, where each index value increases by two. This allows every second element of the data array to be sampled.

Multidimensional Index Sampling

The syntax required to sample a multidimensional array is not immediately obvious. For example, consider the following two-dimensional array:

```
IDL> n = 5
IDL> arr = indgen(n, n)
IDL> print, arr
       0        1        2        3        4
       5        6        7        8        9
      10       11       12       13       14
      15       16       17       18       19
      20       21       22       23       24
```

To extract every second element along each dimension, you might try indexing the array as follows:

```
IDL> index = lindgen((n + 1) / 2) * 2
IDL> print, index
           0           2           4
IDL> print, arr[index, index]
       0       12       24
```

However, this only extracts every other element along the diagonal. To extract the second element along each dimension, you must sample each dimension in turn:

```
IDL> sub = arr[index, *]
IDL> print, sub
```

```
        0        2        4
        5        7        9
       10       12       14
       15       17       19
       20       22       24
IDL> sub = sub[*, index]
IDL> print, sub
        0        2        4
       10       12       14
       20       22       24
```

With array expression indexing, the same result is obtained with a more compact syntax:

```
IDL> sub = (arr[index, *])[*, index]
IDL> print, sub
        0        2        4
       10       12       14
       20       22       24
```

This method may be extended to arrays of higher dimension if necessary:

```
IDL> arr = indgen(n, n, n)
IDL> sub = ((arr[index, *, *])[*, index, *])[*, *, index]
IDL> print, sub
        0        2        4
       10       12       14
       20       22       24

       50       52       54
       60       62       64
       70       72       74

      100      102      104
      110      112      114
      120      122      124
```

2.5   EXPRESSIONS AND ARITHMETIC OPERATORS

In IDL, the term *expression* refers to a combination of variables, constants, and operators that yields a scalar or array of a certain data type. For example, 2.0 + 2.0 is an expression that evaluates to a scalar float value (4.0). Expressions are typically used to create new variables:

```
IDL> x = 2.0 + 2.0
```

Because IDL allows new variables to be created at any time, it is vitally important to understand what happens when an expression contains more than one data type (e.g., a `long` and a `double`).

Type Conversion in Expressions

In languages such as C and Fortran, the variable on the left side of the assignment operator (=) always determines the data type of an expression result. Consider the following C code fragment that computes a factor for converting degrees to radians:

```
double dtr;
dtr = 3.1415927 / 180.0;
```

The expression yields a double-precision result because the variable on the left side of the assignment operator was previously declared as double precision. However, in IDL, variables can be redefined with a new type at any time. There are two ways that the result of an IDL expression is determined.

In the first case, if the variable on the left side of the assignment operator is a scalar, array, or is undefined, then the expression result type is determined by the variables on the right side of the assignment operator:

```
IDL> dtr = 3.1415927 / 180.0
IDL> help, dtr
DTR             FLOAT     =    0.0174533
```

Here the result of the expression is a `float` because both variables on the right side of the assignment operator are `float` constants.

If there are mixed data types on the right side of the assignment operator, then the type of the result is determined by the precedence of the variable types:

```
IDL> arr = indgen(10) * 10.0D
IDL> help, arr
ARR             DOUBLE    = Array[10]
```

Here the result of the expression is a `double` because on the right side of the assignment operator the `double` constant (`10.0D`) takes precedence over the `int` array (`indgen(10)`). In the list of IDL numeric data types shown in Table 2.1, `byte` has the lowest precedence, and `dcomplex` has the highest precedence. When in doubt, you can specify a type by using one of the type conversion functions listed in Table 2.3:

```
IDL> arr = float(indgen(10) * 10)
IDL> help, arr
ARR             FLOAT      = Array[10]
```

In the second case, if the variable on the left side of the assignment statement is a subarray, then the expression result type is determined by the variable on the left side of the assignment operator:

```
IDL> arr = indgen(9)
IDL> arr[0] = 2.0 * 3.1415927
IDL> help, arr[0]
<Expression>    INT       =        6
```

Here the type conversion is done automatically, as if the type conversion function fix had been called. When floating-point types are converted to integers by an assignment statement, the values are truncated, not rounded.

Guarding against Division by an Integer

A common IDL programming error occurs when an integer variable is divided by another integer. For example, say you wish to normalize an array whose type is unknown until runtime:

```
IDL> result = arr / max(arr)
```

If arr is an integer type at runtime (e.g., int, long), the result is an array of zeroes (except for the last element), because integer divisions are truncated:

```
IDL> print, 3 / 4
     0
```

If your code performs division on a variable or array that is not created until runtime and you are expecting a floating-point result, make sure you convert the divisor to float (or double) type:

```
IDL> arr = arr / float(max(arr))
```

Operators

IDL supports a full complement of mathematical operators (e.g. +, −, ^) for performing arithmetic operations. IDL also provides a range of relational (e.g., eq) and Boolean (e.g., and) operators to allow logical tests to be performed on IDL variables. The operators available in IDL are shown in Table 2.6.

Table 2.6   IDL operators.

Operator	Meaning	Precedence level (1 is highest)
( )	Parentheses	1
*	Pointer dereference	2
^	Exponentiation	2
*	Scalar multiplication	3
#	Array multiplication	3
##	Matrix multiplication	3
/	Division	3
mod	Modulus	3
+	Addition	4
-	Subtraction and negation	4
<	Minimum	4
>	Maximum	4
not	Boolean negation	4
eq	Equal to	5
ne	Not equal to	5
le	Less than or equal to	5
lt	Less than	5
ge	Greater than or equal to	5
gt	Greater than	5
and	Boolean AND	6
or	Boolean OR	6
xor	Boolean exclusive OR	6
?:	Ternary operator	7
=	Assignment	8

Operator Precedence

Precedence rules apply when multiple operators are included in a single expression, as in the following example:

```
IDL> print, 5.0 + 10.0 / 5.0
    7.00000
```

Here the division is evaluated first, and the addition is evaluated second, because division takes precedence over addition in IDL. Operators within an expression are applied in a specific order of precedence, depending on the operator type and where it appears in an expression. Operators are grouped into seven levels of precedence, as shown in Table 2.6. Higher-precedence operators are always evaluated before lower-precedence operators in an expression. If several operators in an expression have equal precedence, they are evaluated from left to right.

The safest way to ensure that an expression is evaluated as intended is to enclose subexpressions within parentheses:

```
IDL> print, (5.0 + 10.0) / 5.0
       3.00000
IDL> print, 5.0 + (10.0 / 5.0)
       7.00000
```

Enclosing a subexpression in parentheses ensures that it will be evaluated first. If an expression contains multiple levels of parentheses, the expression is evaluated from the innermost subexpression outwards.

Arithmetic Operations on Arrays

The operators available in IDL allow operations on both scalars and arrays (with the exception of the dereference operator, which only operates on scalar pointers). As discussed previously, it is generally more efficient to perform an arithmetic operation on an array than it is to perform the same operation on each element of the array in a loop. This is an important distinction between IDL and languages such as C or Fortran, where loops are required to process arrays. For example, to normalize an array with 100,000 elements in Fortran-77:

```
nelem = 100000
maxval = arr(1)
do index = 2, nelem
  maxval = max(arr(index), maxval)
end do
do index = 1, nelem
  arr(index) = arr(index) / maxval
end do
```

In IDL, you could construct loop statements to perform the same operation; however, array operations achieve the same result more efficiently:

```
IDL> maxval = max(arr)
IDL> arr = arr / maxval
```

You should always strive to find ways to use array operations in IDL because it will result in programs that are efficient (fast) and contain fewer lines of code.

Operators (with the exception of the pointer dereference operator) can be applied to arrays just as easily as they can be applied to scalars, as shown in the following examples:

```
IDL> a = 2.0
IDL> b = 3.0
IDL> print, a + b
      5.00000
IDL> c = [1, 3, 5, 7]
IDL> d = [2, 2, 2, 2]
IDL> print, c + d
      3       5       7       9
IDL> print, c * d
      2       6      10      14
```

If any one of the variables in an expression is an array, the result will be an array:

```
IDL> a = 10.0
IDL> b = [1.0, 2.0, 3.0, 4.0]
IDL> c = a * b
IDL> help, c
C               FLOAT     = Array[4]
IDL> print, c
      10.0000      20.0000      30.0000      40.0000
```

When the left side of the assignment statement is a subarray and the right side is a scalar, the scalar value is copied into all elements of the subarray:

```
IDL> arr = indgen(9)
IDL> arr[0:6] = 2.0 * 3.1415927
IDL> print, arr
      6       6       6       6       6       6       6
      7       8
```

If an expression contains arrays of different sizes, the result array will have as many elements as the smallest array in the expression (the array with the fewest elements):

```
IDL> print, [10, 10] * [1, 2, 3, 4, 5]
      10      20
```

If an expression contains arrays with different numbers of elements and dimensions, the result array will have as many elements and as many dimensions as the smallest array in the expression:

```
IDL> a = [10, 10, 10, 10, 10, 10, 10]
IDL> b = [[0, 1, 2], [3, 4, 5]]
IDL> print, a * b
       0      10      20
      30      40      50
```

If an expression contains arrays with the same number of elements but different dimensions, the result array will have as many dimensions as the leftmost array in the expression:

```
IDL> a = [10, 10, 10, 10]
IDL> b = [[0, 1], [2, 3]]
IDL> print, a * b
       0      10      20      30
IDL> print, b * a
       0      10
      20      30
```

Operator Precedence and Efficiency of Array Operations

As noted previously, operators in an IDL expression are evaluated in order of precedence. This can have an effect on the efficiency of array operations. For example, say you wish to normalize an array to a maximum value of 100:

```
IDL> arr = dist(256)
IDL> maxval = max(arr)
IDL> arr = arr * 100.0 / maxval
```

Because multiplication takes precedence over division in IDL, the normalization is evaluated as follows:

1. Multiply every element in arr by 100.0.
2. Take the result of step 1 and divide every element by maxval.

Thus every element of the array is operated on twice.

This expression can be rewritten so that each element of the array is operated on only once:

```
IDL> arr = arr * (100.0 / maxval)
```

Because the division is enclosed in parentheses, the division operation now takes precedence, and the normalization is evaluated as follows:

1. Divide 100.0 by maxval (a scalar expression).
2. Multiply every element of arr by the result of step 1.

Now half the number of operations are required, since each element of arr is operated on only once. This can provide significant efficiency gains if you are processing large arrays.

Minimum, Maximum, and Modulo Operators

The minimum operator ($<$) and maximum operator ($>$) return the smaller or larger values of their arguments, respectively:

```
IDL> print, 4 < 5, 5 < 5, 6 < 5
       4       5       5
IDL> print, 9 > 8, 8 > 8, 7 > 8
       9       8       8
```

Negative constants or negated variables on the right side of the minimum or maximum operator must be enclosed in parentheses:

```
IDL> print, 3 > (-1), -3 > (-1)
       3      -1
IDL> print, -5 > (-indgen(9))
       0      -1      -2      -3      -4      -5
      -5      -5      -5
```

The minimum and maximum operators are particularly useful when applied to arrays screening outlier values. For example, to set all negative values in an array to zero, the maximum operator can be used:

```
IDL> arr = [0, 1, 2, -999, 4, 5, -999, 7, 8]
IDL> print, arr > 0
       0       1       2       0       4       5       0
       7       8
```

When both arguments are arrays, the minimum and maximum operators operate on each pair of array elements in turn:

```
IDL> a = [2, 4, 6, 8]
IDL> b = [3, 4, 5, 6]
```

```
IDL> print, a < b
       2      4      5      6
```

The modulo operator (mod) returns the remainder of the first argument divided by the second argument:

```
IDL> print, 9 mod 2
       1
IDL> print, indgen(9) mod 2
       0      1      0      1      0      1      0
       1      0
```

Because of round-off errors, the modulo operator can give incorrect
results when used with real arguments. For example, the result should be
zero in both the following cases:

```
IDL> print, 1.0 mod 0.2, 100.0 mod 0.4
     0.200000    0.399999
```

To avoid round-off errors when computing the remainder of a real argument divided by a real argument, the following method can be used:

```
IDL> a = 1.0
IDL> b = 0.2
IDL> print, a - (b * long(a / b))
     0.000000
```

Array and Matrix Multiplication Operators

As noted previously, arrays in IDL are stored in memory in [column, row]
format. This differs from the normal mathematical concept of a matrix,
which is written in [row, column] format. Therefore, IDL includes two
operators that provide matrix multiplication functionality.

The array multiplication operator (#) multiplies the columns of the
first array argument by the rows of the second array argument:

```
IDL> a = indgen(3, 2) + 1
IDL> b = indgen(2, 3) - 1
IDL> print, a
       1      2      3
       4      5      6
IDL> print, b
      -1      0
       1      2
       3      4
IDL> c = a # b
```

```
IDL> print, c
        -1              -2              -3
         9              12              15
        19              26              33
```

In the first column of the result, the values are equal to

```
a[0, 0] * b[0, 0] + a[0, 1] * b[1, 0]
a[0, 0] * b[0, 1] + a[0, 1] * b[1, 1]
a[0, 0] * b[0, 2] + a[0, 1] * b[1, 2]
```

The result array (c) has the same number of columns as the first array (a), and the same number of rows as the second array (b). The second array must have the same number of columns as the first array has rows.

If the result array is printed using the transpose function, then the result array appears as though a conventional matrix multiplication operation were performed, where the rows of the first array argument are multiplied by the columns of the second array argument:

```
IDL> print, transpose(c)
        -1               9              19
        -2              12              26
        -3              15              33
```

The need to transpose the result of an array multiplication can cause confusion, so IDL also includes a matrix multiplication operator (##). The matrix multiplication operator multiplies the rows of the first array argument by the columns of the second array argument:

```
IDL> a = indgen(2, 4) - 2
IDL> b = indgen(4, 2) + 2
IDL> print, a
      -2      -1
       0       1
       2       3
       4       5
IDL> print, b
       2       3       4       5
       6       7       8       9
IDL> c = a ## b
IDL> print, c
       -10             -13             -16             -19
         6               7               8               9
        22              27              32              37
        38              47              56              65
```

In the first row of the result, the values are equal to

```
a[0, 0] * b[0, 0] + a[1, 0] * b[0, 1]
a[0, 0] * b[1, 0] + a[1, 0] * b[1, 1]
a[0, 0] * b[2, 0] + a[1, 0] * b[2, 1]
a[0, 0] * b[3, 0] + a[1, 0] * b[3, 1]
```

The result array (c) has the same number of rows as the first array (a), and the same number of columns as the second array (b). The second array must have the same number of rows as the first array has columns. When the result array is printed, it appears as though a conventional matrix multiplication operation were performed.

2.6   RELATIONAL AND BOOLEAN OPERATORS

Relational and Boolean operators allow you to perform true/false tests and comparisons on variables in IDL. An understanding of the fundamental nature of these operators is crucial for effective IDL programming.

Relational Operators

The relational operators available in IDL (eq, ne, le, lt, ge, gt) produce a numeric result, where "true" is represented by 1B, and "false" is represented by 0B:

```
IDL> a = 10.0
IDL> b = 20.0
IDL> help, a gt b
<Expression>    BYTE    =    0
IDL> help, a lt b
<Expression>    BYTE    =    1
```

Relational operators are often used in conjunction with an if statement:

```
IDL> if (a lt b) then print, 'True'
True
```

The if statement tests whether a given expression is true. In this case, the expression (a lt b) evaluates to 1B, which is interpreted as true. IDL does not support a dedicated logical data type, such as logical in Fortran. Instead, "true" and "false" are represented by special values, depending on the data type in question as shown in Table 2.7.

Table 2.7   True/false definitions.

Data type	True	False
Integer	Odd nonzero values (e.g., -3, -1, 1, 3, 5)	Zero and even values (e.g., -4, -2, 0, 2, 4, 6)
Floating point	Nonzero values (e.g., -1.0, -0.5, 0.5, 1.0, 3.1415)	Zero (i.e., 0.0)
String	Any string that is not null (e.g., 'Hello', 'IDL')	Null string (i.e., '')

Thus you can rewrite an if statement to explicitly check for a true or false result:

```
IDL> a = 10.0
IDL> b = 20.0
IDL> if (a gt b) eq 0B then print, 'False'
False
IDL> if (a lt b) eq 1B then print, 'True'
True
```

Relational operators can also be applied to array arguments:

```
IDL> a = 5
IDL> b = bindgen(9)
IDL> print, b
   0   1   2   3   4   5   6   7   8
IDL> c = b le a
IDL> print, c
   1   1   1   1   1   1   0   0   0
```

When both arguments are arrays, the relational operator is applied to each pair of corresponding array elements in turn:

```
IDL> a = [2, 4, 6, 8]
IDL> b = [3, 4, 5, 6]
IDL> print, a gt b
   0   0   1   1
```

When applied to array arguments, relational operators provide a way to "mask" values in an array. For example, say you wanted to find the sum of all elements in an array that are greater than or equal to five:

```
IDL> arr = indgen(9)
IDL> print, arr
```

```
     0      1      2      3      4      5      6
     7      8
IDL> mask = arr ge 5
IDL> print, mask * arr
     0      0      0      0      0      5      6
     7      8
IDL> print, total(mask * arr)
     26.0000
```

In this example, the mask is set to zero where the array elements are less than five, and one where the array elements are greater than or equal to five. Thus multiplying the mask by the array returns only the array values that are greater than or equal to five. The total function always returns a float result.

Tip   Equality tests (eq, ne) should be avoided when comparing floating-point variables because the precision of floating-point arithmetic varies between IDL platforms. Instead, test for agreement within a small tolerance that is larger than machine precision:

```
IDL> tol = 1.0e-6
IDL> if (abs(var1 - var2) lt tol) then $
IDL>    print, 'Values agree within tolerance'
```

See the online help for the machar function to determine the machine precision on your platform.

Boolean Operators

The Boolean operators not, and, or, and xor are available in IDL. Boolean operators may be used with any integer type in IDL, and also float and double types (xor can only be used with integer types). Boolean operators behave differently depending on the data type of the argument:

- When operating on integer arguments (byte, int, long, etc.), Boolean operators perform bit-wise operations. That is, each bit in the argument(s) is operated on in turn.
- When operating on floating-point arguments (float, double), Boolean operators return true or false.

This distinction is particularly important to keep in mind when using the not operator, which in other languages (e.g., Fortran) always returns a true or false result, regardless of argument type.

not *Operator*

The not operator performs a bit-wise complement on a single integer argument. Bits in the result are set where corresponding bits in the argument are unset, and vice versa:

```
IDL> arr = byte([0, 1, 2, 3, 4])
IDL> print, not arr
 255 254 253 252 251
IDL> arr = long([0, 1, 2, 3, 4])
IDL> print, not arr
          -1          -2          -3          -4          -5
```

Note the difference in results for an unsigned byte array and a signed long array because signed integers are represented in two's complement form.

The not operator performs a Boolean complement on a single floating-point argument. The result is false if the argument is true, and the result is true if the argument is false:

```
IDL> print, not 1.0
      0.000000
IDL> print, not 3.1415927
      0.000000
IDL> print, not 0.0
      1.00000
```

You should avoid using the not operator to form the Boolean complement of an integer. For example, say you wished to form the Boolean complement of a mask array:

```
IDL> mask = arr ge 5
IDL> print, mask
   0   0   0   0   0   1   1   1   1
IDL> mask = not(arr ge 5)
IDL> print, mask
 255 255 255 255 255 254 254 254 254
```

After the not operator is applied, the mask array no longer conforms to the IDL convention that 1B is true and 0B is false. If this mask array is used later with the expectation that 1B is true, problems can arise. For example, the following does not give the sum of all array elements that are less than five:

```
IDL> print, total(mask * arr)
      9154.00
```

To form the Boolean complement of an integer, you can subtract the variable from 1B:

```
IDL> arr = indgen(9)
IDL> mask = 1B - (arr ge 5)
IDL> print, mask
   1   1   1   1   1   0   0   0   0
IDL> print, total(mask * arr)
      10.0000
```

and *Operator*

The and operator performs a bit-wise AND when operating on a pair of integer arguments. A bit in the result is set if both corresponding bits in the arguments are set; all other bits in the result are unset:

```
IDL> a = [0, 0, 1, 1, 2]
IDL> b = [0, 1, 1, 2, 2]
IDL> print, a and b
      0      0      1      0      2
```

The and operator performs a Boolean AND when operating on a pair of float or double arguments. The result is true if both arguments are true; the result is false otherwise:

```
IDL> a = [0.0, 0.0, 1.0, 1.0, 2.0]
IDL> b = [0.0, 1.0, 1.0, 2.0, 2.0]
IDL> print, a and b
     0.000000     0.000000      1.00000      2.00000
     2.00000
```

The second argument is returned if both arguments are floating point and nonzero.

or *Operator*

The or operator performs a bit-wise OR when operating on a pair of integer arguments. A bit in the result is set if either of the corresponding bits in the arguments is set; all other bits in the result are unset:

```
IDL> a = [0, 0, 1, 1, 2]
IDL> b = [0, 1, 1, 2, 2]
IDL> print, a or b
      0      1      1      3      2
```

The or operator performs a Boolean OR when operating on a pair of float or double arguments. The result is true if either argument is true; the result is false otherwise. You will recall that any nonzero floating-point value is true in IDL:

```
IDL> a = [0.0, 0.0, 1.0, 1.0, 2.0]
IDL> b = [0.0, 1.0, 1.0, 2.0, 2.0]
IDL> print, a or b
      0.000000      1.00000      1.00000      1.00000
      2.00000
```

The first argument is returned if it is nonzero. If the first argument is zero, and the second argument is nonzero, the second argument is returned.

xor *Operator*

The xor operator performs a bit-wise XOR operation on a pair of integer arguments (it does not operate on float or double arguments). If corresponding bits in the arguments are different, the corresponding bit in the result is set; all other bits in the result are unset:

```
IDL> a = [0, 0, 1, 1, 2]
IDL> b = [0, 1, 1, 2, 2]
IDL> print, a xor b
      0      1      0      3      0
```

Combining Relational and Boolean Operators

Relational and Boolean operators are often combined to perform more complicated logical tests. Some examples of logical tests are shown below. Parentheses should be used to ensure that operators and arguments are grouped correctly, and to improve code readability:

```
IDL> a = 100
IDL> b = 120
IDL> print, (a gt 90) and (b gt 90)
   1
```

```
IDL> print, (a gt 110) and (b gt 110)
   0
IDL> print, (a gt 110) or (b gt 110)
   1
IDL> if ((a mod 10) eq 0) and ((b mod 10) eq 0) then print, $
IDL>    'Factors of 10'
Factors of 10
```

Tip   IDL does not "short-circuit" Boolean operators, as can happen in languages such as C or Fortran. In the following examples the logarithm
alog(x) is always evaluated, even if the first relational test (x gt 0.0) is
false:

```
IDL> x = 1.1
IDL> if (x gt 0.0) and (alog(x) gt 0.0) then $
IDL>   print, 'Log is positive'
Log is positive
IDL> x = 1.0
IDL> if (x gt 0.0) and (alog(x) gt 0.0) then $
IDL>   print, 'Log is positive'
IDL> x = 0.0
IDL> if (x gt 0.0) and (alog(x) gt 0.0) then $
IDL>   print, 'Log is positive'
% Program caused arithmetic error: Floating divide by 0
```

When x is equal to zero, the logarithm is still evaluated and an error message is printed. To short-circuit the evaluation of the logarithm, the test
must be rewritten:

```
IDL> x = 0.0
IDL> if (x gt 0.0) then if (alog(x) gt 0.0) then $
IDL>   print, 'Log is positive'
```

Ternary Operator

In the following example, an if statement is used to find the minimum of
two scalars:

```
IDL> x = 10
IDL> y = 5
```

```
IDL> if (x lt y) then z = x else z = y
IDL> print, z
        5
```

An alternative to this statement uses the ternary operator ? : to form a conditional expression:

```
IDL> z = (x lt y) ? x : y
IDL> print, z
        5
```

A conditional expression has the general form

$$expr_1 ? \; expr_2 \; : \; expr_3$$

where $expr_1$ is an expression that yields a true or false result. If the result is true, the value of the conditional expression is set to $expr_2$. If the result is false, the value of the conditional expression is set to $expr_3$. The type of the conditional expression is determined by the type of $expr_2$ or $expr_3$. Since the precedence of the ternary operator is very low (see Table 2.6), parentheses around $expr_1$ are not required. However, parentheses are recommended to visually distinguish $expr_1$ from the possible result values ($expr_2$ and $expr_3$).

Bit Manipulation

Boolean operators can be used to extract sequences of bits from integer variables. For example, to extract the four rightmost (least significant) bits from a byte variable, a mask is created with only the four rightmost bits set:

```
IDL> mask = 8B + 4B + 2B + 1B
IDL> help, mask
MASK            BYTE      =    15
```

To extract the bits, the mask is ANDed with the variable:

```
IDL> word = 35B
IDL> bits = word and mask
IDL> help, bits
BITS            BYTE      =     3
```

This example is depicted in Figure 2.1.

Bit no.	7	6	5	4	3	2	1	0	
Word	0	0	1	0	0	0	1	1	= 35
Mask	0	0	0	0	1	1	1	1	= 15
Result	0	0	0	0	0	0	1	1	= 3

Figure 2.1 Bit masking.

Of the four least significant bits in word, only bit numbers 1 and 0 are set, and the four most significant bits in the argument are "masked." The convention is to number bits in a word from left to right in decreasing order of significance, with the most significant bit (MSB) on the left, and the least significant bit (LSB) on the right.

The "shift and mask" method is often used when extracting bits from an arbitrary location in an integer variable. The bit shift operation in IDL is handled by the ishft function, which accepts two arguments. The first argument is the variable to be shifted, and the second argument specifies how many bit positions to shift (positive implies left shift, negative implies right shift). Vacant bit positions are filled with zero bits. For example, to extract the value of bits 6 and 5 from a byte variable, the bits are shifted five positions right to the zero position, and a mask is applied to the two least significant bits.

```
IDL> word = 35B
IDL> shifted = ishft(word, -5)
IDL> help, shifted
SHIFTED          BYTE       =    1
IDL> mask = 2B + 1B
IDL> bits = shifted and mask
IDL> help, bits
BITS             BYTE       =    1
```

This example is depicted in Figure 2.2.

After all bits in word are shifted right five positions and mask is applied, the result is 1B.

2.7   STRUCTURES

Structures are a special data type that allows variables of different types and sizes to be packaged into one entity (unlike an array, where every element must be the same data type). Two kinds of structures are supported in IDL. The first kind, known as an *anonymous structure,* is a package of

Bit no.	7	6	5	4	3	2	1	0	
Word	0	0	1	0	0	0	1	1	= 35
Shifted	0	0	0	0	0	0	0	1	= 1
Mask	0	0	0	0	0	0	1	1	= 3
Result	0	0	0	0	0	0	0	1	= 1

Figure 2.2 Bit shift and mask.

arbitrary variables. The second kind, known as a *named structure,* is a package of variables that conforms to a template created by the user. Structures are used when it makes sense to collect and store a group of related items (e.g., the name, identification number, and grade for each student in a class).

Anonymous Structures

Anonymous structures are created by enclosing variable name/value pairs within curly brackets {}. In the following example, the name, valid range, and data for a two-dimensional image array are stored in an anonymous structure.

```
IDL> image={name:'Test Image', valid_range:[0.0, 100.0] $
IDL>  data:dist(256)}
```

The name of each variable in the structure must follow the same naming rules as normal IDL variables. The help procedure reveals image to be an array variable of struct type with one element:

```
IDL> help, image
IMAGE           STRUCT    = -> <Anonymous> Array[1]
```

To reveal the contents of the structure, the help procedure is called with the optional structure keyword set:

```
IDL> help, image, /structure
** Structure <1052178>, 3 tags, length=262160, refs=1:
   NAME            STRING    'Test Image'
   VALID_RANGE     FLOAT     Array[2]
   DATA            FLOAT     Array[256, 256]
```

Variables within a structure are accessed by appending the variable name to the structure name with a period separator:

```
IDL> print, image.name
Test Image
```

Structure variables can also be accessed by enclosing a scalar index value in parentheses (not square brackets) after the period:

```
IDL> help, image.(0)
<Expression>    STRING    = 'Test Image'
IDL> help, image.(1)
<Expression>    FLOAT     = Array[2]
IDL> help, image.(2)
<Expression>    FLOAT     = Array[256, 256]
```

The value of any variable within a structure can be modified:

```
IDL> image.data = image.data * (1.0 / max(image.data))
IDL> image.name = 'Normalized Test Image'
IDL> image.valid_range = [0.0, 1.0]
```

However, the type and size of a variable within a structure cannot be modified:

```
IDL> image.data = long(image.data)
IDL> help, image.data
<Expression>    FLOAT     = Array[256, 256]
IDL> image.data = 1
IDL> help, image.data
<Expression>    FLOAT     = Array[256, 256]
IDL> print, image.data[0:4]
      1.00000      1.00000      1.00000      1.00000
      1.00000
```

In this example, attempting to change the type of the structure variable image.data from float to long had no effect. Setting the same structure variable to a scalar value did not change the variable to a scalar value; it just assigned the scalar value to all elements in the array. Setting the same structure variable to a new array overwrites the corresponding elements in the existing array and leaves the other elements unchanged:

```
IDL> image.data = [100, 200, 300]
IDL> print, image.data[0:4]
      100.000      200.000      300.000      1.00000
      1.00000
```

Nested structures can be created by enclosing an existing structure within curly brackets:

```
IDL> sample = {date:'19-Mar-1999', time:'20:02:05', $
IDL>    image:image}
IDL> print, sample.date
```

```
19-Mar-1999
IDL> print, sample.image.name
Normalized Test Image
```

Arrays of Structures

Anonymous structure arrays can be created by calling the replicate function:

```
IDL> image = {name:'Test Image', valid_range:[0.0, 100.0], $
IDL>   data:dist(256)}
IDL> sequence = replicate(image, 10)
```

In this example, an array of structures was created with 10 elements. To access elements of the array, the structure name is followed by an array index in square brackets:

```
IDL> sequence[0].name = 'First Test Image'
IDL> sequence[0].data[0:100] = 1.0
```

In contrast, anonymous structures that are seemingly identical cannot be formed into an array by enclosing the structures in square brackets, as demonstrated in the following example:

```
IDL> a = {name:'Sean', age:32}
IDL> b = {name:'Kate', age:25}
IDL> c = [a, b]
% Conflicting data structures: B,concatenation.
% Execution halted at:  $MAIN$
```

The reason is that even though the structures contain the same type and number of variables, as far as IDL is concerned each anonymous structure is an arbitrary construct, and IDL cannot assume that a and b contain the same types and sizes. Each anonymous structure has a unique internal identifier, which can be seen in the output from help:

```
IDL> help, a, /structure
** Structure <10521f8>, 2 tags, length=12, refs=1:
   NAME            STRING    'Sean'
   AGE             INT              32
IDL> help, b, /structure
** Structure <1053da8>, 2 tags, length=12, refs=1:
   NAME            STRING    'Kate'
   AGE             INT              25
```

The identifiers in this case are <10521f8> and <1053da8>. IDL will refuse to form an array from two (or more) anonymous structures that have different identifers. The best solution to this problem is the use of named structures.

Named Structures

Named structures conform to a template that is created by the user. Once a template is created, it cannot be modified for the remainder of the IDL session. To create a new named structure, the template name is enclosed in curly brackets, followed by variable name/value pairs:

```
IDL> rec = {nav_record, time:0.0, lat:0.0, lon:0.0, $
IDL>    heading:0.0}
```

In this example, a template named nav_record is created containing four variables that encode a navigation fix (time, latitude, longitude, heading). The first instance of this named structure is the variable rec. The variables in the structure are accessed as shown previously:

```
IDL> print, rec.lat, rec.lon
      0.000000      0.000000
```

New instances of the structure can be created by enclosing the template name in curly brackets, or by copying an existing instance of the structure:

```
IDL> xrec = {nav_record}
IDL> xrec.time = 12.25
IDL> yrec = rec
IDL> yrec.time = 13.50
```

Named structure arrays can be created by calling the replicate function:

```
IDL> rec = {nav_record, time:0.0, lat:0.0, lon:0.0, $
IDL>    heading:0.0}
IDL> data = replicate({nav_record}, 100)
IDL> help, data
DATA            STRUCT    = -> NAV_RECORD Array[100]
```

Arrays can also be created by enclosing instances of the named structure in square brackets:

```
IDL> a = {nav_record}
IDL> b = {nav_record}
IDL> c = [a, b]
```

```
IDL> help, c
C                 STRUCT   = -> NAV_RECORD Array[2]
```

Working with Structures

The functions available for working with structures in IDL are shown in Table 2.8.

The n_tags function returns the number of variables (also known as *tags*) in a structure:

```
IDL> image = {name:'Test Image', valid_range:[0.0, 100.0], $
IDL>   data:dist(256)}
IDL> print, n_tags(image)
        3
```

The tag_names function returns the names of each variable in a structure in a string array:

```
IDL> print, tag_names(image)
NAME VALID_RANGE DATA
```

The names are always returned in uppercase. If the optional structure_name keyword is passed to tag_names, the name of the structure is returned (the null string is returned for anonymous structures).

The create_struct function may also be used to create structures and is particularly useful for two reasons:

1. It allows structures (anonymous or named) to be created at runtime. For example, you might not know the contents of a structure until a file is read at runtime, and any given file could contain different combinations of variable types and sizes.
2. It allows you to append new variables to an existing anonymous structure.

Table 2.8   Functions for working with structures.

Function name	Purpose
n_tags()	Return the number of variables (tags) within a structure
tag_names()	Return the name of each variable (tag) within a structure
create_struct()	Create a structure, or append variables to a structure

To create a structure, `create_struct` is called with a sequence of variable name/value pairs as arguments:

```
IDL> image = create_struct('data', dist(256), $
IDL>    'valid_range', [0.0, 100.0])
IDL> help, image.data
<Expression>    FLOAT    = Array[256, 256]
IDL> print, image.valid_range
      0.000000      100.000
```

In this example, a new anonymous structure was created with two variables named `data` and `valid_range`. The optional `create_struct` keyword `name` allows you to specify a named structure.

If the first argument passed to `create_struct` is an existing anonymous structure, then the variable name/value pairs that follow are appended to the existing structure:

```
IDL> image = create_struct('data', dist(256), $
IDL>    'valid_range', [0.0, 100.0])
IDL> image = create_struct(image, 'date', systime())
IDL> help, image.data
<Expression>    FLOAT    = Array[256, 256]
IDL> help, image.date
<Expression>    STRING    = 'Wed Dec 08 13:58:53 1999'
```

The existing structure need not be the first argument passed to `create _struct`. Variable name/value pairs may be prepended or appended to the existing structure depending on where the structure appears in the `create_struct` argument list.

Tip   When you need to merge the contents of two existing structures, the `struct_assign` procedure may be used. See the online help for more information on `struct_assign` and Relaxed Structure Assignment.

2.8   POINTERS

A pointer in IDL is a special variable that does not contain a "value" in the usual sense. Rather, a pointer is simply a reference to an IDL variable. The variable may be any IDL data type, including scalars, arrays, structures, and other pointers. Pointers facilitate the storage of complex collections of data, particularly when the size and type of the data are not known in advance. One situation where pointers are useful is when storing arrays of arbitrary size and type in structures. As described previously, the size and type of a variable in a structure cannot be changed without recreating the structure. However, if you create a pointer and store it in a structure, it can point to an array whose size and type can be modified at any time. For example, you could envision an array of structures where each element in the array is a structure containing an image of arbitrary size, along with an image name, date, and valid range. Pointers are global in scope, which means that a pointer created anywhere in an IDL session is visible at all levels in that IDL session.

The added flexibility of pointers in IDL comes at a price. If you are not careful about managing pointers, variables can become "lost" in your IDL session and you are left with no way to reference them. Pointers are inherently difficult to use safely, and you should exercise caution when you use pointers in your IDL programming. This section encourages the use of pointers while illustrating techniques that help avoid problems.

The functions and procedures available for working with pointers are summarized in Table 2.9.

Types of Pointers

A pointer in IDL can exist in either of two states: *valid* or *invalid*.

• Pointers that point to an IDL variable, or to an undefined variable, are known as valid pointers. Valid pointers may be dereferenced, meaning the variable pointed to may be accessed regardless of whether the variable is defined.

Table 2.9 Functions and procedures for working with pointers.

Name	Purpose
ptr_new()	Return a new pointer
ptrarr()	Return an array of new pointers
ptr_free	Free the memory referenced by a pointer
ptr_valid()	Check the validity of a pointer

- Pointers that do not point to anything are known as invalid pointers. Invalid pointers may not be dereferenced (since they don't point to anything). Pointers in this category include a special kind of pointer known as a null pointer, and any pointer whose memory has been freed.

When a pointer is first created, it may be in either a valid or invalid state. However, just like any other variable in IDL, pointers may be redefined at any time. Thus a pointer that is valid when created may be redefined as invalid, and vice versa.

Creating Pointers

To create a scalar pointer, the ptr_new function is called:

```
IDL> p = ptr_new(1.0)
IDL> help, p
P               POINTER   = <PtrHeapVar1>
```

In this example, a new pointer p is created, which points to a float value of 1.0. To access the variable pointed to by the pointer p, the pointer must be dereferenced. The dereference operator in IDL is an asterisk character placed immediately before the pointer name:

```
IDL> print, *p
    1.00000
```

There are three ways to call ptr_new to create a new pointer. The first way is to create a pointer to an existing variable:

```
IDL> arr = indgen(5)
IDL> ptr1 = ptr_new(arr)
IDL> help, *ptr1
<PtrHeapVar2>   INT       = Array[5]
```

In this example, calling ptr_new with an argument that is an existing variable (arr) creates a pointer (ptr1) that points to the variable (a float index array with five elements). When the pointer is dereferenced, the array that ptr1 points to is exposed.

The second way is to create a pointer to an undefined variable:

```
IDL> ptr2 = ptr_new(/allocate_heap)
IDL> help, *ptr2
<PtrHeapVar3>   UNDEFINED = <Undefined>
```

In this example, calling `ptr_new` with the optional keyword `allocate_heap` creates a pointer (`ptr2`) that points to an undefined variable. When the pointer is dereferenced via `help`, the undefined variable that `ptr2` points to is exposed. The pointer `ptr2` can subsequently be directed to point to a defined variable:

```
IDL> *ptr2 = dist(256)
% Compiled module: DIST.
IDL> help, *ptr2
<PtrHeapVar3>   FLOAT     = Array[256, 256]
```

The third way is to create an invalid (null) pointer:

```
IDL> ptr3 = ptr_new()
IDL> help, *ptr3
% Unable to dereference NULL pointer: PTR3.
% Execution halted at:  $MAIN$
```

In this example, calling `ptr_new` with no arguments creates a null pointer (`ptr3`). Null pointers cannot be dereferenced, and any attempt to dereference a null pointer results in the error message shown. Null pointers are used when a pointer must be created, but the variable to be referenced by the pointer does not yet exist (e.g., in an array of structures, where pointers are used to store variables whose size and type are not known in advance).

To create an array of pointers, the `ptrarr` function is called:

```
IDL> ptr = ptrarr(10, /allocate_heap)
IDL> *ptr[0] = dist(256)
IDL> *ptr[1] = indgen(10)
```

In this example, a pointer array (`ptr`) with 10 elements is created. Setting the `allocate_heap` keyword causes `ptrarr` to create pointers to undefined variables. If the `allocate_heap` keyword is absent, then all pointers in the array will be null pointers.

Note that you can only dereference scalar pointers. For example, the following statement causes an error:

```
IDL> help, *ptr[0:2]
% Expression must be a scalar in this context: $
IDL>    <POINTER   Array[3]>.
% Execution halted at:  $MAIN$
```

Here an attempt was made to dereference three elements of a pointer array; only scalar pointers may be dereferenced.

Freeing Pointers

When using pointers in IDL, it is good practice to have your code clean up after itself. This means not leaving any pointers, or variables that are referenced by pointers, lying around in memory after you are finished using them. For this reason, you should take care to free the memory referenced by a pointer when the pointer is no longer needed.

To release the memory referenced by a pointer, the ptr_free procedure is used:

```
IDL> ptr = ptr_new(10.0)
IDL> ptr_free, ptr
```

Once you have freed the memory referenced by a pointer, the pointer becomes invalid. This means that even though the pointer itself still exists, it can no longer be dereferenced because the memory associated with the pointer has been released:

```
IDL> help, ptr
PTR             POINTER   = <PtrHeapVar1>
IDL> print, *ptr
% Invalid pointer: PTR.
% Execution halted at:  $MAIN$
```

Calling the help procedure shows that while ptr still exists, any attempt to dereference ptr causes an error. However, once the pointer has been freed, the pointer may be redefined with a new type and size (including redefinition as a new pointer).

Checking Pointer Validity

As seen previously, attempts to dereference invalid pointers result in an error, so a method for checking pointer validity is required. To detect invalid pointers, IDL includes the built-in function ptr_valid, which returns true if the argument is a valid pointer, and false otherwise:

```
IDL> ptr = ptr_new(10.0)
IDL> print, ptr_valid(ptr)
   1
IDL> ptr_free, ptr
IDL> print, ptr_valid(ptr)
   0
```

The `ptr_valid` function also provides a way to check for null pointers:

```
IDL> ptr = ptr_new()
IDL> print, ptr_valid(ptr)
   0
```

The `ptr_valid` function accepts any IDL variable as an argument, including undefined variables:

```
IDL> help, zzz
ZZZ             UNDEFINED = <Undefined>
IDL> print, ptr_valid(zzz)
   0
```

Thus, `ptr_valid` returns false for both invalid pointers and any IDL data type that is not a pointer.

Pointer Dereferencing

When a pointer points to an array, it is simple to dereference the pointer and obtain the entire array:

```
IDL> ptr = ptr_new(indgen(4, 4))
IDL> print, *ptr
      0       1       2       3
      4       5       6       7
      8       9      10      11
     12      13      14      15
```

However, to obtain a subarray, indices cannot simply be appended to the pointer variable:

```
IDL> print, *ptr[0, *]
% Expression must be a scalar in this context:
  <POINTER   Array[1]>.
% Execution halted at: $MAIN$
```

The correct method is to enclose the dereferenced array in parentheses and then append indices:

```
IDL> print, (*ptr)[0, *]
      0
      4
      8
     12
```

To dereference pointers that point to other pointers, the dereference operator (*) can be stacked as many times as necessary:

```
IDL> ptr_a = ptr_new(10.0)
IDL> ptr_b = ptr_new(ptr_a)
IDL> print, **ptr_b
     10.0000
```

If a pointer is included in a structure, the dereference operator is placed immediately before the structure name:

```
IDL> rec = {flag:1L, data_ptr:ptr_new(indgen(5))}
IDL> print, *rec.data_ptr
       0     1     2     3     4
```

If a pointer is used to reference a structure containing a pointer, the structure itself must be dereferenced inside parentheses before the pointer contained in the structure can be dereferenced:

```
IDL> struct_ptr = ptr_new(rec)
IDL> print, *(*struct_ptr).data_ptr
       0     1     2     3     4
```

Complex dereferencing operations can make your code difficult to read and understand. You can help improve the readability of dereferencing operations by using well-named intermediate variables that make clear the meaning of the dereferenced variable. For example, say that you've stored a two-dimensional array (an image) within a structure. You've used a pointer to reference the array in the structure because the array size and type are not known until runtime, and you've also used a pointer to reference the structure:

```
IDL> image = dist(256)
IDL> struct = {name:'Test Image',
data_ptr:ptr_new(image)}
IDL> struct_ptr = ptr_new(struct)
```

At some subsequent time, you wish to display the image and print its name. The dereference operations are as follows:

```
IDL> tvscl, *(*struct_ptr).data_ptr
IDL> print, (*struct_ptr).name
Test Image
```

To make the intent of this code more obvious to readers (including your-self), use intermediate variables:

```
IDL> image = *(*struct_ptr).data_ptr
IDL> name = (*struct_ptr).name
IDL> tvscl, image
IDL> print, name
```

Avoiding Pointer Problems

Memory leakage occurs when you neglect to free the memory associated with a pointer. Consider the following example:

```
IDL> ptr = ptr_new(1.0)
IDL> ptr = ptr_new(indgen(100))
```

Here a pointer variable (ptr) is created that points to a float scalar vari-able. Then a pointer with the same name (ptr) is created that points to an int array. What happened to the float scalar variable? As it happens, the variable still exists in memory, but there is no way to reference it because the pointer was redefined. To see a list of all variables in memory that are currently referenced by a pointer, or were previously referenced by a pointer (known collectively as *heap variables*), the help procedure can be called with the heap_variables keyword set:

```
IDL> help, /heap_variables
Heap Variables:
    # Pointer: 2
    # Object : 0

<PtrHeapVar2>   FLOAT    =        1.00000
<PtrHeapVar3>   INT      = Array[100]
```

In this example, the first variable referenced by ptr still exists in mem-ory, but there is no longer a way to reference this variable. To guard against memory leakage, you can test the proposed pointer variable to see if it is already a valid pointer:

```
IDL> if (ptr_valid(ptr) eq 1) then ptr_free, ptr
IDL> ptr = ptr_new(10.0)
```

In this case, the proposed pointer variable ptr is tested for validity. If the proposed variable is already a valid pointer, it is freed by calling ptr_free.

Then the pointer variable ptr is created by calling ptr_new, with no risk of memory leakage.

Another technique for dealing with memory leakage is to use the ptr_valid function in either of the following ways:

- If no argument is supplied, ptr_valid returns a vector of valid pointers to all heap variables in memory.
- If a single heap variable index is supplied as the first argument, and the cast keyword is set, ptr_valid returns a valid pointer to the variable.

Another type of problem can occur when pointers are freed with ptr_free. Consider the following example:

```
IDL> ptr = ptr_new(2.0)
IDL> ptr_free, ptr
IDL> print, *ptr
% Invalid pointer: PTR.
% Execution halted at:  $MAIN$
IDL> help, ptr
PTR             POINTER   = <PtrHeapVar3>
```

Here you can see that even though the pointer was made invalid by calling ptr_free (it can no longer be dereferenced), the pointer still exists in an unhappy "almost dead" state. Pointers in this state are known as *dangling references,* and they will cause a program halt if you attempt to dereference them. To guard against dangling references, check the validity of a pointer before you attempt to dereference it. If your application creates and frees many pointers, you may wish to consider writing a wrapper that handles pointer creation and destruction.

Your last refuge for detecting and avoiding pointer problems is to perform explicit pointer garbage collection. This involves calling a procedure that searches the entire IDL memory space for variables formerly referenced by pointers that have become inaccessible, and then removes every single one of them. To perform pointer garbage collection as a last resort or as a debugging aid, call the heap_gc procedure with the ptr and verbose keywords set:

```
IDL> ptr = ptr_new(dist(256))
IDL> ptr = ptr_new(indgen(10))
IDL> ptr = ptr_new(2.0)
IDL> heap_gc, /ptr, /verbose
```

```
<PtrHeapVar1>    FLOAT     = Array[256, 256]
<PtrHeapVar2>    INT       = Array[10]
```

In this example, the same pointer variable was redefined three times, leaving the first two variables in limbo. When heap_gc is called with the ptr keyword set, it searches the entire IDL memory space for any variables that have become inaccessible because of pointer redefinition and removes them. This is an inefficient operation, which can be avoided by using the techniques shown previously for creating and freeing pointers. The use of heap_gc within IDL programs is strongly discouraged because it obscures pointer bugs.

2.9   ARRAY PROPERTIES

When developing IDL programs, you will sometimes need to obtain information about the properties of an array, such as the number of elements, number of dimensions, the size of each dimension, and the type of the array (long, float, string, etc.). In other cases you may need to find the largest or smallest value within an array, compute statistics from the array, or compute totals along certain array dimensions. For this reason, IDL provides a suite of functions that are designed to return information about the properties of an array, as shown in Table 2.10.

Table 2.10   Functions for determining array properties.

Function name	Returns
n_elements()	Number of array elements
size()	Array size and type information
min()	Minimum array value
max()	Maximum array value
mean()	Mean of array values
variance()	Variance of array values
stddev()	Standard deviation of array values
moment()	Mean, variance, skew, kurtosis, standard deviation, mean absolute deviation
total()	Sum of array values

Number of Array Elements

The n_elements function returns the number of elements in an array:

```
IDL> arr = findgen(32, 32)
IDL> help, arr
ARR               FLOAT     = Array[32, 32]
IDL> print, n_elements(arr)
      1024
```

If the array is undefined (i.e., it does not exist), then a value of zero is returned:

```
IDL> help, foobar
FOOBAR            UNDEFINED = <Undefined>
IDL> print, n_elements(foobar)
         0
```

Tip The n_elements function is commonly used within IDL programs to test whether a variable (array or otherwise) is defined. If n_elements returns zero, the variable is undefined. In interactive mode, the help procedure is usually more convenient for this purpose.

Array Size and Type

The size function returns a long vector that contains size and type information about an input array (or scalar or expression). The optional keywords n_dimensions, dimensions, type, tname, and n_elements return the number of dimensions, dimension sizes, type code (see Table 2.11), type name, and number of elements, respectively:

```
IDL> arr = dist(256)
IDL> help, arr
ARR               FLOAT     = Array[256, 256]
IDL> print, size(arr, /n_dimensions)
         2
IDL> print, size(arr, /dimensions)
      256        256
IDL> print, size(arr, /type)
         4
IDL> print, size(arr, /tname)
```

Table 2.11 IDL Type Codes and Names.

Data type	Type code	Type name
Undefined	0	`'UNDEFINED'`
Byte	1	`'BYTE'`
Integer	2	`'INT'`
Long integer	3	`'LONG'`
Float	4	`'FLOAT'`
Double precision	5	`'DOUBLE'`
Complex float	6	`'COMPLEX'`
String	7	`'STRING'`
Structure	8	`'STRUCT'`
Complex double precision	9	`'DCOMPLEX'`
Pointer	10	`'POINTER'`
Object reference	11	`'OBJREF'`
Unsigned integer	12	`'UINT'`
Unsigned long integer	13	`'ULONG'`
64-bit integer	14	`'LONG64'`
Unsigned 64-bit integer	15	`'ULONG64'`

```
FLOAT
IDL> print, size(arr, /n_elements)
      65536
```

Note The size keywords mentioned are only available in IDL 5.2 and higher.

If no keywords are supplied to size, it returns a long vector containing size and type information about the argument:

```
IDL> arr = dist(256)
IDL> print, size(arr)
          2         256         256           4       65536
```

The contents of the vector returned by size are the following:

1. The number of dimensions (zero if the argument is a scalar or is undefined)
2. The size of each dimension (if one or more dimensions exist)
3. The type code for the argument (zero if the argument is undefined)
4. The number of elements in the argument

To extract array type and size information from the vector returned by size, the following method can be used:

```
IDL> data = dist(32)
IDL> result = size(data)
IDL> ndims = result[0]
IDL> if (ndims gt 0) then $
IDL>    dims = result[1:ndims] else dims = -1L
IDL> type = result[ndims + 1]
IDL> nele = result[ndims + 2]
```

In this example, ndims is the number of dimensions, dims is an array of dimension sizes, type is the type code, and nele is the number of elements.

Minimum and Maximum Values

The min and max functions return the minimum and maximum values of an array:

```
IDL> arr = dist(32)
IDL> print, min(arr), max(arr)
     0.000000      22.6274
```

To avoid scanning the input array twice, the min function can also return the maximum value via the max keyword:

```
IDL> minval = min(arr, max=maxval)
IDL> print, minval, maxval
     0.000000      22.6274
```

The min and max functions both accept an optional argument, which on output contains the one-dimensional array index of the minimum or maximum value, respectively:

```
IDL> maxval = max(arr, index)
IDL> print, index
```

Mean, Variance, and Standard Deviation

The mean, variance, and stddev functions return the mean, variance, and standard deviation of an array:

```
IDL> arr = findgen(10) * 100.0
IDL> print, arr, format='(10f6.1)'
  0.0 100.0 200.0 300.0 400.0 500.0 600.0 700.0 800.0 900.0
IDL> print, mean(arr), variance(arr), stddev(arr)
     450.000       91666.7       302.765
```

The moment function returns the mean, variance, skew, and kurtosis of an array:

```
IDL> result = moment(arr)
IDL> print, result
     450.000       91666.7 2.88252e-008      -1.56164
```

If the optional sdev and mdev keywords are supplied, moment also returns the standard deviation and mean absolute deviation:

```
IDL> result = moment(arr, sdev=sdev, mdev=mdev)
IDL> print, sdev, mdev
     302.765       250.000
```

Totals

The total function returns the total of an array:

```
IDL> arr = indgen(3, 3)
IDL> print, arr
       0       1       2
       3       4       5
       6       7       8
IDL> print, total(arr)
     36.0000
```

An optional argument can be passed to total to specify the dimension along which totals should be computed. For example, to compute totals along the first dimension:

```
IDL> print, total(arr, 1)
     3.00000       12.0000       21.0000
```

To compute totals along the second dimension:

```
IDL> print, total(arr, 2)
      9.00000      12.0000       15.0000
```

Cumulative totals are computed if the optional keyword cumulative is set:

```
IDL> arr = indgen(9)
IDL> print, arr, format='(9i6)'
     0     1     2     3     4     5     6     7     8
IDL> print, total(arr, /cumulative), format='(9f6.1)'
    0.0   1.0   3.0   6.0  10.0  15.0  21.0  28.0  36.0
```

Note   The cumulative keyword is only available in IDL 5.3 and higher.

2.10   LOCATING VALUES WITHIN AN ARRAY

One of the most common tasks when working with arrays is locating elements that meet a certain condition, such as values that are greater than a threshold. The where function is used for this purpose and is one of the most useful array-related functions in IDL.

Finding Values That Meet Selection Critieria

The following example demonstrates how array elements greater than a threshold are found:

```
IDL> arr = indgen(9) * 10
IDL> print, arr
     0     10     20     30     40     50     60
    70     80
IDL> index = where(arr gt 35)
IDL> print, arr[index]
    40     50     60     70     80
```

The where function returns the indices of the nonzero elements in an array or array expression. Thus, in the previous example, where returned the nonzero indices of the expression (arr gt 35) (recall that relational operators in IDL return 0 for false, and 1 for true). So where returned the locations of arrays elements where the expression (arr gt 35) was true. This is easier to see when the relational operator is separated from the where call:

```
IDL> result = arr gt 35
IDL> print, result
   0   0   0   0   1   1   1   1   1
```

The array `result` now contains a value of 1 wherever the expression (`arr gt 35`) is true in `arr`. Now `where` can be called to retrieve the locations of the nonzero elements in `result`:

```
IDL> index = where(result)
IDL> print, index
           4           5           6           7           8
IDL> print, arr[index]
      40        50        60        70        80
```

The expression passed to `where` may be as complicated as desired. For example, to find the array values greater than 35 that are also multiples of four:

```
IDL> index = where((arr gt 35) and ((arr mod 4) eq 0))
IDL> print, arr[index]
      40        60        80
```

You should always account for the possibility that `where` will not find any nonzero values in the input array or expression (i.e., no values meet the prescribed conditions). In this case, `where` returns a scalar long equal to −1:

```
IDL> index = where(arr lt -10000.0)
IDL> help, index
INDEX           LONG      =           -1
```

For this reason the `where` function accepts an optional `count` argument, which returns the number of nonzero elements found:

```
IDL> arr = dist(16)
IDL> print, min(arr), max(arr)
     0.000000       11.3137
IDL> index = where(arr lt -10.0, count)
IDL> print, count
          0
IDL> index = where(arr gt 9.0, count)
IDL> print, count
         25
```

The optional `count` argument is recommended whenever `where` is used within an IDL program.

Working with One-Dimensional Indices from where

When the argument to where is a two-dimensional or higher-dimension array, the returned array of index values always appears as though the input array were one-dimensional:

```
IDL> arr = dist(250, 500)
IDL> help, arr
ARR             FLOAT     = Array[250, 500]
IDL> index = where(arr gt 150.0)
IDL> help, index
INDEX           LONG      = Array[59942]
IDL> print, arr[index[0]]
      150.047
```

You will recall that any array in IDL may be accessed as though it were one-dimensional. Often the index array returned by where can be used in this fashion. However, a transformation is required if you wish to work with multidimensional indices (e.g., column, row), keeping in mind that IDL stores arrays in column-major order:

```
IDL> dims = size(arr, /dimensions)
IDL> print, dims
         250          500
IDL> ncol = dims[0]
IDL> col_index = index mod ncol
IDL> row_index = index / ncol
IDL> print, arr[col_index[0], row_index[0]]
      150.047
```

This method may be extended to higher dimensions if required, and is left as an exercise for the reader.

Finding Values That Don't Meet Selection Critieria

In some cases, you may wish to find the indices of array elements that do not meet a specified condition (i.e., where the result of an expression is false). This is easily accomplished, at the cost of two where calls. First, create an array of relational operator results:

```
IDL> arr = indgen(10)
IDL> test = arr gt 5
```

```
IDL> print, test
0 0 0 0 0 0 1 1 1 1
```

Then use `where` to locate the indices where the test gave true (1) and false (0) values:

```
IDL> true_index = where(test eq 1, true_count)
IDL> false_index = where(test eq 0, false_count)
IDL> print, true_index, false_index
6  7  8  9
0  1  2  3  4  5
```

In IDL 5.4 and later versions this functionality is built into the `where` function via the `complement` and `ncomplement` keywords.

2.11 ARRAY REORDERING

Array reordering refers to operations that change the order of dimensions or elements in an array without changing the total number of elements. Because IDL is optimized for array operations, a good understanding of how to reorder arrays is crucial for effective programming. The functions available for array reordering are summarized in Table 2.12.

Changing Array Dimensions

The `reform` function changes the number or size of dimensions of an array without changing the number of elements. For example, to transform a one-dimensional array to a two-dimensional array:

Table 2.12 Array reordering functions.

Function name	Purpose
reform()	Change array dimensions without changing contents
reverse()	Reverse order of array elements
rotate()	Rotate and/or transpose array
transpose()	Transpose array (reverse dimension order)
shift()	Shift array elements
sort()	Get indices of sorted array elements
uniq()	Get indices of unique elements in a sorted array

```
IDL> arr = [0, 20, 40, 60, 80, 100]
IDL> arr = reform(arr, 3, 2)
IDL> help, arr
ARR               INT      = Array[3, 2]
IDL> print, arr
       0      20      40
      60      80     100
```

The size of each dimension can also be changed by reform without changing the number of dimensions:

```
IDL> arr = indgen(6, 2)
IDL> print, arr
       0       1       2       3       4       5
       6       7       8       9      10      11
IDL> arr = reform(arr, 3, 4)
IDL> print, arr
       0       1       2
       3       4       5
       6       7       8
       9      10      11
```

Any dimensions in the input array that have a size of one (known as *degenerate dimensions*) are automatically removed by reform. This can be useful when extracting a column from a two-dimensional array:

```
IDL> arr = indgen(5, 5)
IDL> col = arr[0, *]
IDL> help, col
COL               INT      = Array[1, 5]
IDL> col = reform(col)
IDL> help, col
COL               INT      = Array[5]
```

To conserve memory, the overwrite keyword may be used with reform to change the dimension information of an array without making a copy of the array:

```
IDL> arr = dist(32)
IDL> help, arr
ARR               FLOAT    = Array[32, 32]
IDL> arr = reform(arr, 32L * 32L, /overwrite)
IDL> help, arr
ARR               FLOAT    = Array[1024]
```

Reversing Array Elements

The reverse function reverses the order of elements in a one-, two-, or three-dimensional array:

```
IDL> arr = indgen(5)
IDL> print, arr
       0       1       2       3       4
IDL> print, reverse(arr)
       4       3       2       1       0
```

When operating on two- or three-dimensional arrays, reverse accepts an optional argument that specifies the dimension to be reversed:

```
IDL> arr = indgen(3, 3)
IDL> print, arr
       0       1       2
       3       4       5
       6       7       8
IDL> print, reverse(arr)
       2       1       0
       5       4       3
       8       7       6
IDL> print, reverse(arr, 1)
       2       1       0
       5       4       3
       8       7       6
IDL> print, reverse(arr, 2)
       6       7       8
       3       4       5
       0       1       2
```

If no optional dimension is passed to reverse, then the first array dimension is reversed by default. The dimension argument uses the values 1, 2, 3 to refer to the first, second, and third dimension.

Rotating Arrays

The rotate function rotates one- or two-dimensional arrays clockwise in 90-degree increments. The first argument is the array to be rotated, and the second argument is the direction flag:

```
IDL> print, arr
       0       1       2       3
       4       5       6       7
       8       9      10      11
IDL> print, rotate(arr, 1)
       8       4       0
       9       5       1
      10       6       2
      11       7       3
IDL> print, rotate(arr, 2)
      11      10       9       8
       7       6       5       4
       3       2       1       0
IDL> print, rotate(arr, 3)
       3       7      11
       2       6      10
       1       5       9
       0       4       8
```

The direction flags 0, 1, 2, 3 specify rotations of 0, 90, 180, and 270 degrees, respectively. When operating on one-dimensional arrays, rotate may change the number of dimensions:

```
IDL> arr = indgen(3)
IDL> help, rotate(arr, 1)
<Expression>    INT       = Array[1, 3]
IDL> print, rotate(arr, 1)
       0
       1
       2
```

Transposing Arrays

The transpose function returns the transpose of an array. That is, it returns an array with the dimension order reversed:

```
IDL> arr = indgen(4, 3)
IDL> print, arr
       0       1       2       3
       4       5       6       7
       8       9      10      11
IDL> help, transpose(arr)
<Expression>    INT       = Array[3, 4]
IDL> print, transpose(arr)
```

```
          0         4         8
          1         5         9
          2         6         10
          3         7         11
```

You can also pass an optional one-dimensional array argument to transpose that defines the new dimension order (the default is to reverse the dimension order):

```
IDL> arr = indgen(2, 4, 6)
IDL> help, transpose(arr)
<Expression>    INT       = Array[6, 4, 2]
IDL> help, transpose(arr, [1, 2, 0])
<Expression>    INT       = Array[4, 6, 2]
```

Shifting Arrays

The shift function shifts array elements along an array dimension. The first argument is the array to be shifted, and the second argument is the shift value. A forward shift is specified by a positive shift value, and a backward shift is indicated by a negative shift value:

```
IDL> arr = indgen(5)
IDL> print, arr
          0         1         2         3         4
IDL> print, shift(arr, 1)
          4         0         1         2         3
IDL> print, shift(arr, -2)
          2         3         4         0         1
```

Elements that are shifted off one end of a dimension are wrapped around to the other end of the dimension. When operating on multi-dimensional arrays, shift shifts elements along each dimension by the request shift value:

```
IDL> arr = indgen(3, 3)
IDL> print, arr
          0         1         2
          3         4         5
          6         7         8
IDL> print, shift(arr, 0, 1)
          6         7         8
          0         1         2
          3         4         5
```

Sorting Arrays

The sort function returns the indices of an array where all array values
have been sorted into ascending order. Because sort returns an array of
indices, the syntax needed to sort an array is as follows:

```
IDL> arr = [50, 30, 60, 40, 10, 20]
IDL> arr = arr[sort(arr)]
IDL> print, arr
      10      20      30      40      50      60
```

If some or all elements of the input array are identical, then sort may
return an array of indices that is not in ascending order:

```
IDL> index = sort([1, 1, 1, 1, 1])
IDL> print, index
            1           2           3           4           0
IDL> print, sort([0, 0, 1, 1, 2, 2])
            1           0           3           2           5
            4
```

This is an artifact of the sort algorithm, which picks a random index as a
starting point for sorting the array, and the results may vary on different
IDL platforms (the previous example is from IDL 5.3 for Windows 98). If
the order of elements in the array must be maintained, the bsort function from the IDL Astronomy Library may be used instead of sort (see
Appendix A).

Finding Unique Array Values

The uniq function returns the indices of the unique values in a sorted
array. Therefore to extract the unique values from an array, it must first
be sorted:

```
IDL> arr = [20, 30, 20, 40, 40, 30, 50, 60, 10]
IDL> arr = arr[sort(arr)]
IDL> arr = arr[uniq(arr)]
IDL> print, arr
      10      20      30      40      50      60
```

In some cases, you may wish to extract unique values from an array
while preserving the order of the elements. First, you obtain the index
arrays from sort and uniq:

```
IDL> arr = [20, 30, 20, 40, 40, 30, 50, 60, 10]
IDL> sort_index = sort(arr)
IDL> uniq_index = uniq(arr[sort_index])
```

Then create an array that contains the indices of the unique values in the input array:

```
IDL> index = sort_index[uniq_index]
IDL> index = index[sort(index)]
IDL> print, arr[index]
      20      30      40      50      60      10
```

2.12 ARRAY RESIZING

Array resizing refers to operations that change the number of elements in an array. This naturally implies that a strategy must be chosen to fill the new array locations. In IDL, the two methods are nearest-neighbor sampling and interpolation. IDL offers several functions for array resizing, and it is important to understand which strategy is used when an array is made larger or smaller. The most commonly used functions for resizing arrays are summarized in Table 2.13.

Resizing by an Integer Factor

The rebin function enlarges or shrinks an array by an integer multiple or factor of the current dimensions:

Table 2.13   Array resizing functions.

Function name	Purpose	Algorithm
rebin()	Resize an *n*-dimensional array by an integer multiple or factor.	Default is linear interpolation for enlarging and neighborhood averaging for shrinking. Nearest-neighbor sampling is optional.
congrid()	Resize a one-, two-, or three-dimensional array to an arbitrary size (user-friendly version).	Default is nearest-neighbor sampling. Linear or cubic convolution interpolation is optional.
interpolate()	Resize a one-, two-, or three-dimensional array to an arbitrary size (generalized version).	Default is linear interpolation. Cubic convolution interpolation is optional.

```
IDL> arr = [20, 40, 60]
IDL> print, rebin(arr, 9, /sample)
      20      20      20      40      40      40      60
      60      60
```

Setting the sample keyword (/sample or sample=1) causes nearest-neighbor sampling to be used for enlarging or shrinking. If the sample keyword is not set (/sample absent or sample=0), then linear interpolation is used for enlarging, yielding quite different results:

```
IDL> print, rebin(arr, 9)
      20      26      33      40      46      53      60
      60      60
```

The last element of the input array is duplicated in the output array. This happens because, although rebin tries to be faithful to the integer enlargement factor (note the values 20, 40, 60 at indices 0, 3, 6), it does not extrapolate past the end of the array. When shrinking an array, rebin uses neighborhood averaging:

```
IDL> arr = indgen(9)
IDL> print, arr
       0       1       2       3       4       5       6
       7       8
IDL> print, rebin(arr, 3)
       1       4       7
```

The rebin function is useful when you wish to create multidimensional grid arrays. For example, a grid of values that increase along the column dimension can be created as follows:

```
IDL> v = indgen(5)
IDL> print, v
       0       1       2       3       4
IDL> x = rebin(v, 5, 3, /sample)
IDL> print, x
       0       1       2       3       4
       0       1       2       3       4
       0       1       2       3       4
```

In this example, the rebin function was used to create a resized array with five columns and three rows.

To create a grid of values that increase along the row dimension, the one-dimensional array must first be reordered by calling reform:

```
IDL> v = indgen(5)
IDL> y = reform(v, 1, 5)
IDL> help, y
Y               INT       = Array[1, 5]
IDL> print, y
      0
      1
      2
      3
      4
IDL> y = rebin(y, 3, 5, /sample)
IDL> print, y
      0       0       0
      1       1       1
      2       2       2
      3       3       3
      4       4       4
```

In this example, the rebin function was used to create a resized array with three columns and five rows.

The rebin function can also be used in conjunction with reform to create index arrays with multiple dimensions:

```
IDL> arr = indgen(3)
IDL> print, rebin(arr, 3, 3, /sample)
      0       1       2
      0       1       2
      0       1       2
IDL> print, rebin(reform(arr, 1, 3), 3, 3, /sample)
      0       0       0
      1       1       1
      2       2       2
IDL> print, rebin(reform(arr, 1, 1, 3), 3, 3, 3, /sample)
      0       0       0
      0       0       0
      0       0       0

      1       1       1
      1       1       1
      1       1       1

      2       2       2
      2       2       2
      2       2       2
```

In these examples, reform is used to transform a one-dimensional vector to a two- or three-dimensional array, which is then resampled to a grid with rebin (this method may be extended to higher dimensions if required).

The following example shows how rebin can be used to compute a two-dimensional sinc function

$$z(x, y) = \sin((x^2 + y^2)^{0.5})/(x^2 + y^2)^{0.5}$$

over the range −10 to 10 in both x and y:

```
IDL> v = findgen(41) * 0.5 - 10.0
IDL> x = rebin(v, 41, 41, /sample)
IDL> y = rebin(reform(v, 1, 41), 41, 41, /sample)
IDL> r = sqrt(x*x + y*y) + 1.0e-6
IDL> z = sin(r) / r
IDL> help, x, y, z
X                 FLOAT     = Array[41, 41]
Y                 FLOAT     = Array[41, 41]
Z                 FLOAT     = Array[41, 41]
```

Adding 10^{-6} to the radius function r avoids the indeteminate value at the origin. The surface z can then be viewed by the surface procedure:

```
IDL> surface, z, x, y
```

Resizing to Arbitrary Size

The congrid function enlarges or shrinks a one-, two-, or three-dimensional array to an arbitrary size. The default is to use nearest-neighbor sampling:

```
IDL> arr = [20, 40, 60]
IDL> print, congrid(arr, 4)
      20      40      60      60
IDL> print, congrid(arr, 5)
      20      40      40      60      60
IDL> print, congrid(arr, 6)
      20      40      40      60      60      60
IDL> print, congrid(arr, 7)
      20      20      40      40      60      60      60
IDL> print, congrid(arr, 8)
      20      20      40      40      60      60      60
      60
```

```
IDL> print, congrid(arr, 9)
      20      20      40      40      40      60      60
      60      60
```

Note how `congrid` favors the right side when resampling the array. This can best be understood by examining the default `congrid` algorithm (`congrid` is a library function written in IDL). In the following example, the number of input elements is three, and the number of output elements is nine:

```
IDL> arr = [20, 40, 60]
IDL> ix = 3
IDL> nx = 9
IDL> index = (float(ix) / float(nx)) * findgen(nx)
IDL> print, index, format='(9f6.2)'
  0.00  0.33  0.67  1.00  1.33  1.67  2.00  2.33  2.67
IDL> index = round(index)
IDL> print, index, format='(9i6)'
      0      0      1      1      1      2      2      2      3
IDL> print, arr[index], format='(9i6)'
      20      20      40      40      40      60      60      60      60
```

When the resampled index array is computed, you can see the largest value is 3, which is larger than the highest index in `arr` (2). Recall that when indices are specified as an array, index values that are out of bounds are silently clipped to the minimum or maximum permitted index values. Thus `congrid` always favors replicating the last value in the array when the default nearest-neighbor sampling algorithm is used.

If the optional `minus_one` keyword is set, then `congrid` uses a slightly different algorithm to compute the resampled index array:

```
IDL> index = (float(ix - 1) / float(nx - 1)) * findgen(nx)
IDL> print, index, format='(9f6.2)'
  0.00  0.25  0.50  0.75  1.00  1.25  1.50  1.75  2.00
IDL> index = round(index)
IDL> print, index, format='(9i6)'
      0      0      1      1      1      1      2      2      2
IDL> print, arr[index], format='(9i6)'
      20      20      40      40      40      40      60      60      60
```

To use linear interpolation when enlarging and shrinking a one- or two-dimensional array, the optional `interp` keyword may be used:

```
IDL> print, congrid(arr, 9, /interp)
      20      26      33      40      46      53      60
      60      60
IDL> print, congrid(arr, 9, /interp, /minus_one)
      20      25      30      35      40      45      50
      55      60
```

Linear interpolation is always used by congrid for three-dimensional arrays.

In summary, congrid provides a quick and convenient way to resize an array. In most cases, congrid is used to resize two-dimensional arrays that are displayed as images, where an extra pixel or two at the edge of an image is not noticeable to the human eye. However, if you wish to have more control over the way arrays are resized, you will probably want to use the interpolate function instead.

Resizing to Arbitrary Size with Customized Interpolation

The interpolate function resizes a one-, two-, or three-dimensional array by using linear, bilinear, or trilinear interpolation between existing array values. The interpolate function differs from congrid in that with interpolate, you specify the exact locations for which you desire interpolated values, as shown in the following example:

```
IDL> arr = [10.0, 20.0, 30.0]
IDL> loc = [0.0, 0.5, 1.0, 1.5, 2.0]
IDL> print, interpolate(arr, loc)
      10.0000      15.0000      20.0000      25.0000
      30.0000
```

The indices for the interpolated data points are specified relative to the indices of the input array (which is why float index values are used for loc). In the previous example, the indices of the input array are 0, 1, and 2. The location array (loc) is then set to give interpolated values at the original indices (0.0, 1.0, 2.0) and at locations between the original values (0.5, 1.5).

To resize a two-dimensional array (such as an image) with interpolate, you must choose an algorithm to compute the locations for the interpolated array values. Consider the following frequency distribution array with 32 columns and rows, which you wish to resize to 500 columns and 300 rows:

```
IDL> a = dist(32, 32)
IDL> nx = 500
IDL> ny = 300
```

The following generalized algorithm is suggested for resizing the array:

```
IDL> dims = size(a, /dimensions)
IDL> xloc = (findgen(nx) + 0.5) * (dims[0] / float(nx)) - 0.5
IDL> yloc = (findgen(ny) + 0.5) * (dims[1] / float(ny)) - 0.5
IDL> b = interpolate(a, xloc, yloc, /grid)
IDL> help, b
B               FLOAT     = Array[500, 300]
```

First, the dimensions of the input array are found by calling size. Then the location arrays in the column (xloc) and row (yloc) dimensions are computed. Finally, interpolate is called to compute the resized array. The optional grid keyword allows the location arrays to have a different size in each output array dimension (otherwise the location arrays must be the same size in each dimension). The resized image can be displayed by calling the image display procedure tvscl:

```
IDL> tvscl, b
```

The same location arrays can also be used to compute a resized array with nearest-neighbor sampling, simply by rounding the location arrays to the nearest integer:

```
IDL> c = interpolate(a, round(xloc), round(yloc), /grid)
IDL> tvscl, c
```

Tip You may wish to investigate some of the other options for array resizing in IDL, such as cubic convolution interpolation via the optional cubic keyword accepted by congrid and interpolate, and the bilinear, krig2d, and interpol functions.

Removing Rows or Columns

In some circumstances, you may wish to remove selected rows or columns from an array. For example, say you have defined an array with

10 columns and 1,000 rows, and you wish to remove rows 16, 200, 545, 762, and 998:

```
IDL> arr = findgen(10, 1000)
IDL> delrow = [16, 200, 545, 762, 998]
```

To make the example more general, size is called to get the number of rows in arr:

```
IDL> dims = size(arr, /dimensions)
IDL> nrows = dims[1]
IDL> help, nrows
NROWS           LONG      =        1000
```

An index array is created to identify the rows you wish to keep. In this array, a value of 1L means the row should be kept, and a value of 0L means the row should be removed:

```
IDL> index = replicate(1L, nrows)
IDL> index[delrow] = 0L
```

Now where is called to return the indices of rows you wish to keep:

```
IDL> keeprow = where(index eq 1)
```

Finally, the rows you wish to keep are extracted:

```
IDL> arr = arr[*, keeprow]
IDL> help, arr
ARR             FLOAT     = Array[10, 995]
```

This method may be applied to remove entries along any dimension in an array.

3 Writing IDL Programs

This chapter describes the process of defining, compiling, and running IDL programs. IDL procedures and functions are explained, as well as the manual and automatic methods that may be used to compile them. The control statements available in IDL are presented, along with examples showing how each statement may be used. Parameter and keyword arguments are covered in detail, and particular attention is paid to argument passing by reference versus value. In this chapter you will also find guidelines for checking input and output arguments in IDL programs. Include files, scripts, journaling, and global variables are described, and the chapter concludes with a description of error-handling mechanisms in IDL and tips for efficient programming.

3.1 DEFINING AND COMPILING PROGRAMS

IDL programs fall into two classes: procedures and functions. Either can be used to create a program in IDL. A procedure normally encapsulates several related operations into one program unit, such as scaling and displaying an image, or opening and reading a file. A function normally encapsulates one operation into a program unit, such as converting a temperature from Fahrenheit to Celsius, and returns a single result variable.

Procedures

Procedures are normally used when more than one variable is passed to or returned from a program. A procedure usually has at least one input argument (although it need not have any) and has one or more output arguments (although it need not have any). For example, if you wanted to read an array of data from a file in a certain format, you would write a procedure that accepted the file name as an input argument and returned the file contents and size as output arguments. Within the procedure you would check to see if the file exists, open it, read the contents in the correct format, and finally close the file. The calling sequence might appear as follows:

```
IDL> read_profile, file, profile, nrec=nrec
```

In this example, the procedure name is read_profile. On entry, the input argument file contains the name of the file to be read. On exit, the output argument profile contains the data read from the file. On exit, the optional keyword nrec contains the number of records read from the file (more about optional keywords later).

A procedure begins with a pro statement and ends with an end statement. The pro statement must contain at least a procedure name and may contain an argument list and/or a keyword list. The convention of capitalizing the pro and end statements is followed in this book although this is not required by IDL (statements in an IDL program are case insensitive, except for the contents of string variables). The following are examples of procedure definitions:

- A procedure with no arguments:
```
PRO HELLO
print, 'Hello world'
END
```

- A procedure with three parameters:
```
PRO READ_IMAGE, IMAGE, DATE, TIME
;statements...
END
```

- A procedure with three parameters and two optional keywords:
```
PRO PRINT_IMAGE, IMAGE, DATE, TIME, $
  LANDSCAPE=LANDSCAPE, COLOR=COLOR
;statements...
END
```

Functions

Functions are programs that return a result via an assignment statement (e.g., y = sin(x)). A function typically has at least one input argument, although it need not have any. For example, if you wished to convert a temperature in degrees Fahrenheit to Celsius, you would write a function that accepted one temperature argument, performed the conversion, and returned the converted temperature on the left side of an assignment. The calling sequence might appear as follows:

```
deg_c = f_to_c(deg_f)
```

In this example, the function name is f_to_c. On entry, the input parameter deg_f contains the temperature value in degrees Fahrenheit. On exit, the variable deg_c contains the Celsius equivalent.

A function begins with a function statement, includes a return statement to return the result to the caller, and ends with an end statement. As with procedures, a function statement must contain at least a function name and may contain an argument list and/or a keyword list. The convention of capitalizing the function and end statements is followed in this book, although this is not required by IDL. The following are examples of function definitions:

- A function with one parameter:
```
FUNCTION F_TO_C, DEG_F
return, (deg_f - 32.0) * (5.0 / 9.0)
END
```

- A function with three parameters and two optional keywords:
```
FUNCTION GET_BOUNDS, IMAGE, LAT, LON, $
  POLAR=POLAR, NORMAL=NORMAL
;statements...
END
```

Naming and Editing Source Files

The standard format for naming an IDL source file is the procedure or function name followed by a .pro extension (e.g., imdisp.pro). IDL is sensitive to the case of source file names on UNIX platforms. This restriction does not exist on non-UNIX platforms, but for the sake of portability, lowercase file names are always recommended for IDL source files (e.g., use imdisp.pro instead of IMDISP.PRO or ImDisp.pro).

On Windows and MacOS platforms, most users edit IDL programs within the IDL Development Environment. Of course, you are free to use any other text editor. On UNIX platforms (including Linux), many users prefer to use the IDL command-line mode with the text editor of their choice, such as `vi` or `emacs`. Other options for UNIX editors are nedit and the IDL Emacs mode (see Appendix A for download details).

Manual Compilation

Procedures or functions can be compiled manually by using the `.com-pile` executive command:

```
IDL> .compile hello.pro
```

The `.pro` extension is assumed if no extension is specified. Multiple procedures or functions may be compiled:

```
IDL> .compile hello.pro imdisp.pro sds_read.pro
```

Once a procedure or function has been compiled manually, it remains resident in memory for the rest of the IDL session, and may be called as often as desired without recompiling. If you modify and recompile the source code for a procedure or function, the new compiled version becomes active in memory and the old version is forgotten. In addition, manually compiling a source file does not recompile any procedures or functions that are called within (unless they are contained in the source file itself).

It is also possible to manually compile procedures or functions with the executive commands `.run` and `.rnew`. These commands will compile procedures or functions in just the same way as the `.compile` command. In addition, if the source file named in the `.run` or `.rnew` command is a "main program," the "main program" will be executed. A main program is *not* the same as a procedure or function. In IDL terminology, a main program is just a sequence of IDL statements terminated by an `end` statement. If the `.rnew` command is used, a side effect is that all variables at the command-line level become undefined. IDL main programs are of limited use because they can only be run from the IDL command line. Most IDL programmers use procedures or functions instead of main programs, so it is perfectly acceptable to use the `.compile` command exclusively for manual compilation at the command line.

Tip Executive commands such as `.compile` can only be used at the IDL command line; they cannot be used in IDL programs. Although it is rarely required, the `resolve_routine` procedure may be used to compile a named procedure or function from within a program.

Automatic Compilation

IDL automatically compiles procedures and functions as they are needed at runtime. If IDL encounters a call to a procedure or function not previously compiled in the current session, it searches the current directory and all directories in the IDL search path for a source file with the same name as the procedure or function call. For example, if the procedure call is

```
IDL> sds_read, 'MAS_911031_03.hdf', data
```

then IDL searches for a source file named `sds_read.pro`. If the procedure is found, it is automatically compiled. For example, the first time the procedure `map_set` is called to create a map projection in a new session, you will see a sequence of compile messages:

```
IDL> map_set, /continents
% Compiled module: MAP_SET.
% Compiled module: CROSSP.
% Compiled module: MAP_CONTINENTS.
% Compiled module: FILEPATH.
```

Note In `idlde` (all platforms), see File/Preferences/Path for the current IDL search path setting. In `idl` (UNIX platforms), see the environment variable `IDL_PATH`.

If the search for a procedure source file is unsuccessful, an error message will be printed and execution will stop:

```
IDL> dingbat, a, b, c
% Attempt to call undefined procedure/function: 'DINGBAT'.
% Execution halted at:  $MAIN$
```

If the search for a function source file is unsuccessful, the behavior is different:

```
IDL> a = dingbat(0.0)
% Variable is undefined: DINGBAT.
% Execution halted at:  $MAIN$
```

Here IDL cannot find a function source file named dingbat.pro in the search path, and it interprets dingbat(0.0) as an attempt to access the first element of an undefined array named dingbat. For historical reasons, IDL allows both square brackets [] and parentheses () to designate arrays; always use square brackets for arrays to avoid confusion.

Finally, if an undefined function is called with only a keyword argument, a syntax error is reported:

```
IDL> a = dingbat(keyword=2.0)

a = dingbat(keyword=2.0)
                ^
% Syntax error.
```

When multiple procedures and/or functions are contained in a source file, the order of routines in the file is important if automatic compilation is to be successful. When IDL automatically compiles a source file, every procedure or function called must meet one of the following conditions:

1. It was previously compiled in the current source file.
2. It was previously compiled in the current IDL session.
3. It can be found in the IDL path and compiled automatically.

For example, consider the following version of hello.pro, where a procedure, and a function called by the procedure, are both contained in the same source file:

```
PRO HELLO
print, 'Hello world'
print, 'The square of 2 is ', square(2)
END

FUNCTION SQUARE, X
return, x * x
END
```

If a new IDL session is started and the procedure is called, IDL attempts to compile it automatically:

```
IDL> hello
% Compiled module: HELLO.
Hello world
% Variable is undefined: SQUARE.
% Execution halted at:  HELLO                   3 hello.pro
%                       $MAIN$
```

IDL compiled the procedure in hello.pro but did not compile the square function. Thus square(2) was interpreted as a reference to an undefined variable.

To solve this problem, and still maintain the convenience of automatic compilation, you can use either of the following techniques:

1. Keep each procedure and function in a separate source file.
2. If related functions and procedures are kept in the same source file, put the primary procedure or function last (i.e., the procedure or function with the same name as the source file itself).

If the second technique was used, hello.pro would be reformatted as follows:

```
FUNCTION SQUARE, X
return, x * x
END

PRO HELLO
print, 'Hello world'
print, 'The square of 2 is ', square(2)
END
```

If a new IDL session is started and hello is called, IDL automatically compiles the square function and the hello procedure:

```
IDL> hello
% Compiled module: SQUARE.
% Compiled module: HELLO.
Hello world
The square of 2 is        4
```

Returning to the Main Level after an Error

If an error in an IDL program causes execution to stop, by default, IDL halts inside the procedure or function that caused the error. For example, consider the following program that uses a function to compute the product of two input variables:

```
FUNCTION PRODUCT, ARG1, ARG2
return, arg1 * arg2
END

PRO HELLO, A, B
print, 'Hello world'
print, 'The product of A and B is ', product(a, b)
END
```

To compile and run the program, the following commands are used:

```
IDL> .compile hello
% Compiled module: PRODUCT.
% Compiled module: HELLO.
IDL> a = 3
IDL> b = 15
IDL> hello, a, b
Hello world
The product of A and B is       45
```

However, if the program is called when an argument is undefined, execution stops inside the product function when the undefined variable is referenced:

```
IDL> hello, a, bbb
Hello world
% Variable is undefined: ARG2.
% Execution halted at:  PRODUCT            2 hello.pro
%                       HELLO              7 hello.pro
%                       $MAIN$
```

The error message shows that IDL halted inside the product function at line 2 of the source file (hello.pro). The product function was called from the hello procedure at line 7 of the source file. Finally, the message shows that hello was called from the main level (the command line).

Because execution halted inside the product function, only the variables defined in this function are now available at the command line. For example:

```
IDL> help, arg1
ARG1            INT       =       3
```

Any variables that were defined at the main level will seem to have "disappeared":

```
IDL> help, a
A              UNDEFINED = <Undefined>
```

In addition, you will see warning messages if you try recompiling the source file after an execution halt:

```
IDL> .compile hello
% Procedure was compiled while active: PRODUCT. Returning.
% Compiled module: PRODUCT.
% Procedure was compiled while active: HELLO. Returning.
% Compiled module: HELLO.
```

After examining any variables in the failed function or procedure, use the `retall` command to return to the main level:

```
IDL> retall
```

You'll eventually get into the habit of typing `retall` whenever an error occurs that halts execution of an IDL program (unless you wish to examine variables in the failed routine).

3.2   CONTROL STATEMENTS

Control statements in IDL allow the programmer to specify the order in which computations will be carried out. This section explains each of the control statements available in IDL. If you are familiar with a procedural language such as C or Fortran, many of the statements will be recognizable. The control statements supported by IDL are listed in Table 3.1.

`if` *Statement*

The `if` statement executes a single statement or a block of statements if a specified condition is true. The following forms are permitted:

```
if condition then statement

if condition then begin
  statement(s)
endif
```

Table 3.1   IDL control statements.

Statement	Purpose
if	If a condition is true, execute statement(s).
case	Select one case to execute from a list of cases.
for	For a specified number of times, execute a statement loop.
while	While a condition is true, execute a statement loop.
repeat	Repeat a statement loop until a condition is true.
return	Return control to the calling function or procedure.
goto	Go to a label.
switch	Branch to a case in a list of cases.*
break	Break out of a loop, case statement, or switch statement.*
continue	Continue execution on the next iteration of a loop.*

* IDL 5.4 or higher is required for the switch, break, and continue statements.

if *condition* then *statement* else *statement*

```
if condition then begin
  statement(s)
endif else begin
  statement(s)
endelse
```

In all forms, *condition* is a scalar expression that evaluates to true or false. In the first two forms, a single statement or block of statements is executed if *condition* is true. In the second two forms, the else statement causes a single statement or a block of statements to be executed when *condition* is false. The else statement block is terminated by endelse, not endif.

The following procedure uses if statements to check whether an integer is even and divisible by a given factor:

```
PRO TEST_IF, NUM, DIV

if ((num mod 2) eq 0) then begin
  print, num, ' is even'
endif

if ((num mod div) eq 0) then begin
  print, num, ' is divisible by ', div
```

```
endif else begin
  print, num, ' is not divisible by ', div
endelse

END
```

The first if statement prints a message if the supplied integer (num) is divisible by two, and the second if statement prints either of two messages depending on whether the integer is divisible by the supplied factor (div) or not.

To run the program:

```
IDL> .compile test_if
IDL> test_if, 100, 5
```

case *Statement*

The case statement selects a single statement or a block of statements to execute based on a match to a scalar expression. The syntax is as follows:

```
case expression of
  exp1:
  exp2: statement
  exp3: begin
          statement(s)
        end
  else: statement
endcase
```

Here, *expression, exp1, exp2,* and *exp3* are scalar expressions. When the first match is found between *expression* and an expression within the case statement, the corresponding statement, or block of statements enclosed by begin and end, is executed (only one matching expression is recognized). After the statement(s) are executed, the case statement terminates and execution continues. If no matches are found, the statement or block of statements following else is executed. If else is omitted, an error will occur and execution will halt. Thus it is good practice to always include an else in a case statement.

The following procedure uses a case statement to execute an IDL display command selected by the user:

```
PRO TEST_CASE

command = ''
```

```
read, command, prompt='Enter an IDL display command: '

cmdlist = ['plot', 'surface', 'tv']
index = where(strlowcase(command) eq cmdlist)

case index[0] of
  0 : plot, sin(findgen(100) * 0.25)
  1 : surface, dist(32)
  2 : begin
        erase
        image = dist(400)
        tvscl, image
      end
  else : print, 'Valid display commands are: ', cmdlist
endcase

END
```

First, a string variable (command) is entered by the user. Then the where function is used to find a match from a list of commands (cmdlist). The case statement then searches for a match to the first element of index. When the 'plot' or 'surface' cases are selected, a single statement is executed. When the 'tv' case is selected, a block of statements is executed. If no match is found, a message is printed.

To run the program:

```
IDL> .compile test_case
IDL> test_case
```

The case statement can also be used in conjunction with relational and Boolean operators. The syntax is as follows:

```
case 1 of
  cond1: statement
  cond2: begin
            statement(s)
         end
  else: statement
endcase
```

Here the expression in the first line of the case statement is a scalar int with a value of 1, which corresponds to true in IDL. In the body of the case statement, *cond1* and *cond2* are expressions containing relational operators that evaluate to either true (1) or false (0), such as (x gt 100). If one of these scalar expressions evaluates to true, then the corresponding statement or block of statements is executed. Otherwise the statement following else is executed.

for *Statement*

The for statement executes a single statement or a block of statements a specified number of times by incrementing or decrementing a loop index variable from a start value to an end value. The following forms are permitted:

```
for i = v1, v2 do statement

for i = v1, v2, inc do statement

for i = v1, v2, inc do begin
  statement(s)
endfor
```

In the first two forms, a single statement is executed on every loop iteration. In the third form, a block of statements enclosed by begin and endfor is executed on every loop iteration. The loop index i starts with a value of v1. On each loop iteration the value of i increases or decreases by inc, depending on whether inc is positive or negative (if inc is not specified, the loop index increments by one on each iteration). When inc is positive, the last iteration occurs the final time i is less than or equal to v2. When inc is negative, the last iteration occurs the final time i is greater than or equal to v2.

The following procedure uses a for loop to create multiple plots:

```
PRO TEST_FOR

erase
for i = 1L, 4L, 1L do begin
  x = findgen(100) * (0.1 * i)
  plot, sin(x) + (2 * i), yrange=[0, 10]
endfor

END
```

To run the program:

```
IDL> .compile test_for
IDL> test_for
```

Tip   The type of the loop index variable is established by the loop start value. If the default `int` type is used for the loop start variable, large loop end values can cause problems:

```
IDL> for i = 0, 40000, 1000 do print, i
% Loop limit expression too large for loop variable type.
  <LONG    (      40000)>.
% Execution halted at:  $MAIN$
```

Here the loop index variable is an `int`, whose type was established by the start value 0. The loop end value of 40,000 is automatically interpreted as a `long` since it is greater than 32,767, and therefore a mismatch exists between the types of the loop start and end values. For this reason, `long` loop control variables are recommended:

```
IDL> for i = 0L, 40000L, 1000L do print, i
```

Floating-point loop variables are permitted, but are not recommended. For example, the following `for` loop terminates earlier than you might expect:

```
IDL> for z = 0.1, 0.5, 0.1 do print, z
      0.100000
      0.200000
      0.300000
      0.400000
```

Notice that the last loop value is only 0.4. This is due to the inherent limited accuracy of floating-point variables. If you need to create floating-point variables inside a loop, the preferred approach is to create a `float` variable from the loop control variable:

```
IDL> for i = 1L, 5L, 1L do print, 0.1 * float(i)
      0.100000
      0.200000
      0.300000
      0.400000
      0.500000
```

while *Statement*

The `while` statement executes a single statement or a block of statements while a specified condition is true. The following forms are permitted:

```
while condition do statement
```

```
while condition do begin
    statement(s)
endwhile
```

In both forms, *condition* is a scalar expression that evaluates to true or false. In the first form, a single statement is executed repeatedly while *condition* is true. In the second form, a block of statements enclosed by begin and endwhile is executed repeatedly while *condition* is true.

The following sample program uses a while loop to echo lines from a text file until the end-of-file is encountered:

```
PRO TEST_WHILE, FILENAME

openr, lun, filename, /get_lun
record = ''
while (eof(lun) ne 1) do begin
  readf, lun, record
  print, record
endwhile
free_lun, lun

END
```

The file is opened by calling openr, and a string variable (record) is created to hold the data for each record in the file. The while loop reads and prints each record in the file, as long as the condition (eof(lun) ne 1) is true. When the end-of-file is reached, the loop ends and the file is closed.

To run the program:

```
IDL> .compile test_while
IDL> file = filepath('crossp.pro', subdir='lib')
IDL> test_while, file
```

repeat *Statement*

The repeat statement executes a single statement or a block of statements until a specified condition is true. The following forms are permitted:

```
repeat statement until condition
```

```
repeat begin
    statement(s)
endrep until condition
```

In both forms, *condition* is a scalar expression that evaluates to true or false. In the first form, a single statement is executed repeatedly until *condition* is true. In the second form, a block of statements enclosed by begin and endrep is executed repeatedly until *condition* is true.

The following sample program uses a repeat loop to count the number of text lines entered until the user enters the string 'done':

```
PRO TEST_REPEAT

text = ''
count = 0
print, 'Enter text (done to quit)'
repeat begin
  read, text
  count = count + 1
endrep until (text eq 'done')
print, 'Number of lines entered: ', count - 1

END
```

A string variable (text) is created to hold the text entered by the user, and an int variable (count) is created to hold the number of lines entered. The repeat loop reads lines of text entered by the user and increments count for each line read. When the user enters the string done, making the condition (text eq 'done') true, the loop ends and the number of lines is printed.

To run the program:

```
IDL> .compile test_repeat
IDL> test_repeat
```

return *Statement*

The return statement causes an immediate exit from the current program unit, and control is returned to the caller. The following forms are permitted:

```
return, result
```

```
return
```

In the first form, *result* is a variable that is returned to the caller. This form is mandatory in functions, which must always return one variable to the caller. The second form is used in procedures, when continuing with the remainder of the procedure is not desired.

In general, you should try to limit each function to one `return` statement. This does not mean that a function should be littered with `goto` statements that jump to a return statement at the end. If a function must have multiple `return` statements, it should be obvious to the caller why the early return occurred (via an error status flag, for example). The following sample program illustrates how this could be done in a function that is designed to open a file for reading:

```
FUNCTION FILEOPEN, FILENAME, ERRTEXT=ERRTEXT

;-Set default return value
result = -1

;- Check that filename is defined
if (n_elements(filename) eq 0) then begin
  errtext = 'Filename is undefined'
  return, result
endif

;- Check that file exists
if ((findfile(filename))[0] eq '') then begin
  errtext = 'Filename was not found'
  return, result
endif

;- Open the file
openr, lun, filename, /get_lun
errtext = ''
return, lun

END
```

If the file name is undefined or the file cannot be found, an invalid logical unit number (`result`) is passed back to the caller, along with a status message (`errtext`) explaining the nature of the error. If the file is opened successfully, a valid logical unit number and an empty error message are passed back to the caller.

To run the program:

```
IDL> .compile fileopen
IDL> file = filepath('crossp.pro', subdir='lib')
IDL> lun = fileopen(file)
```

goto *Statement*

The goto statement jumps to a specified location in the current program unit. The syntax is as follows:

goto, *label*

The destination is specified by *label*, which is inserted at the desired jump point. The format for a goto label is as follows:

label:

Just as in any other programming language, you should be sparing in your use of goto statements in IDL. If you must use a goto, try to only jump forward, and limit yourself to no more than one goto per program unit.

switch *Statement*

The switch statement branches to the first matching case in a list of cases and executes a single statement or a block of statements. IDL 5.4 or higher is required to support switch statements. The syntax is as follows:

```
switch expression of
  exp1:
  exp2: statement
  exp3: begin
          statement(s)
        end
  else: statement
endswitch
```

Here, *expression, exp1, exp2,* and *exp3* are scalar expressions. When the first match is found between *expression* and an expression within the switch statement, the corresponding statement or block of statements is executed and execution falls through to the next case in the list. This is in contrast to the case statement, which terminates once a match has been found. If no matches are found, the statement or block of statements following else is executed. If else is omitted, the switch statement terminates and execution continues. This is also in contrast to the case statement, where execution halts with an error if no matches are found and else is omitted.

The following procedure uses a switch statement to compute the number of days in a given month, with correct accounting for leap years (there is a leap year every year divisible by four, except for years that are both divisible by 100 and not divisible by 400):

```
PRO TEST_SWITCH, MONTH, YEAR

;- Compute number of days in month, with correct
;- accounting for leap years.
;- There is a leap year every year divisible by four,
;- except for years which are both divisible by 100
;- and not divisible by 400

switch long(month) of
   1 :
   3 :
   5 :
   7 :
   8 :
  10 :
  12 : begin
    numdays = 31
    break
  end
   4 :
   6 :
   9 :
  11 : begin
    numdays = 30
    break
  end
   2 : begin
    if ((long(year) mod 4L) eq 0L) then begin
      if ((long(year) mod 100L) eq 0L) and $
         ((long(year) mod 400L) ne 0L) then $
        numdays = 28 else numdays = 29
    endif else begin
      numdays = 28
    endelse
    break
  end
  else : message, 'Illegal MONTH'
endswitch

print, numdays, month, year, $
  format='("There are ", i2, " days in month ",' + $
    'i2, " of year ", i6)'

END
```

The `switch` statement searches for a matching month in the list of cases. For months 1, 3, 5, 7, 8, and 10, no statements are executed, and execution falls through to the next case. For month 12, the number of days is set to 31, and the `break` statement causes an immediate exit from the `switch` statement. Similar logic is followed for months 4, 6, and 9, with the number of days set to 30 when the month is 11, followed by a `break` from the `switch` statement. If the month is 2, then leap year logic is executed followed by a `break`. Finally, if the `else` statement is reached, it means the month was not in the range 1 to 12.

To run the program:

```
IDL> .compile test_switch
IDL> test_switch, 2, 2000
```

`break` *Statement*

The `break` statement causes an immediate exit from a `for`, `while`, or `repeat` loop, or a `case` or `switch` statement. Control is transferred to the next statement after the end of the loop, or an immediate exit from a `case` or `switch` statement. IDL 5.4 or higher is required to support `break` statements. The syntax is

```
break
```

The following procedure uses a `break` statement to break out of a loop that searches an input array for a matching value (this is done more efficiently by the `where` function in IDL):

```
PRO TEST_BREAK, ARR, X

n = n_elements(arr)
i = 0L
while (i lt n) do begin
  if (long(arr[i]) eq long(x)) then break
  i = i + 1L
endwhile

if (i lt n) then begin
  print, 'Matching value found at element ', i
endif else begin
  print, 'No matching values were found'
endelse

END
```

The break statement is used to exit from the loop once a matching value is found. A break statement is preferred over a goto statement in this case because a break only exits the current loop level, rather than an arbitrary number or levels. That said, a goto statement may be appropriate if you must exit from multiple loop levels.

To run the program:

```
IDL> .compile test_break
IDL> test_break, indgen(20), 14
```

continue *Statement*

The continue statement causes the next iteration of a for, while, or repeat loop to be executed. Any statements remaining in the current loop iteration are skipped. IDL 5.4 or higher is required to support continue statements. The syntax is

```
continue
```

The continue statement is useful when it is desirable to stop processing on the current iteration of a loop and continue processing on the next loop iteration. The following procedure reads successive lines from an IDL source code file and prints lines that are not comments in uppercase:

```
PRO TEST_CONTINUE, FILENAME

openr, lun, filename, /get_lun
record = ''
while (eof(lun) ne 1) do begin
  readf, lun, record, format='(a)'
  record = strcompress(record)
  if (strmid(record, 0, 1) eq ';') or $
    (strmid(record, 1, 1) eq ';') then continue
  print, strupcase(record)
endwhile
free_lun, lun

END
```

The continue statement is used to skip to the next iteration of the loop if the current line is a comment (i.e., the first character is a semicolon). Lines that are not comments are then printed in uppercase. This type of logic can be used to avoid processing bad or invalid records in an input file.

To run the program:

```
IDL> .compile test_continue
IDL> file = filepath('crossp.pro', subdir='lib')
IDL> test_continue, file
```

3.3   PARAMETERS AND KEYWORDS

IDL procedures and functions can accept two kinds of arguments: parameters and keywords. A procedure or function normally has at least one parameter, but need not have any. Parameters are typically used to pass arguments that are mandatory in order for a called routine to execute successfully. Keywords are optional arguments that may be passed to the called routine, but are not mandatory (defaults are used for keywords that are not passed).

Parameters

Parameters are used to pass variables and expressions to procedures and functions. For example, a procedure that reads a file of temperature values could be defined as follows:

```
PRO READ_TEMPERATURE, FILE_NAME, TEMP_DATA
```

The first parameter (`file_name`) is an input argument that specifies the name of the file to be read. The second parameter (`temp_data`) is an output argument that will contain the temperature data when the procedure returns to the caller. Parameters are sometimes referred to as positional parameters because their position in the argument list determines how they will be used in the called procedure or function. Parameters are normally used for input and output arguments that are always needed by a procedure or function. When the procedure is called, the parameters take on actual values:

```
IDL> read_temperature, 'temp991201.dat', temp_data
```

Strictly speaking, a parameter is optional if the called routine is designed to proceed whether or not the parameter is present. For example, if a procedure or function has three positional parameters in its definition statement, but only two are passed, then the third positional parameter will be undefined inside the routine. The called routine can execute if it is designed to run in the absence of that parameter. This feature (i.e., optional parameters) can be confusing, so use it with care, and consider whether an optional keyword argument could be used instead.

Keywords

Keywords are optional variables or expressions that may be passed to a called routine, but are not mandatory. Input keywords can be used to specify an argument for which a default is otherwise defined, and also to set a Boolean flag (true or false). Output keywords can be used to return variables that are normally not required by the caller, but that may be required in certain situations. The previous definition of a procedure to read temperature data could be expanded as follows:

```
PRO READ_TEMPERATURE, FILE_NAME, TEMP_DATA, $
  MAXREC=MAXREC, NREC=NREC
```

The first keyword (maxrec) is an input variable that specifies the maximum number of records to read from the file. If the maxrec keyword is not passed, a default value is set inside the procedure. The second keyword (nrec) is used to return the number of records actually read by the procedure.

Using Parameters and Keywords

Input parameters and keywords must necessarily be defined before they are passed to a procedure or function. A well-written procedure or function will check that any mandatory input arguments are defined before doing anything else. Input arguments can be any valid IDL variable or expression. There is no need to define the type or size of input arguments within a called routine because IDL automatically carries the type and size information along with arguments passed into a procedure or function.

Output positional parameters and keywords are usually created inside a procedure or function and therefore need not be defined at the time the procedure or function is called. Output arguments in a procedure or function call can be any valid IDL variable type, with the exception of constants, system variables, expressions, indexed subarrays, and individual structure elements. For example, when calling the built-in where function, the return variable where_count is created within the function:

```
IDL> arr = dist(256)
IDL> help, where_count
WHERE_COUNT     UNDEFINED = <Undefined>
```

```
IDL> loc = where(arr gt 100.0, where_count)
IDL> help, where_count
WHERE_COUNT     LONG      =         34119
```

When keywords are used in a procedure or function call, they may be abbreviated to the shortest unambiguous string. For example, the following two calls to MAP_SET are equivalent:

```
IDL> map_set, position=[0.2, 0.2, 0.6, 0.6]
IDL> map_set, pos=[0.2, 0.2, 0.6, 0.6]
```

Therefore in the procedure or function definition, keywords should be named uniquely enough that the following type of error is avoided:

```
IDL> plot, sin(findgen(100) * 0.2), ym=[0, 1]
% Ambiguous keyword abbreviation: YM.
% Execution halted at:  $MAIN$
```

The error occurs because the plot command accepts both the ymargin and yminor keywords.

Keywords can be used to pass variables or expressions to a called procedure or function, or to return variables from a procedure or function. For example, to make plot create a graph in the lower-left corner of the current display, the position keyword is passed:

```
IDL> plot, sin(findgen(100) * 0.2), $
IDL>   position=[0.1, 0.1, 0.5, 0.5]
```

If plot is called without the position keyword, then a default position is used. The plot procedure must explicitly check whether the position keyword was passed with a legal value and use a default value if the keyword was not passed at all. Keyword checking of this type is always the responsibility of the programmer.

Keywords can also be used as Boolean flags to pass a true/false value to a called routine. There are two ways to set a Boolean keyword flag. Passing a Boolean keyword with a leading slash is the same as setting the keyword equal to 1 (true):

```
IDL> plot, sin(findgen(100) * 0.2), /noerase
IDL> plot, sin(findgen(100) * 0.1), noerase=1
```

Likewise, not setting a Boolean keyword is usually (but not always) the same as setting the keyword equal to 0 (false):

```
IDL> plot, sin(findgen(100) * 0.2)
IDL> plot, sin(findgen(100) * 0.1), noerase=0
```

Some routines may violate this convention and define a default value of 1 (true) for a Boolean keyword (the plot keyword noclip, for example). This behavior is not recommended.

Argument-Passing Mechanism

It is important to understand the mechanism by which arguments (i.e., parameters and keywords) are passed to called routines because it determines which arguments may or may not be modified within a called routine.

For example, consider the following example program named triple.pro, which triples the value of an input argument:

```
PRO TRIPLE, ARG
arg = 3 * arg
END
```

If this procedure is called with an array as the argument, the array values are modified as expected:

```
IDL> arr = [0, 1, 2, 3, 4]
IDL> triple, arr
IDL> print, arr
      0       3       6       9      12
```

However, if this procedure is called with an indexed subarray as the argument, the array values are not modified:

```
IDL> arr = [0, 1, 2, 3, 4]
IDL> triple, arr[0:3]
IDL> print, arr
      0       1       2       3       4
```

The difference in this case is that arrays are passed by *reference* (address), and indexed subarrays are passed by *value*. For the programmer, the implications of passing arguments by reference versus by value are as follows:

- Arguments passed by *reference* may have their type, size, or value modified within a called procedure or function, and the modified argument *is passed* back to the caller.
- Arguments passed by *value* may have their type, size, or value modified within a called procedure or function, but the modified argument *is not passed* back to the caller.

Table 3.2   Arguments passed by reference versus value.

Passed by reference	Passed by value
Scalars	Constants
Arrays	Indexed subarrays
Structures	Structure elements
Undefined variables	System variables
	Expressions

The type of argument determines whether it is passed by reference or by value, as shown in Table 3.2.

The details of the argument-passing mechanism are as follows. When a procedure or function is called, all arguments are saved to temporary values. Copies of the arguments are then created, and the copies may be used or modified during the lifetime of the called routine. When control is returned to the caller, the copies of arguments that were passed by reference are copied back to the corresponding calling arguments. The copies of arguments that were passed by value are destroyed.

Consider the following modified version of triple, which now prints the argument value within the procedure:

```
PRO TRIPLE, ARG
arg = 3 * arg
print, 'Value within triple is ', arg
END
```

When the procedure is called with an array as the argument, the copy of the array is modified within the procedure, and the modified array is returned to the caller:

```
IDL> arr = [0, 1, 2, 3, 4]
IDL> triple, arr
Value within triple is        0       3       6       9      12
IDL> print, arr
       0       3       6       9      12
```

If the argument is an indexed subarray, the copy of the array is modified within the procedure, but the modified array is not returned to the caller:

```
IDL> arr = [0, 1, 2, 3, 4]
IDL> triple, arr[0:3]
Value within triple is        0       3       6       9
```

```
IDL> print, arr
       0       1       2       3       4
```

The reasons for this behavior are straightforward. In the case of a parameter that is a constant, system variable, or expression, it makes no sense
to allow a called routine to modify the parameter, since modification
could involve a change in size, type, or value. In the case of a parameter
that is a subarray or structure element, allowing the parameter to be
modified would imply the possibility of a type conversion or change in
size, neither of which is permitted for a subarray or structure element.

Extra Keywords

When keywords are passed to a procedure or function, it is sometimes
necessary to pass these keywords to another routine from within the
called routine. For example, say you're always forgetting to put your name
and date on plots that you create. What you'd like to do is create a wrapper for the plot procedure that automatically adds your name and the
current date at the bottom of every plot. However, you'd also like to be
able to pass all the usual plot keywords (e.g., title, xrange, yrange, etc.)
to the wrapper program. To do this, the _extra keyword is used as shown
in the following procedure named eplot.pro:

```
PRO EPLOT, X, Y, NAME=NAME, _EXTRA=EXTRA_KEYWORDS

;- Check arguments
if (n_params() ne 2) then $
  message, 'Usage: EPLOT, X, Y'
if (n_elements(x) eq 0) then $
  message, 'Argument X is undefined'
if (n_elements(y) eq 0) then $
  message, 'Argument Y is undefined'
if (n_elements(name) eq 0) then name = 'Joe Average'

;- Plot the data
plot, x, y, _extra=extra_keywords

;- Print name and date on plot
date = systime()
xyouts, 0.0, 0.0, name, align=0.0, /normal
xyouts, 1.0, 0.0, date, align=1.0, /normal

END
```

When `eplot` is called, it accepts any keyword accepted by `plot`, and also prints your name and the date on the plot:

```
IDL> x = findgen(200) * 0.1
IDL> eplot, x, sin(x), xrange=[0, 15], $
IDL>    xtitle='X', ytitle='SIN(X)'
```

By including the `_extra` keyword in the procedure definition, you are instructing IDL to gather any keywords that are not recognized by `eplot` and to package them in a structure named `extra_keywords`. This structure is then passed to `plot` by setting the `_extra` keyword equal to the structure name. The keywords `xrange`, `xtitle`, `ytitle` (and any other keywords recognized by `plot`) are thereby passed to the `plot` procedure.

Extra Keyword Precedence

A keyword passed to a procedure or function via the extra keyword method takes precedence when a keyword with the same name is passed in the argument list. This is best illustrated by the following short procedure named `kplot.pro`:

```
PRO KPLOT, _EXTRA=EXTRA_KEYWORDS

plot, indgen(10), psym=2, _extra=extra_keywords

END
```

When this procedure is called with no keywords, the `plot` procedure uses plot symbol 2 (`psym=2`) to plot the data:

```
IDL> kplot
```

However, if the `psym` keyword is passed when `kplot` is called, the `plot` procedure uses the value of `psym` passed via the extra keyword structure and ignores the explicit setting of `psym=2` in the argument list:

```
IDL> kplot, psym=4
```

If you wish to use a keyword inside a procedure or function that would otherwise be passed via the extra keyword method, you must include the keyword in the procedure or function definition. For example, if you wish to set a default value for `psym` and print its value, you must include the `psym` keyword in the procedure definition, as shown in the following example:

```
PRO KPLOT, PSYM=PSYM, _EXTRA=EXTRA_KEYWORDS

if (n_elements(psym) eq 0) then psym = 2
print, 'PSYM = ', psym
plot, indgen(10), psym=psym, _extra=extra_keywords

END
```

Now the psym keyword is included in the procedure definition, and is not passed by the extra keyword mechanism. Therefore the psym variable may be used inside the procedure (to print its value in this case), and the psym keyword in the plot procedure call is not overridden.

Extra Keyword Passing Mechanism

Keywords passed using the _extra keyword are always passed by value, and therefore cannot be modified by the routine to which they are passed (such as plot in the previous example). However, if the _ref_extra keyword is used instead of _extra in the procedure or function definition, then the keywords are passed by reference and therefore can be modified by the routine to which they are passed.

To demonstrate the difference between passing extra keywords via _extra versus _ref_extra, consider the following example program named test_extra.pro. In the definition of test_val, _extra is used to pass extra keywords from the caller, while in the definition of test_ref, _ref_extra is used. In both test_val and test_ref, _extra is used to pass extra keywords to the function square because _ref_extra can only be used in the definition statement for a procedure or function.

```
FUNCTION SQUARE, ARG, POSITIVE=POSITIVE
result = arg^2
if (arg gt 0) then positive = 1 else positive = 0
return, result
END

PRO TEST_VAL, INPUT, OUTPUT, _EXTRA=EXTRA_KEYWORDS
output = square(input, _extra=extra_keywords)
END

PRO TEST_REF, INPUT, OUTPUT, _REF_EXTRA=EXTRA_KEYWORDS
output = square(input, _extra=extra_keywords)
END
```

When `test_val` is called, `pos_flag` is not set because the extra keywords are passed by value:

```
IDL> .compile test_extra
IDL> test_val, 2.0, output, positive=pos_flag
IDL> help, pos_flag
POS_FLAG        UNDEFINED = <Undefined>
```

However, when `test_ref` is called, `pos_flag` is set to the value determined by the `square` function because the extra keywords are passed by reference:

```
IDL> test_ref, 2.0, output, positive=pos_flag
IDL> help, pos_flag
POS_FLAG        INT      =       1
```

Note   `_ref_extra` is only available in IDL version 5.1 and higher.

3.4   CHECKING PARAMETERS AND KEYWORDS

One of the most effective ways to ensure that a procedure or function runs smoothly is to check the input and output arguments before beginning any processing. IDL performs only the following two tests at runtime when a procedure or function is called:

- Were more parameters passed than were listed in the procedure or function definition?
- Were unrecognized keywords passed and the `_extra` keyword not included in the procedure or function definition?

If either of these tests is true, then an error message is printed and execution is halted. Any further argument checking is your responsibility. Table 3.3 lists the routines in IDL that facilitate argument checking.

Checking Input Parameters and Keywords

A recommended list of checks for input parameters and keywords is shown below, along with an example for each case. For example, consider a hypothetical plotting procedure named `myplot.pro`, which is defined as follows:

Table 3.3   Routines for checking arguments.

Name	Purpose
n_params()	Returns number of parameters passed (not including keywords)
n_elements()	Returns number of elements in a variable (zero means variable is undefined)
size()	Returns size and type information about a variable
arg_present()	Returns true if an argument was present and was passed by reference
message	Prints a message and halts execution

```
MYPLOT, X, Y, POSITION=POSITION
```

The parameters x and y are one-dimensional vectors. Both parameters are required, and they must be the same size. The position keyword must be a one-dimensional vector with four elements if supplied; otherwise the default value is [0.0, 0.0, 1.0, 1.0]. The following input checks are appropriate for this routine:

1. Was the correct number of input parameters passed?

```
if (n_params() ne 2) then $
  message, 'Usage: MYPLOT, X, Y'
```

2. Is each input parameter defined?

```
if (n_elements(x) eq 0) then $
  message, 'X is undefined'
if (n_elements(y) eq 0) then $
  message, 'Y is undefined'
```

3. Does each input parameter have the correct number of dimensions?

```
if (size(x, /n_dimensions) ne 1) then $
  message, 'X must be a 1D array'
if (size(y, /n_dimensions) ne 1) then $
  message, 'Y must be a 1D array'
```

4. Are the input parameters the same size?

```
if (n_elements(x) ne n_elements(y)) then $
  message, 'X and Y must be same size'
```

5. If a keyword was not passed, is a default value set?

```
if (n_elements(position) eq 0) then $
  position = [0.0, 0.0, 1.0, 1.0]
```

6. If a keyword was passed, does it have the correct number of elements?

```
if (n_elements(position) ne 4) then $
  message, 'POSITION must have 4 elements'
```

In these examples, the `message` procedure is used to print an error message and halt execution. You will notice that no type checking was done. For example, the caller can pass `long` or `float` arrays as input. To maintain flexibility, you should allow the caller some latitude in the type of input parameters. After all, one of IDL's strengths is handling different data types. Type conversions are normally handled inside the called procedure or function. If an input parameter is not the correct type (e.g., `long` was passed, but `float` is required), you should wrap the input parameter in the appropriate type conversion function. Otherwise you can make a copy of the input parameter and convert the copy to the correct type. Also, many IDL procedures and functions are designed to accept scalar as well as array arguments, and therefore you should only check the number of dimensions of an argument when a specific type of array is required, such as a one-dimensional vector in the previous example. If your procedure or function is designed to handle scalar or array input arguments, then there is no need to check the number of dimensions.

Don't Modify Input Parameters

You should avoid modifying input parameters. Most people think of input parameters as inviolable and expect that input parameters will have the exact same size, type, and value before and after a procedure or function is called. In the previous example, if the `position` keyword is passed, it must be a one-dimensional vector with four elements. The argument checking for `position` shown previously is acceptable because a default value is assigned if the keyword is undefined, and execution stops only if the keyword has the wrong number of elements.

However, it is not acceptable to modify an input argument (parameter or keyword) that is defined. For example, the following argument check should not be used because it has the potential to modify the `position` keyword:

```
if (n_elements(position) ne 4) then $
  position=[0.1, 0.1, 0.9, 0.9]
```

If `position` has three elements on entry, then this statement will modify the size, value, and potentially the type of `position`.

Checking Boolean Keywords

Boolean keywords are checked using the `keyword_set` function, which returns true if the argument is defined, *and* is a nonzero scalar, *or* an array of any size, type, or value. For example, the `myplot` procedure shown previously could accept an `erase` keyword which causes the screen to be erased if it is set to true. In this case, a formal argument check is not required. Instead, the following code would appear in the body of `myplot` when the decision is made whether or not to erase the screen:

```
if keyword_set(erase) then erase
```

If `erase` is set to true, the screen will be erased. If this method is used, there is no possibility of modifying `erase` (remember that input parameters should not be modified).

This method is preferred over the following argument check:

```
erase = keyword_set(erase)
if (erase) then erase
```

In this case, if `erase` is a nonzero scalar, or an array of any size, type, or value, it will be converted to a scalar `int` equal to 1, which will be returned to the caller. For example, the following array is converted to a scalar by `keyword_set`:

```
IDL> keyval = [0, 1, 2, 3, 4, 5]
IDL> keyval = keyword_set(keyval)
IDL> help, keyval
KEYVAL          INT     =       1
```

Another case where you may wish to use a Boolean keyword within a procedure or function is to pass it to another routine that accepts a Boolean keyword with the same name. In this case, simply call `keyword_set` in the argument list:

```
plot, x, y, erase=keyword_set(erase)
```

Tip   Don't use `keyword_set` to check non-Boolean keywords, because `keyword_set` only checks whether the keyword is set to true in a Boolean sense. For keywords that carry a value (e.g., a `position` keyword that must have four elements), use the `n_elements` function to check whether the keyword is defined and has the correct number of elements.

Checking Output Parameters and Keywords

Output arguments must be passed by reference if they are to be created or modified within a called routine and returned to the caller. The arg_present function is used to check for arguments that can be modified inside a called routine. If a parameter or keyword was present in the calling sequence, and the parameter or keyword was passed by reference, arg_present returns true. For example, the myplot procedure shown previously could have an optional xrange keyword, which returns the range chosen for the axis in the displayed plot. In this case, the following argument check is used:

```
if arg_present(xrange) then $
  xrange = [min(x) - 1.0, max(x) + 1.0]
```

In the case of mandatory output parameters, arg_present allows you to detect parameters that cannot be modified. For example, if the myplot procedure computed a line of best fit, it would require the output parameters slope and intercept. The argument check would appear as follows:

```
if (arg_present(slope) ne 1) then $
  message, 'SLOPE cannot be modified'
if (arg_present(intercept) ne 1) then $
  message, 'INTERCEPT cannot be modified'
```

3.5   SCRIPTS, INCLUDE FILES, AND JOURNALING

If a text file contains a list of IDL statements, the statements can be executed in IDL by typing the "at" character (@) followed by the name of the file. This feature allows

- the creation of scripts which execute several IDL procedures or functions in sequence;
- sequences of statements to be included in IDL procedures and functions;
- journaled IDL sessions to be replayed.

Scripts

A script is a file containing a list of IDL commands that are executed in sequence, just as you would type them at the command line. Scripts are executed at the command line by prefacing the script name with the "at" character (@). For example, the following script named earth.pro creates a global map projection with color-filled continents:

```
map_set, /aitoff, /isotropic
map_continents, /fill
map_grid, /label
```

To execute this script at the command line:

```
IDL> @earth
```

A script that is executed at the command line may contain any IDL statement that may be typed at the command line, including executive commands such as .compile. However, statement blocks are not permitted in scripts. Thus the following single-line for loop is permitted in a script:

```
for index = 0, 10 do print, index
```

However, the following multiline for loop is not permitted in a script because it contains a statement block (starting at begin):

```
for index = 0, 10 do begin
  print, index
endfor
```

It is possible to bypass this behavior by including multiple statements on one line separated by the & character:

```
for index = 0, 10 do begin & print, index & endfor
```

This method of defining a loop should only be used in a script or on the command line. In procedures and functions, one statement per line is preferred for code readability.

Include Files

An include file contains a sequence of IDL statements that are inserted in a procedure or function at compile time. Include files may contain any statement that is legal in a procedure or function, including multiline statement blocks. For example, the following physical constants could be contained in an include file named fundamental_constants.inc:

```
planck_constant    = 6.6260755d-34 ; Joule second
light_speed        = 2.9979246d+8  ; meters per second
boltzmann_constant = 1.380658d-23  ; Joules per Kelvin
rad_c1 = 2.0d0 * planck_constant * light_speed^2
rad_c2 = (planck_constant * light_speed) / boltzmann_constant
```

To include the file in a function named `planck.pro` that computes monochromatic Planck radiance ($mW/cm^2/sr/cm^{-1}$) given wavenumber (cm^{-1}) and temperature (K), the include file name is prefaced by the "at" character (@):

```
FUNCTION PLANCK, V, T
@fundamental_constants.inc
vs = 1.0D2 * v
return, vs^3 * ((rad_c1 * 1.0D5) / $
  (exp(rad_c2 * (vs / t)) - 1.0D0))
END
```

The include file is silently inserted into the function at compile time:

```
IDL> .compile planck
% Compiled module: PLANCK.
IDL> print, planck(1100.0, 300.0)
      81.511538
```

Tip   Beware of clashes between the names of variables defined in the include file and variables defined in the procedure or function. For this reason, unique and descriptive names are recommended for variables defined in include files.

Journaling

A journal of an IDL session can be created by calling the `journal` procedure:

```
IDL> journal
```

The default journal file `idlsave.pro` is created in the current directory. The `journal` procedure accepts one optional parameter specifying the path and name of the journal file:

```
IDL> journal, 'mydemo.pro'
```

Journaling ends when `journal` is called without any arguments, or when the IDL session ends. To replay a journal file, simply use the "at" character (@):

```
IDL> @mydemo
```

3.6 GLOBAL VARIABLES

IDL offers several mechanisms for using global variables. A global variable is one that is visible at any level, whether at the command line or within a called procedure or function. IDL maintains a number of read-only global variables (also known as *system variables*) that reflect the state of the current session, such as the IDL version number, the size of the color table, and the name of the currently selected graphics device. In addition, writable system variables exist that may be used to change the default behavior of IDL; these should be used with care. You can also define new writable system variables; however, these are usually required only in exceptional circumstances. System variable names begin with an exclamation mark (!) to distinguish them from normal variable names. Finally, IDL allows global common blocks to be defined.

Read-Only System Variables

It is quite common to require some information about the current IDL session within a procedure or function. For example, you may wish to know which version of IDL is running if you are using a version-dependent routine (e.g., a function that was added in IDL 5.2). Or you may wish to use a system variable to obtain a mathematical constant. Some commonly used read-only system variables are shown in Table 3.4.

You will see some of these read-only system variables used in example programs in subsequent chapters of this book. For more information, see the online help topic "System Variables." The system variable `!d.flags` contains information about the current graphics device and is described in detail in Appendix E.

Writable System Variables

Writable system variables may be used to modify the default behavior of IDL globally. That is, when you change the value of a writable system variable,

Table 3.4   Commonly used read-only system variables.

System variable	Meaning
!dtor	Degrees to radians conversion factor
!radeg	Radians to degrees conversion factor
!pi	π (single precision)
!dpi	π (double precision)
!version.release	IDL version number (string, e.g., '5.3')
!version.os_family	Platform identifier ('Windows', 'MacOS', 'unix', or 'vms')
!d.flags	Bitmask containing information about the current graphics device
!d.n_colors	Number of possible colors in palette
!d.name	Name of the current graphics device
!d.table_size	Size of the color table
!d.window	Index of current graphics window
!d.x_vsize	Viewable horizontal size of current graphics device (in pixels)
!d.y_vsize	Viewable vertical size of current graphics device (in pixels)
!x.window	Horizontal coordinates of current plot (normalized units)
!y.window	Vertical coordinates of current plot (normalized units)

the change is visible at all levels. For example, the system variable !p.font controls the font used by IDL to create plotted characters. The default value is −1, which tells IDL to use platform-independent vector fonts for plotted characters as shown in the following example:

```
IDL> print, !p.font
         -1
IDL> x = findgen(200) * 0.1
IDL> y = sin(x)
IDL> plot, x, y
```

If !p.font is set to 0, IDL uses platform-dependent hardware fonts for plotted characters. However, keep in mind that a modified global variable is visible at all levels in IDL, so that all plots will use alternate fonts. A good strategy is to save the current value of the system variable, modify it only as long as needed, and then restore the value:

```
IDL> entry_font = !p.font
IDL> !p.font = 0
IDL> plot, x, y
IDL> !p.font = entry_font
```

Table 3.5   Commonly used writable system variables.

System variable	Meaning
!p.multi	Configures multipanel plots
!p.font	Selects default font for plotted characters
!order	Controls image display order (bottom up or top down)
!path	The current search path for procedures and functions
!except	Controls math error behavior

Some commonly used writable system variables are listed in Table 3.5. Some of these writable system variables will be encountered in subsequent chapters.

User-Defined System Variables

IDL allows you to define system variables if the need arises. You should always think carefully before defining a new system variable; there may be another way to achieve your goal, such as using a pointer. User-defined system variables can clutter the name space of IDL if used indiscriminately, since they cannot be deleted once they are created.

To create a new system variable, the defsysv procedure is used:

```
IDL> defsysv, '!plot_info', 10.0
IDL> help, !plot_info
<Expression>    FLOAT     =      10.0000
```

By default, system variables created by defsysv are writable:

```
IDL> !plot_info = -32.0
IDL> help, !plot_info
<Expression>    FLOAT     =      -32.0000
```

However, read-only system variables can be created by adding an optional nonzero argument to defsysv, as shown in the following example, where the speed of light is defined in meters per second:

```
IDL> defsysv, '!speed_of_light', 2.9979246d+8, 1
IDL> help, !speed_of_light
<Expression>    DOUBLE    =      2.9979246e+008
IDL> !speed_of_light = 123.45
% Attempt to write to a readonly variable: !SPEED_OF_LIGHT.
% Execution halted at:  $MAIN$
```

Once a system variable has been created, its type and size cannot be changed:

```
IDL> !plot_info = 64L
IDL> help, !plot_info
<Expression>    FLOAT    =        64.0000
```

In this case, even though the system variable was assigned a long value of 64, the type was automatically converted to float. Any attempt to change the size of a system variable will result in an error:

```
IDL> !plot_info = indgen(10)
% Conflicting data structures: <INT Array[10]>,!PLOT_INFO.
% Execution halted at:  $MAIN$
```

To remove user-defined system variables, you can either exit IDL and start a new session, or issue the .reset_session executive command at the IDL command line to reset the session:

```
IDL> .reset_session
IDL> help, !plot_info
% Not a legal system variable: !PLOT_INFO.
% Execution halted at:  $MAIN$
```

Note   The .reset_session command destroys all user-defined variables, including pointers, structures, and objects, and removes all references to user-defined procedures or functions that have been previously compiled. Therefore, you should use .reset_session sparingly, if ever.

To check for the existence of a system variable, the exist keyword is used in conjunction with defsysv to return a logical variable that is true (1) if the system variable exists, and false (0) otherwise:

```
IDL> defsysv, '!plot_info', 2.0
IDL> defsysv, '!plot_info', exist=exist
IDL> help, exist
EXIST           LONG      =            1
IDL> defsysv, '!plot_nothing', exist=exist
IDL> help, exist
EXIST           LONG      =            0
```

| Tip | If you must create system variables, use unique names to avoid clutter-ing the name space. For example, if your IDL application is named `mul-tispec`, then create system variables with names such as `multispec_state`, `multispec_options`, and so on. |

Common Blocks

Common blocks with global scope may be created in IDL. Once a common block is created, any program unit that references the common block may access the variables contained within it. The syntax for defining a common block is

> `common` *block_name, var1, var2, var3,...*

where *block_name* is the name of the common block, and *var1*, *var2*, and *var3* are variables to be stored in the common block. The first procedure or function to reference the common block defines the number of variables contained within the common block. Procedures and functions that subsequently reference the common block can read or write variables in the common block, but cannot change the type of any variable, or the total number of variables. Variables that appear as parameters in the current program unit may not be stored in a common block. Common blocks remain in existence until either the current IDL session ends or a `.reset_session` executive command is issued.

The following procedures use a common block to store a long integer value along with the time the value was set.

```
PRO SET_NUMBER

common set_number_info, number, time
number = 0L
read, prompt='Enter a number: ', number
time = systime()

END

PRO GET_NUMBER
```

```
common set_number_info, number, time
print, 'The last number set was ', number, ' at ', time

END
```

If the `set_number` procedure is called to set a value, a subsequent call to `get_number` will print the value:

```
IDL> set_number
Enter a number: 12345
IDL> get_number
The last number set was 12345 at Fri Dec 08 15:10:06 2000
```

The use of common blocks to pass variables within a single program or among related programs is generally discouraged because it tends to make program maintenance difficult. For example, if you have defined 10 variables in a common block and you wish to add one more variable, you must exit IDL and start a new session (or reset the session) in order to do so. Pointers and structures provide a much cleaner and safer method for passing information and should be used instead of common blocks whenever possible.

3.7   ERROR HANDLING

When IDL encounters a fatal error in a procedure or function, the default behavior is to stop execution in the routine that caused the error. This default behavior may be modified by calling the `on_error` procedure, which accepts a single scalar argument specifying the default error behavior. Table 3.6 lists the possible `on_error` argument values.

In most cases, the default behavior is appropriate, because if your procedure or function crashes, IDL will stop inside the failed routine at the point where the error occurred, and you can inspect the size, type, and

Table 3.6   Argument values for `on_error`.

Value	Behavior when error occurs
0	Stop in the routine that caused the error (default)
1	Return to the main level
2	Return to the caller of the routine that caused the error
3	Return to the routine that caused the error

value of variables. However, for utility routines that have been debugged and tested, and are called often, you may wish to return to the caller of the routine that caused the error:

```
on_error, 2
```

Intercepting Errors

If you wish to manually intercept errors and provide your own error-handling code, the catch procedure can be used. When a catch error handler is established, control is transferred to the start of the code block associated with the error handler. For example, consider the following function named ncdf_isncdf, which returns true if a given file exists in netCDF format, and false otherwise:

```
FUNCTION NCDF_ISNCDF, FILE

;- Check arguments
if (n_params() ne 1) then $
  message, 'Usage: RESULT = NCDF_ISNCDF(FILE)'
if (n_elements(file) eq 0) then $
  message, 'Argument FILE is undefined'

;- Establish error handler
catch, error_status
if (error_status ne 0) then return, 0

;- Attempt to open the file
ncid = ncdf_open(file)

;- Close the file and return to caller
ncdf_close, ncid
return, 1

END
```

The call to catch establishes the error handler and creates the variable error_status, which is set to zero. In the event of a subsequent error, error_status is set to a nonzero error code and control is transferred to the first statement after the initial catch statement. In this case, the error-handling code is a simple if statement that returns false to the caller if error_status is nonzero. This statement is initially skipped because `error_status` is set to zero. The next statement executed is the call to `ncdf_open`, which attempts to open `file` in netCDF mode. If `file` does not exist, is not readable, or is not netCDF format, this statement would normally cause an error:

```
IDL> file = filepath('ctscan.dat', subdir='examples/data')
IDL> ncid = ncdf_open(file)
% NCDF_OPEN: Unable to open the file
"C:\RSI\IDL53\examples/data\ctscan.dat". (NC_ERROR=19)
% Execution halted at:  $MAIN$
```

However, because an error handler was established, control will be transferred to the `if` statement if an error occurs, and false will be returned to the caller:

```
IDL> print, ncdf_isncdf(file)
     0
```

However, if the file is netCDF format, such as the sample data file `sao.nc` available from `http://www.gumley.com`, then the call to `ncdf_open` is successful, and true is returned to the caller:

```
IDL> print, ncdf_isncdf('sao.nc')
     1
```

Note   Error handlers established with `catch` override the error-handling behavior set by `on_error`. To trap errors that occur only during I/O operations, use the `on_ioerror` procedure (see the online help for `on_ioerror` for more information). Type conversions are classed as I/O operations by IDL. For example, `on_ioerror` may be used to catch errors encountered when converting from `string` to `float` type.

If you wish to obtain further information about an error that was handled by `catch`, the `help` procedure can be used to obtain the error message text that would have been printed if the error had not been trapped. In the previous example, the error-handling code would be modified as follows:

```
if (error_status ne 0) then begin
  help, /last_message, output=errtext
```

```
    print, errtext[0]
    return, 0
endif
```

The first element of `errtext` contains the error message, and the second element tells you which source line of the routine caused the error.

Error handlers established by `catch` are automatically canceled when control is returned to the caller. However, if it is necessary to cancel an error handler within a procedure or function (e.g., to read a file after it has been opened), the optional `cancel` keyword may be passed to `catch`:

```
catch, /cancel
```

This causes the error handler for the current procedure or function to be canceled. It does not affect error handlers defined in any other routines.

Math Errors

On systems that support the IEEE floating-point arithmetic standard, IDL is able to detect math errors such as overflow, underflow, and divide-by-zero. In these cases, IDL substitutes the special floating-point values `NaN` (not a number) or `Inf` (infinity) for the value that caused the error:

```
IDL> print, sqrt(-1.0)
        -NaN
% Program caused arithmetic error: Floating illegal operand
IDL> print, 1.0 / 0.0
        Inf
% Program caused arithmetic error: Floating divide by 0
```

The default behavior is to continue execution and print a warning message when control is returned to the command line. To change the default behavior, you can change the system variable `!except`, as shown in Table 3.7.

Table 3.7 Values for system variable `!except`.

Value	Behavior when math error occurs
0	Do not print a warning.
1	Print a warning when control returns to the command line (default).
2	Print a warning when the exception occurs.

Note
If you wish to check the math error status without printing a warning message, set !except to zero and call the check_math function (see the online help for check_math for more information).

The finite function may be used to check for the presence of NaN and Inf. This function returns true wherever an argument (scalar or array) is finite, and false otherwise:

```
IDL> a = [0.0, 1.0, sqrt(-1.0), 4.0, 1.0 / 0.0]
% Program caused arithmetic error: Floating divide by 0
% Program caused arithmetic error: Floating illegal operand
IDL> print, finite(a)
   1   1   0   1   0
```

To locate nonfinite values and set them to a missing value, use the finite function in conjunction with where to return the indices of the nonfinite numbers:

```
IDL> missing = -999.9
IDL> index = where(finite(arr) eq 0, count)
IDL> if (count gt 0) then arr[index] = missing
IDL> print, arr
      0.000000      1.00000     -999.900      4.00000
     -999.900
```

Tip
Don't use the not operator to locate nonfinite values because not operates in a bit-wise fashion on integers. If the not operator performs a Boolean negation on the result of finite, then a subsequent call to where will not return the indices of the nonfinite values:

```
IDL> print, not finite(a)
 254 254 255 254 255
IDL> print, where(not finite(a))
           0            1            2            3            4
```

Resetting the IDL Session

If for some reason you wish to reset the current IDL session without having to exit, use the .reset_session executive command at the command line:

```
IDL> .reset_session
```

This command resets most (but not all) of the state of the current session to the way it existed at IDL startup. Of particular note are the following items:

- Control is returned to the main level.
- All user-opened files are closed except the journal file (if open) and any output files connected to graphics devices.
- All local variables and user-defined system variables are destroyed.
- All common blocks, pointers, object references, and user-defined structures are destroyed.
- Compiled versions of user-defined functions and procedures are removed from memory.
- All graphics windows are closed and all widgets are destroyed.

This command should be used sparingly. It is not a good idea to make it a daily IDL programming habit because resetting the session makes it easy to avoid fixing problems such as memory leaks.

3.8   EFFICIENT PROGRAMMING

There are several easy ways to make IDL programs more efficient, meaning they take less time and use less memory. By following a few simple rules, you will get into the habit of writing efficient IDL programs.

Conserving Memory

The method by which IDL evaluates statements determines the amount of memory required by a given statement. For example, consider the following statements:

```
IDL> a = dist(500, 500)
IDL> a = a + 1.0
```

Here a floating-point array is created with 500 columns and 500 rows, where each element occupies 4 bytes. Thus the size of the array is $500 \times 500 \times 4$ bytes = 1 million bytes. In the second statement, IDL creates a new array to hold the result of the addition, assigns the result to the new array, and then frees the memory occupied by the old version of the array. Thus the memory required by this operation is 2 million bytes.

The `temporary` function can be used to reduce the memory required by this kind of operation. The `temporary` function returns a temporary copy of a single input argument and sets the argument to undefined type. Thus the following statement only requires 1 million bytes of memory:

```
IDL> a = temporary(a) + 1.0
```

This method can only be used when the array in question appears once on the right side of an assignment statement. In the following example, the array becomes undefined before the `max` function is called:

```
IDL> a = temporary(a) * (1.0 / max(a))
% MAX: Variable is undefined: A.
% Execution halted at:   $MAIN$
```

If multiple operations are performed on the array, they can be performed one step at a time to conserve memory:

```
IDL> a = dist(500, 500)
IDL> maxval = max(a)
IDL> a = temporary(a) / maxval
```

When an array is replaced by a subarray, it is not immediately obvious how `temporary` should be used to conserve memory. For example, `temporary` saves no memory if it is used in the following way:

```
IDL> a = dist(256)
IDL> b = temporary(a[0:63, 0:63])
IDL> help, a, b
A               FLOAT     = Array[256, 256]
B               FLOAT     = Array[64, 64]
```

The subarray `a[0:63, 0:63]` is passed to `temporary` by value and therefore cannot be modified. However, the following method does conserve memory because `a` is passed to `temporary` by reference, and a subarray is extracted from the array returned by `temporary`:

```
IDL> a = dist(256)
IDL> b = (temporary(a))[0:63, 0:63]
IDL> help, a, b
A               UNDEFINED = <Undefined>
B               FLOAT     = Array[64, 64]
```

Using Efficient Methods

There is just about always more than one way to carry out an operation in IDL. The trick is finding a method that is fast. For example, say you wish to find the sum of all elements greater than 100.0 in a frequency distribution array with 500 columns and 1,000 rows. The first method shown uses a loop over all elements, with an if test on each element:

```
IDL> a = dist(500, 1000)
IDL> sum = 0.0
IDL> for i = 0L, n_elements(a) - 1L do $
IDL>    if (a[i] gt 100.0) then sum = sum + a[i]
```

On a modest Windows PC, this operation requires 2.36 seconds. Another method uses the where and total functions:

```
IDL> index = where(a gt 100.0, count)
IDL> if (count gt 0) then sum = total(a[index])
```

This method cuts the time to 0.44 seconds. A third method uses the gt operator to select the elements greater than 100.0:

```
IDL> sum = total(a * (a gt 100.0))
```

The time required in this case is 0.28 seconds. Thus a judicious selection of method reduced the runtime by a factor of 10 in this case. When speed is important, methods that do not use loops are preferred.

Tip

The systime function may be used to time an operation. When called with no arguments, it returns a time/date string. However, when called with a single nonzero argument, systime returns the number of seconds elapsed since midnight on January 1, 1970, according to the system clock. Thus you simply need to call systime before and after the operation in question and then print the difference:

```
IDL> t0 = systime(1) & sum = total(a * (a gt 100.0)) & $
IDL>    t1 = systime(1)
IDL> print, t1 - t0
     0.28000009
```

Input and Output

A common scenario in the real world goes something like this: You've acquired a set of data, either from measurement or simulation. The data set exists in a file on disk in a format that is specific to the sensor or environment that generated the data. Your task is to read the data into IDL in order to analyze and/or visualize it. The data set could be as simple as a text file containing two columns of numbers, or as complex as a satellite image containing millions of measurements and dozens of items of information that describe the data (known as *metadata*). You also may want to read or write industry-standard data formats (e.g., TIFF, DICOM) or self-describing platform-independent formats such as netCDF or HDF.

Fortunately, IDL is very capable when it comes to reading and writing data in a variety of formats. Just like C and Fortran, IDL reads and writes formatted (ASCII) and unformatted (binary) data sets. The wide variety of data types built into IDL, and the availability of arrays and structures, ensures that it can handle just about any ASCII or binary data set. IDL also includes built-in support for reading and writing common image and scientific data formats.

This chapter covers reading and writing formatted ASCII text and numeric data to standard input and output and data files on disk. Reading and writing unformatted binary data is covered in detail, including techniques for dealing with platform-dependent byte ordering. The chapter concludes with coverage of the netCDF and HDF scientific data formats—formats that provide the means to create platform-independent, self-describing data sets.

4.1   STANDARD INPUT AND OUTPUT

Reading and writing data in ASCII text format is one of the most common tasks in IDL. This section discusses reading data from the standard input (the keyboard) and writing data to the standard output, the screen. The procedures and functions used for standard input and output (I/O) are shown in Table 4.1.

Writing to Standard Output

The print procedure writes formatted ASCII data to the standard output. If you are using the IDL Development Environment (idlde), the standard output is the Output Log window. If you are using the IDL Command Line (idl), the standard output is the command line.

The general syntax for the print procedure is

print, *arg₁*, *arg₂*, ... , *argₙ*

A simple example is the classic

```
IDL> print, 'Hello world'
Hello world
```

IDL has default rules to determine how the output from print should be formatted. For example, float values are printed with six digits of precision:

```
IDL> print, findgen(3)
      0.000000      1.00000      2.00000
```

Although the default formatting rules are often adequate, there will be times when you need to specify the output format exactly. For this pur-

Table 4.1   Procedures and functions for standard I/O.

Name	Purpose
print	Write formatted data to standard output
read	Read formatted data from standard input
reads	Read formatted data from a string
string()	Write formatted data to a string

pose, `print` uses Fortran-style format codes that are set with the `format` keyword. For example, to print the system variable `!pi` (pi represented as a `float`) with three digits after the decimal point:

```
IDL> print, !pi, format='(f7.3)'
  3.142
```

The most commonly used format codes are listed in Table 4.2.

The same formatting can be repeated for multiple values:

```
IDL> print, findgen(5), format='(5f7.3)'
  0.000  1.000  2.000  3.000  4.000
```

Multiple format codes separated by commas can be used to create a format sequence:

```
IDL> print, 2, !pi, format='(i4, 2x, f7.3)'
   2    3.142
```

Table 4.2 **Commonly used format codes.**

Code	Output
iN.M	Integer value with up to N characters (.M is optional; however, if .M is used, any blank positions in the rightmost M characters are filled with zeroes)
fN.M	Single-precision value with up to N characters, and M digits after the decimal point
dN.M	Double-precision value with up to N characters, and M digits after the decimal point
eN.M	Floating-point value in exponential format with up to N characters, and M digits after the decimal point*
aN	String with up to N characters (if N is omitted, all characters in the input string are printed)
Nx	Skip N character positions
/	Start a new line
$	Suppress new line (on output only)
:	Terminate output if no more arguments are available

* The number of digits in the exponent may vary between platforms (e.g., 1.0e+02 versus 1.0e+002). Also, e in the format code produces e in the printed value (e.g., 1.0e+002), while E in the format code produces E in the printed value (e.g., 1.0E+002).

Repeated format codes can be specified using parentheses:

```
IDL> print, 2, !pi, 4, 2*!pi, format='(2(i4, 2x, f7.3))'
   2    3.142    4    6.283
```

The following rules apply when multiple format codes are used:

- Format codes are always used from left to right.
- If there are more format codes than values to be printed, format codes are used from left to right until all values have been printed.
- If there are more values to be printed than format codes, then after the last format code is used, a new line is printed and the format codes are used again from left to right:

```
IDL> print, findgen(6), format='(2f7.3)'
  0.000  1.000
  2.000  3.000
  4.000  5.000
```

Strings may be used in a format sequence, but they must be enclosed in double quotes:

```
IDL> print, !pi, format='("The value of pi is ", f9.7)'
The value of pi is 3.1415927
```

String values may be printed using the a format code to print either the entire string or a certain number of characters:

```
IDL> print, 'Hello world', format='(a)'
Hello world
IDL> print, 'Hello world', format='(a7)'
Hello w
```

For the i, f, d, and e format codes, the number of characters N must include any spaces and a minus sign, decimal point, and exponent if needed. If N is not large enough to accommodate a value, then asterisks are printed to indicate a format overflow:

```
IDL> print, 12345.6, format='(f7.1)'
12345.6
IDL> print, 12345.6, format='(f6.1)'
******
```

Any value that does not match the type of the corresponding format code is printed as though it were converted to the type indicated by the format code (however, it is not actually converted). For example, a byte value is printed as though it were converted to float if the f format code is used:

```
IDL> print, 128B, format='(f8.3)'
 128.000
```

If the data types of the value and the corresponding format code are incompatible (say you tried to print a string in exponential notation), then an error message is printed:

```
IDL> print, 'Hello world', format='(e7.3)'
% Type conversion error: Unable to convert given
  STRING to Double.
% Detected at:  $MAIN$
*******
```

Reading from Standard Input

The read procedure reads formatted ASCII data from the standard input. If you are using the IDL Development Environment (idlde), the standard input is the Command Input window. If you are using the IDL Command Line (idl), the standard input is the command line.

The general syntax for the read procedure is

read, arg_1, arg_2, ... , arg_n

For example, to prompt the user to enter a value:

```
IDL> read, npoints, prompt='Enter number of points: '
IDL> help, npoints
```

If you executed the previous two commands and entered a numeric value, you will notice that npoints was created as a float. If the return value is undefined when read is called, and no format keyword is specified, then the default type for the return value is float. Thus if you enter a nonnumeric value in the previous example, an error occurs:

```
% READ: Input conversion error.
% Execution halted at:  $MAIN$
```

To read a variable of a specific type, you must create the variable before read is called. To read a long value, first create a long variable:

```
IDL> npoints = 0L
IDL> read, npoints, prompt='Enter number of points: '
Enter number of points: 32
IDL> help, npoints
NPOINTS         LONG      =          32
```

To read a `string` value, first create a `string` variable:

```
IDL> name = ''
IDL> read, name, prompt='Enter your name: '
Enter your name: Joe Average
IDL> help, name
NAME            STRING    = 'Joe Average'
```

Format codes are not normally used when reading formatted data from standard input because they increase the likelihood of a formatting error. However, format codes may be used if desired:

```
IDL> year = 0L
IDL> read, year, prompt='Enter year (YYYY): ', format='(i4)'
Enter year (YYYY): 2000
IDL> help, year
YEAR            LONG      =         2000
```

If the input variable does not exist before `read` is called, then the variable type will be `float` regardless of the format code:

```
IDL> read, z, format='(i6)'
: 123456
IDL> help, z
Z               FLOAT     =       123456.
```

Free-Format Input

When a `read` statement is executed without a `format` keyword, this is known as *free-format input*. When numeric input is expected from the user, free-format input is recommended because it allows some flexibility in the way the input data is entered. However, there are a few rules to follow for numeric free-format input:

- Input values must be separated by commas, spaces, tabs, or newlines.
- If the current input line does not contain enough values to fulfill the read request, then subsequent input lines are read until sufficient values are obtained.
- If the current input line contains more values than are required to fulfill the read request, the extra values are ignored.

When a `string` variable is read via free-format input, all characters on the current input line are read, and the next variable (if there is one) is read from the next input line (i.e., each `string` variable is read from a separate input line):

```
IDL> a = ' '
IDL> b = ' '
IDL> read, a, b
: First line
: Second line
IDL> help, a, b
A               STRING    = 'First line'
B               STRING    = 'Second line'
```

Reading from a String

The reads procedure reads data from an existing string variable. The general syntax for the reads procedure is

reads, arg_1, arg_2, . . . , arg_n

For example, to read long values of year, month, and day from a string variable:

```
IDL> date = '1999/06/24'
IDL> year = 0L
IDL> month = 0L
IDL> day = 0L
IDL> reads, date, year, month, day, $
IDL>   format='(i4, 1x, i2, 1x, i2)'
IDL> print, year, month, day
      1999             6           24
```

The formatting rules that apply to the read procedure also apply to the reads procedure. The format keyword may be used, or else free-format rules apply.

Writing to a String

The string function writes (converts) data to a string variable. The general syntax for the string function is

text = string(*arg*)

where *arg* is a variable of numeric or string type. Often the string function is called with a format keyword to specify the format of the resulting string variable:

```
IDL> year = 2000
IDL> month = 1
```

```
IDL> day = 27
IDL> date = string(year, month, day, $
IDL>  format='(i4, "/", i2.2, "/", i2.2)')
IDL> print, date
2000/01/27
```

Double quotes are used to enclose the forward slash character because the format sequence itself is a string variable enclosed in single quotes.

Legal and Illegal read *Arguments*

Arguments supplied to the read procedure must be passed by reference because read must be able to modify the size, type, or value of the arguments. Arguments that are passed by reference include scalar variables, arrays, structures, and undefined variables. Arguments that are passed by value to read are illegal, including constants, subarrays, structure elements, system variables, and expressions. For example, say you try to read a single element of an array:

```
IDL> flags = intarr(3)
IDL> read, flags[0], prompt='Enter flag value: '
% READ: Expression must be named variable in this context:
  <INT ( 0)>.
% Execution halted at:  $MAIN$
```

In the example above, read detected that subarray flags[0] was passed by value, and therefore execution was stopped and an error message was printed. However, it is perfectly legal to read an entire array, since arrays are passed by reference:

```
IDL> flags = intarr(3)
IDL> read, flags, prompt='Enter 3 flag values: '
Enter 3 flag values: 1, 2, 3
IDL> print, flags
       1       2       3
```

Likewise, structure elements cannot be passed to read because they are passed by value:

```
IDL> contact = {area:0L, phone:0L, zip:0L}
IDL> read, contact.area, prompt='Enter area code: '
% READ: Expression must be named variable in this context:
  <LONG ( 0)>.
% Execution halted at:  $MAIN$
```

However, complete structures can be passed to `read` because they are passed by reference:

```
IDL> contact = {area:0L, phone:0L, zip:0L}
IDL> read, contact, prompt='Enter area code, phone, zip: '
Enter area, phone, zip: 555, 3394819, 53706
IDL> print, contact
{       555    3394819      53706}
```

4.2 WORKING WITH FILES

The next step in reading and writing data involves working with files on disk. The basic operations are opening, closing, and obtaining information about files. There are essentially two kinds of arbitrary data files that IDL handles in this context (not including standard formats such as TIFF, netCDF, etc.):

- Formatted files containing data in ASCII text format, such as tabular columns of numbers
- Unformatted files containing data of any type in raw binary form (e.g., 32-bit `long` integers)

IDL is equally capable of handling either form. Table 4.3 lists the procedures and functions available for working with formatted and unformatted files in IDL.

Table 4.3 Procedures and functions for working with files.

Name	Purpose
openr	Open an existing file for read only
openw	Open a new file for read or write
openu	Open an existing file for updating (read or write)
findfile()	Return names of files in the current directory
dialog_pickfile()	Graphical file selector
fstat()	Return information about an open file
eof()	Check for end-of-file
close	Close a file
free_lun	Free a logical unit number and close a file

Opening Files

In order to read or write a formatted or unformatted file, you must first open the file and assign a logical unit number. Read and write operations are then performed using the logical unit number to reference the file. The relevant procedures are openr, openw, and openu, as described in Table 4.3. The openr procedure opens an existing file for reading only; writing is not permitted as long as the file remains open. The openw procedure opens a new file for reading or writing. If the file existed previously, it is overwritten. The openu procedure opens an existing file for updating, which includes both reading and writing.

Each open procedure assigns a logical unit number that references the file. An error message will be printed and execution will stop if for any reason the file cannot be opened. The logical unit number is a scalar long that may be set (hard-wired) to a value in the range 1 to 99:

```
IDL> lun = 20L
IDL> openw, lun, 'test.dat'
```

However, it is preferable to allow IDL to assign a free logical unit by passing the optional get_lun keyword:

```
IDL> openw, lun, 'test.dat', /get_lun
```

When get_lun is passed to openr, openw, or openu, an unused logical unit number in the range 100 to 128 is assigned (logical unit numbers 0, −1, and −2 are reserved for standard input, standard output, and standard error, respectively). Likewise, the free_lun procedure closes the file and returns the logical unit number to the pool of unused logical unit numbers (see the description of free_lun in the subsequent section "Closing Files"). The open procedures accept a number of other keywords (see the online help for more information).

Tip   On the Windows platform in IDL 5.3 and earlier versions, it is recommended that the optional binary and noautomode keywords be set when opening a file for reading, writing, or updating. When a file is opened in IDL for Windows, by default no translation of carriage-return/line-feed (CR/LF) pairs is done. However, some IDL procedures (e.g., printf) cause IDL to switch to a mode where CR/LF pairs are converted to a single LF.

Using the `binary` and `noautomode` keyword in conjunction with `openr`, `openw`, or `openu` prevents IDL from switching translation modes and prevents potential errors that may occur when the current file pointer position is obtained. In IDL 5.4 this problem is fixed, so the Windows platform reads and writes data the same way as all other IDL platforms. In IDL 5.4 the `binary` and `noautomode` keywords are accepted by the open procedures, but are completely ignored.

Selecting a File

If you are opening a new file for writing, then all you need to do is decide on a name (and perhaps a directory) for the new file. However, if you are opening an existing file, then you need some way to select the file name from the files available on disk.

The `findfile` function, when called without any arguments, returns a string array containing the names of all files in the current directory:

```
IDL> list = findfile()
IDL> print, list
hurric.dat test.dat hello.pro square.pro
```

When `findfile` is called with a `string` argument, a string array is returned containing all matching files:

```
IDL> list = findfile('data/*.nc')
IDL> print, list
data/image.nc data/sao.nc
```

The null string (`' '`) is returned if no files are found that match the string argument. The asterisk character (`'*'`) is treated as a wildcard, so that the following statement returns a list of all files in the current directory with the extension `.dat`:

```
IDL> list = findfile('*.dat')
```

Sometimes a graphical interface for selecting a file is more convenient and user-friendly. The `dialog_pickfile` function provides a standard Open File dialog that allows you to select a file from the current directory, or any directory on your system:

```
IDL> file = dialog_pickfile()
```

If the `filter` keyword is used to pass a `string` variable, then only files matching the `filter` string are displayed:

```
IDL> file = dialog_pickfile(filter='*.dat')
```

Obtaining Information about Files

The `fstat` function returns information about an open file, including the size, read status, and expanded path name. The information is returned in a structure, with each field in the structure containing a particular item. For example, to obtain information about the sample data file `hurric.dat`:

```
IDL> file = filepath('hurric.dat', subdir='examples/data')
IDL> openr, lun, file, /get_lun
IDL> info = fstat(lun)
IDL> help, info.size, info.read, info.name
<Expression>    LONG    =         149600
<Expression>    BYTE    = 1
<Expression>    STRING  = 'C:\RSI\IDL53\examples\data\
  hurric.dat'
IDL> free_lun, lun
```

For the complete list of fields in the structure returned by `fstat`, see the online help.

When reading a file, it is often desirable to know whether the end-of-file has been reached, so that read operations can be terminated. The `eof` function returns true if the end-of-file (EOF) has been reached, and false otherwise. For example, the file `hurric.dat` mentioned in the previous example has a size of 149,600 bytes (it is actually a two-dimensional image array, but here it is read as a one-dimensional vector):

```
IDL> file = filepath('hurric.dat', subdir='examples/data')
IDL> openr, lun, file, /get_lun
IDL> print, eof(lun)
     0
IDL> data = bytarr(149600)
IDL> readu, lun, data
IDL> print, eof(lun)
     1
IDL> free_lun, lun
```

Closing Files

The close procedure is used to close files that were opened with a hard-wired logical unit number (i.e., without the get_lun keyword):

```
IDL> lun = 50
IDL> openr, lun, 'test.dat'
IDL> close, lun
```

The free_lun procedure is used to close files that were opened with the get_lun keyword:

```
IDL> openr, lun, 'test.dat', /get_lun
IDL> free_lun, lun
```

The free_lun procedure has the advantage that the logical unit number lun is returned to the pool of logical unit numbers available to subsequent open statements that include the get_lun keyword. If free_lun is not used to close the file, the logical unit number is not freed for future use.

Finally, to close all files in an IDL session, regardless of how they were opened, the optional all keyword may be passed to close:

```
IDL> close, /all
```

4.3 READING AND WRITING FORMATTED (ASCII) FILES

Formatted files contain data in a text format, such as columns of numbers in a table. This type of file is commonly used because it is human readable and easy to port between software applications and hardware platforms (e.g., between a Fortran program on a UNIX workstation and a spreadsheet on a MacOS platform). Formatted files are, however, slower to read and write than unformatted binary files, and generally require more disk space than the corresponding binary data. The procedures used for formatted I/O are listed in Table 4.4.

Table 4.4 Procedures for formatted I/O.

Name	Purpose
readf	Read data from a formatted file
printf	Write data to a formatted file

Reading a Formatted File

The readf procedure reads data from an open formatted file. The general syntax for the readf procedure is

readf, lun, *arg₁*, *arg₂*, ... , *argₙ*

Reading data from a formatted file of a known size is easy in IDL. For example, if a formatted data file contains 10 columns and 100 records (rows) of integer data where every integer occupies 6 spaces, the following statements can be used to read the entire file:

```
IDL> openr, lun, 'input.dat', /get_lun
IDL> data = lonarr(10, 100)
IDL> readf, lun, data, format='(10i6)'
IDL> free_lun, lun
```

In this example, openr was used to open the file for read-only on logical unit lun. The input array data was created with the correct type and size, and the entire file was read with readf. The format of each record was specified via the format keyword (the format code and free-format input rules that apply to read and reads also apply to readf). The file was then closed by calling free_lun.

However, you're more likely to have to read a formatted file that has a known format but an unknown length (some files may have a couple of hundred records, and some may have a couple of thousand records). Your first instinct might be to try and determine the number of records in the file, which would then allow you to read the entire file with a single readf as in the previous example. However, in practice, it is usually easier to use a while loop to read records from the file sequentially until the end of the file is reached. For example, say you had a file containing several thousand aircraft position readings (time, latitude, longitude, heading) in the following format:

```
22:02:13.34UTC -29.9345S -116.0234W 234.2
22:02:14.33UTC -29.9357S -116.0232W 234.1
22:02:15.34UTC -29.9362S -116.0230W 234.1
22:02:16.35UTC -29.9367S -116.0228W 234.2
22:02:17.36UTC -29.9373S -116.0226W 234.2
22:02:18.34UTC -29.9378S -116.0224W 234.3
```

The following function named read_position.pro will read the contents of this file into an array of structures, where each element of the output array contains one input record:

```
FUNCTION READ_POSITION, FILE, MAXREC=MAXREC

;- Check arguments
if (n_elements(file) eq 0) then $
  message, 'Argument FILE is undefined'
if (n_elements(maxrec) eq 0) then $
  maxrec = 10000L

;- Open input file
openr, lun, file, /get_lun

;- Define record structure and create array
fmt = '(2(i2, 1x), f5.2, 4x, f8.4, 2x, f9.4, 2x, f5.1)'
record = {hour:0L, min:0L, sec:0.0, $
  lat:0.0, lon:0.0, head:0.0}
data = replicate(record, maxrec)

;- Read records until end-of-file reached
nrecords = 0L
recnum = 1L
while (eof(lun) ne 1) do begin

  ;- Read this record (jumps to bad_rec: on error)
  on_ioerror, bad_rec
  error = 1
  readf, lun, record, format=fmt
  error = 0

  ;- Store data for this record
  data[nrecords] = record
  nrecords = nrecords + 1L

;- Check if maximum record count exceeded
  if (nrecords eq maxrec) then begin
    free_lun, lun
    message, 'Maximum record reached: increase MAXREC'
  endif

  ;- Check for bad input record
  bad_rec:
  if (error eq 1) then $
    print, 'Bad data at record ', recnum
  recnum = recnum + 1

endwhile
```

```
;- Close input file
free_lun, lun

;- Trim data array and return it to caller
data = data[0 : nrecords - 1]
return, data
```

```
END
```

The function returns an array of structures:

```
IDL> result = read_position('position.dat')
IDL> print, result[0].sec, result[0].lat
      13.3400      -29.9345
```

After checking the input arguments, the file is opened. Then an anonymous structure (record) is created to hold a single record, and an output array of structures (data) is created to hold all records read from the file. A while loop is started that reads a single record, stores it in the output array, and increments the record counter. The while loop executes as long as the file pointer is not at the end-of-file (the eof function returns true when the file pointer is at the end-of-file). The on_ioerror procedure is used to handle any errors when reading from the input file, such as a record with an invalid format. Bad record numbers are printed and are not stored in the output array. If the maximum number of input records is exceeded, the function halts, and an error message is printed. When the loop terminates, the input file is closed, and the output array is trimmed of empty records and returned to the caller.

Note how the structure variable record was used to read a record from the file:

```
readf, lun, record, format=fmt
```

A common mistake is to try and read each record into individual elements of the output array:

```
readf, lun, data[nrecords], format=fmt
```

This statement causes execution to stop, and the following error message is printed:

```
% Attempt to store into an expression: <STRUCT    Array[1]>.
% Execution halted at:  READ_POSITION     21 read_position.pro
%                       $MAIN$
```

The error occurs because data[nrecords] is a subarray that is passed by value to readf, and is therefore an illegal argument because it cannot be modified by readf.

Tip The ddread function written by Fred Knight may be used to read arbitrary formatted files with an unknown number of columns and rows (see the Searchable Library Database in Appendix A for download details).

Writing a Formatted File

The printf procedure writes data to a formatted file that has been opened for writing or updating. The general syntax for the printf procedure is

printf, lun, arg_1, arg_2, ... , arg_n

The free-format output and format code rules that apply to print also apply to printf. For example, to write an array to a formatted file:

```
IDL> data = lindgen(10, 100)
IDL> openw, lun, 'output.dat', /get_lun
IDL> printf, lun, data, format='(10i6)'
IDL> free_lun, lun
```

When writing formatted files, you should try to preserve the precision of floating-point variables, while recognizing that real-world measurements have a finite number of significant digits. Single-precision float values have about 7 digits of precision, while double-precision double values have about 14 digits of precision. Therefore you should use the appropriate number of digits when writing float and double values. Exponential notation provides the easiest and most general way to achieve this goal. To preserve all digits in a float variable, the appropriate format code is e14.6, and for double values the format code is e21.13:

```
IDL> print, -1.0 * !pi, format='(e14.6)'
-3.141593e+000
IDL> print, -1.0D * !dpi, format='(e21.13)'
-3.1415926535898e+000
```

On the Windows platform, IDL prints three exponent digits as shown in the previous example. On all other platforms, two exponent digits are printed.

If your IDL program produces a great deal of printed output, you may wish to redirect the output to a file rather than the terminal. If you use printf (instead of print) in your program, it's easy to send the printed output to the screen by default, or to an output file if required. This is possible because the logical unit number −1 is reserved for standard output. The following procedure, named redirect.pro, shows how this technique may be implemented:

```
PRO REDIRECT, OUTFILE=OUTFILE

;- Select logical unit for output
if (n_elements(outfile) eq 1) then begin
  openw, outlun, outfile, /get_lun
endif else begin
  outlun = -1
endelse

;- printf is used in the program for output
printf, outlun, 'Starting program execution at ', systime()

;- Body of program goes here

;- Close the output file if needed
if (outlun gt 0) then free_lun, outlun

END
```

When the procedure is executed without any arguments, output is directed to the screen. However, if the outfile keyword is set to the name of an output file, output is instead directed to the file:

```
IDL> redirect
Starting program execution at Sat Jan 29 15:22:37 2000
IDL> redirect, outfile='out.dat'
```

If the outfile keyword is defined, then an output file is opened and the logical unit number is returned by openw. Otherwise the logical unit number is set to −1, which corresponds to the standard output. In the body of the program, printf is used instead of print for printed output. Finally, if outfile is defined, the output file is closed.

Tip Formatted output to a file is limited to 80 columns by default (output past 80 columns is truncated). To increase the default output width, use the width keyword when the openw or openu procedure is called:

```
IDL> openw, lun, 'wide.dat', /get_lun, width=150
IDL> printf, lun, findgen(100), format='(10f10.2)'
IDL> free_lun, lun
```

4.4 READING AND WRITING UNFORMATTED (BINARY) FILES

Unformatted files contain data in a raw binary format. For example, an unformatted file might contain an image with 256 rows and 256 columns, where each image element is a 16-bit signed int. Or a file might contain multiple records, where each record contains a mix of data types. Both kinds of unformatted file can be read and written in IDL. The procedures and functions used for unformatted I/O are listed in Table 4.5.

Reading an Unformatted File (Single Data Type)

The readu procedure reads data from an open unformatted file. The general syntax for the readu procedure is

readu, lun, arg_1, arg_2, ... , arg_n

If an unformatted file contains only one kind of binary data (e.g., byte), and the file size is known in advance, then reading the contents of the file

Table 4.5 Procedures and functions for unformatted I/O.

Name	Purpose
readu	Read data from an unformatted file
point_lun	Reposition the file pointer in an open file
writeu	Write data to an unformatted file
assoc()	Associate a logical unit number with a variable
save	Save variables in a portable IDL-specific format
restore	Restore variables from a save file

is straightforward. For example, the file ctscan.dat (from the IDL example data directory) contains an image with 256 columns and 256 rows, where each element is a byte value:

```
IDL> file = filepath('ctscan.dat', subdir='examples/data')
IDL> openr, lun, file, /get_lun
IDL> data = bytarr(256, 256)
IDL> readu, lun, data
IDL> free_lun, lun
IDL> tvscl, data
```

In this example, the filepath function was used to obtain the full path and name of ctscan.dat in the IDL installation directory. Then the file was opened with openr (openr, openw, or openu may be used to open an unformatted file). A byte array of the required size was created with bytarr, and the data was read with readu. Finally the file was closed with free_lun, and the image was displayed with tvscl.

If the size of the file is not known in advance, but the size of each record is known, the following method can be used. In the following example, the example data file hurric.dat contains an image that is known to have 440 pixels per row, where each pixel is a byte value. However, the number of rows is not known, so the file is queried to determine the file size:

```
IDL> file = filepath('hurric.dat', subdir='examples/data')
IDL> openr, lun, file, /get_lun
IDL> info = fstat(lun)
IDL> ncols = 440L
IDL> nrows = info.size / ncols
IDL> data = bytarr(ncols, nrows)
IDL> readu, lun, data
IDL> free_lun, lun
IDL> tvscl, data
```

After the file was opened, the fstat function was called to obtain information about the file and returned a structure named info. The structure field info.size (the size of the file in bytes) was then used along with the number of columns (ncols) to create a byte array of the correct size. Then the image was read with readu, the file was closed with free_lun, and the image was displayed with tvscl.

ID	Year	Month	Day	Hour	Minute	Pressure	Temper-ature	Dew-point	Speed	Direction
long	int	int	int	int	int	float	float	float	float	float

Figure 4.1 Schematic form of records for an automated weather station.

Reading an Unformatted File (Mixed Data Types)

Unformatted data files may contain more than one data type per record. For example, say an unformatted file from an automated weather station contains readings obtained once every minute for up to 24 hours, and each record in the file contains the following information:

- One long value containing the station identification number
- Five int values containing the year, month, day, hour, and minute
- Five float values containing the pressure, temperature, dewpoint, wind speed, and wind direction

Represented in schematic form, each record appears as shown in Figure 4.1.

An array of anonymous structures provides a convenient way to read multiple records in this format. The following read_weather function uses a similar technique to the previous read_position function, except that binary data is read instead of ASCII data:

```
FUNCTION READ_WEATHER, FILE

;- Check arguments
if (n_elements(file) eq 0) then $
  message, 'Argument FILE is undefined'

;- Open the input file
openr, lun, file, /get_lun

;- Define record structure, and create data array
record = {id:0L, year:0, month:0, day:0, hour:0, minute:0, $
  pres:0.0, temp:0.0, dewp:0.0, speed:0.0, dir:0.0}
data = replicate(record, 24L * 60L)

;- Read records from the file until EOF
nrecords = 0
while (eof(lun) ne 1) do begin
  readu, lun, record
```

```
    data[nrecords] = record
    nrecords = nrecords + 1
endwhile

;- Close the input file
free_lun, lun

;- Trim the data array, and return it to caller
data = data[0 : nrecords - 1]
return, data
```

END

On return from read_weather, the result is an array of structures containing all records read from the file. To check the 10th pressure and temperature values:

IDL> print, data[9].pres, data[9].temp

Reading a Fortran-77 Unformatted File

The previous examples demonstrate how to read files that are compatible with Fortran-77 unformatted direct access mode. However, files that are written in Fortran-77 unformatted sequential access mode have extra information attached to the beginning and end of each data record. IDL can read (and write) these files if the optional f77_unformatted keyword is used in conjunction with the openr, openw, or openu procedures. For example, consider the following Fortran-77 program:

```
c ... Fortran-77 program to produce unformatted output
      implicit none
      integer a(10)
      real b(5)
      integer index
      do index = 1, 10
        a(index) = index
      end do
      do index = 1, 5
        b(index) = real(index * 10)
      end do
      open(30, file='idltest.dat',
    &  form='unformatted', access='sequential')
      write(30) a
```

```
write(30) b
close(30)
end
```

When this program is compiled and run, it produces an output file name idltest.dat. To read the contents of this file in IDL on the same platform:

```
IDL> openr, lun, 'idltest.dat', /get_lun, /f77_unformatted
IDL> a = lonarr(10)
IDL> b = fltarr(5)
IDL> readu, lun, a
IDL> readu, lun, b
IDL> free_lun, lun
IDL> print, a, format='(10i4)'
   1   2   3   4   5   6   7   8   9  10
IDL> print, b, format='(5f5.1)'
 10.0 20.0 30.0 40.0 50.0
```

Repositioning the File Pointer

Whenever you open an unformatted file with openr, openw, or openu, the logical unit number of the open file has an associated file pointer. The file pointer points to the position in the file where the next read or write request will begin. Every time a read or write request is issued, the file pointer is moved the appropriate number of bytes further along in the file.

The point_lun procedure allows you to reset the file pointer to a new position. For example, say you're reading a file containing 512 columns and 512 rows of byte data, which was originally read from a magnetic tape. The file contains a header of 1,024 bytes that was inserted by the program that wrote the tape. You want to skip the header and go right to the data:

```
IDL> openr, lun, 'tapefile.dat', /get_lun
IDL> point_lun, lun, 1024L
IDL> data = bytarr(512, 512)
IDL> readu, lun, data
IDL> free_lun, lun
```

When the file is opened the file pointer is set to zero. To reposition the file pointer just after the header, point_lun is called, and the data is read from the file.

If you wish to get the current position of the file pointer, the `cur_ptr` field in the structure returned by the `fstat` function contains the current file pointer value (in bytes from the beginning of the file):

```
IDL> info = fstat(lun)
IDL> position = info.cur_ptr
```

Byte Swapping (or Big-Endian versus Little-Endian)

If you have ever tried to port binary data from a UNIX platform to a PC platform, then you probably already know something about the problem of byte swapping. This problem arises because hardware vendors represent multibyte binary data in two different ways:

- Most significant byte first (big-endian)
- Least significant byte first (little-endian)

Therefore if you transfer a binary data file that contains multibyte data types from a big-endian to a little-endian platform or vice versa, you must be prepared to account for differences in byte order. All numeric data types in IDL except `string` and `byte` are affected (formatted files containing ASCII data are unaffected).

The following platforms supported by IDL are big-endian: Sun Solaris (Ultra), SGI IRIX, IBM AIX, HP-UX, MacOS (PowerPC). The remaining platforms supported by IDL are little-endian: Windows (all versions), Linux (x86), Sun Solaris (x86), Compaq Tru 64 UNIX, Compaq VMS.

There are a couple of ways to avoid dealing with byte swapping. First, if you only work with formatted ASCII files, there will never be a problem. However, formatted ASCII files are rather inefficient for storing large data sets, so this solution is often unsatisfactory. Second, you could restrict your programming to one platform only. For example, if your organization uses PC-compatible computers only, the byte ordering of binary data files will always be little-endian.

However, when you port binary data files between big-endian and little-endian platforms, the issue of byte swapping must be addressed. Fortunately, IDL offers several ways to deal with this problem. Say you have an application written in IDL (or C or Fortran) that creates binary data files on an SGI IRIX platform (big-endian). You would like to visualize the data in IDL on either the SGI or a PC running Windows NT (little-endian). Thus you need to be able to read the data files on big-endian or little-endian platforms. This can be accomplished by setting the optional keyword `swap_if_little_endian` when opening the file with `openr`, `openw`, or `openu`:

```
IDL> openr, lun, 'sgi.dat', /get_lun, /swap_if_little_endian
```

If this statement is executed on a big-endian platform, subsequent read or write statements proceed normally. However, if this statement is executed on a little-endian platform (such as a PC running Windows NT), then all data types other than `byte` or `string` are byte-swapped as they are read or written. Likewise, the `swap_if_big_endian` keyword achieves the same result on big-endian platforms:

```
IDL> openr, lun, 'sgi.dat', /get_lun, /swap_if_big_endian
```

A limitation of this technique is that it requires you to remember which platform was used to create the binary data file, and to code the appropriate keyword into any procedures or functions that read the file.

A more sophisticated technique involves using IDL to automatically check your binary data and determine whether byte swapping is required. For example, say you have a program (IDL or C or Fortran) that writes binary data files, and it can be run on IBM AIX (big-endian) and Linux (little-endian) platforms. You'd like to be able to read the binary data files in IDL on any platform and have IDL take care of any byte swapping automatically. The solution is to check a couple of values in the data file (say, a date and a time) to see if they are within the expected range. For example, the expected range for a year value might be between 1970 and 2100. If the year value is stored in a `long` variable, then a byte-swapped year value would be outside the expected range:

```
IDL> year = 1999L
IDL> print, swap_endian(year)
-821624832
```

Here the `swap_endian` function was used to swap the byte order of the variable `year`. This function can be used to swap the byte order of any variable passed to it, including arrays and structures.

To modify the previously shown `read_weather` function to handle byte swapping automatically, the following lines are inserted after the structure of a record is defined, and before the `while` loop:

```
;- Read the first record, then reset file pointer
readu, lun, record
point_lun, lun, 0L

;- Set default byte-swapping flag to false
swap_flag = 0

;- Check whether byte-swapping is required
year = record.year
hour = record.hour
test = (year lt 1970) or (year gt 2100) or $
  (hour lt 0) or (hour gt 23)
if test then begin
  year = swap_endian(year)
  hour = swap_endian(hour)
  test = (year lt 1970) or (year gt 2100) or $
  (hour lt 0) or (hour gt 23)
  if test then begin
    free_lun, lun
    message, 'File format is incorrect', /continue
    return
  endif else begin
    swap_flag = 1
  endelse
endif
```

After the file is opened, the first record is read, and the file pointer is reset to the beginning of the file with `point_lun`. A range test is performed on the `year` and `hour` values from the first `record`. If either the `year` or `hour` value is out of range, both values are byte-swapped by the `swap_endian` function. If either value is still out of range after byte swapping, the file must be in the wrong format, so the file is closed, an error message is printed, and control returns to the calling program. If the byte-swapped values are both within range, the byte-swapping flag `swap_flag` is set to true.

Once the byte-swapping flag is set correctly, adding the following line to the `while` loop immediately after the `readu` statement will take care of any byte swapping:

```
if swap_flag then record = swap_endian(record)
```

Using this method enables `read_weather` to read the input data correctly on any IDL platform, regardless of whether the data file was created on a big-endian or little-endian platform.

Writing Binary Data to an Unformatted File

The writeu procedure writes binary data to an open unformatted file. The general syntax for the writeu procedure is

writeu, lun, arg_1, arg_2, ... , arg_n

Arrays can usually be written with one statement:

```
IDL> data = dist(256)
IDL> openw, lun, 'dist.dat', /get_lun
IDL> writeu, lun, data
IDL> free_lun, lun
```

When writing binary data to a file, it can be helpful to first write a header record that records the size and type of the data contained in the file. The output of the size function is well suited to this task. For example:

```
IDL> data = dist(256)
IDL> info = size(data)
IDL> print, info
          2         256         256           4       65536
```

The array info is of long type and contains the following information about data:

- Number of dimensions (2)
- Dimension sizes (256, 256)
- Data type code (4)
- Number of elements (65,536)

The size of the info array is determined by the number of dimensions in data. So if you wanted to write the array data to a file, you would first write a header array containing the data size and type information, followed by the data itself:

```
IDL> openw, lun, 'dist.dat', /get_lun
IDL> info = size(data)
IDL> info_size = n_elements(info)
IDL> header = [info_size, info]
IDL> writeu, lun, header
IDL> writeu, lun, data
IDL> free_lun, lun
```

After the file was opened, the size information for the array data was stored in the array info. Then the long array header was created, containing the number of elements in the info array, followed by the info array values. The header array and data array were then written to the file, and the file was closed. When you subsequently read the file, you would first read the header, and then use the make_array function to create an array of the correct size and type to hold the data:

```
IDL> openr, lun, 'dist.dat', /get_lun
IDL> info_size = 0L
IDL> readu, lun, info_size
IDL> info = lonarr(info_size)
IDL> readu, lun, info
IDL> data = make_array(size=info)
IDL> readu, lun, data
IDL> free_lun, lun
```

After opening the file, the number of elements in the size information array info was read. The long array info was then created using lonarr and read using readu. The make_array function was then used to create a data array matching the size and type information in info, the data was read, and the file was closed. This technique works for multidimensional arrays containing any numeric IDL data type (it does not work for strings, structures, pointers, or object references).

Programs to Write and Read Portable Binary Data

The previous technique for writing and reading binary data is now implemented in two procedures named binwrite and binread. The binwrite procedure allows you to write one or more arrays to an open binary unformatted file. The binread procedure allows you to read one or more arrays from a binary unformatted file created by binwrite in first-in/first-out order. Byte swapping is handled automatically by binread, via a long "magic value" that is stored in the first 4 bytes of the header for each array. The source for binwrite.pro is shown below:

```
PRO BINWRITE, LUN, DATA

;- Check arguments
if (n_elements(lun) eq 0) then $
  message, 'LUN is undefined'
if (n_elements(data) eq 0) then $
  message, 'DATA is undefined'
```

```
;- Check that file is open
result = fstat(lun)
if (result.open eq 0) then $
  message, 'LUN does not point to an open file'

;- Check that data type is allowed
type_name = size(data, /tname)
if (type_name eq 'STRING') or $
   (type_name eq 'STRUCT') or $
   (type_name eq 'POINTER') or $
   (type_name eq 'OBJREF') then $
   message, 'DATA type is not supported'

;- Check that DATA is an array
if (size(data, /n_dimensions) lt 1) then $
  message, 'DATA must be an array'

;- Create header array
magic_value = 123456789L
info = size(data)
info_size = n_elements(info)
header = [magic_value, info_size, info]

;- Write header and data to file
writeu, lun, header
writeu, lun, data

END
```

First the program checks to see that a file is open for writing on logical unit number lun. It then checks to see that the input data type is supported, and that the input variable is an array. Then a header containing a "magic" value, a size variable, and an information array is constructed. The "magic" value allows binread to determine whether or not byte swapping is required, and the size variable indicates the number of words in the array size/type array. Finally the header and array are written to disk.

The accompanying binread procedure reads data file created by binwrite, regardless of whether the platform used to write the data file was little-endian or big-endian:

```
PRO BINREAD, LUN, DATA

;- Check arguments
if (n_elements(lun) eq 0) then $
  message, 'LUN is undefined'
if (arg_present(data) eq 0) then $
  message, 'DATA cannot be modified'

;- Check that file is open
result = fstat(lun)
if (result.open eq 0) then $
  message, 'LUN does not point to an open file'

;- Read magic value
magic_value = 0L
readu, lun, magic_value

;- Decode magic value to see if byte swapping is required
swap_flag = 0
if (magic_value ne 123456789L) then begin
  magic_value = swap_endian(magic_value)
  if (magic_value eq 123456789L) then begin
    swap_flag = 1
  endif else begin
    message, 'File was not written with BINWRITE'
  endelse
endif

;- Read the header, swapping if necessary
info_size = 0L
readu, lun, info_size
if swap_flag then info_size = swap_endian(info_size)
info = lonarr(info_size)
readu, lun, info
if swap_flag then info = swap_endian(info)

;- Read the data, swapping if necessary
data = make_array(size=info)
readu, lun, data
if swap_flag then data = swap_endian(temporary(data))

END
```

First, the program checks that a file is open for reading on logical unit number `lun`. Then the first 4 bytes are read into a `long` integer, and the resulting value is checked to see if it matches the "magic" value. If a match is found (with or without byte swapping), then the remainder of the header is read and swapped if necessary. Finally a result array is created by calling `make_array`, and the data is read and returned to the caller.

In the following example, two arrays are written with `binwrite`:

```
IDL> a = dist(256)
IDL> b = lindgen(1000)
IDL> openw, lun, 'test.dat', /get_lun
IDL> binwrite, lun, a
IDL> binwrite, lun, b
IDL> free_lun, lun
```

To read the two arrays with `binread`:

```
IDL> openr, lun, 'test.dat'
IDL> binread, lun, a
IDL> binread, lun, b
IDL> free_lun, lun
IDL> help, a, b
A               FLOAT     = Array[256, 256]
B               LONG      = Array[1000]
```

Because `binread` takes care of any byte swapping that may be required, data files written in IDL with `binwrite` can be read on any IDL platform, whether the platform is big-endian or little-endian. An additional benefit of `binwrite` and `binread` is the simple file format, which allows you to easily read and write compatible files in other applications (e.g., C, Fortran, Python, Matlab).

Reading Binary Data via an Associated Variable

In the previous sections, you saw how to read binary data using the `readu` procedure. You can also read (and write) binary data by referencing a special kind of variable known as an *associated variable*, which is created by the `assoc` function. For example, the IDL example data file `people.dat` contains two images and is stored as a `byte` array with dimensions [192, 192, 2]:

```
IDL> file = filepath('people.dat', subdir='examples/data')
IDL> openr, lun, file, /get_lun
IDL> chunk = bytarr(192, 192)
IDL> image = assoc(lun, chunk)
IDL> tvscl, image[0]
IDL> tvscl, image[1]
IDL> free_lun, lun
```

In this example, the filepath function was used to obtain the full path and name of people.dat, and the file was opened with openr. Then a byte array named chunk was created to define the type and size of each image chunk in the file. The assoc function was then used to associate a variable named image with the file. Note that only the type (byte) and size ([192, 192]) are taken from the array chunk; its value is ignored. Then the first and second elements of the associated array image were displayed with tvscl, and the file was closed.

Associated variables are especially useful when an input file contains many sequential chunks of data. In the following example, an animation of a beating heart is created using 15 consecutive image frames from the example data file abnorm.dat:

```
IDL> file = filepath('abnorm.dat', subdir='examples/data')
IDL> openr, lun, file, /get_lun
IDL> chunk = bytarr(64, 64)
IDL> image = assoc(lun, chunk)
IDL> for i = 0, 14 do tvscl, rebin(image[i], 256, 256)
```

In this example, after the file was opened, the associated variable image was created, which references sequential chunks of image data, each 64 pixels by 64 rows in size. Then a loop was started to read each image frame, magnify it four times via the rebin function, and display it with tvscl.

Saving and Restoring IDL Variables

The save and restore procedures may be used to write and read variables in a portable (i.e., platform independent) IDL-specific binary format. These procedures are useful when you wish to save binary data for later use in IDL, whether on the host platform or another platform, and you have no intention of using the files outside IDL.

The general syntax for the save procedure is

save, *arg$_1$*, *arg$_2$*, ... , *arg$_n$*

For example:

```
IDL> data = dist(256)
IDL> save, data, filename='dist.dat'
```

If the `filename` keyword is not passed, the default output filename is `idlsave.dat`. If no variables are passed as arguments, or the `/variables` keyword is passed, then all variables in the current program unit are saved.

The `restore` procedure restores all IDL variables in a saved file. If you executed the `save` statement shown above, exited IDL, and then started a new IDL session, you could restore the array data:

```
IDL> restore, 'dist.dat'
IDL> help, data
DATA              FLOAT      = Array[256, 256]
```

If the `/verbose` keyword is passed to `restore`, the name of each restored variable will be listed.

4.5 SCIENTIFIC AND SPECIALIZED DATA FORMATS

IDL includes built-in support for a variety of standard scientific data formats used in the geophysical science, medical imaging, astronomy, and space science communities. Scientific data formats are designed to overcome many of the limitations of unformatted binary data files. For example, in the previous discussion of unformatted binary data files, it was always assumed that the format of a data file was known (e.g., the size, type, and number of elements). However, this requires that documentation accompany a data file, so that others can read and decipher it. This type of documentation can often be inaccurate, insufficient, or missing altogether. Scientific data formats include information about the size, type, name, and structure of data inside the file itself, so that in theory all you need to do is tell users which data format was used (e.g., netCDF), and they can then discover everything they need to know about the contents of the file.

The main advantages of using a standard scientific data format are the following:

- Portability: Data can be read or written on all supported platforms, regardless of host byte order.
- Self-describing data: Everything you need to know about the size and type of the data in a file is stored in the file itself.

- Mixed data types: Data of different types and sizes can be stored in one file.
- Widely available read/write software: Standard data formats support a wide variety of environments, including C, C++, Fortran (77 and 90), Java, and Matlab.

The scientific data formats with built-in support in IDL are listed in Table 4.6. Each format provides its own calling interface, which hides the details of the underlying physical file format from the caller. Of the data formats listed in Table 4.6, netCDF and HDF are described in this chapter in more detail. For more information on built-in support in IDL for the HDF-EOS and CDF formats, see the online documentation.

Tip The astronomy community has developed a robust IDL library for reading and writing data in the FITS (Flexible Image Transport System) format. For more information, see Appendix A.

IDL also contains built-in support for a number of specialized formats including DICOM (medical imaging), GeoTIFF (geographic imagery), SYLK (spreadsheet), and WAV (audio). The names of the IDL routines for working with these formats are listed in Table 4.7. For more information on reading and writing these formats in IDL, see the online help (WAV support is available in IDL 5.3 and higher).

4.6   READING AND WRITING NETCDF FILES

The data format known as netCDF (network Common Data Form) was developed by the Unidata Program Center at the University Corporation

Table 4.6   Scientific data formats with built-in support in IDL.

Format	Developer	URL
netCDF	UCAR	http://www.unidata.ucar.edu
HDF	NCSA	http://hdf.ncsa.uiuc.edu
HDF-EOS	EOS Project, NASA GSFC	http://hdfeos.gsfc.nasa.gov
CDF	NSSDC, NASA GSFC	http://nssdc.gsfc.nasa.gov/cdf

Table 4.7   Specialized formats supported by IDL.

Format	Relevant routines
DICOM	`query_dicom(), read_dicom()`
GeoTIFF	`read_tiff(), query_tiff(), write_tiff`
SYLK	`read_sylk(), write_sylk()`
WAV	`query_wav(), read_wav(), write_wav`

for Atmospheric Research in Boulder, Colorado. The data model in netCDF is simple and flexible. The basic building blocks of netCDF files are variables, attributes, and dimensions:

- Variables are scalars or multidimensional arrays. The IDL data types supported by netCDF are `string`, `byte`, `int`, `long`, `float`, and `double`.
- Attributes contain supplementary information about a single variable or an entire file. Attributes that contain information about a variable (e.g., units, valid range, scaling factor) are known as *variable attributes*. Attributes that contain information about a file (e.g., creation date) are known as *global attributes*. Attributes may be scalars or one-dimensional arrays, and the supported data types are `string`, `byte`, `int`, `long`, `float`, or `double`.
- Dimensions are `long` scalars that record the size of one or more variables.

The structure of a hypothetical netCDF file containing an image from an earth-orbiting satellite is shown below:

```
Name:
      image.nc
      Dimensions:
      xsize = 1200
      ysize = 600
Variables:
      byte image[xsize, ysize]
            long_name = 'Imager visible channel'
            units = 'Counts'
            valid_range = 0, 255
      double time[ysize]
            long_name = 'Seconds since 0000 UTC, Jan 1 1970'
            units = 'seconds'
            valid_range = 0.0D+0, 10.0D+308
```

```
Global Attributes:
    title = 'GOES Image'
    history = 'Created Wed Jul 14 14:15:01 1993'
```

The file described above is named image.nc (.nc is the conventional extension for netCDF files), and it contains two variables. The first variable (image) is a float array with 1,200 columns and 600 rows. The variable attributes associated with image (long_name, units, and valid_range) identify the source, physical units, and valid range of image. The second variable time has 600 elements. Since both time and image share the dimension ysize, it can be assumed that time is the time value for each row in image. The time variable also has attributes named long_name, units, and valid_range. Finally, the file has two global attributes (title and history) that record information about what the file contains and when it was created.

In the examples that follow, real netCDF files are used for demonstration purposes. If you wish to run the examples, please download the following sample data files from http://www.gumley.com:

- image.nc

- sao.nc

The most commonly used routines for working with netCDF files are listed in Table 4.8.

Reading a Variable from a netCDF file

Variables in netCDF files are referenced by name. For example, to read and display the variable 'image' from the netCDF file image.nc:

```
IDL> cdfid = ncdf_open('image.nc')
IDL> varid = ncdf_varid(cdfid, 'image')
IDL> ncdf_varget, cdfid, varid, data
IDL> ncdf_close, cdfid
IDL> tvscl, data
```

In this example, the file was opened with the ncdf_open function, returning the file identifier cdfid. The ncdf_varid function was used to get the variable identifier varid for the variable named 'image'. The procedure ncdf_varget was then called to read the entire contents of the variable, and the file was closed by the procedure ncdf_close. The resulting array data was displayed with tvscl.

Table 4.8   Commonly used netCDF routines.

Name	Purpose
`ncdf_open()`	Open a netCDF file
`ncdf_close`	Close a netCDF file
`ncdf_varid()`	Return a variable identifier
`ncdf_varget`	Read a variable
`ncdf_attget`	Read an attribute
`ncdf_inquire()`	Return file information
`ncdf_varinq()`	Return variable information
`ncdf_attname()`	Return an attribute name
`ncdf_create()`	Create a netCDF file
`ncdf_dimdef()`	Create a dimension
`ncdf_vardef()`	Create a variable
`ncdf_attput`	Write attribute data
`ncdf_control`	Begin or end define mode
`ncdf_varput`	Write variable data

If you wish to read a subset of a variable, the `ncdf_varget` procedure accepts the optional subsetting keywords `offset`, `count`, and `stride`:

```
IDL> cdfid = ncdf_open('image.nc')
IDL> varid = ncdf_varid(cdfid, 'image')
IDL> ncdf_varget, cdfid, varid, data, $
IDL>   offset=[600, 0], count=[256, 256], stride=[2, 2]
IDL> ncdf_close, cdfid
IDL> tvscl, data
```

In this example, starting at column 600 and row 0, a 256 by 256 subset of the variable was read, skipping every second element in the column and row dimensions. Note that any or all of the keywords `offset`, `count`, or `stride` may be used in combination (you don't have to use them all).

The subsetting keywords are defined as follows:

- `offset`: The first element in each dimension to be read (zero-based; default is `[0, 0, . . . . , 0]`)

- count: The number of elements to be read in each dimension (default is from the current offset to the last element in each dimension)
- stride: The sampling interval along each dimension (default is [1, 1, . . . , 1], which samples every element)

If the chosen offset, count, or stride causes the dimension limits for the variable to be exceeded, IDL reads as much data as possible without exceeding the variable dimensions and prints a warning message:

```
IDL> ncdf_varget, cdfid, varid, data, $
IDL>    offset=[600, 0], count=[256, 512], stride=[2, 2]
% NCDF_VARGET: Requested read is larger than the available data.
  The 1 dimension of the extracted data has been reduced to the
  maximum available size of 600.
```

Reading an Attribute from a netCDF file

Attributes in netCDF are referenced by name. For example, to read the attribute 'long_name' associated with the variable 'PRECIP' from the netCDF file sao.nc:

```
IDL> cdfid = ncdf_open('sao.nc')
IDL> varid = ncdf_varid(cdfid, 'PRECIP')
IDL> ncdf_attget, cdfid, varid, 'long_name', attvalue
IDL> print, attvalue
precipitation amount
```

In this example, the ncdf_open function is called to open the file and return the file identifier cdfid. The ncdf_varid function returns the variable identifier varid for the variable named 'PRECIP'. Finally the ncdf_attget procedure is called to read the attribute 'long_name' associated with varid.

To read a global attribute from the same file, a slightly different ncdf_attget syntax is used:

```
IDL> ncdf_attget, cdfid, 'filetime', attvalue, /global
IDL> ncdf_close, cdfid
IDL> print, attvalue
15Z 14 JUL 93
```

To indicate that 'filetime' is a global attribute, ncdf_attget is called without the varid argument, and the global keyword is set.

Discovering the Contents of a netCDF file

The previous examples show how to read data from a netCDF file when you know that a particular variable or attribute exists. However, you will sometimes need to read data from a netCDF file whose contents are not known in advance. In this case, your first task is to discover what is contained in the file. Then you can decide which part(s) of the file you want to read.

To discover the contents of a netCDF file, inquiry routines can be called to determine the name, type, and size of all variables and attributes in the file. For convenience, the built-in netCDF inquiry routines can be wrapped in a function. The following function, when given a file identifier `cdfid`, returns a string array containing the names of all variables in an open netCDF file. The null string `''` is returned if no variables are found.

```
FUNCTION NCDF_VARDIR, CDFID

;- Check arguments
if (n_params() ne 1) then $
  message, 'Usage: RESULT = NCDF_VARDIR(CDFID)'
if (n_elements(cdfid) eq 0) then $
  message, 'Argument CDFID is undefined'

;- Set default return value
varnames = ''

;- Get file information
fileinfo = ncdf_inquire(cdfid)
nvars = fileinfo.nvars

;- If variables were found, get variable names
if (nvars gt 0) then begin
  varnames = strarr(nvars)
  for index = 0L, nvars - 1L do begin
    varinfo = ncdf_varinq(cdfid, index)
    varnames[index] = varinfo.name
  endfor
endif

;- Return the result
return, varnames

END
```

After checking the input parameters and setting a default return value, the ncdf_inquire function is called to return a structure containing information about the file. The structure field nvars (number of variables) is then extracted. If the number of variables is greater than zero, the string array varnames is created to hold the list of variable names. Then a loop is started that calls ncdf_varinq to inquire about each variable and store the name of each variable in the array varnames. Finally, the result is returned to the caller.

For example, to obtain a list of all variable names in the netCDF file sao.nc:

```
IDL> cdfid = ncdf_open('sao.nc')
IDL> varnames = ncdf_vardir(cdfid)
IDL> help, varnames
VARNAMES        STRING    = Array[25]
IDL> print, varnames
id region time lat lon elev T TD PSL ALTIM SPD DIR GUST WX
  ZCL CC cloudtype VIS Ptend delP PRECIP reftime_PRECIP
  Tmax Tmin remarks
IDL> ncdf_close, cdfid
```

A similar function can be written to return attribute names. The following function, when given a file identifier cdfid and a variable name varname, returns a string array containing the names of all attributes associated with the variable. If varname is the null string ' ', a string array containing the names of all global attributes is returned. The null string is returned if no attributes are found.

```
FUNCTION NCDF_ATTDIR, CDFID, VARNAME

;- Check arguments
if (n_params() ne 2) then $
  message, 'Usage: RESULT = NCDF_ATTDIR(CDFID, VARNAME)'
if (n_elements(cdfid) eq 0) then $
  message, 'Argument CDFID is undefined'
if (n_elements(varname) eq 0) then $
  message, 'Argument VARNAME is undefined'

;- Set default return value
attnames = ''

;- Get attribute information
if (varname eq '') then begin
```

```
  fileinfo = ncdf_inquire(cdfid)
  natts = fileinfo.ngatts
endif else begin
  varid = ncdf_varid(cdfid, varname)
  varinfo = ncdf_varinq(cdfid, varid)
  natts = varinfo.natts
endelse

;- If attributes were found, get attribute names
if (natts gt 0) then begin
  attnames = strarr(natts)
  for index = 0L, natts - 1L do begin
    if (varname eq '') then begin
      name = ncdf_attname(cdfid, index, /global)
    endif else begin
      name = ncdf_attname(cdfid, varid, index)
    endelse
    attnames[index] = name
  endfor
endif

;- Return the result
return, attnames

END
```

First, the input parameters are checked and a default return value is set. If global attributes are requested, then `ncdf_inquire` is called to return the number of global attributes; otherwise `ncdf_varinq` is called to return the number of attributes associated with the named variable. If the number of attributes is greater than zero, the string array `attnames` is created to hold the list of attribute names. Then a loop is started that calls `ncdf_attname` to return the name of each attribute and store the name in the array `attnames`. Finally, the result is returned to the caller.

For example, to obtain a list of all attribute names associated with the variable PRECIP in the netCDF file `sao.nc`:

```
IDL> attnames = ncdf_attdir(cdfid, 'PRECIP')
IDL> help, attnames
ATTNAMES        STRING    = Array[3]
IDL> print, attnames
long_name units _FillValue
```

To obtain a list of all global attribute names:

```
IDL> attnames = ncdf_attdir(cdfid, '')
IDL> help, attnames
ATTNAMES        STRING    = Array[4]
IDL> print, attnames
title version history filetime
```

Writing to a netCDF file

In order to write a variable to a netCDF file, you first define the variable name and type, and then you write the data for that variable. For example, the following statements will write the contents of the example data file ctscan.dat to a netCDF file.

First, load the data from ctscan.dat:

```
IDL> file = filepath('ctscan.dat', subdir='examples/data')
IDL> openr, lun, file, /get_lun
IDL> data = bytarr(256, 256)
IDL> readu, lun, data
IDL> free_lun, lun
```

Then create a new netCDF file and define the variable:

```
IDL> cdfid = ncdf_create('ctscan.nc', /clobber)
IDL> xdimid = ncdf_dimdef(cdfid, 'xdim', 256)
IDL> ydimid = ncdf_dimdef(cdfid, 'ydim', 256)
IDL> varid = ncdf_vardef(cdfid, 'image', $
IDL>   [xdimid, ydimid], /byte)
```

Finally, write the attributes and data:

```
IDL> ncdf_attput, cdfid, varid, 'long_name', $
IDL>   'CT scan from IDL examples'
IDL> ncdf_attput, cdfid, 'creation_date', systime(), /global
IDL> ncdf_control, cdfid, /endef
IDL> ncdf_varput, cdfid, varid, data
IDL> ncdf_close, cdfid
```

In this example, the file is created by calling the ncdf_create function. The clobber keyword causes the file to be overwritten if it exists. When you create a new netCDF file with ncdf_create, the file is automatically put into "define" mode, which means that new variables, attributes, and dimensions can be added to the file. The dimensions for this variable are then defined by calling the ncdf_dimdef function (a dimension can be shared by several variables). A variable named image is created with dimensions given by xdimid and ydimid. If a data type keyword is not set when ncdf_vardef is called (e.g., /byte), the default type is float. The variable attribute long_name is then added to describe the contents of image, and the global attribute creation_date is added. When all definitions are complete, the ncdf_control procedure is called to end "define" mode, and thereby enter "data" mode (the file must be in data mode to write variables). Finally, data is written to the file by calling the ncdf_varput procedure, and the file is closed.

Standard Attributes

In order to introduce a degree of interoperability for netCDF files, the netCDF user community has come up with a set of standard attribute names and definitions to describe variables. Using these standard attributes makes netCDF files easier to understand and more portable. Table 4.9 describes the standard attributes commonly used in netCDF files. These standard attributes are also often used in HDF Scientific Data Set files, as described in the following section on HDF.

Table 4.9   Standard netCDF attributes.

Attribute name	Definition
long_name	A text string that describes a variable in detail (e.g., 'Northwards velocity component').
units	A text string that describes the units of a variable (e.g., 'meters/second').
valid_range	A two-element array containing the valid minimum and maximum values for a variable (e.g., [0.0, 50.0]). The type of this attribute should be the same as the variable type.
scale_factor	A multiplier to be applied to a variable after it is read (allows float values to be stored as short or byte). The type of this attribute should be the same as the desired unscaled variable type (e.g., float).
add_offset	An offset to be added to a variable after it is read, and after scale_factor (if present) is applied. The type of this attribute should be the same as the desired unscaled variable type (e.g., float).
_FillValue	A value indicating that no data were written. The type of this attribute should be the same as the variable type.

Coordinate Variables

Coordinate variables contain an array of values representing a quantity that corresponds to a dimension. For example, say you created a netCDF file containing a vertical profile of atmospheric temperatures (in degrees Kelvin) at a number of different pressure levels. It would be natural to create a dimension named Pressure in this case, as shown in the following example:

```
IDL> cdfid = ncdf_create('profile.nc', /clobber)
IDL> dimid = ncdf_dimdef(cdfid, 'Pressure', 10)
IDL> varid = ncdf_vardef(cdfid, 'Temperature', [dimid], /float)
IDL> ncdf_attput, cdfid, varid, 'units', 'K'
IDL> ncdf_control, cdfid, /endef
IDL> data = 300.0 - 5.0 * findgen(10)
IDL> ncdf_varput, cdfid, varid, data
```

To store the actual pressure value (in hectoPascals) at each atmospheric level, you can create a coordinate variable named Pressure, which also uses the Pressure dimension:

```
IDL> ncdf_control, cdfid, /redef
IDL> dimid = ncdf_dimid(cdfid, 'Pressure')
IDL> varid = ncdf_vardef(cdfid, 'Pressure', [dimid], /float)
IDL> ncdf_attput, cdfid, varid, 'units', 'hPa'
IDL> ncdf_control, cdfid, /endef
IDL> data = 1000.0 - 15.0 * findgen(10)
IDL> ncdf_varput, cdfid, varid, data
IDL> ncdf_close, cdfid
```

Coordinate variables are distinguished by having a single dimension with the same name as the variable name, and they may be used in the same way as other variables (e.g., attributes may be added as shown in the example). Examples of uses for coordinate variables include defining time step intervals for data stored as a time sequence; or defining grid coordinates for data stored on an *n*-dimensional grid.

4.7   READING AND WRITING HDF FILES

The data format known as HDF (Hierarchical Data Format) was developed at the National Center for Supercomputing Applications in Urbana-Champaign, Illinois. HDF offers a variety of data models, including multidimensional arrays, tables, images, annotations, and color palettes. In the sections that follow, the HDF Scientific Data Sets (SDS) data model is described because it is the most flexible model in HDF, and it shares similar features with netCDF. That is, the basic building blocks of HDF SDS files are variables, attributes, and dimensions (see the preceding section on netCDF for a definition of these terms). Therefore in the following discussion, *HDF* actually refers to the HDF Scientific Data Sets (SDS) data model in HDF Version 4.x.

In the examples that follow, real HDF files are used for demonstration purposes. If you wish to run the examples, please download the following sample data files from http://www.gumley.com:

- EarthProbe5_31_99.hdf

- Manassas.hdf

The most commonly used routines for working with HDF Scientific Data Sets are listed in Table 4.10.

Reading a Variable from a HDF file

Variables in HDF files are referenced by name. For example, to read an array of global atmospheric ozone data from the variable 'TOTAL_OZONE' in the HDF file EarthProbe5_31_99.hdf:

```
IDL> hdfid = hdf_sd_start('EarthProbe5_31_99.hdf')
IDL> index = hdf_sd_nametoindex(hdfid, 'TOTAL_OZONE')
IDL> varid = hdf_sd_select(hdfid, index)
IDL> hdf_sd_getdata, varid, data
IDL> hdf_sd_endaccess, varid
IDL> hdf_sd_end, hdfid
IDL> tvscl, data
```

In this example, the file is opened by calling the hdf_sd_start function, which returned the file identifier hdfid. The hdf_sd_nametoindex function is called to get the index of the variable named 'TOTAL_OZONE', and then hdf_sd_select is called to return the variable identifier varid (a variable index represents an extra layer of abstraction in HDF files that is not present in netCDF files). To read the contents of the variable, the hdf_sd_getdata procedure is called. Finally, access to the variable is ended by calling hdf_sd_endaccess, and the file is closed by calling hdf_sd_end.

Table 4.10   Commonly used HDF Scientific Data Set routines.

Name	Purpose
hdf_sd_start()	Open a HDF file in SDS mode*
hdf_sd_end	Close a HDF file in SDS mode
hdf_sd_nametoindex()	Return variable index
hdf_sd_select()	Return variable identifier
hdf_sd_getdata	Read variable data
hdf_sd_endaccess	End access to a variable
hdf_sd_attrfind()	Return attribute index
hdf_sd_attrinfo	Read attribute data
hdf_sd_attrfind()	Return global attribute index
hdf_sd_attrinfo	Read global attribute data
hdf_sd_fileinfo	Return file information
hdf_sd_getinfo	Return variable information
hdf_sd_attrinfo	Return attribute name
hdf_sd_start()	Create a HDF file
hdf_sd_create()	Create a variable
hdf_sd_dimgetid()	Create a dimension
hdf_sd_dimset	Set dimension information
hdf_sd_adddata	Write variable data
hdf_sd_attrset	Write attribute data

* Several routines are listed twice to show they have more than one function (e.g., open an existing file, or create a new file).

If you wish to read a subset of a variable, then the hdf_sd_getdata procedure accepts the optional subsetting keywords start, count, and stride:

```
IDL> hdfid = hdf_sd_start('EarthProbe5_31_99.hdf')
IDL> index = hdf_sd_nametoindex(hdfid, 'TOTAL_OZONE')
IDL> varid = hdf_sd_select(hdfid, index)
IDL> hdf_sd_getdata, varid, data, $
IDL>   start=[0, 100], count=[100, 1], stride=[2, 1]
IDL> hdf_sd_endaccess, varid
IDL> hdf_sd_end, hdfid
IDL> plot, data
```

In this example, starting at column 0 and row 100, a 100 by 1 subset of the variable was read, skipping every second element in the column dimension. Note that any or all of the keywords start, count, or stride may be used in combination.

The subsetting keywords are defined as follows:

- start: The first element in each dimension to be read (zero-based; default is [0, 0, . . . , 0])
- count: The number of elements to be read in each dimension (default is from the current offset to the last element in each dimension)
- stride: The sampling interval along each dimension (default is [1, 1, . . . , 1], which samples every element)

If the chosen start, count, or stride causes the dimension limits for the variable to be exceeded, IDL halts execution and prints an error message:

```
IDL> hdf_sd_getdata, varid, data, $
IDL>   start=[0, 100], count=[1000, 1], stride=[2, 1]
% HDF_SD_GETDATA: Cannot read 1999 elements.
  Only 288 are present.
% Execution halted at:  $MAIN$
```

Using a Wrapper Procedure to Read a Variable

The use of a wrapper procedure makes reading HDF variables simpler and less error prone. The following procedure reads a single variable from a previously opened HDF file. The identifier of the HDF file is given by the input argument hdfid, and the name of the variable to be read is given by the input argument varname. The data read from the variable is returned in the output argument data:

```
PRO HDF_SD_VARREAD, HDFID, VARNAME, DATA, $
  _EXTRA=EXTRA_KEYWORDS

;- Check arguments
if (n_params() ne 3) then $
  message, 'Usage: HDF_SD_VARREAD, HDFID, VARNAME, DATA'
if (n_elements(hdfid) eq 0) then $
  message, 'Argument HDFID is undefined'
if (n_elements(varname) eq 0) then $
  message, 'Argument VARNAME is undefined'
```

```
if (arg_present(data) eq 0) then $
  message, 'Argument DATA cannot be modified'

;- Get index of the requested variable
index = hdf_sd_nametoindex(hdfid, varname)
if (index lt 0) then $
  message, 'SDS was not found: ' + varname

;- Select and read the SDS
varid = hdf_sd_select(hdfid, index)
hdf_sd_getdata, varid, data, _extra=extra_keywords
hdf_sd_endaccess, varid

END
```

First, the input arguments are checked (extra keywords are passed to
`hdf_sd_varget`). Then the index of the requested variable is obtained,
and an error message is printed if the variable is not found. Finally the
variable data is read. To read a global map of atmospheric ozone data
from the HDF file `EarthProbe5_31_99.hdf`:

```
IDL> hdfid = hdf_sd_start('EarthProbe5_31_99.hdf')
IDL> hdf_sd_varread, hdfid, 'TOTAL_OZONE', ozone
IDL> hdf_sd_end, hdfid
IDL> help, ozone
OZONE           INT       = Array[288, 180]
```

Reading an Attribute from a HDF File

Attributes in HDF are referenced by name. For example, to read the
attribute `'valid_range'` associated with the surface elevation variable
`'CELO: ELEVATION'` in the HDF file `Manassas.hdf`:

```
IDL> hdfid = hdf_sd_start('Manassas.hdf')
IDL> index = hdf_sd_nametoindex(hdfid, 'CELO: ELEVATION')
IDL> varid = hdf_sd_select(hdfid, index)
IDL> attindex = hdf_sd_attrfind(varid, 'valid_range')
IDL> hdf_sd_attrinfo, varid, attindex, data=attvalue
IDL> hdf_sd_endaccess, varid
IDL> print, attvalue
   17134   17394
```

In this example, the `hdf_sd_nametoindex` function is called to get the
index of the variable named `'CELO: ELEVATION'`, and then `hdf_sd_select`

returns the variable identifier `varid`. The index of the attribute `'valid_range'` is returned by `hdf_sd_attrfind`, and `hdf_sd_attrinfo` is called to read the attribute data.

To read a global attribute (the data set title) from the same file, a slightly different `hdf_sd_attrfind` and `hdf_sd_attrinfo` syntax is used:

```
IDL> attindex = hdf_sd_attrfind(hdfid, 'TITL: Title')
IDL> hdf_sd_attrinfo, hdfid, attindex, data=attvalue
IDL> hdf_sd_end, hdfid
IDL> print, attvalue
MANASSAS, VA - 24000
```

Here, `hdf_sd_attrfind` is called with file identifier `hdfid` and global attribute name `'TITL: Title'` as arguments, returning the attribute index `attindex`. Then `hdf_sd_attrfind` is called to read the attribute data.

Discovering the Contents of a HDF file

All the HDF examples shown so far have assumed that a particular variable or attribute is known to exist in a given file. However, if you obtain a HDF file whose contents are not known in advance, you will need to inventory the contents of the file before you can decide which part(s) of the file you want to read. Inquiry routines allow you to determine the name, type, and size of all variables and attributes in the file. The following function named `hdf_sd_vardir.pro`, when given a HDF file identifier `hdfid`, returns a string array containing the names of all variables in the file (the null string `' '` is returned if no variables are found):

```
FUNCTION HDF_SD_VARDIR, HDFID

;- Check arguments
if (n_params() ne 1) then $
  message, 'Usage: RESULT = HDF_SD_VARDIR(HDFID)'
if (n_elements(hdfid) eq 0) then $
  message, 'HDFID is undefined'

;- Set default return value
varnames = ''

;- Get file information
hdf_sd_fileinfo, hdfid, nvars, ngatts
```

```
;- If variables were found, get variable names
if (nvars gt 0) then begin
  varnames = strarr(nvars)
  for index = 0L, nvars - 1L do begin
    varid = hdf_sd_select(hdfid, index)
    hdf_sd_getinfo, varid, name=name
    hdf_sd_endaccess, varid
    varnames[index] = name
  endfor
endif


;- Return the result
return, varnames

END
```

After checking the input parameters, `hdf_sd_fileinfo` is called to return the number of variables and global attributes in the file. If the number of variables is greater than zero, the string array `varnames` is created to hold the list of variable names. Then a loop is started that calls `hdf_sd_select` to select a variable, `hdf_sd_getinfo` to get the variable name, and `hdf_sd_endaccess` to end access to the variable. The name of each variable is stored in the array `varnames`. Finally, the result is returned to the caller.

For example, to obtain a list of all variable names in the HDF file `EarthProbe5_31_99.hdf`:

```
IDL> hdfid = hdf_sd_start('EarthProbe5_31_99.hdf')
IDL> varnames = hdf_sd_vardir(hdfid)
IDL> print, varnames
TOTAL_OZONE LATITUDE LONGITUDE REFLECTIVITY
```

To obtain information on a specific variable, the `hdf_sd_getinfo` function is used:

```
IDL> index = hdf_sd_nametoindex(hdfid, 'LATITUDE')
IDL> varid = hdf_sd_select(hdfid, index)
IDL> hdf_sd_getinfo, varid, ndims=ndims, dims=dims, type=type
IDL> print, ndims, dims
          1          180
IDL> print, type
FLOAT
IDL> hdf_sd_endaccess, varid
IDL> hdf_sd_end, hdfid
```

Using a similar method, you can obtain a list of all attributes associated with a variable or all global attributes associated with a file. For example, when given a file identifier `hdfid` and a variable name `varname`, the following function named `hdf_sd_attdir.pro` returns a string array containing the names of all attributes associated with the variable. If `varname` is the null string `''`, a string array containing the names of all global attributes is returned (the null string is returned if no attributes are found):

```
FUNCTION HDF_SD_ATTDIR, HDFID, VARNAME

;- Check arguments
if (n_params() ne 2) then $
  message, 'Usage: RESULT = HDF_SD_ATTDIR(HDFID, VARNAME)'
if (n_elements(hdfid) eq 0) then $
  message, 'HDFID is undefined'
if (n_elements(varname) eq 0) then $
  message, 'VARNAME is undefined'

;- Set default return value
attnames = ''

;- Get attribute information
if (varname eq '') then begin
  hdf_sd_fileinfo, hdfid, nvars, natts
endif else begin
  index = hdf_sd_nametoindex(hdfid, varname)
  varid = hdf_sd_select(hdfid, index)
  hdf_sd_getinfo, varid, natts=natts
endelse

;- If attributes were found, get attribute names
if (natts gt 0) then begin
  attnames = strarr(natts)
  for index = 0L, natts - 1L do begin
    if (varname eq '') then begin
      hdf_sd_attrinfo, hdfid, index, name=name
    endif else begin
      hdf_sd_attrinfo, varid, index, name=name
    endelse
    attnames[index] = name
  endfor
endif
```

```
;- End access to this variable if necessary
if (varname ne '') then hdf_sd_endaccess, varid

;- Return the result
return, attnames

END
```

If global attributes are needed, then `hdf_sd_fileinfo` is called to return the number of global attributes. Otherwise the desired variable is selected by calling `hdf_sd_nametoindex` and `hdf_sd_select`, and `hdf_sd_getinfo` is called to return the number of attributes associated with the variable. If the number of attributes is greater than zero, the string array `attnames` is created to hold the list of attribute names. Then a loop is started that calls `hdf_sd_attrinfo` to return the name of each attribute and store the name in the array `attnames`.

To obtain a list of all attribute names associated with the variable `TOTAL_OZONE` in the HDF file `EarthProbe5_31_99.hdf`:

```
IDL> hdfid = hdf_sd_start('EarthProbe5_31_99.hdf')
IDL> attnames = hdf_sd_attdir(hdfid, 'TOTAL_OZONE')
IDL> hdf_sd_end, hdfid
IDL> print, attnames
scale_factor scale_factor_err add_offset add_offset_err
  calibrated_nt long_name units format cordsys
  _FillValue valid_range
```

To obtain a list of all global attribute names in the HDF file `Manassas.hdf`:

```
IDL> hdfid = hdf_sd_start('Manassas.hdf')
IDL> attnames = hdf_sd_attdir(hdfid, '')
IDL> hdf_sd_end, hdfid
IDL> print, attnames
PRID: Profile Identification PDOC: Profile Document Reference
  PRVS: Profile Version TITL: Title DAID: Data Identification
  DCDT: Dataset Creation Date
```

Writing to a HDF file

To write a variable to a HDF file, you must first define the variable name, size, and type, and then write the required data. In the following example, the contents of the example image `ctscan.dat` are written to a HDF file. First, the data is read from `ctscan.dat`:

```
IDL> file = filepath('ctscan.dat', subdir='examples/data')
IDL> openr, lun, file, /get_lun
IDL> data = bytarr(256, 256)
IDL> readu, lun, data
IDL> free_lun, lun
```

Then a new HDF file is created, the variable name, size, and type are defined, and the dimensions are created:

```
IDL> hdfid = hdf_sd_start('ctscan.hdf', /create)
IDL> varid = hdf_sd_create(hdfid, 'image', [256, 256], /byte)
IDL> dimid = hdf_sd_dimgetid(varid, 0)
IDL> hdf_sd_dimset, dimid, name='xdim'
IDL> dimid = hdf_sd_dimgetid(varid, 1)
IDL> hdf_sd_dimset, dimid, name='ydim'
```

Finally the data is written to the file, along with a variable attribute and a global attribute, and the file is closed:

```
IDL> hdf_sd_adddata, varid, data
IDL> hdf_sd_attrset, varid, 'long_name', $
IDL>    'CT scan from IDL examples'
IDL> hdf_sd_attrset, hdfid, 'creation_date', systime()
IDL> hdf_sd_endaccess, varid
IDL> hdf_sd_end, hdfid
```

In this example, the file is created by calling the hdf_sd_start function with the create keyword set. A variable named image with dimensions [256, 256] of byte type is created by calling hdf_sd_create (if a data type keyword such as /byte is not set when hdf_sd_create is called, the default type is float). The dimensions are created by calling hdf_sd_dimgetid and hdf_sd_dimset for each dimension. The data is written by calling hdf_sd_adddata. The variable attribute long_name is added to describe the contents of image, and the global attribute creation_date is added to record the date and time when the file was created.

To add a variable named frequency to this file that also uses the dimensions xdim and ydim, simply use the existing dimension names:

```
IDL> hdfid = hdf_sd_start('ctscan.hdf', /rdwr)
IDL> varid = hdf_sd_create(hdfid, 'frequency', $
IDL>    [256, 256], /float)
IDL> dimid = hdf_sd_dimgetid(varid, 0)
IDL> hdf_sd_dimset, dimid, name='xdim'
IDL> dimid = hdf_sd_dimgetid(varid, 1)
```

```
IDL> hdf_sd_dimset, dimid, name='ydim'
IDL> hdf_sd_adddata, varid, dist(256)
IDL> hdf_sd_endaccess, varid
IDL> hdf_sd_end, hdfid
```

Coordinate Variables

In the previous section on netCDF, the concept of coordinate variables was introduced (coordinate variables contain an array of values representing a quantity that corresponds to a dimension). The following example duplicates the example shown in the netCDF section, where a new file is created containing a vertical profile of atmospheric temperature:

```
IDL> hdfid = hdf_sd_start('profile.hdf', /create)
IDL> varid = hdf_sd_create(hdfid, 'Temperature', [10], /float)
IDL> dimid = hdf_sd_dimgetid(varid, 0)
IDL> hdf_sd_dimset, dimid, name='Pressure'
IDL> data = 300.0 - 2.5 * findgen(10)
IDL> hdf_sd_adddata, varid, data
IDL> hdf_sd_attrset, varid, 'units', 'K'
IDL> hdf_sd_endaccess, varid
```

Next a coordinate variable named Pressure, which also uses the Pressure dimension, is created to store the actual pressure value at each atmospheric level:

```
IDL> varid = hdf_sd_create(hdfid, 'Pressure', [10], /float)
IDL> dimid = hdf_sd_dimgetid(varid, 0)
IDL> hdf_sd_dimset, dimid, name='Pressure'
IDL> data = 1000.0 - 15.0 * findgen(10)
IDL> hdf_sd_adddata, varid, data
IDL> hdf_sd_attrset, varid, 'units', 'hPa'
IDL> hdf_sd_endaccess, varid
IDL> hdf_sd_end, hdfid
```

To determine if a given variable is a coordinate variable, the hdf_sd_iscoordvar function may be called. When passed, a variable identifier, hdf_sd_iscoordvar, returns true (1) if the variable is a coordinate variable, and false (0) otherwise.

5

Direct Graphics

The Direct Graphics system is the basic environment in which graphical displays are created in IDL. One of the main advantages of IDL over other languages used for data analysis (e.g., C, Fortran) is that analysis and graphical display are closely linked. As soon as a new data set is read or created in IDL, it can be visualized in a variety of different ways. It is important to obtain a good understanding of IDL graphics fundamentals in order to make full use of the capabilities of IDL.

This chapter begins with an overview of the functioning of the Direct Graphics system and explains its device-oriented nature. An outline of the differences between 8-bit and 24-bit display modes follows, along with detailed instructions on how each mode can be selected when a new IDL session begins. The concept of graphics windows, and the procedures used to manipulate them, are described. Next the differences between Indexed Color mode and Decomposed Color mode are discussed, along with the features of each mode related to graphics colors and the color table. The chapter ends with a section on troubleshooting common IDL display problems.

5.1 GRAPHICS DEVICES

Since IDL was developed in the early 1980s, it has supported a system known as Direct Graphics, which is built to a "device"-oriented model. That is, you select a particular graphics device (such as the screen, or a printer) and then draw graphics on that device. For example, when you start a new IDL session, the default graphics device is the screen display. If you display an image, it appears in a graphics window on the screen:

```
IDL> tvscl, dist(256)
```

Other graphics devices include a PostScript renderer (which sends output to a file), a Printer device (which renders graphics directly on a local or networked printer), and a memory-based Z-buffer (which allows hidden line and surface removal). Table 5.1 lists the most commonly used graphics devices in the IDL Direct Graphics system (see the online help for a complete list of supported devices).

The WIN, MAC, and X graphics devices are only available on the Windows, MacOS, and UNIX platforms, respectively. The remaining graphics devices are available on all IDL platforms (the current graphics device name is given by the system variable !d.name) with the exception of the METAFILE device that is available in IDL 5.4 and later versions on Windows platforms only.

The Direct Graphics system does not "remember" what has been displayed. For example, if you've created a plot on the WIN device, and you wish to save it in a PostScript file, you must switch to the PostScript graphics device and redisplay the plot (of course, operations such as this can be handled in software, but at a basic level the same principle applies). The main advantage of the Direct Graphics system is that it is fast and easy to use, both at the IDL command line and within IDL programs. In addition the availability of the PostScript and Printer devices makes it possible to produce publication-quality graphics.

Table 5.1   Commonly used graphics devices.

Device name	Description	Device type
WIN	Windows	Screen display
MAC	MacOS	Screen display
X	X-Windows (UNIX)	Screen display
PS	PostScript	File
PRINTER	Local or network printer	Printer
METAFILE	Windows Enhanced Metafile	File
Z	Z-buffer	Memory
CGM	Computer Graphics Metafile	File
PCL	HP Page Control Language	File
NULL	Null device (no output)	Memory

Selecting a Graphics Device

The `set_plot` procedure selects a named graphics device. All subsequent graphics output is sent to the selected graphics device until another `set_plot` call is made, or the IDL session ends. As mentioned previously, the default graphics device at startup is the screen display; thus the following command should display a plot on-screen:

```
IDL> plot, indgen(10)
```

To select the PostScript device, render the same plot, and switch back to the entry graphics device:

```
IDL> entry_device = !d.name
IDL> set_plot, 'PS'
IDL> plot, indgen(10)
IDL> device, /close_file
IDL> set_plot, entry_device
```

In this example, the PostScript output was directed to a file in the current directory with the default name `idl.ps`. When the plot file was closed, the entry graphics device was reselected. This method for reselecting the entry graphics device is recommended as it saves you having to remember the entry device name.

Configuring the Graphics Device

The `device` procedure can be used to configure certain properties of the currently selected graphics device. The `device` keywords most commonly used for configuring the graphics device are shown in Table 5.2.

The following `device` keywords are of particular importance:

- The `retain` keyword determines how backing store is maintained for the `WIN`, `MAC`, and `X` graphics devices only. That is, it determines how the contents of graphics windows will be refreshed when windows are moved in front of or behind each other. For Direct Graphics, the recommended setting is `retain=2`, which means IDL is responsible for maintaining backing store.

- The `decomposed` keyword activates or deactivates decomposed color on the `WIN`, `MAC`, and `X` graphics devices only. This is explained in more detail later in this chapter; suffice to say that if decomposed color is turned on (`decomposed=1`), the color table is bypassed. For Direct

Table 5.2   Commonly used `device` **keywords for graphics device configuration.**

Keyword	Purpose	Supported devices
`retain`	Set backing store mode	`WIN,MAC,X`
`decomposed`	Set decomposed color on or off	`WIN,MAC,X`
`set_character_size`	Set graphics character size	All devices
`pseudo_color`	Set 8-bit PseudoColor mode*	`MAC,X`
`index_color`	Set 8-bit PseudoColor mode	`PRINTER, METAFILE`
`true_color`	Set 24-bit TrueColor mode*	`MAC,X, PRINTER,METAFILE`

* For the `MAC` and `X` devices, these keywords only have an effect before the first graphics window is created in an IDL session; they have no effect after the first graphics window is created.

Graphics, the recommended setting is `decomposed=0`, which means the color table is used to determine displayed colors.

- The `set_character_size` keyword sets the size of graphics characters. The main reason for changing this setting is that default graphics character sizes vary between IDL platforms. Setting the size explicitly ensures consistent behavior on all platforms. Commonly used settings include `set_character_size=[10, 12]` and `set_character_size=[6, 9]`.

The remaining keywords in Table 5.2 are described later in this chapter.

Tip   The Z-buffer (`Z`) graphics device may be configured to provide a pixel-based 8-bit display device that exists only in memory. This is useful for scripted IDL applications that run in the background on UNIX platforms because no X-server connection is required to use the Z-buffer device (i.e., you need not be logged in). For example, the following commands configure the Z-buffer as an 800 by 600 pixel display with 256 colors:

```
IDL> set_plot, 'Z'
IDL> device, z_buffering=0, set_resolution=[800, 600], $
IDL>   set_colors=256, $
IDL>   set_character_size=[10, 12]
```

Because the Z-buffer is not a window graphics device, the `window`, `wset`, `wshow`, and `wdelete` procedures explained in Section 5.3 are not supported. The width and height of the Z-buffer device is limited only by available memory.

5.2   DISPLAY MODES

The Direct Graphics system in IDL can operate in either of two display modes: 8-bit mode or 24-bit mode. The choice of display mode is governed by the graphics hardware available on your computer and by your personal preference. Either mode can be used to produce publication-quality graphical output.

8-Bit Display Mode

In 8-bit display mode (also known as PseudoColor mode), each pixel on the display device has an associated 8-bit intensity, which can range from 0 to 255 (2^8 levels). The intensity value of each pixel is used as an index into the color table, which has a maximum of 256 entries. Each entry in the color table contains a red/green/blue (RGB) triplet that determines the color for the corresponding intensity. For example, all pixels with an intensity of 16 point to the 17th entry in the color table. If the 17th entry in the color table contains the RGB triplet (0, 0, 255), then all pixels with an intensity of 16 are colored bright blue. Since 8-bit mode supports a maximum of 256 (2^8) intensity levels, a maximum of 256 colors can be displayed simultaneously. All IDL graphics devices support 8-bit mode. On the `WIN`, `MAC`, and `X` graphics devices, other applications on the desktop may already be using some of the available 256 colors, so that IDL can only use a portion of the color table.

24-Bit Display Mode

In 24-bit display mode (also known as TrueColor mode), each pixel on the display device has an associated 24-bit RGB intensity (8 bits each for red, green, and blue). The color for each pixel is determined by the additive mixture of red, green, and blue intensities for that pixel. For example, if a pixel has the RGB intensity (255, 255, 0), then that pixel is colored bright yellow. Since 24-bit mode supports 256 intensity levels in red, green, and blue, a maximum of 16,777,216 colors (256^3) can be displayed simultaneously. A special feature of 24-bit mode is its ability to emulate 8-bit mode, where the color table determines the color of each pixel. This behavior is off by default when IDL is running in 24-bit mode, but it may be turned on at any time.

Display Mode Comparison

A comparison of the features in 24-bit display mode versus 8-bit display mode is shown in Table 5.3. Each display mode offers features that are attractive to different IDL users. For example, if you wish to display 24-bit TrueColor images, you will probably prefer 24-bit display mode (24-bit images can be displayed in 8-bit display mode, but first they must be quantized to reduce the number of colors to a maximum of 256). In fact, 24-bit display mode is usually a good choice because it allows a variety of image types to be displayed, and it allows the maximum range of colors. In general, 24-bit mode is recommended if your graphics hardware supports it.

Some IDL users prefer to use 8-bit mode because of one special feature. In 8-bit mode, whenever the color table is modified, the modifications are

Table 5.3   Display mode feature comparison.

Feature	24-bit mode	8-bit mode
Able to display 8-bit PseudoColor images	Yes	Yes
Able to display 24-bit TrueColor images	Yes	No*
Maximum simultaneous colors	16,777,216	256
Color table determines displayed colors	Optional	Always
Immediate updates when color table changes	No[†]	Yes
Supported graphics devices	WIN, MAC, X, PRINTER, METAFILE	All

* The PS (PostScript) graphics device can display TrueColor images. On other graphics devices, TrueColor images must be quantized to 8 bits for display in 8-bit mode.
[†] While IDL does not automatically update displayed graphics when the color table is changed in 24-bit mode, it is relatively simple to write programs that handle the update.

immediately reflected in any graphics that are currently displayed. For example, in 8-bit mode, modifying the color table with xloadct will cause a previously displayed image to change as well:

```
IDL> device, decomposed=0
IDL> loadct, 0
IDL> tvscl, dist(256)
IDL> xloadct
```

If IDL is running in 8-bit mode, the image will immediately reflect any changes you make in the xloadct dialog. However, if IDL is running in 24-bit mode, the image does not automatically reflect the color table changes, and you must redisplay it:

```
IDL> tvscl, dist(256)
```

If you require this feature, and you feel more comfortable running IDL in 8-bit display mode, then by all means do so.

Obtaining Display Mode Information

Information about the current display mode is contained in several system variables and may also be obtained by calling the device procedure, as shown in Table 5.4. The device commands shown are permitted on the WIN, MAC, and X graphics devices only.

Table 5.4   Display mode information.

Information	System variable or command
Name of current graphics device	!d.name
Size of color table	!d.table_size
Number of simultaneous colors	!d.n_colors
Name of current display mode*	device, get_visual_name=name
Bit depth of current display mode*	device, get_visual_depth=depth
Decomposed color mode[†]	device, get_decomposed=mode
Screen size	device, get_screen_size=size
General information	help, /device

* Command available in IDL 5.1 and higher.
[†] Command available in IDL 5.2 and higher.

For example, IDL 5.4 running on a Windows platform in 24-bit display mode returns the following information:

```
IDL> print, !d.name, !d.table_size, !d.n_colors
WIN         256    16777216
IDL> device, get_visual_name=name
IDL> device, get_visual_depth=depth
IDL> device, get_decomposed=mode
IDL> print, name, depth, mode
TrueColor          24          1
IDL> help, /device
Available Graphics Devices: CGM HP METAFILE NULL PCL PRINTER
  PS WIN Z
Current graphics device: WIN
   Screen Resolution: 1280x1024
   Simultaneously displayable colors: 16777216
   Number of allowed color values: 16777216
   System colors reserved by Windows: 0
   IDL Color Table Entries: 256
   NOTE: this is a TrueColor device
   Using Decomposed color
   Graphics Function: 3 (copy)
   Current Font: System,    Current TrueType Font: <default>
   Default Backing Store: None.
```

Note   The size of the color table (!d.table_size) and the number of simultaneous colors available (!d.n_colors) are two separate pieces of information, even though they may have the same value when IDL is running in 8-bit mode. The size of the color table can never exceed 256, regardless of display mode. The number of simultaneous colors cannot exceed 256 when IDL is running in 8-bit mode, but it can be up to 16,777,216 when IDL is running in 24-bit mode.

Selecting a Display Mode: Windows and MacOS Platforms

On Windows and MacOS platforms, the amount of memory on your graphics card determines which resolutions and display modes are available. IDL will run in whatever mode is indicated by the current desktop settings. You cannot change display modes within an IDL session. For example, if you started IDL in 24-bit mode and wish to change to 8-bit mode, you must exit IDL, change your desktop settings, and then restart IDL.

To change the desktop settings (and hence the IDL display mode), exit from any current IDL sessions, and do the following:

- For Windows: Right-click on the desktop, and select "Properties", "Settings", "Colors". If you select "256 Colors", then IDL will run in 8-bit mode. If you select "High Color (16-bit)" or "True Color (24- or 32-bit)", then IDL will run in 24-bit mode.
- For MacOS: Open the Monitors and Sound control panel, and select "Monitor". If you select "256 Colors", then IDL will run in 8-bit mode. If you select "Thousands of Colors" or "Millions of Colors", then IDL will run in 24-bit mode.

To verify the display mode after starting a new IDL session, you must first create a graphics window and then inquire about the display depth. In the following example, IDL is running in 24-bit mode:

```
IDL> window, /free
IDL> device, retain=2, decomposed=0
IDL> device, get_visual_depth=depth
IDL> print, depth
        24
```

In 8-bit mode, IDL must share the color table with the desktop, so fewer than 256 colors will be available. In the following example, IDL is running in 8-bit mode on a Windows platform:

```
IDL> window, /free
IDL> device, retain=2
IDL> device, get_visual_depth=depth
IDL> print, depth
         8
IDL> print, !d.table_size
        236
```

Selecting a Display Mode: UNIX Platforms

On UNIX platforms, the graphics hardware and X server on your local terminal determine which display modes can be used by IDL. This is true whether you are logged in at the system console or logged in remotely. If you are logged in to a remote computer, the display modes available to IDL are determined by the graphics hardware and X server on your local terminal, not the remote computer. Once a display mode is selected in an IDL session, it cannot be changed. For example, if you started IDL in 24-bit mode and you wish to change to 8-bit mode, you must exit and then restart IDL.

By default, IDL will try to run in 24-bit mode. If 24-bit mode is not available, IDL will start in 8-bit mode. The following examples show how you can select 24-bit mode or 8-bit mode at startup.

- Example 1: You wish to run in 24-bit mode, and the terminal supports 24-bit mode.

```
% idl
IDL Version 5.4 (IRIX mipseb). (c) 2000, Research Systems, Inc.
Installation number: 12345-0.
Licensed for use by: Wicked Widgets Corp.

IDL> device, true_color=24
IDL> window, /free
IDL> device, retain=2, decomposed=0
IDL> device, get_visual_depth=depth
IDL> print, depth
        24
```

In this case, the device procedure is called with the true_color=24 keyword to request IDL to use 24-bit mode if possible. Then window is called to create the first graphics window in the session, at which time the display mode is selected (the display mode is not selected until the first graphics window is created). Finally, device is called with the get_visual_depth keyword to verify the display depth.

- Example 2: You wish to run in 24-bit mode, but the terminal only supports 8-bit mode.

```
% idl
IDL Version 5.4 (IRIX mipseb). (c) 2000, Research Systems, Inc.
Installation number: 12345-0.
Licensed for use by: Wicked Widgets Corp.

IDL> device, true_color=24
IDL> window, /free
% Unsupported X Windows visual (class: TrueColor, depth: 24).
  Substituting default (class: PseudoColor, Depth: 8).
IDL> device, retain=2
```

```
IDL> device, get_visual_depth=depth
IDL> print, depth
          8
```

When window is called to create the first graphics window in the session, IDL determines that 24-bit mode is not supported and reverts to 8-bit mode. Calling device with the get_visual_depth keyword verifies that IDL is running in 8-bit mode.

■ Example 3: You wish to run in 8-bit mode, and the terminal supports 8-bit mode.

```
% idl
IDL Version 5.4 (IRIX mipseb). (c) 2000, Research Systems, Inc.
Installation number: 12345-0.
Licensed for use by: Wicked Widgets Corp.

IDL> device, pseudo_color=8
IDL> window, /free
IDL> device, retain=2
IDL> device, get_visual_depth=depth
IDL> print, depth
          8
```

The device procedure is called with the pseudo_color=8 keyword to request IDL to use 8-bit mode if possible. After window is called to create the first graphics window in the session, device is called with the get_visual_depth keyword to return the display depth. In this case, IDL was able to start in 8-bit mode. When running IDL in 8-bit mode, it is recommended that you close any other nonessential applications such as web browsers or image viewers to allow IDL to use as many of the 256 desktop colors as possible (even then, IDL may get fewer than 200 colors to work with).

Tip Linux users should note that some X servers will not allow you to run IDL in 8-bit mode if the X server was started in 16-, 24-, or 32-bit mode. Linux users should also note that IDL Direct Graphics will not function correctly if the X server is started in 16-bit mode. If your Linux X server is running in 16-bit mode and you wish to use IDL Direct Graphics, you must shut down the X server and restart it in 8- or 24-bit mode.

Selecting a Display Mode via a Startup File

A startup file is a text file containing a sequence of IDL commands that will be executed every time a new IDL session is started. This is an ideal way to ensure the display mode is set automatically whenever you start IDL. The following startup file named idl_startup.pro was used in preparing all the Direct Graphics examples in this book:

```
if (!version.os_family eq 'unix') then device, true_color=24
window, /free, /pixmap, colors=-10
wdelete, !d.window
device, retain=2, decomposed=0, set_character_size=[10, 12]
device, get_visual_depth=depth
print, 'Display depth: ', depth
print, 'Color table size: ', !d.table_size
```

The startup file selects a display mode, sets several display properties, and then prints a status report for the user. First, if the host operating system is UNIX, device is called to request 24-bit display mode. Then window is called to create the first graphics window in the session, at which time the display mode is selected (the /pixmap keyword creates an "invisible" window). Next, wdelete is called to delete the graphics window. Then device is called with

- retain=2 to have IDL manage graphics window backing store
- decomposed=0 to set decomposed color off (this only has an effect in 24-bit mode)
- set_character_size=[10, 12] to specify the vector font size

Finally, the display depth and color table size are printed.

To force selection of 8-bit mode on a UNIX platform, the first line is modified as follows:

```
if (!version.os_family eq 'unix') then device, pseudo_color=8
```

If a startup file is used, IDL must be told where to find it. In the IDL Development Environment (idlde), select "File", "Preferences", "Startup", and enter your startup file location in the Startup File dialog box. If you are running the IDL command line (idl) on a UNIX system, you must set the environment variable IDL_STARTUP to the full path and name of the startup file.

For example, if you store a startup file named `idl_startup.pro` in your login directory, the syntax would be as follows (depending on your shell):

```
% setenv IDL_STARTUP $HOME/idl_startup.pro        (C shell)
$ export IDL_STARTUP=$HOME/idl_startup.pro        (Korn shell)
```

5.3   GRAPHICS WINDOWS

When the `WIN`, `MAC`, or `X` graphics device is selected, graphics output is directed to a window on the computer screen. If no graphics windows exist (e.g., when a new IDL session is started), the first plotting or image display command will open a new graphics window automatically. The procedures for working with graphics windows are shown in Table 5.5.

Creating a Window

The `window` procedure creates a new graphics window:

```
IDL> window, 1
IDL> plot, sin(findgen(200) * 0.1)
```

The `window` argument is the index of the window to be created (if no argument is supplied, the index is assumed to be zero). In this example, a new graphics window with an index of 1 was created, and a plot was created in the window.

The `window` keyword `free` instructs IDL to open a new graphics window with the next available index:

```
IDL> window, /free
```

This removes the burden of remembering which index values have already been assigned to open windows.

Table 5.5   Procedures for working with graphics windows.

Name	Purpose
window	Create a new window
wset	Make an existing window the current window
wdelete	Delete an existing window
wshow	Expose, hide, or iconify an existing window
erase	Erase the contents of an existing window

To create a window with a specific size, rather than the default size of 640 by 512 pixels, `window` accepts the optional keywords `xsize` and `ysize`, which specify the window width and height in pixels:

```
IDL> window, /free, xsize=800, ysize = 600
```

Whenever a new window is created, it becomes the *current window*. All subsequent graphics output is directed to the current window unless or until

- a new graphics window is created (thus becoming the current window)
- another graphics window is designated the current window
- another graphics device is selected

Multiple graphics windows can exist on-screen. If multiple windows are created by calling `window` repeatedly, then the last graphics window created is the current window.

Note   The current window index is stored in the system variable `!d.window`.

Working with Existing Windows

The `wset` procedure makes an existing window the current window:

```
IDL> window, 0
IDL> window, 1
IDL> plot, sin(findgen(200) * 0.1)
IDL> wset, 0
IDL> plot, cos(findgen(200) * 0.1)
```

In this example two graphics windows are created (indices 0 and 1). A sine wave is plotted in window 1, which is the current window because it is the most recently created window. Then `wset` is called to make window 0 the current window, and a cosine wave is plotted. The `wset` procedure is particularly important when developing IDL applications that use more than one graphics window.

The `wdelete` procedure deletes an existing graphics window:

```
IDL> wdelete, 1
```

The argument is the index of the window to be deleted. If the current window is to be deleted, then the system variable !d.window can be used to specify the window index:

```
IDL> wdelete, !d.window
```

The wshow procedure exposes (i.e., brings to the front) an existing graphics window:

```
IDL> wshow, 0
```

The argument is the index of the window to be exposed (the window restored by wshow does *not* become the current window). To iconify (minimize) an existing window, the iconic keyword is set:

```
IDL> wshow, 0, /iconic
IDL> wshow, 0
```

The erase procedure erases the contents of an existing graphics window:

```
IDL> erase
```

The window color is set to the default background color, which is stored in the system variable !p.background. The default background color is zero, which corresponds to black in many of the predefined IDL color tables, including the default grayscale color table. Thus the window color is usually set to black. However, erase accepts an optional argument specifying the color table index to be used for the window. For example, to set the window color to the highest index in the color table:

```
IDL> erase, !d.table_size - 1
```

The highest index in many of the predefined IDL color tables corresponds to white.

Invisible Graphics Windows (Pixmaps) and Animation

For some applications it is useful to be able to create graphics windows that exist only in memory. Graphics windows of this type are known in IDL as *pixmap windows*. A pixmap window acts just like a normal graphics window in every way except one: a pixmap window is invisible. To create a pixmap window, the window procedure is called with the optional pixmap keyword set:

```
IDL> window, /free, /pixmap
IDL> plot, indgen(10)
```

Pixmap windows are useful when animation is required. Rectangular regions can be copied rapidly from a pixmap window to the current graphics window by calling the `device` procedure with the `copy` keyword. In the following example, a plot is created in a pixmap window, and the contents of the window are copied to the current window:

```
IDL> xsize = 640
IDL> ysize = 512
IDL> window, /free, /pixmap, xsize=xsize, ysize=ysize
IDL> pixwin = !d.window
IDL> x = findgen(200) * 0.1
IDL> y = sin(x)
IDL> plot, x, y
IDL> window, /free, xsize=xsize, ysize=ysize
IDL> device, copy=[0, 0, xsize, ysize, 0, 0, pixwin]
```

The syntax for the `device` procedure in this case is

device, copy=[x_0, y_0, *xsize*, *ysize*, x_1, y_1, *source_window*]

where x_0 and y_0 are the bottom left *x* and *y* coordinates in the source window; *xsize* and *ysize* are the width and height of the region to be copied; x_1 and y_1 are the bottom left *x* and *y* coordinates in the current graphics window (the destination); and *source_window* is the index of the source graphics window.

The following example program, named `brownian.pro`, creates an animation of simulated Brownian motion by using a pixmap window.

```
PRO BROWNIAN

;- Create visible window, and initialize plot
xsize = 640
ysize = 512
window, /free, xsize=xsize, ysize=ysize
viswin = !d.window
plot, [0], /nodata, xrange=[-1, 1], yrange=[-1, 1]

;- Create pixmap window, and copy visible window
window, /free, /pixmap, xsize=xsize, ysize=ysize
pixwin = !d.window
device, copy=[0, 0, xsize, ysize, 0, 0, viswin]

;- Set animation parameters
```

```
nframes = 250
npoints = 50
temp = 0.02
seed = -1L
x = randomn(seed, npoints) * 0.1
y = randomn(seed, npoints) * 0.1

;- Create Brownian motion animation in visible window
wset, viswin
for i = 1L, nframes do begin
  device, copy=[0, 0, xsize, ysize, 0, 0, pixwin]
  plots, x, y, psym=1
  x = x + temp * randomn(seed, npoints)
  y = y + temp * randomn(seed, npoints)
endfor

END
```

First, a visible graphics window is created and plot axes are established. Then a pixmap window is created, and the contents of the visible
window are copied to the pixmap window. Next, the animation parameters are set. The speed and fluidity of the animation can be adjusted by
modifying these parameters (the randomn function creates an array of
normally distributed random numbers). Finally, a loop commences to
plot each frame in the animation. Before each new frame is plotted, the
old frame is erased by copying the plot background from the pixmap window. The initial and final states of the animation are shown in Figure 5.1.

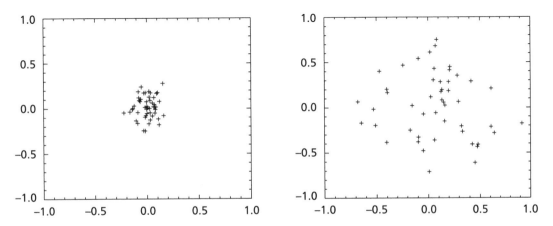

Figure 5.1 Initial and final states of Brownian motion animation.

Scrolling Graphics Windows

Graphics windows created by `window` can be larger than the dimensions of the visible screen, but the off-screen portion is not easily viewed:

```
IDL> window, /free, xsize=700, ysize=1400
```

In this example, the graphics window is taller than most visible displays. However, the lower part of the window cannot be seen easily. It is possible to create graphics windows with scrollbars by using the IDL Graphical User Interface (GUI) toolkit, which is described in more detail in Chapter 9. For example, the following commands create a graphics window with actual dimensions of 700 by 1,400 pixels, and a viewable size of 700 by 700 pixels:

```
IDL> base = widget_base()
IDL> draw = widget_draw(base, xsize=700, ysize=1400, $
IDL>   x_scroll_size=700, y_scroll_size=700)
IDL> widget_control, base, /realize
IDL> scrollwin = !d.window
```

The details of `widget_base`, `widget_draw`, and `widget_control` are explained more fully in Chapter 9. For the purpose of this chapter it is sufficient to note that a graphics window with scrollbars is created. The scrolling graphics window functions in most respects just like a normal graphics window:

```
IDL> wset, scrollwin
IDL> surface, dist(256)
```

However, the scrolling graphics window is unique in at least two respects:

- If the edges of the frame around the window are dragged to a new size, the graphics window itself does not automatically change size.
- If the graphics window is deleted by calling `wdelete`, the frame around the window remains.

5.4   WORKING WITH COLORS

IDL can display a wide variety of color plots and images because of its flexible modes for working with color. IDL supports two different color models (Indexed Color and Decomposed Color), and each model is appropriate for certain tasks. However, from the programmer's point of view, the essential question is "How do I make a pixel on the display green?" (or yellow, or magenta, or gray, etc.). In order to answer this question, it is first necessary to gain an understanding of color models in IDL. You may notice certain similarities in the following discussion of color models when compared to the discussion of display modes at the begininning of this chapter. Display modes and color models are necessarily related because they reflect the fundamental properties of graphics devices. However, it is important to understand color models as a separate concept because either color model can, in certain circumstances, be used when IDL is running in 8-bit or 24-bit display mode.

Color Models

Indexed Color is the default color model on all graphics devices when IDL is running in 8-bit mode. It may also be used if the WIN, MAC, or X graphics device is selected and IDL is running in 24-bit mode. When this model is active, 8-bit intensity values are used as indexes into the color table, which in turn determines the displayed color. Thus to create a plot with a certain color, you must load the appropriate information into the color table, and then select the index in the color table that contains the desired color. When 8-bit images are displayed and the Indexed Color model is active, image intensities are mapped to indexes in the color table, which then determines the color displayed for each image pixel.

Decomposed Color is the default color model if the WIN, MAC, or X graphics device is selected and IDL is running in 24-bit mode. It may also be used if the PRINTER graphics device is selected, regardless of display mode. When this model is active, 24-bit RGB intensity values are used directly to determine the displayed color, bypassing the color table entirely (the color table still exists in memory, however). To create a plot with a certain color, the individual color components (red, green, and blue) are specified directly. When 24-bit images are displayed, the combination of red, green, and blue image channels determines the color displayed on-screen for each image pixel. The supported devices and display modes for each color model are summarized in Table 5.6.

Indexed Color

Indexed Color is the most commonly used color model in IDL. Most IDL programmers are familiar with the concept of the color table and are com-

Table 5.6   Color model support

Color model	Devices	Display modes
Indexed Color	All graphics devices	8-bit
	WIN, MAC, X	24-bit
Decomposed Color	WIN, MAC, X	24-bit
	PRINTER, METAFILE	8-bit or 24-bit

fortable working with this model. When this model is in use, colors are specified via the color table. For example, to display a bright green plot:

```
IDL> device, decomposed=0
IDL> tvlct, 0B, 255B, 0B, 128
IDL> plot, sin(findgen(200) * 0.1), color=128
```

In this example, tvlct is called to load the RGB triplet (0, 255, 0) into the color table at index 128 (the first color table index is zero, and the maximum index is !d.table_size - 1). Then plot is called to plot a sine wave, with the optional color keyword specifying that color index 128 should be used for plotting. The RGB triplet (0, 255, 0) corresponds to minimum red, maximum green, and minimum blue. By loading different RGB triplets into the color table, you can use different colors (e.g., red, yellow, magenta, cyan) for plotting.

Tip   If you are running IDL in 24-bit mode, Decomposed Color is the default when a new IDL session begins. To select Indexed Color, you must explicitly turn off Decomposed Color with the command device, decomposed=0. This command has no effect when run in 8-bit mode. When the Indexed Color model is active, the output from the command help, /device will contain the text "NOT using Decomposed color".

In addition to defining individual entries in the color table, you can also redefine the entire color table using your own RGB vectors. When a new IDL session is started, a Grayscale color table is loaded by default. However, you can redefine the contents of the color table by supplying new RGB triplets for the entire color table. For example, to display an image with a color table that transitions from bright red to white:

```
IDL> ncolors = !d.table_size
IDL> redvec = replicate(255B, ncolors)
IDL> grnvec = byte((findgen(ncolors) / $
IDL>   float(ncolors - 1)) * 255. 0)
IDL> bluvec = grnvec
IDL> tvlct, redvec, grnvec, bluvec
IDL> tvscl, dist(256)
```

In this example, tvlct is called to load RGB vectors into the color table. The red vector (redvec) contains the maximum value (255B) in all entries, while the green and blue vectors (grnvec, bluevec) contain a linear ramp from 0 to 255. Thus the first entry in the color table is red, and the last entry is white, with a smooth transition in between. A frequency distribution image is created by calling dist and is displayed by calling tvscl.

Note   If the image appears in Grayscale, then IDL is running in 24-bit mode with the Decomposed Color model active. To use the Indexed Color model, you must execute the command device, decomposed=0 as explained previously.

Working with the Color Table

As shown in the previous example, the color table may be modified at will. The procedures for working with the color table are listed in Table 5.7.

The tvlct procedure either sets or gets the contents of the color table. The syntax for tvlct is

tvlct, *red, green, blue, (start)*

Table 5.7   Procedures for color table modification.

Name	Purpose
tvlct	Set or get the contents of the color table
loadct	Load a predefined color table
xloadct	Load and modify predefined color tables
xpalette	Create custom color tables

The *red, green,* and *blue* arguments are byte vectors that can have up to !d.table_size elements. Each element of the *red, green,* and *blue* vectors contains a value between 0B and 255B that specifies the red, green, and blue intensity for the corresponding index in the color table. The additive mixture of red, green, and blue determines the color for that index. The optional argument *start* is the starting index in the color table where the *red, green,* and *blue* vectors are loaded (the start index is zero by default).

To get the contents of the color table, the optional keyword get is used:

```
IDL> tvlct, r, g, b, /get
IDL> help, r, g, b
R               BYTE      = Array[256]
G               BYTE      = Array[256]
B               BYTE      = Array[256]
```

The loadct procedure loads one of 41 predefined color tables. The syntax for loadct is

    loadct, *table*

The *table* argument is the color table number, as shown in the following example, where the "Rainbow" color table is loaded, and a frequency distribution image is displayed:

```
IDL> loadct, 13
IDL> tvscl, dist(256)
```

If loadct is called without arguments, the list of available color tables is printed and the user is prompted to enter a table number. The loadct procedure also accepts the optional bottom and ncolors keywords, which specify the start index in the color table, and the number of colors to be loaded.

The xloadct procedure provides a graphical user interface for loading and modifying predefined color tables. For example, to display an image and then modify the color table:

```
IDL> tvscl, dist(256)
IDL> xloadct
```

If IDL is running in 8-bit mode, any changes you make to the color table in xloadct are immediately shown in the image. However, if IDL is running in 24-bit mode, you must redisplay the image to see the changes (the next section discusses this in more detail). The xloadct procedure also accepts the optional bottom and ncolors keywords.

The xpalette procedure provides a graphical user interface that allows you to interactively edit the color table by modifying any RGB triplet in the color table:

```
IDL> xpalette
```

Color Table Updates in 24-Bit Mode

When IDL is running in 24-bit mode, changes to the color table are not automatically reflected in an image (or any other graphic) displayed on-screen. For example:

```
IDL> tvscl, dist(256)
IDL> xloadct
```

If IDL is running in 24-bit mode and the Red-Purple color table is selected, the image does not reflect the updated color table until it is redisplayed:

```
IDL> tvscl, dist(256)
```

This behavior in 24-bit mode is due to the device-based nature of the IDL Direct Graphics system. Because this system works at a low level (i.e., it talks directly to the graphics hardware), xloadct does not automatically "tell" tvscl that the image needs to be redisplayed. The update happens automatically in 8-bit mode because only 256 colors are available on the entire desktop, and any application that changes the color table changes all colors on the desktop immediately.

However, it is possible to write programs that take care of color table updates in 24-bit mode automatically. For example, the xloadct procedure allows a named routine to be called whenever the user modifies the color table. Consider the following procedures, named tvscl24.pro and xloadct24.pro:

```
PRO TVSCL24, IMAGE, DATA=DATA
case 1 of
  n_elements(image) gt 0 : begin
    print, 'Normal image display'
    tvscl, image
  end
  n_elements(data) gt 0 : begin
    print, 'Color table was updated'
```

```
   tvscl, data
  end
  else : message, 'Usage: TVSCL24, IMAGE'
endcase
END

PRO XLOADCT24, IMAGE
xloadct, updatecallback='tvscl24', updatecbdata=image
END
```

The tvscl24 procedure accepts a single argument, a two-dimensional image array:

```
IDL> image = dist(256)
IDL> tvscl24, image
```

The xloadct24 procedure also accepts a single argument, the same two-dimensional image array that was passed to tvscl24:

```
IDL> xloadct24, image
```

Now whenever xloadct modifies the color table, the image is redisplayed. When xloadct is called within xloadct24, two optional keywords are passed. The updatecallback keyword is set to the name of the user-written procedure to be called whenever xloadct modifies the color table (tvscl24 in this case). The updatecbdata keyword is set to a variable that is passed to the user-written procedure via the data keyword. So if tvscl24 is called and the variable passed by the data keyword is defined, it signals that xloadct modified the color table, and therefore the image is redisplayed.

Decomposed Color

The WIN, MAC, and X devices can use the Decomposed Color model when IDL is running in 24-bit mode. As mentioned previously, when this model is active, the color table is bypassed (although it remains in memory). Decomposed Color is the default when a new IDL session begins in 24-bit mode. However, if Indexed Color is active in 24-bit mode, Decomposed Color can be activated by calling device with the decomposed keyword set to 1:

```
IDL> device, decomposed=1
```

Tip   When the Decomposed Color model is active, the output from the command `help, /device` will contain the text "`Using Decomposed color`".

Because color-handling in IDL is rather different when Decomposed
Color is active, it is typically used only in the following cases:

- Creating plots where more than 256 colors must be displayed simultaneously
- Displaying TrueColor images

To specify a plotting color when Decomposed Color is active, the RGB
combination that gives the desired color must be encoded in a `long`
scalar, where the least significant 8 bits contain the red intensity, the next
most significant 8 bits contain the green intensity, and the most significant 8 bits contain the blue intensity. For example, to create a yellow plot
(maximum red, maximum green, minimum blue):

```
IDL> device, decomposed=1
IDL> r = 255L
IDL> g = 255L
IDL> b = 0L
IDL> color = r + (g * 256L) + (b * 256L^2)
IDL> plot, sin(findgen(200) * 0.1), color=color
```

Decomposed color values can also be specified as `long` integers in
hexadecimal form. To repeat the previous yellow plot:

```
IDL> color = '00FFFF'XL
IDL> plot, sin(findgen(200) * 0.1), color=color
```

The hexadecimal value `'00FFFF'XL` specifies blue first, then green, then
red, when read from left to right.

When the Decomposed Color model is active, TrueColor images can
be displayed regardless of the contents of the color table because the
color table is bypassed completely. The image colors on-screen depend
only on the red, green, and blue intensities in each image channel. For
example, to display the TrueColor image contained in the example data
file `rose.jpg`:

```
IDL> file = filepath('rose.jpg', subdir='examples/data')
IDL> read_jpeg, file, image
```

```
IDL> device, get_decomposed=entry_decomposed
IDL> device, decomposed=1
IDL> erase
IDL> tv, image, true=1
IDL> device, decomposed=entry_decomposed
```

In this example, the current Decomposed Color state is saved, the image is displayed, and the original Decomposed Color state is restored.

The Decomposed Color model may be used when the PRINTER or METAFILE graphics device is selected. However, instead of using the device keyword decomposed (which is not supported by these devices), you must set the true_color keyword:

```
IDL> device, /true_color
```

To switch the PRINTER or METAFILE device back to Indexed Color (the default), set the index_color keyword:

```
IDL> device, /index_color
```

5.5   DISPLAY MODE TROUBLESHOOTING

The following section addresses some common questions and problems related to IDL display modes.

Why are my plots always colored red, no matter which color I specify? Or, why are my images always displayed in Grayscale, no matter which color table I have loaded?
IDL is running in 24-bit display mode with Decomposed Color active. To deactivate Decomposed Color:

```
IDL> device, decomposed=0
```

This command is included in the startup file recommended earlier in this chapter.

How do I know if Decomposed Color is active?
If IDL is running in 24-bit mode, the following command will return the Decomposed Color setting in IDL 5.2 and higher:

```
IDL> device, get_decomposed=decomposed
IDL> print, decomposed
       1
```

A value of 1 indicates the Decomposed Color model is active.

In earlier versions of IDL the only way to check the Decomposed Color setting is as follows:

```
IDL> help, /device
```

If the Decomposed Color model is in use, the phrase "Using Decomposed Color" will be seen in the help output.

Why don't the colors in the graphics window change when I load a new color table or modify the current color table?

IDL is running in 24-bit display mode, and the color table changes will not be reflected in the graphics window until you redisplay the image or plot (see "Color Table Updates in 24-Bit Mode" in Section 5.4).

How do I know if IDL is running in 8-bit or 24-bit display mode?

If at least one graphics window has been created in the current IDL session, the following command may be used in IDL 5.1 and higher to return the bit depth:

```
IDL> device, get_visual_depth=depth
IDL> print, depth
        24
```

If the bit depth is greater than 8, then IDL is running in 24-bit display mode. It is possible for the bit depth to be a value other than 24 when IDL is running in 24-bit display mode. For example, if IDL is running on a Windows platform where the desktop setting is "High Color (16 bit)":

```
IDL> device, get_visual_depth=depth
IDL> print, depth
        16
```

Alternatively, you can use the following command in IDL versions 5.0 and above to return the visual class name:

```
IDL> device, get_visual_name=name
IDL> print, name
TrueColor
```

If the returned visual class name is 'TrueColor' or 'DirectColor', then IDL is running in 24-bit display mode.

In earlier versions of IDL the system variable !d.n_colors may be used as an indicator. If !d.n_colors is greater than 256, IDL is running in 24-bit mode.

How do I find the size of the color table?

If at least one graphics window has been created in the current IDL session, the system variable !d.table_size contains the size of the color table:

```
IDL> print, !d.table_size
      236
```

If IDL is running in 8-bit display mode, the color table size is a maximum of 256, and often is less. If IDL is running in 24-bit display mode, the color table size is always 256.

Why do all the colors on my desktop flash in an annoying way when I select or move the cursor over an IDL graphics window?

Color flashing occurs when IDL is running in 8-bit display mode and is using a private colormap. A private colormap is used when there are not enough colors available for IDL to share with the desktop. To see what kind of colormap IDL is using, use the command

```
IDL> help, /device
```

To fix this problem, exit from your IDL session, try one of the following suggestions, and then restart IDL to see if the problem is gone.

1. Close any other applications you have running, particularly color-hungry applications like web browsers. On UNIX systems, if you wish to have the Netscape web browser running in the background, you can force it to use a small number of colors using the -ncols option:

```
% netscape -ncols 32 &
```

2. If you are running IDL on a UNIX system that uses the Common Desktop Environment (CDE), click on the desktop icon that shows a color palette. Then select "Colors", "Number of Colors", "Most Colors for Applications", and restart the desktop for the changes to take effect.

3. If you are using an IDL startup file, check that it does not try to allocate a particular number of colors:

```
window, colors=256
```

In 8-bit display mode, there are never 256 colors available, and you should never assume a particular number of colors (256 or otherwise). In a startup file, it is much better to use the following command:

```
window, colors=-10
```

which attempts to allocate as many colors as possible for IDL in a shared colormap, while leaving 10 colors for the desktop (for menus, buttons, icons, etc.).

4. If you are running IDL on a UNIX system, check that IDL is not directed to use a particular number of colors in your X resources file `$HOME/.Xdefaults`:

```
idl.colors: 256
```

If you find this entry in your X resources file, or the system X resources file (location is system dependent), remove it and reinitialize your X resources with the shell command

```
% xrdb -merge $HOME/.Xdefaults
```

Note that color flashing does not occur if IDL is running in 24-bit display mode.

I have a Linux system and I've tried everything suggested above, but my desktop colors still flash when I select or move the cursor over a graphics window.

If your Linux system is using an 8-bit desktop, then the window manager may take all the desktop colors by default, leaving IDL with no option but to use a private colormap (and therefore causing color flashing). If this happens, your options are

1. Restart your X server in 24-bit mode.
2. Reconfigure your X server so it uses fewer colors.
3. Learn to live with color flashing (it's not the end of the world!).

***Why do the contents of my IDL graphics window get erased when I move
another window over the graphics window? (This also happens when I
minimize or maximize a window.)***

Backing store is not being maintained for this graphics window. To force
IDL to maintain backing store for all graphics windows, use the command

```
IDL> device, retain=2
```

This command is included in the startup file recommended earlier in this
chapter.

***Why is the color table a different size every time I start IDL in 8-bit
mode?***

This is normal behavior. The size of the color table depends on how many
colors IDL can obtain from the desktop, so you should never assume a
particular color table size. Instead, always use the system variable
`!d.table_size` to find the size of the color table.

Why is the color table size very small when I run IDL in 8-bit mode?

If the color table is small, it means other applications on your desktop
(e.g., web browsers, image viewers) are using up most of the 256 colors
available on an 8-bit desktop. Exit IDL, close all nonessential applications, and restart IDL.

***Why are the vector font sizes different when I run my IDL program on a
different platform?***

The size of the IDL vector fonts is potentially different on every IDL platform. However, you can set the default vector font size as shown in the
following example:

```
IDL> device, set_character_size=[10, 12]
```

The first element of the keyword array is the character width, and the second element is the character height (in device units, such as pixels). This
command is included in the startup file recommended earlier in this
chapter.

How can I determine the status of the current IDL graphics device?

The command `help, /device` will list the status of your current IDL
graphics device. The following examples are from Windows and UNIX

platforms. At least one graphics window should be opened in the IDL session to ensure that the information reported by help is accurate.

For a Windows platform running IDL 5.3 in 24-bit mode:

```
IDL> window, /free
IDL> help, /device
Available Graphics Devices: CGM HP NULL PCL PRINTER PS WIN Z
Current graphics device: WIN
    Screen Resolution: 1280x1024
    Simultaneously displayable colors: 16777216
    Number of allowed color values: 16777216
    System colors reserved by Windows: 0
    IDL Color Table Entries: 256
    NOTE: this is a TrueColor device
    Using Decomposed color
    Graphics Function: 3 (copy)
    Current Font: System,    Current TrueType Font: <default>
    Default Backing Store: None.
    Window Status:  (ID: Type(x, y, backing store))
        32: Window ( 640, 512,          Pixmap)
```

For a UNIX (Linux) platform running IDL 5.1 in 8-bit mode:

```
IDL> window, /free
IDL> help, /device
Available graphics_devices: CGM HP LJ NULL PCL PRINTER PS
  REGIS TEK X Z
Current graphics device: X
    Server: X11.0, The XFree86 Project, Inc, Release 3310
    Display Depth, Size: 8 bits, (1024,768)
    Visual Class: PseudoColor (3)
    Bits Per RGB: 6
    Physical Color Map Entries (Used / Total): 197 / 256
    Colormap: Shared, 197 colors.  Translation table: Enabled
    Graphics pixels: Combined,  Dither Method: Ordered
    Write Mask: 255 (decimal) ff (hex)
    Graphics Function: 3 (copy)
    Current Font: <default>,    Current TrueType Font: <default>
    Default Backing Store: Req from Server.
    Window Status: -----------
    id typ(   x,  y,  backing store)
    32: Win( 640, 512, Req from Server)
```

Why do I get the following error message when running IDL on a UNIX platform?

```
% WINDOW: Unable to connect to X Windows display: :0
% WINDOW: Unable to open X Windows display.
        Is your DEVICE environment variable set correctly?
% Execution halted at:  $MAIN$
```

Either you do not have an X server running on your local terminal, or your DISPLAY environment variable is not set correctly. For example, if you are logged in at the console of a terminal named vortex:

```
% setenv DISPLAY vortex:0          (C shell)
$ export DISPLAY=vortex:0          (Korn shell)
```

Why do I get the following error message when I create a graphics window on a Linux platform?

```
% Unsupported X Windows visual (class: StaticGray, depth: 0).
  Substituting default (class: , Depth: 0).
```

This problem occurs when the window manager is configured to use 16-bit color. As of IDL 5.4, 16-bit color mode is not supported for Direct Graphics (this may change in future IDL versions). The only modes supported are 8-bit and 24-bit color. You can either reconfigure your display to use 8-bit or 24-bit color (e.g., by editing /etc/X11/XF86Config), or else exit your window manager and restart it in a different mode as shown in the following two examples:

```
% startx --bpp 8
```

or

```
% startx --bpp 24
```

and then starting a new IDL session.

6

Plotting Data

One of the most common uses of IDL is to create plots. You might want to quickly plot the results of an experiment or computation to see if there is a trend, or to check for anomalies, or you might need to create a publication-quality figure for inclusion in a scientific or technical paper. If you work in the geosciences, you might need to plot geographically distributed data on a map. Whatever your plotting needs may be, there is usually a way to get the job done in IDL. The interactive nature of IDL means that you may need to redisplay the plot several (or many!) times on-screen in order to configure it precisely the way you wish. However, the flexibility of the low-level plotting routines in IDL means that you can tweak plot settings until the graph is just right.

This chapter begins with a description of the types of plots that can be created in IDL and the coordinate systems available for plotting. The chapter continues with detailed information on how plots may be customized, including plot and axis properties; plot colors; and titles, labels, and mathematical symbols. Specialized plot types including error bar, histogram, and bar plots are described. Next, techniques for creating contour, mesh, and shaded surface plots are covered, and the chapter concludes with map projections and methods for plotting geographic data.

6.1   PLOTTING OVERVIEW

The Direct Graphics system in IDL offers a variety of ways to create plots of your data. Two-dimensional graph types include line, scatter, polar, bar, histogram, and contour plots. Three-dimensional graph types include mesh surfaces and shaded surfaces. Plot characteristics such as axes, titles, symbols, colors, and linestyles can be adjusted in a variety of ways. The procedures used to create plots in IDL are summarized in Table 6.1.

Line Plots

The plot procedure is the most commonly used routine for creating line plots in IDL (scatter plots and polar plots are variations of this plot type). The general syntax for plot is

```
plot, x, y
```

where x is a vector of ordinate values, and y is a vector of coordinate values. For example, the plot procedure can be used to create a plot of the sine function over the interval zero to 2π:

```
IDL> x = findgen(101) * (0.01 * 2.0 * !pi)
IDL> y = sin(x)
IDL> plot, x, y
```

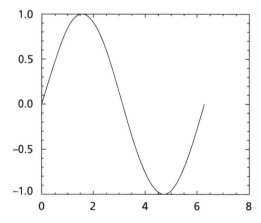

When plot is called, the default behavior is as follows:

1. Erase the contents of the current window (a new window is created if none exists).

Table 6.1   Plotting procedures.

Name	Purpose
plot	Plot a line graph
oplot	Overplot a line graph on axes created by plot
plots	Plot a line graph in one of three coordinate systems
axis	Create a new axis
contour	Plot contours
surface	Plot a mesh surface
shade_surf	Plot a shaded surface

2. Establish appropriate data coordinates for the input data.
3. Draw axes (including labels and tick marks).
4. Draw a line connecting each data point.

Note   The contour, surface, and shade_surf procedures also follow this default behavior when creating a new plot.

If a single vector argument is passed to plot, the data points are plotted against the corresponding element number in the input vector:

```
IDL> plot, y
```

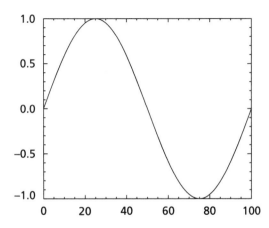

The `plot` procedure accepts the keywords shown in Table 6.2. In addition, see Section 6.3 for other keywords accepted for plot customization.

Overplotting

The `oplot` procedure overplots data on an existing set of axes. The general syntax for `oplot` is

```
oplot, x, y
```

where x and y are vectors of ordinate and coordinate data, respectively. In the following example, two data sets are overplotted on existing axes:

```
IDL> x = findgen(101) * (0.01 * 2.0 !pi)
IDL> plot, x, sin(x)
IDL> oplot, x, sin(-x)
IDL> oplot, x, sin(x) * cos(x)
```

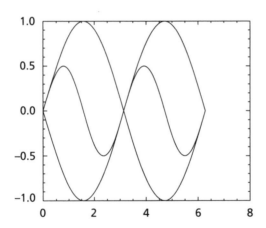

If a single vector argument is passed to `oplot`, the data points are plotted against the corresponding element number in the input vector. The `oplot` procedure also accepts the `polar`, `min_value`, `max_value`, and `nsum` keywords accepted by `plot`.

Scatter Plots

The `plot` procedure may be used to create scatter plots by setting the optional `psym` keyword to a code specifying the symbol to be plotted:

Table 6.2   `plot` **keywords.**

Keyword	Purpose
`/polar`	Create a polar plot (default: create a cartesian plot)
`/ynozero`	*y*-axis minimum is not zero when all points are positive (default: *y*-axis minimum is zero when all points are positive)
`min_value`	Minimum coordinate to plot (default: data minimum)
`max_value`	Maximum coordinate to plot (default: data maximum)
`nsum`	Number of values to average when plotting (default: no averaging)

```
IDL> x = findgen(100)
IDL> y = x + (20.0 * randomu(-1L, 100))
IDL> plot, x, y, psym=1
```

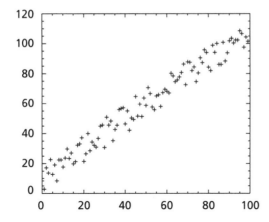

The `psym` value selects one of nine predefined symbols as shown in Table 6.3. User-defined symbols may be created with the `usersym` procedure; see the online help for more information.

A positive symbol code causes only the symbol to be plotted at each data point, and a negative symbol code causes a symbol to be plotted at each point along with a line connecting all the points:

```
IDL> plot, x, y, psym=-5
```

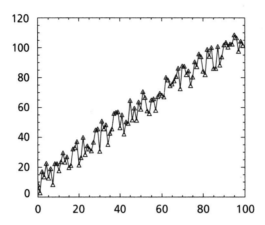

Table 6.3   Symbol codes.

Symbol	Code
None	0
Plus	1
Asterisk	2
Dot	3
Diamond	4
Triangle	5
Square	6
Cross	7
User defined	8

Polar Plots

The `plot` procedure may be used to create polar plots by setting the optional `polar` keyword. In this case, the general syntax for `plot` is

```
plot, r, t, /polar
```

where r is a vector of radius values, and t is a vector of angles in radians. In the following example, a spiral is plotted in polar form:

```
IDL> r = findgen(100) * 0.01
IDL> t = 4.0 * !pi * r
IDL> plot, r, t, /polar
```

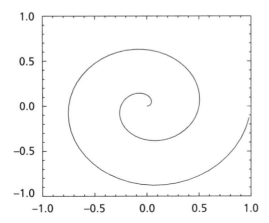

Plot Coordinates

Direct Graphics supports the following plot coordinate systems: data, normal, and device.

Data coordinates are established when plot, axis, contour, surface, or shade_surf are called, and a mapping is established from data values to locations in the current graphics window or graphics device. The mapping is saved in the global system variables !x, !y, and !z, and it remains in effect until the next command is issued that creates a new mapping. A data coordinate mapping is tailored for the graphics window or graphics device that was current at the time the plotting command was issued. Thus when you switch to a different graphics window or device, you must issue a new plotting command to create new data coordinates.

Normal coordinates are always in effect, regardless of any plotting commands. In this system, the lower-left corner of the current graphics window or graphics device has the x, y-coordinates (0.0, 0.0), and the upper-right corner has the x, y-coordinates (1.0, 1.0). Normal coordinates are useful because they allow positions to be specified independently of the size or aspect of the current graphics window or graphics device. For example, the coordinate (0.5, 0.5) is always at the center in normal coordinates, whether the window or device has a square or rectangular aspect.

Device coordinates are always in effect and reflect the most fundamental level of addressing graphics windows and devices. In this system, the lower-left corner of the current window or graphics device has the coordinates (0, 0), and the upper-right corner has the coordinates (*xsize* - 1, *ysize* - 1), where *xsize* and *ysize* are the width and height of the window or device in pixels. The width and height can vary tremendously, depending on the graphics device selected. For example, a graphics window might be 640 pixels wide by 512 pixels high. However, the PostScript device in default portrait mode is 17,780 pixels wide by 12,700 pixels high.

Tip   The horizontal and vertical size of the current graphics window or device (in pixels) is given by the system variables !d.x_vsize and !d.y_vsize, respectively.

Coordinate Conversions

The convert_coord function may be used to convert between data, normal, and device coordinates. The general syntax for convert_coord is

result = convert_coord(x, y, /*to_coordinate*)

where x and y are scalars or vectors containing the input coordinates (a z input argument is optional), and result is an array with three columns representing the (*x, y, z*) components of the output coordinates, and as many rows as there are elements in x and y. The default input coordinates are data coordinates, and the output coordinates are selected by /*to_coordinate*, which can be one of to_data, to_normal, or to_device. In the following example, the data coordinates of a plotted line are converted to normal coordinates:

```
IDL> x = findgen(5) + 1.0
IDL> y = 1.0 / x
IDL> window, /free
IDL> plot, x, y
IDL> result = convert_coord(x, y, /to_normal)
IDL> print, result[0, *]
     0.156255
     0.355474
     0.554693
```

```
       0.753911
       0.953130
IDL> print, result[1, *]
       0.953130
       0.523443
       0.380213
       0.308599
       0.265630
```

The input coordinate type may be selected explicitly by setting one of the optional convert_coord keywords data, normal, or device.

Tip To convert between rectangular, polar, cylindrical, and spherical coordinates, the cv_coord function may be used. This type of coordinate conversion is independent of graphics window or device size. See the online help for more information.

Plotting in Normal and Device Coordinates

The plots procedure plots lines or points in data coordinates by default, but also offers the option of plotting in normal or device coordinates. The general syntax for plots is

```
plots, x, y
```

where x and y are vectors of ordinate and coordinate data, respectively. If a single vector argument is passed, the data points are plotted against the corresponding element number in the input vector. The default is to plot a line joining the data points in data coordinates. However, if the optional /normal keyword is set, the supplied data points are plotted in normal coordinates, and if the optional /device keyword is set, the supplied data points are plotted in device coordinates. In the following example, lines are plotted between opposite corners of the current window:

```
IDL> window, /free
IDL> plots, [0.0, 1.0], [0.0, 1.0], /normal
IDL> plots, [0.0, 1.0], [1.0, 0.0], /normal
```

System Variables

There are several global system variables that reflect the state of the most recent plot and affect the state of the next plot. The plot-related system variables in IDL are listed in Table 6.4. All system variables listed in Table 6.4 are writable, with the exception of !d. For the detailed contents of each system variable (each is a structure with multiple fields), see the online help.

It is possible to change the default behavior of Direct Graphics plots by changing fields in the !p, !x, !y, or !z system variables. For example, the default behavior of the plot procedure is to plot a solid line. However, changing the linestyle field of !p to a value of 2 causes a dashed line to be plotted instead:

```
IDL> print, !p.linestyle
           0
IDL> !p.linestyle = 2
IDL> plot, indgen(10)
IDL> !p.linestyle = 0
```

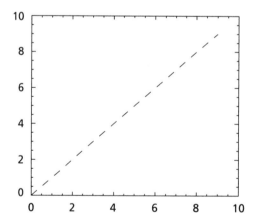

This behavior may at first glance seem desirable. However, because system variables have global scope, changing a field such as !p.linestyle means every subsequent plot will be affected. If you wished to create five plots in sequence, each with a different linestyle, you would need to set !p.linestyle five times.

Fortunately, plot properties can also be adjusted by passing optional keywords to the plotting procedure in question (e.g., plot). This method is preferred because it allows the properties of a plot to be set at the time

Table 6.4   Plot-related system variables.

Variable	Purpose
!p	General plot properties
!x	*x*-axis properties
!y	*y*-axis properties
!z	*z*-axis properties
!d	Graphics window/device properties (read-only)

the plot is created without affecting the properties of subsequent plots. With one major exception (!p.multi), every field in the !p, !x, !y, and !z system variables has a corresponding keyword that can be used for plot configuration. Another advantage of this method is that keywords passed to plotting procedures override the values set in global variables. Thus the following method is preferred for setting the linestyle of a plot:

```
IDL> plot, indgen(10), linestyle=2
```

6.2   PLOT POSITIONING

Plots are normally positioned automatically by IDL to fill the current graphics window or device. However, there may be situations where you wish to take control of plot positioning. For example, you might want to create two plots side by side, or you may require a plot to have an aspect ratio (the ratio of height to width) of 1, regardless of the current graphics window or device size.

Specifying a Plot Position

The keyword position can be used to specify the location for a plot, and is accepted by the plot, contour, surface, shade_surf, and map_set procedures. For example, to position two plots side by side:

```
IDL> window, /free, xsize=640, ysize=512
IDL> x = findgen(200) * 0.1
IDL> plot, x, sin(x), $
IDL>   position=[0.1, 0.1, 0.45, 0.9]
IDL> plot, x, cos(x), $
IDL>   position=[0.55, 0.1, 0.9, 0.9], /noerase
```

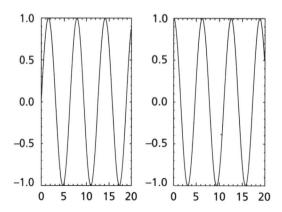

The position keyword is a vector of the form $[x_1, y_1, x_2, y_2]$ in normal coordinates, where x_1 and y_1 are the positions of the left end of the x-axis and lower end of the y-axis, and x_2 and y_2 are the positions of the right end of the x-axis and upper end of the y-axis. Titles and axis labels are drawn outside the area defined by position, so enough space must be allowed around the axis edges when a position vector is specified. An advantage of specifying the position in normal coordinates is that the relative position is maintained regardless of the size of the current graphics window or device.

Tip   The position of the most recent plot is contained in the system variables !x.window (x_1, x_2) and !y.window (y_1, y_2).

The aspect ratio of the plots in the previous example will remain the same as long as the window or device aspect ratio remains the same. However, if the aspect ratio of the window or device changes, the aspect ratio of the plots will change:

```
IDL> window, /free, xsize=800, ysize=300
IDL> plot, x, sin(x), $
IDL>    position=[0.1, 0.1, 0.45, 0.9]
IDL> plot, x, cos(x), $
IDL>    position=[0.55, 0.1, 0.9, 0.9], /noerase
```

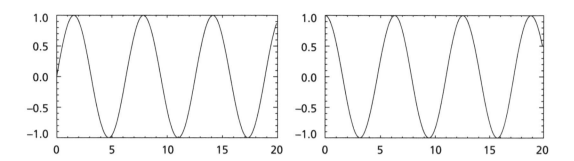

Now the plots are wider than taller. Often you'd like to be sure that a plot will have the same aspect ratio regardless of the size of the current display. One way to achieve this is to compute a position vector that takes into account the desired aspect ratio and the size of the current graphics window or device.

Computing a Plot Position

The following function named getpos.pro returns a position vector in normal coordinates for a given aspect ratio (ratio of height to width). If an input position vector is passed via the optional position keyword, then the output position vector is sized to fit within the input position vector while maintaining the requested aspect ratio. The optional margin keyword can be used to specify a margin in normal coordinates.

```
FUNCTION GETPOS, ASPECT, POSITION=POSITION, MARGIN=MARGIN

;- Check arguments
if (n_params() ne 1) then $
  message, 'Usage: RESULT = GETPOS(ASPECT)'
if (n_elements(aspect) eq 0) then $
  message, 'Argument ASPECT is undefined'

;- Check keywords
if (n_elements(position) eq 0) then $
  position = [0.0, 0.0, 1.0, 1.0]
if (n_elements(margin) eq 0) then margin = 0.1

;- Get range limited aspect ratio and margin input values
aspect_val = (float(aspect[0]) > 0.01) < 100.0
margin_val = (float(margin[0]) > 0.0) < 0.49
```

```
;- Compute aspect ratio of position vector in this window
xsize = (position[2] - position[0]) * !d.x_vsize
ysize = (position[3] - position[1]) * !d.y_vsize
cur_aspect = ysize / xsize

;- Compute aspect ratio of this window
win_aspect = float(!d.y_vsize) / float(!d.x_vsize)

;- Compute height and width in normalized units
if (aspect_val ge cur_aspect) then begin
  height = (position[3] - position[1]) - 2.0 * margin
  width  = height * (win_aspect / aspect_val)
endif else begin
  width  = (position[2] - position[0]) - 2.0 * margin
  height = width * (aspect_val / win_aspect)
endelse

;- Compute and return position vector
xcenter = 0.5 * (position[0] + position[2])
ycenter = 0.5 * (position[1] + position[3])
x0 = xcenter - 0.5 * width
y0 = ycenter - 0.5 * height
x1 = xcenter + 0.5 * width
y1 = ycenter + 0.5 * height
return, [x0, y0, x1, y1]

END
```

First, the input arguments and keywords are checked, and defaults are assigned if the input keywords are undefined. The desired aspect ratio value is extracted and limited to the range 0.01 to 100.0, and the margin value is extracted and limited to the range 0.0 to 0.49. Next, the aspect ratio of the input position vector within the current display is computed. Then the aspect ratio of the current display (regardless of position) is computed. An if statement tests to see if the desired aspect ratio is greater than the current aspect ratio. If true, the output height is that of the input position vector minus margins, and the output width is scaled to give the desired aspect ratio. If not true, the output width is that of the input position vector minus margins, and the output height is scaled to give the desired aspect ratio. Finally, the output position vector is computed with reference to the center of the input position vector.

To create a plot with an aspect ratio of 1.0 (equal height and width) and a default margin of 0.1:

```
IDL> window, /free
IDL> x = findgen(200) * 0.1
IDL> pos = getpos(1.0)
IDL> plot, x, sin(x), position=pos
```

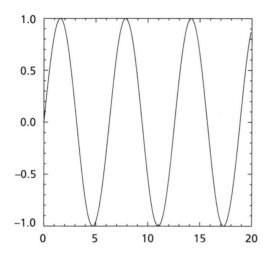

To create a plot with an aspect ratio of 1.5 (height is 1.5 times width) and a margin of 0.2:

```
IDL> pos = getpos(1.5, margin=0.2)
IDL> plot, x, sin(x), position=pos
```

To create a plot with an aspect ratio of 1.0 in the bottom half of the current display:

```
IDL> plot, x, sin(x)
IDL> pos = getpos(1.0, position=[0.0, 0.0, 1.0, 0.5])
IDL> plot, x, sin(x), position=pos
```

Positioning Multiple Plots

The global system variable !p.multi offers a built-in mechanism for positioning multiple plots. For example, to place four plots on the display:

```
IDL> !p.multi = [0, 2, 2, 0, 0]
IDL> x = findgen(200) * 0.1
IDL> plot, x, sin(x)
IDL> plot, x, sin(x) * x^2
IDL> plot, x, randomu(1, 200) * x, psym=1
IDL> plot, x, 4.0 * !pi * x * 0.1, /polar
```

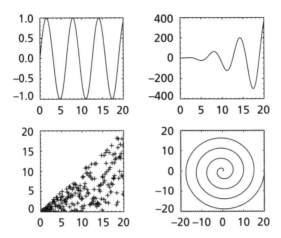

The system variable !p.multi is a long vector with five elements, and is honored by the plot, contour, surface, and shade_surf procedures. The second element of !p.multi specifies the number of plot columns, and the third element specifies the number of plot rows (you can leave the other elements set to zero). In the previous example, !p.multi is set to create two columns and two rows of plots on the display. When the first plot is created, the contents of the display are erased unless the noerase keyword is set, and subsequent plots fill the remaining rows. When all rows are filled, the next plot erases the display and starts again at top left.

To disable multiple plots, simply reset all elements of !p.multi to zero (the default):

```
IDL> !p.multi = 0
IDL> plot, x, sin(x) * x^2
```

Tip   You will notice that the size of the axis labels is adjusted when !p.multi is used to position multiple plots. This behavior may or may not be desirable for your needs. If you wish to position multiple plots manually (without changing text sizes), use position vectors instead of !p.multi.

6.3   PLOT CUSTOMIZATION

Direct Graphics plots are highly customizable. Plot properties such as position, title, and character size; linestyle, thickness, and color; and axis ranges, tick positions, and labels can all be adjusted. As explained in the previous section, optional keywords are the preferred method for changing the properties of a plot.

General Plot Properties

The keywords listed in Table 6.5 are commonly used to customize the appearance of Direct Graphics plots. The plot procedure accepts all keywords shown in Table 6.5, while the oplot and plots procedures accept color, linestyle, thick, psym, symsize, and /noclip. For the complete list of keywords supported by plot, oplot, and plots, see the online help for each procedure.

The following example demonstrates a selection of these keywords:

```
IDL> x = findgen(200) * 0.1
IDL> plot, x, sin(x), $
IDL>    title='SIN(X) vs. X', subtitle='A sample IDL plot', $
IDL>    charsize=1.25, font=1, linestyle=3, $
IDL>    thick=2.0, psym=-1
```

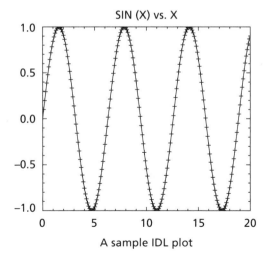

Table 6.5 Common plot customization keywords.

Keyword	Purpose
position	Position vector (default: automatic)
title	Title string (default: no title)
subtitle	Subtitle string (default: no subtitle)
charsize	Character size* (default: 1.0)
charthick	Character thickness (default: 1)
font	Character font index (-1, 0, or 1; default: -1)
color	Color index (default: highest color table index)
linestyle	Linestyle[†] (0–5; default: 0)
thick	Line thickness (default: 1.0)
ticklen	Tick length[‡] (default: 0.02)
psym	Symbol code (0–8, default: 0)
symsize	Symbol size (default: 1.0)
/xlog	Create logarithmic *x*-axis (default: create linear *x*-axis)
/ylog	Create logarithmic *y*-axis (default: create linear *y*-axis)
/noerase	Don't erase display (default: erase display before plotting)
/nodata	Create axes only (default: create axes and plot data)
/noclip	Don't clip data (default: clip the data to axis range)

* The size of title is 1.25 times the value of charsize.

[†] Line styles 0–5 are solid, dotted, dashed, dash/dot, dash/dot/dot/dot, and long dashes.

[‡] Tick length is expressed as a fraction of the axis width or height. Negative tick lengths create outward pointing tick marks.

General Axis Properties

The plot procedure draws axes around all sides of a plot by default. If a specific axis range is not requested, IDL estimates an axis range that is appropriate for the input data. Axis labels, major (large) tick marks, and minor (small) tick marks are also drawn. Axis titles are left blank by default.

Axis properties can be customized by passing axis-specific keywords to the plot, contour, surface, or shade_surf procedures. The keywords listed in Table 6.6 are commonly used to customize the properties of plot axes.

Table 6.6 Common axis customization keywords.

Keyword	Purpose
[xyz]range	Axis range (default: automatic)
[xyz]title	Title string (default: no title)
[xyz]charsize	Character size* (default 1.0)
[xyz]style	Axis style (0–31, default 0)
[xyz]thick	Axis and tick mark thickness (default 1.0)
[xyz]margin	Margin at axis edges (default x: [10, 3], y: [4, 2])
[xyz]minor	Number of minor tick intervals (default: automatic)
[xyz]ticklen	Tick length[†] (default 0.02)
[xyz]gridstyle	Grid style[‡] (0–5, default 0)
[xyz]tickformat	Tick label format code (default: automatic)
[xyz]ticks	Number of major tick intervals (default: automatic)
[xyz]tickv	Array of tick values (default: automatic)
[xyz]tickname	Array of tick labels (default: automatic)
[xyz]tick_get	Return an array of tick values

* Relative to the overall character size set by the charsize keyword.

[†] Fraction of axis width or height; overrides the overall tick length set by the ticklen keyword.

[‡] Style values (0–5) have the same meaning as linestyles. Set tick lengths to 1.0 to create a grid.

Configuring Axis Range and Style

By default, axes are drawn as a box around the plotted data, with the limits of each axis spanning the data range. The axis limits can be adjusted by using the plot keywords xrange and yrange, which specify the minimum and maximum limits for the x- and y-axes:

```
IDL> x = findgen(200) * 0.1
IDL> y = sin(x)
IDL> plot, x, sin(x), xrange=[0, 13.5]
```

You will notice that IDL adjusts the x-axis limits to what it thought was a more reasonable range of 0 to 15. To force the exact axis range specified in the xrange keyword, you must add the keyword xstyle=1:

```
IDL> plot, x, y, xrange=[0, 13.5], xstyle=1
IDL> plot, x, y, xrange=[0, 13.5], xstyle=1, $
IDL>   yrange=[-2.5, 2.5], ystyle=1
```

The values allowed for the [xyz]style keywords are listed in Table 6.7. The [xyz]style keywords can be used to modify several axis properties at once by combining values in an additive fashion. For example, to specify an exact *x*-axis range and draw axes on one side of the plot only:

```
IDL> plot, x, y, xstyle=8, yrange=[-2, 2], ystyle=1+8
```

Tip   To create a reversed axis, simply reverse the axis limits in the [xyz]range keyword.

If the independent (*y*-axis) data values are all greater than zero and a yrange keyword is not specified, then by default the *y*-axis lower limit will be zero:

```
IDL> plot, x, y + 100.0
```

To override this behavior, set the plot keyword ynozero:

```
IDL> plot, x, y + 100.0, /ynozero
```

The same effect can be achieved by setting the [xyz]style keyword to 16, as shown in Table 6.7.

Creating Axes

The axis procedure may be used to create customized axes on existing plots. This is often required when one or more variables with different units

Table 6.7   Values for [xyz]style keywords.

Value	Meaning
1	Use the exact range specified by xrange or yrange.
2	Leave a margin at either end of the axis range.
4	Do not draw the axis on either side of the plot.
8	Draw the axis on the lower or left side only.
16	Do not force the *y*-axis lower limit to zero.

are plotted with respect to the same ordinates. For example, the velocity and distance of a falling body could be plotted on the same graph as a function of time. First, a time sequence of time, velocity, and distance is computed:

```
IDL> t = findgen(11)     ; time
IDL> a = 9.8             ; acceleration due to gravity
IDL> v = a * t           ; velocity
IDL> x = 0.5 * a * t^2   ; distance
```

To plot velocity and distance versus time:

```
IDL> plot, t, x, /nodata, ystyle=4, $
IDL>   xmargin=[10, 10], xtitle='Time (sec)'
IDL> axis, yaxis=0, yrange=[0, 100], /save, $
IDL>   ytitle='Velocity (meters/sec, solid line)'
IDL> oplot, t, v, linestyle=0
IDL> axis, yaxis=1, yrange=[0, 500], /save, $
IDL>   ytitle='Distance (meters, dashed line)'
IDL> oplot, t, x, linestyle=2
```

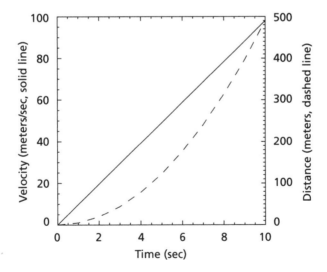

First the plot procedure is called to create the *x*-axis without plotting any data (/nodata). The *y*-axes are suppressed by the ystyle keyword. Then axis is called to create the left-hand *y*-axis (yaxis=0). The /save keyword causes the scaling established by axis to be saved for subsequent overplotting (otherwise the scaling is unchanged). Velocity data are overplotted as a solid line. Finally, the right-hand *y*-axis is created, and the distance data are overplotted as a dashed line.

Logarithmic Axes

The plotting keywords /xlog and /ylog cause logarithmic axes to be created. These keywords are accepted by the plot, axis, contour, surface,
and shade_surf procedures. For example, to plot an exponential curve:

```
IDL> x = findgen(200) * 0.1 + 1.0
IDL> plot, x, x^3, /ylog
```

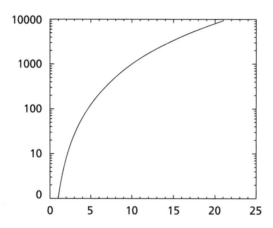

If the range of a logarithmic axis spans less than a decade (a power of
10), then only the axis endpoints are labeled:

```
IDL> x = findgen(200) * 0.005 + 1.0
IDL> plot, x, x^3, /ylog
```

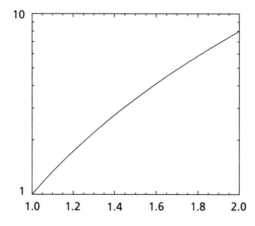

This problem can be overcome by creating custom tick marks and labels.

Tick Marks and Labels

The [xyz]ticks, [xyz]tickv, [xyz]tickname, and [xyz]tickformat plotting keywords may be used to set the number, values, labels, and format of axis tick marks, respectively. These keywords are accepted by the plot, axis, contour, surface, and shade_surf procedures. A case where custom ticks are required was shown in the previous example, where a logarithmic *y*-axis spanned less than a decade and IDL only labeled the *y*-axis endpoints. You can add tick marks and labels within a decade on a logarithmic plot by creating custom *y*-axes with the axis procedure:

```
IDL> plot, x, x^3, /ylog, ystyle=4
IDL> axis, yaxis=0, /ylog, yticks=6, $
IDL>   ytickv=[1, 2, 4, 6, 8, 10]
IDL> axis, yaxis=1, /ylog, yticks=6, $
IDL>   ytickv=[1, 2, 4, 6, 8, 10], $
IDL>   ytickname=replicate(' ', 6)
```

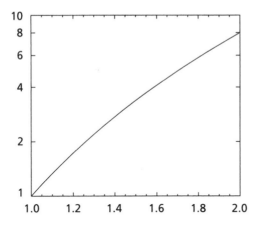

The initial plot command creates the plot but suppresses the *y*-axes. The first axis command creates the left *y*-axis (yaxis=0) with six tick marks specified by the yticks keyword and the tick values specified by the ytickv keyword. The second axis command creates the right *y*-axis (yaxis=1) with tick marks at the same locations, but with the tick labels suppressed by specifying blank characters in the ytickname keyword (if ytickname is not specified, the tick labels are derived from the tick values).

The plotting keyword [xyz]tickformat may be used to customize the format of tick labels by specifying a format code, as described in Table 4.2.

For example, exponential format may be used to give a consistent label appearance on a logarithmic plot:

```
IDL> x = findgen(200) * 0.1 + 1.0
IDL> plot, x, x^3, /ylog, ytickformat='(e8.1)'
```

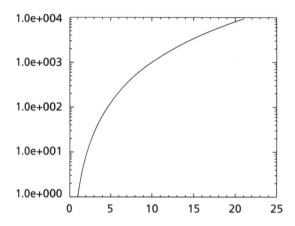

As explained in Chapter 4, the number of digits in the exponent may vary between platforms (the figure in this example is from a Windows platform).

Tip The [xyz]tickformat keyword may also be used to pass the name of a function that performs user-defined label formatting. To label an axis with dates or times, the label_date function may be used in conjunction with the [xyz]tickformat keyword. See the online help for more information.

6.4   PLOT COLORS

The plotting keyword color may be used to select colors other than the defaults. The color keyword is supported by the plot, oplot, plots, axis, contour, surface, and shade_surf procedures. Colors are specified differently depending on which color model (Indexed or Decomposed) is active.

Indexed Colors

If the Indexed color model is active, plotting colors are specified by loading appropriate values into the color table and then selecting the appropriate color table index. The default plot color is determined by the highest color table index, and the default background color is determined by color table index 0.

For example, to create a green plot:

```
IDL> device, decomposed=0
IDL> tvlct, 0, 255, 0, 1
IDL> plot, sin(findgen(200) * 0.1), color=1
```

First, the Indexed color model was selected by calling the device procedure. Then the red, green, and blue components were loaded into the color table at index 1 by calling tvlct, and plot was called with the color keyword used to specify the index in the color table.

The following procedure named loadcolors.pro loads 16 plotting colors into the color table. The colors are loaded starting at index 0 by default, or at the index specified by the bottom keyword. The names of the colors can be returned by the names keyword.

```
PRO LOADCOLORS, BOTTOM=BOTTOM, NAMES=NAMES

;- Check arguments
if (n_elements(bottom) eq 0) then bottom = 0

;- Load graphics colors
red = [   0, 255,   0, 255,   0, 255,   0, 255, $
          0, 255, 255, 112, 219, 127,   0, 255]
grn = [   0,   0, 255, 255, 255,   0,   0, 255, $
          0, 187, 127, 219, 112, 127, 163, 171]
blu = [   0, 255, 255,   0,   0,   0, 255, 255, $
        115,   0, 127, 147, 219, 127, 255, 127]
tvlct, red, grn, blu, bottom

;- Set color names
names = [ 'Black', 'Magenta', 'Cyan', 'Yellow', $
          'Green', 'Red', 'Blue', 'White', $
          'Navy', 'Gold', 'Pink', 'Aquamarine', $
          'Orchid', 'Gray', 'Sky', 'Beige' ]

END
```

To create a color plot using the colors loaded by `loadcolors`, simply
select the index corresponding to the desired color:

```
IDL> loadcolors
IDL> x = findgen(200) * 0.1
IDL> plot, x, sin(x), color=4
```

This example creates a plot where the background is black and the
plot color is green. To create a plot in a graphics window where the background, axes, and data are different colors, a little trickery is required. For
example, try the following after calling `loadcolors`:

```
IDL> plot, x, sin(x), /nodata, background=7, color=4
IDL> oplot, x, sin(x), color=1
```

First, `plot` is called with the `nodata` keyword set, which instructs `plot` to
create the axes without plotting the data. The background color (white) is
set by the `background` keyword, and the axis color (green) is set by the
`color` keyword. Creating a plot without plotting any data may seem odd,
but that's the way it's done in IDL. Finally the data is overplotted by calling `oplot` with the `color` keyword set to 1 (magenta).

Tip The `background` keyword has no effect when the PostScript graphics
device is selected. To set a color background in this case, use the `poly-
fill` procedure to fill the entire drawable area with the selected color:

```
IDL> polyfill, [0.0, 1.0, 1.0, 0.0, 0.0], $
IDL> [0.0, 0.0, 1.0, 1.0, 0.0], /normal, color=13
```

Decomposed Colors

When the Decomposed color model is active, plotting colors are specified
as long integers in hexadecimal format in blue/green/red order. The
default plot color is white, and the default background color is black.

For example, to create a blue plot:

```
IDL> device, decomposed=1
IDL> color = 'FF0000'XL
IDL> plot, sin(findgen(200) * 0.1), color=color
```

Table 6.8   Decomposed plotting colors.

Color	Hex value
Black	'000000'XL
Magenta	'FF00FF'XL
Cyan	'FFFF00'XL
Yellow	'00FFFF'XL
Green	'00FF00'XL
Red	'0000FF'XL
Blue	'FF0000'XL
White	'FFFFFF'XL
Navy	'730000'XL
Gold	'00BBFF'XL
Pink	'7F7FFF'XL
Aquamarine	'93DB70'XL
Orchid	'DB70DB'XL
Gray	'7F7F7F'XL
Sky	'FFA300'XL
Beige	'7FABFF'XL

In this example, the hexadecimal value 'FF0000'XL represents maximum blue (FF), minimum green (00), and minimum red (00). A selection of decomposed plotting colors is listed in Table 6.8.

Tip

Remember, when IDL is running in 24-bit mode, you can switch between the Indexed and Decomposed color models by calling the device procedure with the decomposed keyword set to 0 or 1. Thus you could create a plot in Indexed Color, switch to Decomposed Color to display a True-Color image, and then switch back to Indexed Color to plot a legend, all in the same graphics window.

6.5   TITLES, LABELS, AND SYMBOLS

The plotting keywords title, subtitle, and [xyz]title may be used to set plot and axis titles. These keywords are supported by the plot, axis, contour, surface, and shade_surf procedures. In addition, labels may be placed at arbitrary locations by calling the xyouts procedure, which plots a text string. Finally, mathematical symbols may be included as part of any title or text label.

Titles

Plot titles may be specified by the title, xtitle, and ytitle keywords, which are set to string variables containing the desired text:

```
IDL> x = findgen(500) * 0.1
IDL> y = x + 10.0 * sin(x)^2
IDL> plot, x, y, title='Sample #11', $
IDL>   xtitle='Hours', ytitle='Temperature (C)'
```

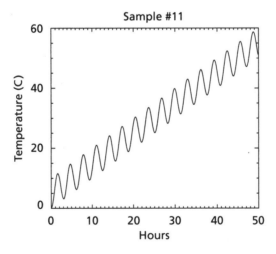

The default text fonts in IDL are known as vector fonts, since they are drawn by plotting vectors. Vector fonts are available on all IDL graphics devices, and they provide text and symbols of reasonable quality. There are 17 sets of vector fonts (3 through 20), which provide a range of typefaces and symbols (see the "Fonts" chapter in the online help document "IDL Reference" for more information). Chapter 8 describes the font types available in IDL (vector, hardware, and TrueType) in more detail.

When vector or TrueType fonts are selected, formatting commands can be embedded in `string` variables to enable different fonts and font properties to be selected. A selection of commonly used font-formatting commands is shown in Table 6.9.

For example, to create a plot of a simulated carbon dioxide spectral absorption feature:

```
IDL> x = findgen(100) * 0.1 - 5.0
IDL> y = 1.0 - exp(-(x^2))
IDL> title  = '!3CO!D2!N Spectral Absorption Feature!X'
IDL> xtitle = '!3Wavenumber (cm!U-1!N)!X'
IDL> ytitle = '!3Transmittance!X'
IDL> plot, x + 805.0, y, title=title, xtitle=xtitle, $
IDL>    ytitle=ytitle
```

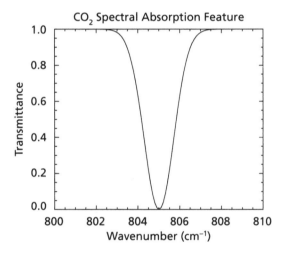

Table 6.9   **Common font-formatting commands.**

Command	Meaning
!3	Select Simplex Roman font (default)
!4	Select Simplex Greek font
!6	Select Complex Roman font
!X	Revert to entry font
!C	Begin new line
!D	Select subscript level and character size
!U	Select superscript level and character size
!N	Select normal level and character size

Labels

The xyouts procedure may be used to create plot labels. The general syntax for xyouts is

xyouts, x, y, *string*

where x and y are the label coordinates, and *string* is the label string. For example, to add a date label to the current graphics window or device:

```
IDL> date = systime()
IDL> xyouts, 0.0, 0.0, date, /normal
```

The label is plotted in the lower-left corner of the display and is left-justified by default. The string variable date contains the label to be plotted. The normal keyword specifies that the first two arguments are in normal coordinates (the default is data coordinates).

The most commonly used keywords accepted by xyouts are listed in Table 6.10. In addition, xyouts accepts the plotting keywords charsize, charthick, font, and color as shown in Table 6.5.

The alignment keyword allows you to specify whether the label should be left-, center-, or right-justified:

```
IDL> xyouts, 0.5, 0.0, 'Page 1 of 5', $
ID>L>    normal, alignment=0.5
IDL> xyouts, 1.0, 0.0, 'IDL Graphics Lab', $
IDL>    /normal, alignment=1.0
```

The first label is centered at the supplied normal coordinates by setting alignment=0.5. The second label is right-justified by setting alignment=1.0. Labels are often positioned using normal coordinates to make plot labeling independent of data values, especially when multiple plots

Table 6.10   Commonly used xyouts **keywords.**

Keyword	Purpose
alignment	Text alignment (0.0 = left, 0.5 = center, 1.0 = right, default 0.0)
orientation	Text orientation (degrees counterclockwise, default 0.0)
/normal	Input position is in normal coordinates
/data	Input position is in data coordinates (default)
/device	Input position is in device coordinates
width	On return, contains width of string in normal coordinates

with the same format are created from different data sets. In other cases where you wish to highlight a feature in the plotted data, such as highlighting a peak or local minimum, data coordinates (the xyouts default) may be used instead to position the label.

Tip The legend procedure from the IDL Astronomy Library may be used to combine lines, plot symbols, and labels to create plot legends. See Appendix A for download details.

Mathematical Symbols

It is possible to use IDL font formatting directly to plot text that contains mathematical and Greek symbols. However, it is much easier to use the TeXtoIDL package developed by Matthew W. Craig (see Appendix A for download details). TeXtoIDL allows font-formatting strings to be constructed using a TeX-like syntax. For example, to print the Greek letter rho with an exponent of 2, followed by a plus sign, and then a 2 followed by the uppercase Greek letter gamma with a subscript of ij:

```
IDL> text = textoidl('\rho^2 + 2\Gamma_{ij}')
IDL> print, text
!7q!X!U2!N + 2!7C!X!Dij!N
IDL> xyouts, 0.5, 0.5, text, charsize=5, $
IDL>    /normal, align=0.5, font=-1
```

$$\rho^2 + 2\Gamma_{ij}$$

TeXtoIDL supports vector fonts (font index −1, the default) on all graphics devices, and if the PostScript device is selected, hardware fonts are supported (font index 0). To use hardware fonts on the PostScript device, set the font keyword equal to 0 in the call to textoidl, and also in the call to the plotting command (xyouts in this example):

```
IDL> set_plot, 'PS'
IDL> device, filename='textoidl.ps'
IDL> font = 0
```

```
IDL> text = textoidl('\rho^2 + 2\Gamma_{ij}', font=font)
IDL> xyouts, 0.5, 0.5, text, charsize=5, $
IDL>   /normal, align=0.5, font=font
IDL> device, /close_file
```

$$\rho^2 + 2\Gamma_{ij}$$

To view the TeX sequences supported by TeXtoIDL along with the corresponding mathematical symbol, call the `showtex` procedure:

```
IDL> showtex
```

Vector fonts

\alpha α	\beta β	\gamma γ	\delta δ	\epsilon ϵ
\zeta ζ	\eta η	\theta θ	\iota ι	\kappa κ
\lambda λ	\mu μ	\nu ν	\xi ξ	\pi π
\rho ρ	\sigma σ	\tau τ	\upsilon υ	\phi ϕ
\chi χ	\psi ψ	\omega ω	\varpi π	\varepsilon ϵ
\varphi φ	\vartheta ϑ	\Gamma Γ	\Delta Δ	\Theta Θ
\Lambda Λ	\Xi Ξ	\Pi Π	\Sigma Σ	\Upsilon Υ
\Phi Φ	\Psi Ψ	\Omega Ω	\aleph $\aleph$	\ast $\cdot$
\cap $\cap$	\cdot $\cdot$	\cup $\cup$	\exists $\exists$	\infty ∞
\in $\in$	\equiv $\equiv$	\pm $\pm$	\div $\div$	\subset $\subset$
\superset $\supset$	\leftarrow $\leftarrow$	\downarrow $\downarrow$	\rightarrow $\rightarrow$	\uparrow $\uparrow$
\neq $\neq$	\propto $\propto$	\sim $\sim$	\partial ∂	\nabla ∇
\angle $\angle$	\times $\times$	\geq $\geq$	\leq $\leq$	\' '
\prime '	\circ $\circ$			

Superscripts are indicated by the "^" character, and subscripts are indicated by the "_" character. If more than one character is to be superscripted or subscripted, the character sequence should be enclosed in curly brackets "{}". To create the simulated absorption feature plot shown in the previous section using TeXtoIDL formatting:

```
IDL> x = findgen(100) * 0.1 - 5.0
IDL> y = 1.0 - exp(-(x^2))
IDL> plot, x + 805.0, y, charsize=1.25, $
IDL>   title = textoidl('CO_2 Spectral Absorption Feature'), $
IDL>   xtitle = textoidl('Wavenumber \nu (cm^{-1})'), $
IDL>   ytitle = textoidl('Transmittance \tau')
```

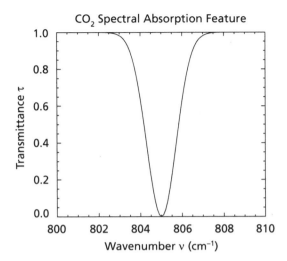

CO_2 Spectral Absorption Feature

6.6 ERROR BAR, HISTOGRAM, AND BAR PLOTS

Several other two-dimensional plot types may be created in IDL using either built-in or user-written procedures. In this section, a user-written procedure for plotting error bars is described that offers more flexibility than the corresponding built-in routines. Next, the `histogram` function is described, along with a procedure to compute and plot histograms of data arrays. Finally, the built-in procedure for creating bar plots in IDL is described.

Error Bar Plots

If you are plotting experimental data, you may need to plot error bars for each data point. IDL has several built-in procedures that enable error bars to be plotted, but they lack the ability to specify important options such as color and thickness. The following procedure named `err_plot.pro` allows you to plot error bars on top of an existing set of plotted data. The optional `width` keyword sets the error bar width in normal coordinates. The `_extra` keyword allows any keywords accepted by `plots` to be passed to this procedure.

```
PRO ERR_PLOT, X, YLOW, YHIGH, WIDTH=WIDTH, $
  _EXTRA=EXTRA_KEYWORDS

;- Check arguments
if (n_params() ne 3) then message, $
  'Usage: ERR_PLOT, X, YLOW, YHIGH'
if (n_elements(x) eq 0) then $
  message, 'Argument X is undefined'
if (n_elements(ylow) eq 0) then $
  message, 'Argument YLOW is undefined'
if (n_elements(yhigh) eq 0) then $
  message, 'Argument YHIGH is undefined'

;- Check keywords
if (n_elements(width) eq 0) then width = 0.02

;- Plot the error bars
for index = 0L, n_elements(x) - 1L do begin

  ;- Plot vertical bar using data coordinates
  xdata = [x[index], x[index]]
  ydata = [ylow[index], yhigh[index]]
  plots, xdata, ydata, /data, noclip=0, $
    _extra=extra_keywords

  ;- Compute horizontal bar width in normal coordinates
  normalwidth = (!x.window[1] - !x.window[0]) * width

  ;- Plot horizontal bar using normal coordinates
  lower = convert_coord(x[index], ylow[index], $
    /data, /to_normal)
  upper = convert_coord(x[index], yhigh[index], $
    /data, /to_normal)
  xdata = [lower[0] - 0.5 * width, lower[0] + 0.5 * width]
  ylower = [lower[1], lower[1]]
  yupper = [upper[1], upper[1]]
  plots, xdata, ylower, /normal, noclip=0, $
    _extra=extra_keywords
  plots, xdata, yupper, /normal, noclip=0, $
    _extra=extra_keywords

endfor

END
```

First, the input arguments are checked. A loop is started to plot each error bar. Each vertical bar is plotted in data coordinates by calling plots, which can plot lines in both data and normal coordinates (oplot only works in data coordinates). The error bar width is then computed as a fraction of the plot width (given by the system variable !x.window) in normal coordinates. The center of each horizontal bar tail is found by calling the function convert_coord, which in this case converts from data to normal coordinates. Then the *x*- and *y*-coordinates of the horizontal bar tails are computed, and plotted by calling plots (the noclip=0 keyword causes the error bars to be clipped to the plot window).

You can then plot error bars where every data point has the same error value:

```
IDL> x = findgen(10)
IDL> y = randomu(-1L, 10) + 10
IDL> plot, x, y, yrange=[9.5, 11.5]
IDL> err = 0.1
IDL> err_plot, x, y-err, y+err
```

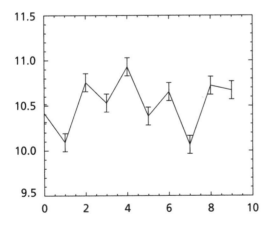

You can also plot error bars where every data point has its own error value:

```
IDL> plot, x, y, yrange=[9.5, 11.5]
IDL> err = findgen(10) * 0.025
IDL> err_plot, x, y-err, y+err
```

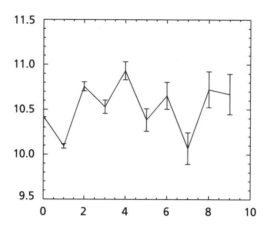

Histogram Plots

Histograms are computed with the histogram function. To compute the histogram of an image array with a default histogram bin size of 1.0:

```
IDL> data = dist(32)
IDL> hist = histogram(data)
IDL> print, hist[0:4]
           1           8          16          20          24
```

By default, the lower edge of the first histogram bin starts at the minimum data value. The last histogram bin straddles the maximum data value (the left edge of this bin is a multiple of the bin size). Thus the first element in hist is the number of elements in data that are in the range $0.0 \leq data < 1.0$, the second element in hist is the number of elements in data that are in the range $1.0 \leq data < 2.0$, and so on.

Computing the histogram array is the easy part. Plotting it correctly is a little more involved. The online documentation for the plot procedure says that setting psym=10 will plot data as a histogram. However, to use this plot feature, you must first compute a sensible histogram bin size (the default bin size of 1.0 is inappropriate if your data range is smaller than 1.0), then compute the coordinates of each bin, and finally call the plot procedure.

To simplify this process, the following procedure named hist_plot.pro computes and plots the histogram of a given input array. The optional min and max keywords specify the data range used to compute the histogram, and the binsize keyword specifies the bin size. If the normalize keyword is set, the histogram will be normalized to the total number of values in the input array (this is useful for comparing histograms of different data sets). If the fill keyword is set, the plotted histogram will be filled. The _extra keyword allows any keywords accepted by plot to be passed to this procedure.

```
PRO HIST_PLOT, DATA, MIN=MIN_VALUE, MAX=MAX_VALUE, $
  BINSIZE=BINSIZE, NORMALIZE=NORMALIZE, FILL=FILL, $
  _EXTRA=EXTRA_KEYWORDS

;- Check arguments
if (n_params() ne 1) then message, 'Usage: HIST_PLOT, DATA'
if (n_elements(data) eq 0) then message, 'DATA is undefined'

;- Check keywords
if (n_elements(min_value) eq 0) then min_value = min(data)
if (n_elements(max_value) eq 0) then max_value = max(data)
if (n_elements(binsize) eq 0) then $
  binsize = (max_value - min_value) * 0.01
binsize = binsize > ((max_value - min_value) * 1.0e-5)

;- Compute histogram
hist = histogram(float(data), binsize=binsize, $
  min=min_value, max=max_value)
hist = [hist, 0L]
nhist = n_elements(hist)

;- Normalize histogram if required
if keyword_set(normalize) then $
  hist = hist / float(n_elements(data))

;- Compute bin values
bins = lindgen(nhist) * binsize + min_value

;- Create plot arrays
x = fltarr(2 * nhist)
x[2 * lindgen(nhist)] = bins
x[2 * lindgen(nhist) + 1] = bins
y = fltarr(2 * nhist)
y[2 * lindgen(nhist)] = hist
y[2 * lindgen(nhist) + 1] = hist
y = shift(y, 1)
```

```
;- Plot the histogram
plot, x, y, _extra=extra_keywords

;- Fill the histogram if required
if keyword_set(fill) then $
  polyfill, [x, x[0]], [y, y[0]], _extra=extra_keywords

END
```

First, the input arguments are checked. If the `min_value` and `max_value` keywords are not set, the default range for the histogram is defined by the minimum and maximum data values. If the `binsize` keyword is not specified, the bin size is computed to give 100 histogram bins. Next, the histogram (`hist`) is computed. If the `normalize` keyword is set, the histogram is normalized. Then, the bin edge coordinates (x and y) are computed (each bin requires a pair of coordinates in the *x* and *y* directions). Finally, the histogram is plotted with lines connecting each pair of bin coordinates, and if the `fill` keyword is set, the histogram is filled.

To plot the histogram of a two-dimensional array:

```
IDL> hist_plot, dist(256), $
IDL>   xtitle='Intensity', ytitle='Frequency'
```

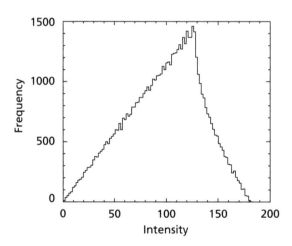

Bar Plots

Bar plots are created by calling the `bar_plot` procedure. For example, to create a bar plot showing the growth in the number of IDL-related web sites over a five-year period:

```
IDL> sites = [20, 55, 102, 235, 350]
IDL> years = ['1995', '1996', '1997', '1998', '1999']
IDL> bar_plot, sites, barnames=years
```

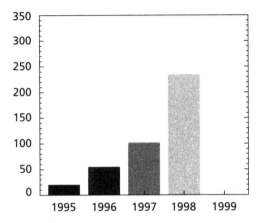

The argument sites contains the bar values. The keyword barnames is set to a string array containing the name of each bar (bars are unlabeled if the barnames keyword is not used).

You can see that IDL selects default colors that span the current color table. However, you can specify a color for each bar using the colors keyword. In addition, titles can be specified with the title, xtitle, and ytitle keywords:

```
IDL> xtitle = 'Year'
IDL> ytitle = 'Number of sites'
IDL> title  = 'IDL Web Sites Worldwide'
IDL> loadcolors
IDL> bar_plot, sites, $
IDL>   barnames=years, colors=[1, 2, 3, 4, 5], $
IDL>   title=title, xtitle=xtitle, ytitle=ytitle, /outline
```

Here the loadcolors procedure from Section 6.4 is called to load 16 graphics colors into the color table. When bar_plot is called, the colors keyword is used to select a color for each bar. The outline keyword causes an outline to be drawn around each bar.

6.7 CONTOUR PLOTS

Data sets that are a function of two dimensions may be visualized as contour plots in IDL Direct Graphics. Contour plots may be produced for any data set defined as $z = f(x, y)$, regardless of whether x and y are defined at regular grid intervals. An example of a regularly gridded data set would be global surface temperature from a numerical weather prediction model, defined at evenly spaced latitudes and longitudes. An example of an irregularly gridded data set would be surface temperature measurements acquired by weather stations throughout the continental United States. Contour plots in IDL require a little effort to configure, but the results are worthwhile.

In the following discussion of contour plotting, a regularly gridded data set that simulates atmospheric total ozone is used as an example:

```
IDL> z = randomu(-100L, 50, 50)
IDL> for i = 0, 4 do z = smooth(z, 15, /edge)
IDL> ; total ozone
IDL> z = (z - min(z)) * 15000.0 + 100.00
IDL> ; longitude
IDL> x = findgen(50) - 100.0
IDL> ; latitude
IDL> y = findgen(50) + 10.0
```

The z array represents total column ozone in Dobson units. The x and y arrays represent the grid locations where z is defined, in longitude (degrees East), and latitude (degrees North), respectively.

Contour Plotting Overview

The contour procedure plots the contours of two-dimensional data sets defined on regular grids, or of data sets that are a function of two dimensions but are defined at irregular intervals. The general syntax for contour is

```
contour, z, x, y
```

where z is a two-dimensional array if the input data are regularly gridded, and x and y are optional vectors or arrays specifying regularly spaced ordinate values on the x- and y- axes. If the input data are irregularly defined, z is a vector of function values, and x and y are vectors describing the points where z is defined.

The minimal argument list for contour contains a two-dimensional array of regularly gridded data:

```
IDL> contour, z
```

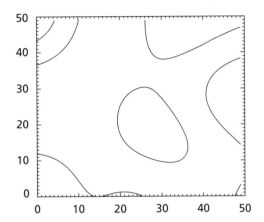

However, when a two-dimensional data set is contoured, it is usually possible to define vectors that describe the data intervals on the *x*- and *y*-axes. These vectors may be passed as optional arguments to contour to define the data grid:

```
IDL> contour, z, x, y
```

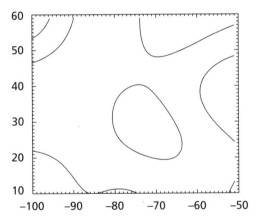

The optional arguments x and y can also be two-dimensional arrays, where each element of x describes the *x*-axis location of the corresponding element in z, and each element of y describes the *y*-axis location of the corresponding element of z.

If contour levels are not specified, IDL chooses default contour levels (usually between 3 and 8 levels). Specific contour levels may be selected via the levels keyword:

```
IDL> levels = [150, 200, 250, 300, 350, 400, 450, 500]
IDL> contour, z, levels=levels
```

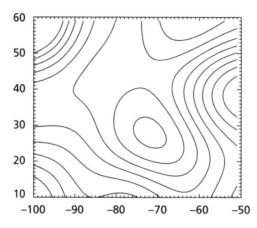

You will notice that contour levels are not labeled by default. To label contour levels, the c_labels keyword is set to a vector with the same number of elements as levels, with nonzero values indicating the levels to be labeled. For example, to label every second level:

```
IDL> c_labels = [0, 1, 0, 1, 0, 1, 0, 1]
IDL> contour, z, x, y, levels=levels, c_labels=c_labels
```

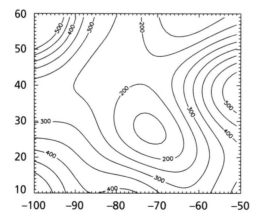

Tip   Avoid the contour keyword nlevels for setting the number of contour levels. IDL treats the nlevels keyword as a suggestion only, and often chooses to plot more or fewer contour levels than requested.

Table 6.11 **Commonly used** contour **keywords.**

Keyword	Purpose
levels	Contour levels (default: automatic)
c_labels	Contour label flags (default: no labels)
c_charsize	Contour label size (default 1.0)
c_charthick	Contour label thickness (default 1.0)
c_annotation	Contour label strings (default: level values)
c_colors	Contour line colors (default: highest color table index)
c_linestyle	Contour linestyle (0–5, default 0)
c_thick	Contour line thickness (default 1.0)
/irregular	Irregularly gridded input (default: regularly gridded input)
/overplot	Overplot on existing axes (default: create axes)
/fill	Fill contours (default: don't fill contours)
/cell_fill	Fill contours via cell-fill (default: don't fill contours)
min_value	Minimum data value to plot (default: data minimum)
max_value	Maximum data value to plot (default: data maximum)

The most commonly used keywords accepted by the contour procedure are listed in Table 6.11; for the complete list of keywords supported
by contour, see the online help. The contour procedure also accepts all
plot customization keywords listed in Table 6.5 except for the following:
linestyle, psym, and symsize. In addition, contour accepts all axis customization keywords listed in Table 6.6.

Contouring Irregularly Spaced Data

When the input data set is defined at irregular intervals, contour can perform a Delaunay triangulation to interpolate the input data to a regular
grid. For example, the simulated ozone data set could be sampled at 250
random locations (one tenth of the number of points in the two-dimensional data set):

```
IDL> npts = 250
IDL> xrnd = randomu(-100L, npts) * 50.0
IDL> yrnd = randomu(-200L, npts) * 50.0
IDL> xran = x[xrnd]
```

```
IDL> yran = y[yrnd]
IDL> zran = z[xrnd, yrnd]
IDL> help, zran, xran, yran
ZRAN            FLOAT     = Array[250]
XRAN            FLOAT     = Array[250]
YRAN            FLOAT     = Array[250]
IDL> plot, xran, yran, psym=1, /ynozero
```

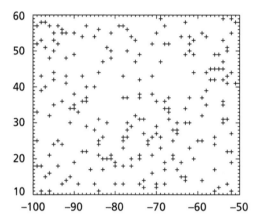

The distribution of points can be seen in the previous plot, where each symbol represents one sampling location. When the input data set consists of irregularly spaced points, the z, x, and y arguments must be supplied to contour, and the optional irregular keyword must be set:

```
IDL> contour, zran, xran, yran, /irregular, $
IDL>    levels=levels, c_labels=c_labels
```

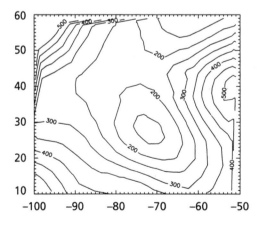

Filled Contours

The `contour` procedure color-fills contour regions when the `fill` or `cell_fill` keywords are set. Colors for the filled regions are specified as indices in the color table and are passed via the `c_colors` keyword. A color table with the appropriate number of colors must be loaded, and the Indexed color model must be in effect. In the following example, a color-filled contour plot of the simulated ozone data set is created.

First, the desired contour levels (`levels`), the number of fill colors (`ncolors`), and the start index in the color table (`bottom`) are defined:

```
IDL> levels = [150, 200, 250, 300, 350, 400, 450, 500]
IDL> nlevels = n_elements(levels)
IDL> ncolors = nlevels + 1
IDL> bottom = 1
```

Next, the plotted contour levels (`c_levels`), labeling flags (`c_labels`), and color indices (`c_colors`) are defined, and the color table is loaded by calling `loadct`:

```
IDL> c_levels = [min(z), levels, max(z)]
IDL> c_labels = [0, replicate(1, nlevels), 0]
IDL> c_colors = indgen(ncolors) + bottom
IDL> loadct, 33, ncolors=ncolors, bottom=bottom
```

The minimum and maximum data values are added to the array of plotted contour levels (`c_levels`) because color-filling begins at the lowest contour level and ends at the highest contour level. If the minimum and maximum values are not included in the level array, the regions below the lowest contour level and above the highest contour level are not filled (below the 150 contour and above the 500 contour in this case). There are (`nlevels + 1`) elements in `c_colors` because the color-filled regions are between each pair of plotted contour levels in `c_levels`. If there are more contour levels than color indices in `c_colors`, the color indices are repeated cyclically for all filled regions.

Finally, the color-filled regions are drawn and the contour lines and labels are overplotted with two separate calls to `contour`:

```
IDL> contour, z, x, y, $
IDL>    levels=c_levels, c_colors=c_colors, /fill, $
IDL>    xstyle=1, ystyle=1, title='Simulated Total Ozone', $
IDL>    xtitle='Longitude', ytitle='Latitude'
IDL> contour, z, x, y, $
IDL>    levels=c_levels, c_labels=c_labels, /overplot
```

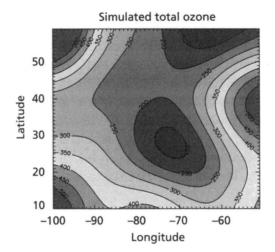

Filled contour regions are drawn with the first call to contour. The axis customization keywords xstyle and ystyle ensure the axes fit the x and y data range exactly. Contour lines and labels are drawn with the second call to contour.

Tip   In certain cases, the default region-filling algorithm invoked by the fill keyword may fail. The cell_fill keyword causes an alternative algorithm to be used. This algorithm may give better results when your data set has missing values screened out with the min_value or max_value keywords, or when your data set is plotted on a map projection (the optional contour arguments x and y are required in this case and must be in ascending order).

6.8   MESH AND SHADED SURFACE PLOTS

Surface plots may be created for data sets that are a function of two dimensions. The two forms available are meshes consisting of closely spaced lines and shaded surfaces, both with hidden line/surface removal. Irregularly gridded data sets must be interpolated to a regular grid before they can be displayed as a surface.

In the following discussion, a two-dimensional sinc function defined over the range −10 to 10 in both *x* and *y* is used as an example:

```
IDL> v = findgen(41) * 0.5 - 10.0
IDL> x = rebin(v, 41, 41, /sample)
IDL> y = rebin(reform(v, 1, 41), 41, 41, /sample)
IDL> r = sqrt(x^2 + y^2) + 1.0e-6
IDL> z = sin(r) / r
```

Mesh Surface Plots

The `surface` procedure plots a surface mesh for two-dimensional data sets defined on regular grids. The general syntax for `surface` is

```
surface, z, x, y
```

where z is a two-dimensional array, and x and y are optional vectors or arrays specifying regularly spaced ordinate values on the *x*- and *y*-axes. If x and y are two-dimensional arrays, each element of x describes the *x*-axis location of the corresponding element in z, and each element of y describes the *y*-axis location of the corresponding element of z.

When the optional x and y arguments are not supplied, the *x*- and *y*-axes are simply element numbers:

```
IDL> surface, z, charsize=1.5
```

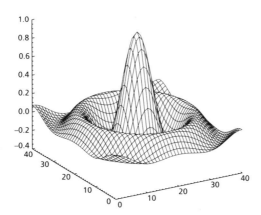

When the optional x and y arguments are supplied as vectors or arrays, the *x*- and *y*-axes reflect the ordinate values of the data set:

```
IDL> surface, z, x, y, charsize=1.5
```

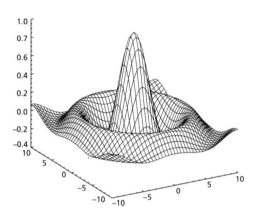

The most commonly used keywords accepted by the surface procedure are listed in Table 6.12; for the complete list of keywords supported by surface, see the online help. The surface procedure also accepts all plot customization keywords listed in Table 6.5 except for psym and symsize. In addition, surface accepts all axis customization keywords listed in Table 6.6.

The viewpoint can be adjusted by setting the az and ax keywords, which specify the rotation of the surface about the *z*- and *x*-axes:

```
IDL> surface, z, x, y, az=60, charsize=1.5
IDL> surface, z, x, y, ax=60, charsize=1.5
```

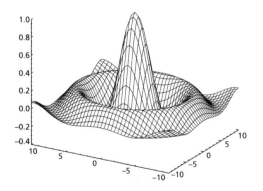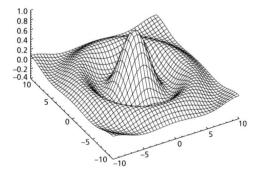

Table 6.12   Commonly used `surface` **keywords.**

Keyword	Purpose
`az`	Angle of rotation about *z*-axis* (counterclockwise, default 30 degrees)
`ax`	Angle of rotation about *x*-axis (counterclockwise, default 30 degrees)
`shades`	Color index for each *z*-level (default: highest color table index)
`skirt`	Value on *z*-axis where an edge skirt is drawn (default: no skirt)
`/lower_only`	Plot lower surface only (default; plot lower and upper surfaces)
`/upper_only`	Plot upper surface only (default; plot lower and upper surfaces)
`min_value`	Minimum data value to plot (default: data minimum)
`max_value`	Maximum data value to plot (default: data maximum)
`/zlog`	Create logarithmic *z*-axis (default; create linear *z*-axis)

* Plot is rotated about *z*-axis first, then *x*-axis.

The color shade at each level in the *z* direction may be specified by setting the `shades` keyword to an array of color index values:

```
IDL> loadcolors
IDL> bottom = 16
IDL> loadct, 13, bottom=bottom
IDL> shades = bytscl(z, top=!d.table_size - 1 - bottom) + $
IDL>    byte(bottom)
IDL> surface, z, x, y, charsize=1.5, shades=shades, $
IDL>    color=0, background=7
```

Graphics colors are loaded in the lowest 16 color table entries by calling `loadcolors`, and the "Rainbow" color table is loaded in the remaining color table entries by calling `loadct`. An array of color index values in the range `bottom` to `!d.table_size` is created by calling `bytscl`. Finally the surface is plotted by calling `surface` with the `shades` keyword set to the array of shading values, and the `color` and `background` keywords set to provide a black plot color on a white background.

A skirt may be added around the edges of the surface by setting the `skirt` keyword to the value on the *z*-axis where the skirt should be drawn:

```
IDL> surface, z, x, y, skirt=-0.2, $
IDL>    zrange=[-0.2, 1.0], zstyle=1, charsize=1.5
```

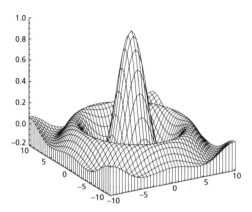

Irregularly Spaced Data

If your data set is spaced at irregular intervals, you must resample the data to a regular grid before using surface or shade_surf to display the data. This is accomplished by the triangulate and trigrid procedures. For example, the two-dimensional sinc function used in the previous examples (arrays x, y, z) can be sampled at 150 irregularly spaced pseudo-random points:

```
IDL> xindex = randomu(-100L, 150) * 40.0
IDL> yindex = randomu(-200L, 150) * 40.0
IDL> xran = x[xindex, 0]
IDL> yran = y[0, yindex]
IDL> zran = z[xindex, yindex]
IDL> help, xran, yran, zran
XRAN            FLOAT     = Array[150]
YRAN            FLOAT     = Array[150]
ZRAN            FLOAT     = Array[150]
```

To show the distribution of data points, the location of each point can be plotted on a two-dimensional grid:

```
IDL> plot, xran, yran, psym=1
```

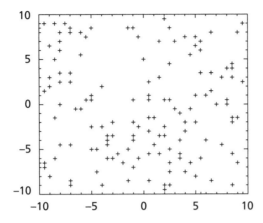

The triangulate procedure and trigrid function allow the data set to be resampled to a regular grid using the Delaunay triangulation method:

```
IDL> triangulate, xran, yran, triangles
IDL> zgrid = trigrid(xran, yran, zran, triangles, $
IDL>    xgrid=xgrid, ygrid=ygrid)
IDL> surface, zgrid, xgrid, ygrid, charsize=1.5
```

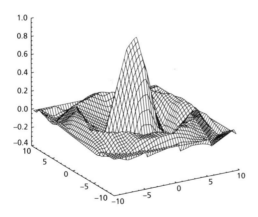

The triangulate procedure computes a list of triangles, and the trigrid function uses this information to compute the resampled data set by interpolation. By default, linear interpolation is used to produce a grid of dimensions 51 by 51 that spans the input *x*- and *y*-coordinates. The trigrid keywords xgrid and ygrid return vectors of *x*- and *y*-ordinates for the interpolated data.

To customize the grid spacing and limits of the interpolated data, tri-grid accepts two optional arguments. The spacing argument is a two-element vector specifying the grid spacing in the *x* and *y* directions. The limits argument is a four-element vector specifying the grid limits in the form [*xmin, ymin, xmax, ymax*]. In addition, smooth interpolation using quintic polynomials can be specified by setting the quintic keyword:

```
IDL> spacing = [0.2, 0.2]
IDL> limits = [-10.0, -10.0, 10.0, 10.0]
IDL> zgrid = trigrid(xran, yran, zran, triangles, $
IDL>    spacing, limits, $
IDL>    xgrid=xgrid, ygrid=ygrid, /quintic)
IDL> surface, zgrid, xgrid, ygrid, charsize=1.5
```

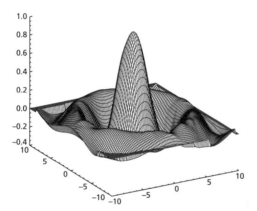

Even with a finer grid spacing and quintic interpolation, the resampled data set zgrid is not as smooth as the original two-dimensional data set because of the limited number of irregularly spaced points defining zran. In real-world applications, be sure to examine the resampled data set carefully for artifacts that may be introduced by the resampling.

Shaded Surface Plots

The shade_surf procedure renders a shaded surface for two-dimensional data sets defined on regular grids. The general syntax for shade_surf is

```
shade_surf, z, x, y
```

where z is a two-dimensional array, and x and y are optional vectors or arrays specifying regularly spaced ordinate values on the *x*- and *y*-axes (if x and y are not passed, the *x*- and *y*-axes are simply element numbers). If x and y are two-dimensional arrays, each element of x describes the *x*-axis location of the corresponding element in z, and each element of y describes the *y*-axis location of the corresponding element of z:

```
IDL> shade_surf, z, x, y, charsize=1.5
```

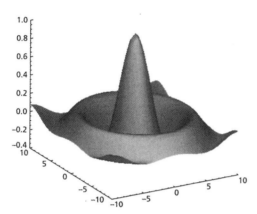

The most commonly used keywords accepted by the shade_surf procedure are listed in Table 6.13; for the complete list of keywords supported by shade_surf, see the online help. The shade_surf procedure also

Table 6.13 Commonly used shade_surf **keywords.**

Keyword	Purpose
az	Angle of rotation about *z*-axis* (counterclockwise, default 30 degrees)
ax	Angle of rotation about *x*-axis (counterclockwise, default 30 degrees)
shades	Color index for each *z*-level[†] (default: highest color table index)
image	Return the shaded surface as an image
pixels	Maximum image size in pixels[‡] (default: defined by graphics window)
min_value	Minimum data value to plot (default: data minimum)
max_value	Maximum data value to plot (default: data maximum)
/zlog	Create logarithmic *z*-axis (default; create linear *z*-axis)

* Plot is rotated about *z*-axis first, then *x*-axis.

[†] See the previous section on mesh surface plots for an example.

[‡] Only applies to graphics devices with scalable pixels. Of the most commonly used graphics devices, only the PostScript and CGM devices have scalable pixels.

accepts all plot customization keywords listed in Table 6.5 except for `linestyle`, `noerase`, `psym`, and `symsize`. In addition, `shade_surf` accepts all axis customization keywords listed in Table 6.6.

A shaded surface can be a useful way to visualize a two-dimensional data set that is not a smoothly varying function. To demonstrate, a surface elevation example data set is loaded and displayed as a shaded surface:

```
IDL> restore, filepath('marbells.dat', subdir='examples/data')
IDL> help, elev
ELEV            INT        = Array[360, 460]
IDL> loadct, 0
IDL> shade_surf, elev, charsize=1.5
```

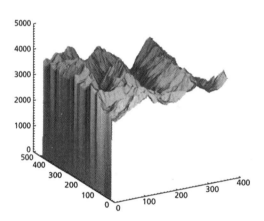

In this data set, zero indicates a missing value. The surface is generated over the entire data range by default, and a curtain is seen on the left where zero values exist in the elevation data. The optional `min_value` keyword can be used to specify the lower bound for data to be rendered, but first a suitable minimum value must be found:

```
IDL> min_value = min(elev)
IDL> min_index = where(elev gt 0, min_count)
IDL> if (min_count gt 0) then $
IDL>   min_value = min(elev[min_index])
IDL> help, min_value
MIN_VALUE       INT        =     2666
IDL> shade_surf, elev, min_value=min_value, charsize=1.5
```

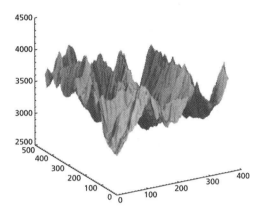

First a default minimum value (min_value) is set. Then where is called to return the indices (min_index) of elements with values greater than zero. If one or more indices were found, then the minimum elevation greater than zero is found. Finally shade_surf is called to render the surface.

Tip   When PostScript output is selected, shade_surf plots may appear jagged or pixelated. This occurs because the surface is rendered as an image, and the default number of image pixels is often too small on the PS (Post-Script) device. To remedy this problem, the optional shade_surf keyword pixels may be used to specify the maximum size (e.g., pixels=1000) of the rendered image in pixels. This keyword is honored on graphics devices that have scalable pixels (notably the PS and CGM devices) and is ignored on all other graphics devices.

The usual axis keywords (xrange, xstyle, xtitle, etc.) can be used to customize the axes of a shaded surface. In the following example, latitude and longitude vectors are defined for the elevation data set, and the *z*-axis is scaled to provide a more realistic view of the elevation data:

```
IDL> lon = (findgen(360) / 359.0) * 7.0 - 90.0
IDL> lat = (findgen(460) / 459.0) * 5.0 + 35.0
IDL> shade_surf, elev, lon, lat, min_value=min_value, $
IDL>   zrange=[0, 7000], zstyle=1, charsize=1.5
```

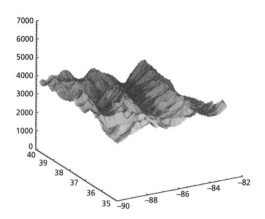

Combined Mesh and Shaded Surface Plots

Combined mesh and shaded surface plots can be created by calling shade_surf and surface in sequence. The two-dimensional sinc function defined at the beginning of this section is used as an example:

```
IDL> loadcolors
IDL> bottom = 16
IDL> loadct, 33, bottom=bottom
IDL> shades = bytscl(z, top=(!d.table_size - 1 - bottom)) + $
IDL>   byte(bottom)
IDL> shade_surf, z, x, y, /save, shades=shades, $
IDL>   background=7, color=0, charsize=1.5
IDL> position = [!x.window[0], !y.window[0], $
IDL>   !x.window[1], !y.window[1]]
IDL> surface, z, x, y, position=position, $
IDL>   /t3d, /noerase, /upper_only, $
IDL>   xstyle=4, ystyle=4, zstyle=4, color=0
```

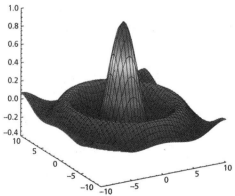

Graphics colors are loaded in the lowest 16 color table entries by calling loadcolors, and the "Blue-Red" color table is loaded in the remaining color table entries by calling loadct. An array of color shade indices is created by calling bytscl. The shaded surface is plotted by calling shade_surf, with the save keyword set to save the axis-scaling transformation, and the shades keyword specifying the color shade indices for the surface. Then the position of the shaded surface is saved in the vector position. Finally the mesh overlay is plotted by calling surface, with the position keyword specifying the same position as the previous shaded surface; the t3d keyword set to use the existing axis-scaling transformation; the noerase keyword set to not erase the shaded surface; the upper_only keyword set to plot a mesh on the top surface only; and the xstyle, ystyle, and zstyle keywords set to suppress drawing the *x*-, *y*-, and *z*-axes.

Tip   Struan Gray has produced an informative guide to plotting surfaces in IDL, including how to create transparency effects and intersecting surfaces. See Appendix A for details.

6.9   MAPPING

Map projections may be defined in IDL Direct Graphics. When a map projection is in effect, the data coordinates for the current graphics window or device correspond to longitude (*x*-axis) and latitude (*y*-axis) in fractional degrees, and the oplot, plots, xyouts, and contour procedures plot in terms of longitude and latitude. Continental outlines and map grids can also be overplotted. Longitudes in IDL range from –180W to +180E, with Greenwich at 0 degrees. Latitudes range from –90S at the South Pole to +90N at the North Pole, with the equator at 0 degrees.

Creating a Map Projection

The map_set procedure establishes a map projection for the current graphics window or device. The general syntax for map_set is

```
map_set, lat, lon, rot
```

where lat and lon are the latitude and longitude in degrees at the center of the projection, and rot is the clockwise rotation of the map projection in degrees. If lat and lon are not supplied, the default latitude and longitude is (0, 0). If rot is not supplied, the default rotation is zero. The default projection is cylindrical equidistant and spans the entire Earth:

```
IDL> map_set
IDL> map_continents
```

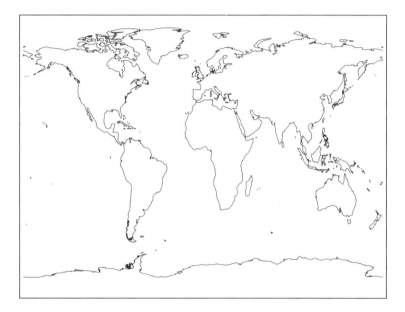

The default behavior of map_set is to erase the display and draw a border around the edges of the map. The map_continents procedure is called in this example to plot low-resolution continental outlines. To select a different projection center, lat and lon arguments are passed:

```
IDL> map_set, 0, 135
IDL> map_continents
```

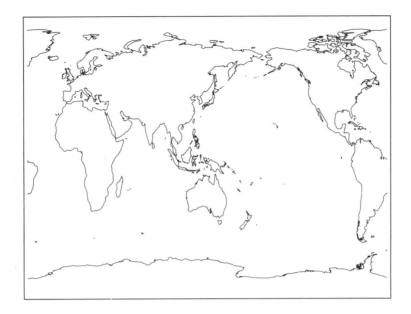

When map_set is called, a new set of data coordinates is established. Subsequent calls to plotting procedures such as oplot, plots, xyouts, and contour will use the map coordinates (longitude is *x*, latitude is *y*) until either a new map projection is established or a new set of data coordinates is established by calling plot, axis, contour, surface or shade_surf. If you select a graphics window with a different size, or another graphics device (e.g., PostScript), you must re-establish the map projection by calling map_set.

For example, to plot 100 random locations on a map projection:

```
IDL> lon = randomu(-100L, 100) * 360.0 - 180.0
IDL> lat = randomu(-200L, 100) * 180.0 - 90.0
IDL> map_set, /aitoff, /horizon
IDL> map_continents
IDL> oplot, lon, lat, psym=1
```

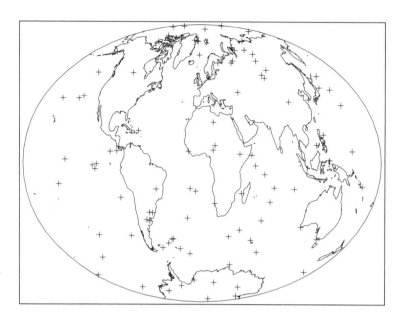

In this example, map_set was called to create an Aitoff projection with a horizon plotted. Then oplot was called to plot a symbol at each random location. Note how longitude is plotted in the *x* direction, and latitude is plotted in the *y* direction.

Tip   To check whether a map projection is in effect, the system variable !x.type may be examined. If the value of !x.type is 3, then a map projection exists.

Configuring a Map Projection

In addition to the default cylindrical equidistant projection, the map_set procedure supports a number of other projections, as described in Table 6.14. A projection is selected by the appropriate keyword shown in the table.

The map_set procedure also accepts a number of keywords that configure other aspects of a map projection. The most commonly used key-

Table 6.14 `map_set` **projections.**

Keyword	Projection
`/aitoff`	Aitoff
`/albers`	Albers equal area conic
`/azimuthal`	Azimuthal equidistant
`/conic`	Lambert conformal conic*
`/cylindrical`	Cylindrical equidistant
`/goodeshomolosine`	Goode's Homolosine
`/gnomic`	Gnomic
`/hammer`	Hammer-Aitoff equal area
`/lambert`	Lambert azimuthal equal area
`/mercator`	Mercator
`/miller`	Miller cylindrical
`/mollweide`	Mollweide
`/orthographic`	Orthographic
`/robinson`	Robinson
`/satellite`	Satellite[†]
`/sinusoidal`	Sinusoidal
`/stereographic`	Stereographic
`/transverse_mercator`	Transverse Mercator*

* The Clarke 1866 ellipsoid is used for the Lambert conformal conic and transverse Mercator projections by default. The optional `map_set` keyword `ellipsoid` allows a custom ellipsoid to be defined; see the online help for details.

[†] The `map_set` keyword `sat_p` must be supplied when using the satellite projection; see the online help for details.

words accepted by `map_set` are listed in Table 6.15. For the complete list of keywords supported by `map_set`, see the online help.

In the following example, an orthographic projection centered on Southeast Asia is created:

```
IDL> map_set, 15, 110, /orthographic, /isotropic, /horizon
IDL> map_continents
IDL> map_grid
```

Table 6.15   Commonly used `map_set` **keywords.**

Keyword	Purpose
/isotropic	Set same map scale in x and y directions (default: scale map to fit window)
limit	Map projection limits* (default: whole Earth)
scale	Scale for isotropic map (default: scale to fit window)
position	Position for map projection in normal coordinates[†] (default: automatic)
xmargin	Margin at left and right edges in character units[‡] (default: automatic)
ymargin	Margin at bottom and top edges in character units[‡] (default: automatic)
title	String containing map title (default: no map title drawn)
charsize	Character size (default 1.0)
color	Character and border color (default: highest color table index)
/advance	Advance to next position in multipanel plot (default: erase window)
/noborder	Do not draw map border (default: draw map border)
/noerase	Do not erase window (default: erase window)
/continents	Plot low-resolution continent outlines (default: no outlines plotted)
/horizon	Plot horizon if applicable (default: no horizon plotted)

* A vector with four elements of the form [*latmin, lonmin, latmax, lonmax*], or a vector with eight elements of the form [$lat_0, lon_0, lat_1, lon_1, lat_2, lon_2, lat_3, lon_3$].

[†] A vector with four elements of the form [x_0, y_0, x_1, y_1].

[‡] A scalar margin value, or a vector with two elements specifying left/right or bottom/top margins.

The isotropic keyword causes the map projection to have an aspect ratio of 1.0, rather than the default behavior that adjusts the aspect ratio to fit the current display. Setting the horizon keyword causes a horizon to be plotted. The map_continents and map_grid procedures are called to plot low-resolution continent outlines and a map grid, respectively.

When the system variable !p.multi is used to create multipanel map projections, the map_set keyword advance must be used to advance to the next panel, as shown in the following example:

```
IDL> !p.multi = [0, 2, 2, 0, 0]
IDL> map_set, 0, 0, /aitoff, /advance, $
IDL>    title='Aitoff', $
IDL>    /horizon, /continents
IDL> map_set, -30, -70, /stereographic, /advance, $
IDL>    title='Stereographic', $
IDL>    /horizon, /continents, /isotropic
IDL> map_set, -90, 0, /orthographic, /advance, $
IDL>    title='Orthographic', $
IDL>    /horizon, /continents, /isotropic
IDL> map_set, 0, 0, /mercator, /advance, $
IDL>    title='Mercator', /continents
IDL> !p.multi = 0
```

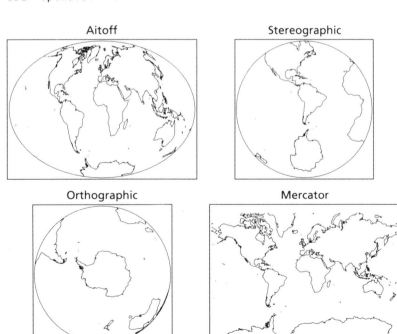

| Aitoff | Stereographic |
| Orthographic | Mercator |

Selecting Map Limits

Most map projections in IDL display the entire Earth by default. However, you can zoom in on a particular region in several ways. The first is via the map_set keyword scale, which sets the scale of the map projection relative to the size of the Earth. For example, to create a sinusoidal projection centered on North America at a scale of 1:75,000,000:

```
IDL> map_set, 45, -90, /sinusoidal, scale=75e6
IDL> map_continents
```

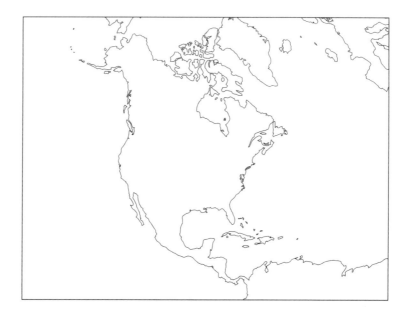

Note how the map projection fills the entire graphics display. A particular scale value will create a map at the same scale regardless of the size of the graphics window. This feature is particularly useful for creating map projections of different regions of the Earth at a consistent scale, such as in the following illustration of the relative sizes of the Australian and North American continents:

```
IDL> map_set, -25, 135, /lambert, scale=100e6, $
IDL>    position=[0, 0, 0.5, 1.0]
IDL> map_continents
IDL> map_set, 45, -90, /lambert, scale=100e6, $
IDL>    position=[0.5, 0.0, 1.0, 1.0], /noerase
IDL> map_continents
```

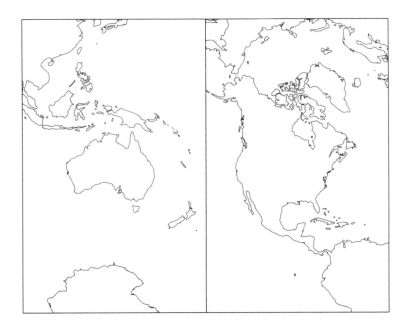

Another method for specifying map projection limits uses the map_set keyword limit to define the edges or corners of the projection. For example, to create a Lambert projection containing Greenland:

```
IDL> map_set, 72.5, -45, /lambert, /isotropic, $
IDL>   limit=[55, -75, 90, -15]
IDL> map_continents
```

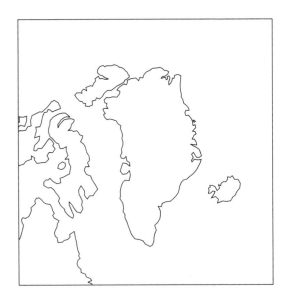

In this example, limit defines the minimum latitude (+55N), minimum longitude (−75W), maximum latitude (+90N), and maximum longitude (−15W) for the map projection. The projection in this case does not necessarily fill the entire display, and the map scale depends on the display size and limits chosen. Thus if the display size changes, the map scale changes as well.

Continental Outlines

The map_continents procedure plots continental outlines on map projections. Low-resolution coastline data is used by default, which is often sufficient for large-scale map projections. However, high-resolution coastline data containing finer detail can be added during the initial installation of IDL.

For example, the low-resolution coastline data for Florida and the Bahamas is shown below:

```
IDL> map_set, 27.5, -82.0, /lambert, scale=10e6
IDL> map_continents
```

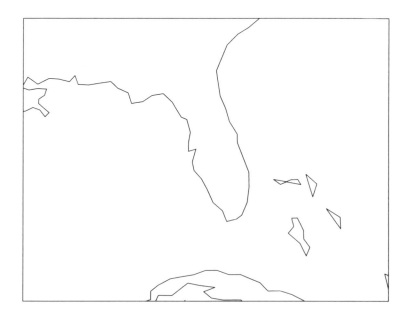

To view the high-resolution continental outlines, use the map_continents keywords hires and coasts:

```
IDL> erase
IDL> map_continents, /hires, /coasts
```

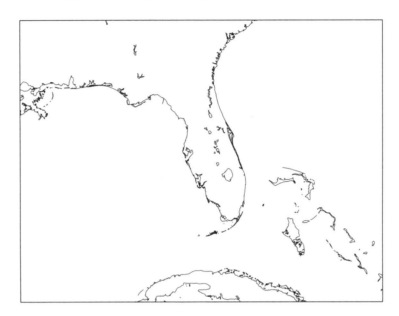

Note that both coastlines and inland lakes are drawn in this case. Be warned that over certain land areas (e.g., North America) thousands of lakes will be drawn, which can take a significant amount of time. If you prefer to just see the high-resolution continental outlines without lakes or small islands, use the `hires` keyword only. The most commonly used `map_continents` keywords are listed in Table 6.16.

Table 6.16   **Commonly used** `map_continents` **keywords.**

Keyword	Purpose
`color`	Color index for continental outlines or fills
`/coasts`	Plot coastlines including islands and lakes
`/countries`	Plot world political boundaries (as of 1993)
`/fill_continents`	Fill continental outlines
`/hires`	Plot high-resolution continental outlines
`/usa`	Plot state outlines in the United States

Tip   If high-resolution coastline data are not installed, a warning message appears when the map_continents keyword hires is used. High-resolution coastline data may be added to an existing IDL installation by running the IDL installer from CD-ROM and selecting "Custom Installation".

Map Grid Lines

The map_grid procedure plots grid lines on map projections. The default is to draw grid lines with the latitude and longitude grid spacing determined automatically:

```
IDL> map_set, 50, 10, /lambert, scale=25e6
IDL> map_continents, /hires
IDL> map_continents, /countries, /hires
IDL> map_grid, label=1
```

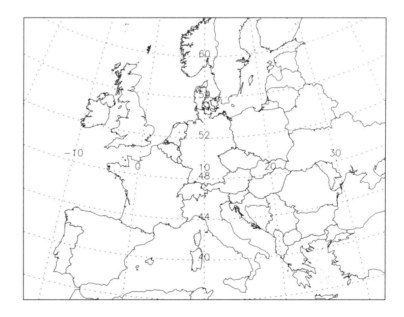

In this example, latitude parallels are drawn at 4-degree intervals, and longitude meridians are drawn at 10-degree intervals.

The default behavior of map_grid may be modified by a number of keywords, as shown in Table 6.17, which lists the most commonly used map_grid keywords.

If the map projection extends to the edges of the map border on all sides, then a box-style map grid may be drawn around the edges of the projection by setting the box_axes keyword. In the following example, a box-style grid is drawn, and custom latitude and longitude intervals are specified by the using the map_grid keywords latdel and londel:

```
IDL> map_set, 50, 10, /lambert, scale=25e6, $
IDL>   xmargin=[2, 2], ymargin=[2, 4], $
IDL>    title='Western and Central Europe!C'
IDL> map_continents, /hires
IDL> map_continents, /countries, /hires
IDL> map_grid, /box, latdel=5, londel=5, charsize=0.75
```

Table 6.17   Commonly used map_grid **keywords.**

Keyword	Purpose
/box_axes	Draw box-style lat/lon grid
charsize	Character size (default 1.0)
color	Color index for grid lines (default: highest color table index)
glinestyle	Grid linestyle* (0–5, default 1)
glinethick	Grid line thickness (default 1)
/label	Grid labeling flag[+] (default: no grid labels)
latalign	Latitude label alignment (0.0 = left, 0.5 = center, 1.0 = right, default 0.5)
latdel	Latitude grid increment in degrees (default: automatic)
latlab	Longitude at which latitude labels are drawn (default: center)
lats	Array of user-specified latitude grid values
lonalign	Longitude label alignment (0.0 = left, 0.5 = center, 1.0 = right, default 0.5)
londel	Longitude grid increment in degrees (default: automatic)
lonlab	Latitude at which longitude labels are drawn (default: center)
lons	Array of user-specified longitude grid values

* Grid linestyle codes correspond to the linestyle codes shown in Table 6.5.

[+] If label is set (i.e., /label), every grid line is labeled. If label is set to an integer *n*, every *n*th grid line is labeled.

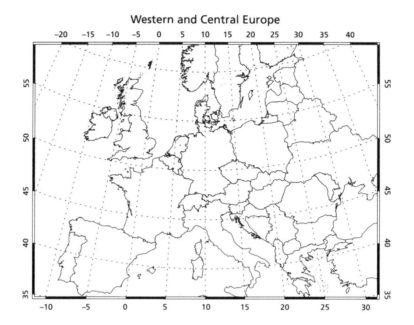

First, the map projection is created by calling map_set, with the xmargin and ymargin keywords used to leave room for a title and the grid labels. The title string has a carriage-return font positioning code appended (!C) to leave room for grid labels along the top of the projection border. Continental outlines and political boundaries are plotted at high-resolution by calling map_continents. Finally, a grid is plotted by calling map_grid with latitude and longitude intervals set to 5 degrees, and character size set to 0.75 for the grid labels.

Contour Plots on Map Projections

The contour procedure may be used to plot contours on a map projection. As an example, the simulated total ozone data set described in Section 6.7 is recreated:

```
IDL> z = randomu(-100L, 50, 50)
IDL> for i = 0, 4 do z = smooth(z, 15, /edge)
IDL> z = (z - min(z)) * 15000.0 + 100.0
IDL> x = findgen(50) - 100.0
IDL> y = findgen(50) + 10.0
```

Then a map projection is created, and the contours are plotted:

```
IDL> map_set, 35.0, -75.0, /mercator, scale=50e6
IDL> map_continents
IDL> map_grid
IDL> levels = [150, 200, 250, 300, 350, 400, 450, 500]
IDL> c_labels = [0, 1, 0, 1, 0, 1, 0, 1]
IDL> contour, z, x, y, levels=levels, c_labels=c_labels, $
IDL>    /overplot
```

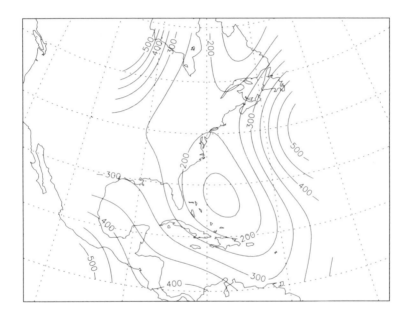

In this example, the x coordinate array contains longitude values ranging from −100 to −51 (100W to 51W), and the y coordinate array contains
latitude values ranging from 10 to 59 (10N to 59N). The map_set procedure is called to create a Mercator projection centered at 35N, −75W at a
scale of 1:50,000,000, and continents and gridlines are overlaid. Then contour is called to plot the contours of the atmospheric ozone data set
(note the use of the overplot keyword to force contour to use the existing
x- and y-axis scaling).

Likewise, filled contours can be plotted on a map projection, as
described in Section 6.8. The x- and y-coordinate vectors or arrays passed
to contour must be in ascending order when filled contours are plotted
on a map projection. First, the levels for color filling and labeling are
defined as shown in Section 6.8:

```
IDL> levels = [150, 200, 250, 300, 350, 400, 450, 500]
IDL> nlevels = n_elements(levels)
IDL> ncolors = nlevels + 1
IDL> bottom = 1
IDL> c_levels = [min(z), levels, max(z)]
IDL> c_labels = [0, replicate(1, nlevels), 0]
IDL> c_colors = indgen(ncolors) + bottom
IDL> loadct, 33, ncolors=ncolors, bottom=bottom
```

Then the map projection is created, filled contours are plotted, and contour lines are drawn (the contour keyword cell_fill is recommended when plotting filled contours on a map projection). Finally, continental outlines and a map grid are plotted:

```
IDL> map_set, 35.0, -75.0, /mercator, scale=50e6
IDL> contour, z, x, y, levels=c_levels, c_colors=c_colors, $
IDL>   /cell_fill, /overplot
IDL> contour, z, x, y, levels=c_levels, c_labels=c_labels, $
IDL>   /overplot
IDL> map_continents
IDL> map_grid
```

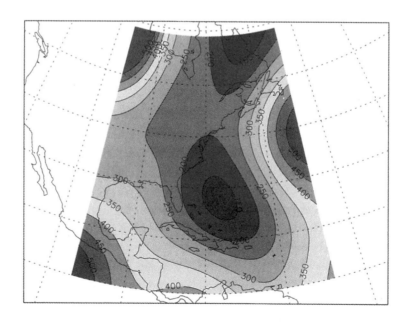

Displaying Regularly Gridded Images on Map Projections

The `map_image` function allows images defined on regular latitude and longitude grids to be displayed on map projections. The general syntax for `map_image` is

```
image = map_image(data, x0, y0, xsize, ysize)
```

where `data` is an input two-dimensional array defined on a regular geographic grid where longitude and latitude are in ascending order; `image` is an output two-dimensional array of data resampled to the map projection; and `x0`, `y0`, `xsize`, and `ysize` are output scalars that define the offset and size of the resampled array when it is displayed as an image. The input two-dimensional array is assumed to span the range −180W to +180E and −90S to +90N if no input range is specified.

For example, consider the following example data set that depicts global surface elevation:

```
IDL> openr, lun, filepath('worldelv.dat',$
IDL>    subdir='examples/data'), /get_lun
IDL> elev = bytarr(360, 360)
IDL> readu, lun, elev
IDL> free_lun, lun
IDL> elev = shift(elev, 180, 0)
IDL> tvscl, elev
```

The elevation data in `worldelv.dat` is defined on a longitude grid that starts at 0 degrees and proceeds eastward for 360 grid points spaced at 1-degree intervals. The `map_image` function requires that the grid not cross +180E, so `elev` is shifted along the first dimension to create a grid that spans the range −180W to +180E. Finally the elevation data is displayed by calling the `tvscl` procedure, which is discussed in more detail in the following chapter.

The next step is to create a map projection and resample the image to the map projection:

```
IDL> map_set, 20, 80, /orthographic, /isotropic, /noborder
IDL> image = map_image(elev, x0, y0, xsize, ysize)
IDL> tvscl, image, x0, y0, xsize=xsize, ysize=ysize
```

An orthographic map projection centered on the Indian subcontinent is created by calling `map_set` to provide a view of the Himalayas. Then `map_image` is called to compute the resampled image. The arguments `x0`, `y0`, `xsize`, and `ysize` are used by `tvscl` to correctly position and size the image.

The `map_image` function supports a number of optional keywords that allow the resampled image to be customized, as shown in Table 6.18.

The world elevation data can be resampled at a finer resolution using the keywords shown in Table 6.18:

```
IDL> map_set, 20, 80, /orthographic, /isotropic, /noborder
IDL> image = map_image(elev, x0, y0, xsize, ysize, $
IDL>    latmin=-90, lonmin=-180, latmax=90, lonmax=180, $
IDL>    compress=1, scale=0.05)
IDL> tvscl, image, x0, y0, xsize=xsize, ysize=ysize
```

```
IDL> color = !d.table_size - 1
IDL> map_continents, color=color
IDL> map_grid, color=color
```

Table 6.18   `map_image` **keywords.**

Keyword	Purpose
`lonmin`	Minimum longitude in input grid (default −180E)
`lonmax`	Maximum longitude in input grid (default +180W)
`latmin`	Minimum latitude in input grid (default −90S)
`latmax`	Maximum latitude in input grid (default +90S)
`compress`	Interpolation compression flag* (default 4)
`scale`	Scale factor for output image[†] (default 0.02)
`/bilinear`	Resample via bilinear interpolation (default: nearest neighbor)
`min_value`	Minimum data value to resample (default: data minimum)
`max_value`	Maximum data value to resample (default: data maximum)
`missing`	Value for missing pixels[‡] (default 0)

* When compress is set to n, the resampling is applied to every nth row and column in the input array. Setting `compress=1` produces the best results.

[†] Determines the resolution of the output image on graphics devices with scalable pixels (i.e., the PS and CGM devices). Setting `scale` to a higher value (e.g., 0.05) produces better results. This keyword is ignored on graphics devices that do not have scalable pixels.

[‡] Resampled image pixels outside the map projection boundaries or pixels that contain values outside the allowed range are set to the missing value. On the PostScript device, the default missing value is 255.

The latmin, lonmin, latmax, and lonmax keywords explicitly define the edges of the regular latitude and longitude grid on which elev is defined. The compress keyword causes every row and column to be resampled, and the scale keyword increases the resolution of the output image. Finally, the image is displayed by calling tvscl, and continent outlines and grid lines are overlaid by calling map_continents and map_grid.

Tip   The map_patch function may also be used to resample regularly gridded images to map projections; see the online help for details.

7

Displaying Images

Image display has long been a specialty of IDL. Few other data analysis environments offer the flexibility of IDL when it comes to reading, manipulating, and displaying digital images. This chapter begins with a definition of the two image types that can be displayed in IDL: PseudoColor and TrueColor. The built-in procedures available for displaying images are described, followed by a discussion of image scaling techniques, including histogram clipping and equalization. The chapter continues with a description of how images may be resized and positioned to fit the display. Methods for displaying TrueColor images are described next, followed by specialized instructions for displaying images on the PostScript and Printer graphics devices. Finally an IDL procedure is developed that builds on the ideas presented in the chapter and provides flexible and device-independent image display.

The images shown in this chapter are included in the IDL installation directory in a subdirectory named examples/data. To simplify reading these files, the following function named imdata is used throughout this chapter to load sample images:

```
FUNCTION IMDATA, FILE, NX, NY

;- Load an example image
openr, lun, filepath(file, subdir='examples/data'), /get_lun
image = bytarr(nx, ny)
readu, lun, image
```

```
free_lun, lun
return, image

END
```

IMAGE FUNDAMENTALS

There are two basic types of images that may be displayed in IDL: Pseudo-Color and TrueColor. PseudoColor images are associated with a color table that defines the color displayed for each image pixel. TrueColor images combine red, green, and blue intensities for each image pixel to determine the color displayed. IDL is equally adept at displaying each image type, regardless of the output graphics device.

There is necessarily some overlap between the description of image types in this chapter and the description of display modes and color models in Chapter 5. However, it is important to realize that regardless of the display mode, color model, or graphics device used by IDL, an image is simply a representation of a two-dimensional scene that takes the form of an array in memory. The purpose of this chapter is to describe how images of different types may be displayed on IDL graphics devices, taking into account any differences between the abstract representation of the image in memory and the physical characteristics of the display device.

PseudoColor Images

PseudoColor images are two-dimensional arrays with dimensions of the form [*nx, ny*] where *nx* is the number of columns and *ny* is the number of rows. PseudoColor image arrays may be of any numeric data type; however, only 8-bit `byte` representations may be displayed. If the native data type of the image is not `byte`, scaling to `byte` type is required to display the image. The scaling may be done automatically by IDL, or it may be done manually.

PseudoColor images are displayed using the Indexed color model described in Chapter 5. That is, the 8-bit intensity for each element in the image array is an index that points to an entry in the color table. For example, an 8-bit intensity value of zero points to the first entry in the color table. If the first entry in the color table contains the Red/Green/Blue triplet (255, 0, 0), array elements with a value of zero will be displayed as red. Grayscale images are a special case of PseudoColor images, where the color table contains only black, white, and shades of gray. Each element in such an image represents a grayscale intensity where the minimum intensity is black, the maximum intensity is white, and values in between represent shades of gray.

Note PseudoColor images may be displayed on the WIN, MAC, and X graphics devices when IDL is running in either 8-bit or 24-bit display mode. However, if IDL is running in 24-bit display mode, Decomposed Color must be turned off, as explained in Chapter 5. PseudoColor images may also be displayed on the CGM, PCL, PRINTER, PS, and Z graphics devices.

TrueColor Images

TrueColor images are three-dimensional arrays with dimensions of the form [3, *nx*, *ny*], [*nx*, 3, *ny*], or [*nx*, *ny*, 3] where *nx* is the number of columns, *ny* is the number of rows, and the remaining dimension contains the red, green, and blue (RGB) image components. TrueColor image arrays may be of any numeric data type; however, only 8-bit byte representations may be displayed. Scaling to byte type is usually required if the native data type is not byte.

TrueColor images are displayed using the Decomposed color model described in Chapter 5. The color displayed for each element in the image is determined by the additive mixture of 8-bit intensities in the red, green, and blue channels.

Note TrueColor images may be displayed on the WIN, MAC, and X graphics devices when IDL is running in 24-bit display mode. If IDL is running in 8-bit mode, TrueColor images must be converted to PseudoColor form to be displayed on these devices. TrueColor images may also be displayed on the PRINTER and PS devices. However, TrueColor images must be converted to PseudoColor form in order to be displayed on the CGM, PCL, and Z graphics devices.

7.2   IMAGE DISPLAY ROUTINES

The `tv` and `tvscl` procedures are used to display images in IDL. Both these procedures can display either PseudoColor or TrueColor images. The first line and element of the image array is displayed in the bottom-left corner of the screen by default, and subsequent rows are displayed from the bottom up. When displaying images in graphics windows, each element in the image array is displayed as one pixel on the screen.

Displaying Unscaled Images: `tv`

The `tv` procedure displays images as though the image array were converted directly to `byte` values without scaling. The syntax for `tv` is

```
tv, image, [x0], [y0], [keywords]
```

where `image` is the image array to be displayed, `x0` and `y0` are optional arguments specifying the horizontal and vertical offset of the first image pixel from the lower-left corner of the display (the default is 0, 0), and *keywords* are optional keywords. If the image array is not `byte` type, it is displayed as though the array were converted to `byte` type, and only the least significant 8 bits were displayed. The displayed image values are clipped to the range `zero` to `!d.table_size - 1`.

For example, a PseudoColor image of a hurricane with a maximum intensity of 100 may be created from the sample image `hurric.dat` as follows:

```
IDL> hurric = imdata('hurric.dat', 440, 340)
IDL> maxval = max(hurric)
IDL> hurric = hurric * (100.0 / maxval)
IDL> print, min(hurric), max(hurric)
      18.5185       100.000
```

To display this image in shades of gray:

```
IDL> window, /free, xsize=440, ysize=340
IDL> loadct, 0
IDL> tv, hurric
```

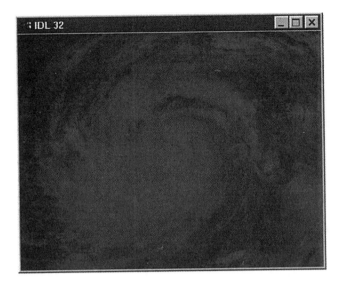

The loadct command loads the grayscale color table, and the tv command displays the image. On most IDL displays, the image will appear dark because tv simply maps the image values directly to indices in the color table. Thus, in this example, color indices 18B to 100B are used to display the image. To enhance the image contrast, the image values must be scaled to span the entire range of color table indices.

Displaying Scaled Images: tvscl

The tvscl procedure displays images as though the image array were converted to linearly scaled byte values that span the entire range of color table indices (zero to !d.table_size - 1). The syntax for tvscl is

tvscl, image, [x0], [y0], [*keywords*]

where image is the image array to be displayed, x0 and y0 are optional arguments specifying the horizontal and vertical offset of the first image pixel from the lower-left corner of the display (the default is 0, 0), and *keywords* are optional keywords.

To display a scaled version of the PseudoColor hurricane image from the previous example in shades of gray:

```
IDL> window, /free, xsize=440, ysize=340
IDL> loadct, 0
IDL> tvscl, hurric
```

This image is noticeably brighter than the previous image that was displayed using `tv` because `tvscl` linearly maps the minimum array value to the lowest index in the color table (`0B`) and the maximum array value to the highest index in the color table (`!d.table_size - 1`). By using the entire color table, the image contrast is enhanced. The only drawback of `tvscl` is that you cannot specify the range of input data values to be scaled; it always uses minimum to maximum.

To display a color image, simply load a different color table:

```
IDL> loadct, 1
IDL> tvscl, hurric
```

On most IDL systems, this produces a color image in shades of blue. If a grayscale image is displayed on your system, then IDL is running in 24-bit mode with Decomposed Color mode active. You must turn off Decomposed Color mode to display a PseudoColor image:

```
IDL> device, decomposed=0
IDL> tvscl, hurric
```

To highlight either the brightest or darkest areas of an image, the > or < operators may be used:

```
IDL> tvscl, hurric > 150
IDL> tvscl, hurric < 150
```

Bottom-up versus Top-down Display

By default, tv and tvscl display the first row of an image array at the bottom of the graphics display, and subsequent rows are displayed going up the display. The system variable !order controls this behavior. Setting !order to 0 (the default) causes images to be displayed in bottom-up orientation, and setting !order to 1 causes images to be displayed in top-down orientation.

Both tv and tvscl support the optional keyword order, which overrides the value of !order. Setting the keyword order=0 means bottom-up image display, and order=1 means top-down image display, regardless of the value of !order. When writing an IDL application, it is best to use the order keyword explicitly (use zero as the default) when calling tv or tvscl so that no particular value for !order is assumed. Remember that system variables like !order are global in scope and can potentially be changed by other applications in your IDL session.

Keywords for tv and tvscl

The most commonly used keywords accepted by the tv and tvscl procedures are listed in Table 7.1.

Table 7.1   Commonly used tv and tvscl keywords.

Keyword	Purpose
order	Set display order (0 = bottom up, 1 = top down)
xsize	Set width of displayed image* (default units: pixels)
ysize	Set height of displayed image (default units: pixels)
true	Set dimension of RGB components[†] (1 = first, 2 = second, 3 = third)
channel	Set display channel (1 = red, 2 = green, 3 = blue)

* The xsize and ysize keywords are explained in more detail in Section 7.6. These keywords are recognized only when the PS or PRINTER graphics devices are selected and are otherwise ignored.
[†] The true and channel keywords are explained in more detail in Section 7.5.

7.3   CUSTOMIZING IMAGE SCALING

Eventually you will need to exert finer control over the way an image is scaled. For example, you may wish to specify the range of image values to be scaled, rather than accepting the default behavior of tvscl, which scales from minimum to maximum value. In addition, you may wish to specify the range of color indices used to display the image.

Image Scaling via bytscl

The bytscl function returns a linearly scaled byte version of an input array. The syntax for bytscl is

```
image = bytscl(array, [keywords])
```

where array is the array of image data (which may be of any numeric type), and image is the resulting scaled byte array. The bytscl function accepts the optional keywords listed in Table 7.2.

To compare tvscl and bytscl, the following example shows scaled images of a human brain X ray (see Figure 7.1):

```
IDL> cereb = imdata('cereb.dat', 512, 512)
IDL> loadct, 0
IDL> window, /free, xsize=512, ysize=512
IDL> tvscl, cereb
IDL> tv, bytscl(cereb, min=100, max=240, $
IDL>    top=(!d.table_size - 1))
```

Figure 7.1 (b) shows higher contrast than Figure 7.1 (a) because bytscl was used to scale the input image over the range 100 to 240, rather than

Table 7.2   Optional bytscl **keywords.**

Keyword	Purpose
min	Set minimum input value to be scaled* (default: data minimum)
max	Set maximum input value to be scaled[†] (default: data maximum)
top	Set top color index for result[‡] (default: 255B)
/nan	Exclude IEEE NaN values (default: NaN values are included)

* The result is set to 0B where input array values are less than or equal to min.
[†] The result is set to top where input array values are greater than or equal to max.
[‡] The bottom color index value in the result is always 0B.

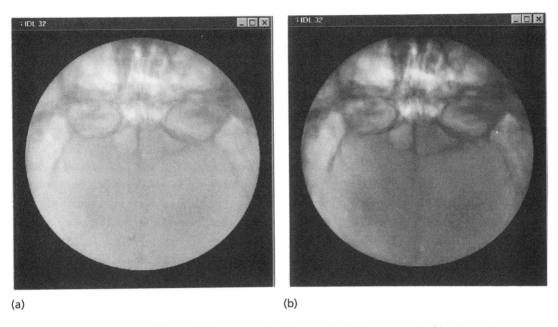

(a)   (b)

Figure 7.1 Human brain X ray: (a) image scaled by `tvscl`**; (b) image scaled by** `bytscl`**.**

minimum to maximum. The `min` and `max` keywords specify the range of input data values to be scaled. Image values between `min` and `max` are linearly mapped to output `byte` values in the range `0B` to `top`. The `min` and `max` keywords can also be used individually to set either the minimum or maximum input value. Only the `bytscl` procedure allows you to specify the input data range for image scaling; neither `tv` nor `tvscl` offers this feature. Consequently `bytscl` is often preferable for custom image scaling.

Tip   To display images that have been previously scaled with `bytscl`, use the `tv` procedure instead of the `tvscl` procedure; otherwise you run the risk of negating your customized image scaling.

In addition to specifying the input data scaling range, it is also sometimes desirable to specify the range of color indices for the scaled `byte` image. The `bytscl` function provides the `top` keyword for this purpose, but always sets the bottom color index to `0B`. The following technique allows both the bottom color table index and the number of color table indices to be specified:

```
IDL> bottom = 16
IDL> ncolors = 64
IDL> loadct, 0, bottom=bottom, ncolors=ncolors
IDL> tv, bytscl(cereb, min=100, max=240, $
IDL>    top=(ncolors - 1)) + byte(bottom)
```

In this example, the variables `bottom` and `ncolors` specify the bottom index in the color table and the number of color table indices, respectively. Then the grayscale color table is loaded into the specified color table indices, and the scaled image is displayed. The scaled image values are "shifted" into the desired range of color table indices by adding the `bottom` value (the conversion to `byte` ensures the type of the scaled image is not changed inadvertently).

This technique is useful enough to encapsulate in a wrapper for the `bytscl` function. The following function named `imscale` returns a scaled `byte` version of an input image array. The optional keyword `range` is a vector with two elements that specifies the minimum and maximum input array value to be used for scaling. The optional keywords `bottom` and `ncolors` specify the bottom color table index and number of colors for the scaled image, respectively.

```
FUNCTION IMSCALE, IMAGE, RANGE=RANGE, $
  BOTTOM=BOTTOM, NCOLORS=NCOLORS

;- Check arguments
if (n_params() ne 1) then $
  message, 'Usage: RESULT = IMSCALE(IMAGE)'
if (n_elements(image) eq 0) then $
  message, 'Argument IMAGE is undefined'

;- Check keywords
if (n_elements(range) eq 0) then begin
  min_value = min(image, max=max_value)
  range = [min_value, max_value]
endif
if (n_elements(bottom) eq 0) then bottom = 0B
if (n_elements(ncolors) eq 0) then $
  ncolors = !d.table_size - bottom

;- Return the scaled image
```

```
scaled = bytscl(image, min=range[0], max=range[1], $
  top=(ncolors - 1)) + byte(bottom)
return, scaled

END
```

First, the input arguments are checked. If the range variable does not exist, it is created by finding the input array minimum and maximum. If the bottom or ncolors variables do not exist, they are assigned default values. Finally, bytscl is called to create the scaled byte image, which is returned to the caller. To recreate the scaled image from the previous example:

```
IDL> tv, imscale(cereb, range=[100, 240], $
IDL>    bottom=bottom, ncolors=ncolors)
```

Color Table Splitting

The technique of using different parts of the color table for different purposes is known as *color table splitting*. For example, you may wish to reserve some entries in the color table for plotting titles, axes, or contours on top of an image, or you may wish to display multiple images in the same graphics window where each image has its own color table. In the following example, the lowest 16 entries in the color table are reserved for plotting colors, and the rest of the color table is used for displaying an image of the M51 galaxy:

```
IDL> galaxy = imdata('m51.dat', 340, 440)
IDL> loadcolors
IDL> bottom = 16
IDL> loadct, 0, bottom=bottom
IDL> window, /free
IDL> tv, imscale(galaxy, bottom=bottom)
```

First, the image array galaxy is loaded by calling imdata. Plotting colors are loaded in the first 16 color table indices by calling the loadcolors procedure described in Chapter 6. Then bottom is defined to specify the bottom color table index, and the grayscale color table is loaded by calling loadct. A new window is created by calling window, and the scaled image is computed by calling imscale and displayed by calling tv. The output image is thus scaled over the range 16B to !d.table_size - 1, and the first 16 color table indices are reserved for plot overlays:

```
IDL> plots, [340/2, 350], [440/2, 240], $
IDL>    /device, color=1
IDL> xyouts, 350, 240, 'Center of the M51 galaxy', $
IDL>    /device, color=1
```

Displaying Multiple Images with Separate Color Tables

When IDL is running in 8-bit display mode, you can split the color table into sections to enable multiple images to be displayed with different color tables. For example, an image can be displayed with a grayscale color table using the first 64 entries in the color table:

```
IDL> ctscan = imdata('ctscan.dat', 256, 256)
IDL> window, /free, xsize=700, ysize=400
IDL> bottom = 0
IDL> ncolors = 64
IDL> loadct, 0, bottom=bottom, ncolors=ncolors
IDL> tv, imscale(ctscan, bottom=bottom, ncolors=ncolors)
```

A second image can be displayed with a rainbow color table using the next 64 entries in the color table:

```
IDL> hurric = imdata('hurric.dat', 440, 340)
IDL> bottom = 64
```

```
IDL> ncolors = 64
IDL> loadct, 13, bottom=bottom, ncolors=ncolors
IDL> tv, imscale(hurric, bottom=bottom, ncolors=ncolors), $
IDL>   300, 0
```

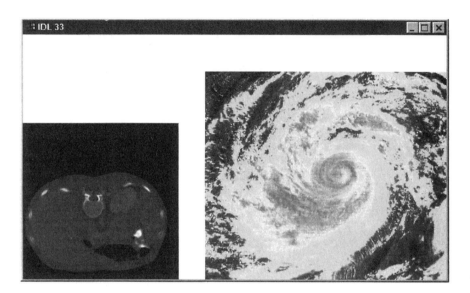

If IDL is running on a 24-bit display, it is not necessary to split the color table to display multiple images, because changing the color table on a 24-bit display does not affect any images that have been displayed previously. On a 24-bit display, the following method is used instead:

```
IDL> device, decomposed=0
IDL> loadct, 0
IDL> tv, imscale(ctscan)
IDL> loadct, 13
IDL> tv, imscale(hurric), 300, 0
```

Tip In this respect, the PS (PostScript) and PRINTER graphics devices act as though they are 24-bit displays, because changing the color table on these devices does not affect *previously* displayed images.

Histogram Clipping

When scaling an image, you must choose the range of image values to be mapped to scaled byte values. In many of the previous examples, the minimum and maximum image values were used by default for this purpose. However, if the image contains a few low or high values, the minimum or maximum value in the image may not give a good indication of the best scaling range for the image. One technique for determining the scaling range for an image is to examine the image histogram. To display the histogram of an X-ray image, the hist_plot procedure described in Chapter 6 is used:

```
IDL> cereb = imdata('cereb.dat', 512, 512)
IDL> hist_plot, cereb, /normal, /fill, xstyle=3, $
IDL>   title='X-Ray Histogram', $
IDL>   xtitle='Pixel Value', ytitle='Fraction of Pixels'
```

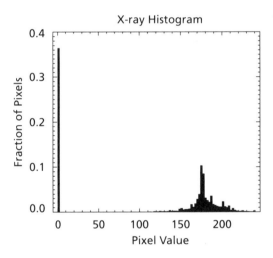

The histogram shows that most of the image values are in the range 125 to 225, with a spike at 0 indicating that a significant number of pixels have zero values. To find an appropriate scaling range automatically, the zero values must first be screened out. Then the histogram must be analyzed to determine where to set the scaling range endpoints. One technique for finding this range is known as *histogram clipping*, where a certain percentage of the total number of pixels are "clipped" from the upper and lower limits of the histogram. The clipped edges of the histogram then define the scaling range.

The following function (imclip) implements the histogram clipping technique. Given an input array image, it returns a two-element vector that specifies the scaling range for the input array. The optional keyword percent specifies the percentage of the total number of pixels to be clipped from the histogram edges (the default is 2 percent from either edge).

```
FUNCTION IMCLIP, IMAGE, PERCENT=PERCENT

;- Check arguments
if (n_params() ne 1) then $
  message, 'Usage: RESULT = IMCLIP(IMAGE)'
if (n_elements(image) eq 0) then $
  message, 'Argument IMAGE is undefined'

;- Check keywords
if (n_elements(percent) eq 0) then percent = 2.0

;- Get image minimum and maximum
min_value = min(image, max=max_value)

;- Compute histogram
nbins = 100
binsize = float(max_value - min_value) / float(nbins)
hist = histogram(float(image), binsize=binsize)
bins = lindgen(nbins + 1) * binsize + min_value

;- Compute normalized cumulative sum
sum = fltarr(n_elements(hist))
sum[0] = hist[0]
for i = 1L, n_elements(hist) - 1L do $
  sum[i] = sum[i - 1] + hist[i]
sum = 100.0 * (sum / float(n_elements(image)))

;- Find and return the range
range = [min_value, max_value]
index = where((sum ge percent) and $
  (sum le (100.0 - percent)), count)
if (count ge 2) then $
  range = [bins[index[0]], bins[index[count - 1]]]
return, range

END
```

First the input arguments are checked, and a default value is assigned for `percent` if required. The image minimum and maximum are obtained by calling `min`, and the image histogram is computed by calling `histogram`. Then the cumulative sum of the histogram is computed and is converted to a normalized percentage. Finally, the indices of image values that fall within the clipping range are found (the minimum and maximum image values are used if the search is unsuccessful).

Note   A loop is used to compute the cumulative sum in `imclip` to provide compatibility with all versions of IDL 5.x. In IDL 5.3 and higher versions, the `total` function may be used instead if the `cumulative` keyword is set.

To find the scaling range for the X ray image with zero values screened out, and then plot the range edges on the previous histogram:

```
IDL> index = where(cereb gt 0)
IDL> range = imclip(cereb[index])
IDL> print, range
      131.800      216.760
IDL> oplot, [range[0], range[0]], [0.0, 1.0], linestyle=2
IDL> oplot, [range[1], range[1]], [0.0, 1.0], linestyle=2
```

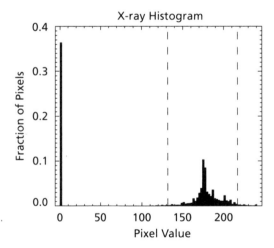

To display the scaled image, the output from `imclip` can be passed to `imscale` via the `range` keyword:

```
IDL> window, /free, xsize=512, ysize=512
IDL> tv, imscale(cereb, range=imclip(cereb[index]))
```

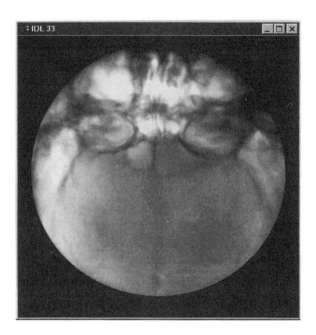

If you prefer less contrast in the image, you can adjust the clipping range via the percent keyword:

```
IDL> tv, imscale(cereb, range=imclip(cereb[index], $
IDL>   percent=1))
```

Histogram Equalization

Another method for increasing image contrast involves redistributing the intensities in the image histogram. This is accomplished by the hist_equal function, which has the following syntax:

```
result = hist_equal(image, [keywords])
```

where image is an array of image data (which may be of any numeric type), and result is a histogram-equalized byte image. For example, the X ray image shown in the previous example may be enhanced and displayed as follows:

```
IDL> tv, hist_equal(cereb, top=(!d.table_size - 1))
```

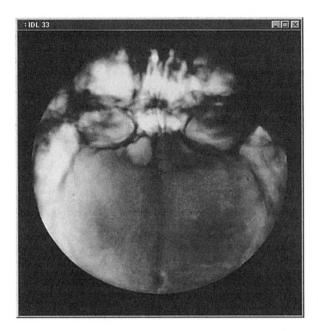

The keywords accepted by the hist_equal function are listed in Table 7.3. In addition, you may wish to try the h_eq_ct and h_eq_int procedures, which histogram-equalize the color table based on a subregion of an input image.

7.4   SIZING THE IMAGE TO FIT THE GRAPHICS DEVICE

In all the previous examples, you will have noticed that tv and tvscl assume a one-to-one correspondence between the elements of the image array and the pixels in a graphics window. This means that if the image array has 440 columns and 340 rows, the displayed image is 440 pixels wide and 340 pixels tall. However, it is often convenient to size an image to fit the current graphics window or device while maintaining the image aspect ratio (the ratio of height to width). Also, it is often desirable to center the image.

For window-based direct graphics devices such as the WIN, MAC, and X devices, the image itself is resized to fit the current graphics window, and is centered by specifying the offset from the bottom-left corner of the window. In the following example, a small image (size 256 by 256) of a

Table 7.3 Optional `hist_equal` **keywords.**

Keyword	Purpose
`minv`	Set minimum input value to consider* (default: 0)
`maxv`	Set maximum input value to consider[†] (default: data maximum)
`top`	Set top color index for result[‡] (default: 255B)
`binsize`	The bin size used when computing the histogram[§] (default: 1)

* The result is set to 0B where input array values are less than or equal to `minv`.

[†] The result is set to `top` where input array values are greater than or equal to `maxv`.

[‡] The bottom color index value in the result is always 0B.

[§] The `binsize` keyword is ignored when the input array is of `byte` type.

computed tomography scan is resized and offset for display in a larger graphics window (size 600 by 600):

```
IDL> ctscan = imdata('ctscan.dat', 256, 256)
IDL> image = congrid(ctscan, 500, 500)
IDL> window, /free, xsize=600, ysize=600
IDL> loadct, 0
IDL> x0 = 50
IDL> y0 = 50
IDL> tvscl, image, x0, y0
```

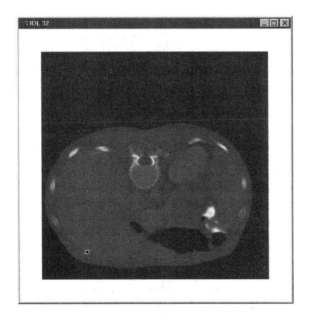

First, the image is read by calling `imdata` and then resized by calling `congrid`. Then `window` is called to create a graphics window slightly larger than the resized image. The grayscale color table is loaded by calling `loadct`, and the image is displayed by calling `tvscl`. The optional `tvscl` arguments `x0` and `y0` specify the horizontal and vertical offset of the displayed image from the bottom-left corner of the graphics window. In this example, the size of the graphics window and the size and offset of the displayed image were chosen to give the desired result. However, it is much more convenient to compute the size and offset required to make an image fit an existing graphics window (or other graphics device) of arbitrary size.

Tip   As mentioned in Section 2.12, the `congrid` function may not resize an array with sufficient accuracy for your purposes. If this is the case, you may wish to resize the image array via the `interpolate` function, using the technique described in "Resizing to Arbitrary Size with Customized Interpolation."

Computing Image Size and Offset Automatically

The following procedure named `imsize.pro` computes the offset (`x0, y0`) and size (`xsize, ysize`) required to make an image fit the current graphics window or device, while maintaining the original image aspect ratio. If a particular aspect ratio is desired, it may be specified via the optional `aspect` keyword. If a particular position is required, a four-element position vector may be specified via the optional `position` keyword. Finally, if the caller wishes to set a margin around the image, the optional `margin` keyword specifies the margin in normal coordinates (the default margin is 0.1). This procedure calls the `getpos` function described in Chapter 6.

```
PRO IMSIZE, IMAGE, X0, Y0, XSIZE, YSIZE, ASPECT=ASPECT, $
  POSITION=POSITION, MARGIN=MARGIN

;- Check arguments
if (n_params() ne 5) then $
  message, 'Usage: IMSIZE, IMAGE, X0, Y0, XSIZE, YSIZE'
if (n_elements(image) eq 0) then $
  message, 'Argument IMAGE is undefined'
```

```
if (n_elements(position) eq 0) then $
  position = [0.0, 0.0, 1.0, 1.0]
if (n_elements(margin) eq 0) then margin = 0.1

;- Get image dimensions
result = size(image)
ndims = result[0]
if (ndims ne 2) then message, 'IMAGE must be a 2D array'
dims = result[1 : ndims]

;- Get aspect ratio for image
if (n_elements(aspect) eq 0) then $
  aspect = float(dims[1]) / float(dims[0])

;- Get approximate image position
position = getpos(aspect, position=position, margin=margin)

;- Compute lower left position of image (device units)
x0 = round(position[0] * !d.x_vsize) > 0L
y0 = round(position[1] * !d.y_vsize) > 0L

;- Compute size of image (device units)
xsize = round((position[2] - position[0]) * !d.x_vsize) > 2L
ysize = round((position[3] - position[1]) * !d.y_vsize) > 2L

;- Recompute the image position based on actual image size
position[0] = x0 / float(!d.x_vsize)
position[1] = y0 / float(!d.y_vsize)
position[2] = (x0 + xsize) / float(!d.x_vsize)
position[3] = (y0 + ysize) / float(!d.y_vsize)

END
```

First, the input arguments are checked, and default values are assigned if necessary. The size function is called to obtain the dimensions (dims) of the input image, and the image aspect ratio (aspect) is computed (the ratio of height to width). The getpos function is called to compute an approximate position vector (position) for the image. The position vector is used to compute the image offset (x0, y0) and size (xsize, ysize) values for the current graphics window or device (recall that !d.x_vsize and !d.y_vsize represent the viewable width and height of the current graphics device). Finally, the position vector in normal coordinates is recomputed to take account of the rounding used in determining the offset and size.

To fit an image to a graphics window, the image offset and size values are computed and the image is resized for display:

```
IDL> window, /free
IDL> imsize, ctscan, x0, y0, xsize, ysize
IDL> image = congrid(ctscan, xsize, ysize)
IDL> loadct, 0
IDL> tvscl, image, x0, y0
```

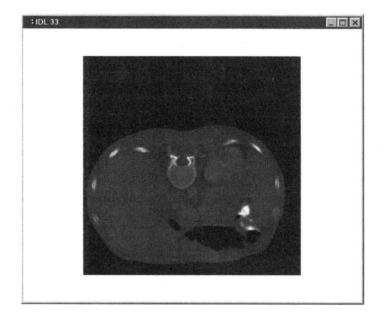

In this example, the congrid function is used to resize the image to the computed xsize and ysize values, and the x0 and y0 values are passed to tvscl to position the image correctly. As long as imsize is called whenever the size of the graphics display changes, the image will be sized to fit the display while maintaining aspect ratio.

Tip   The technique implemented in imsize.pro for computing image size and offset also works when the PS (PostScript) or PRINTER graphics devices are selected. However, on these devices the image itself is not resized. Rather, the size of the displayed image is specified with the xsize and ysize keywords that are accepted by tv and tvscl. See Section 7.6 for details.

7.5   DISPLAYING TRUECOLOR IMAGES

TrueColor images may be displayed by either the tv or tvscl procedures. If the current graphics device is the WIN, MAC, or X device in 24-bit display mode, then TrueColor images may be displayed directly by tv or tvscl without modification. TrueColor images may also be displayed when the PS or PRINTER graphics devices are selected. If the current graphics device is the WIN, MAC, or X device in 8-bit display mode, or graphics devices other than the PS or PRINTER devices, then TrueColor images must be quantized before they can be displayed by tv or tvscl.

The examples in this section use a TrueColor image of a rose:

```
IDL> file = filepath('rose.jpg', subdir='examples/data')
IDL> read_jpeg, file, rose
IDL> help, rose
IMAGE           BYTE      = Array[3, 227, 149]
```

Displaying TrueColor Images in 24-Bit Display Mode

Two methods are available for displaying TrueColor images when a WIN, MAC, or X graphics device is selected and IDL is running in 24-bit display mode. The first method uses the optional true keyword accepted by tv and tvscl to specify the image dimension containing the red, green, and blue image components:

```
IDL> window, /free, xsize=227, ysize=149
IDL> device, decomposed=1
IDL> tv, rose, true=1
IDL> device, decomposed=0
```

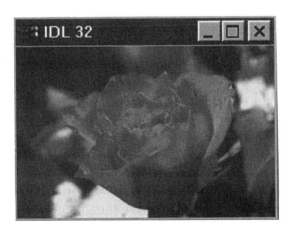

Decomposed Color mode is activated by calling `device` to ensure that the color table is bypassed, allowing the combined RGB intensities to map directly to displayed colors. The image is displayed by calling `tv` with the keyword `true=1` to specify that the first dimension of `image` contains the RGB components (`true` is set to 2 or 3 if the second or third dimension contains the RGB components). Finally, Decomposed Color is turned off by calling `device`. If `tvscl` is used instead of `tv`, the scaling range is determined by the minimum and maximum values of the entire array. This can have undesirable side effects if one RGB component contains significantly smaller or larger values than the other components, so the `tv` procedure is typically used instead of `tvscl` to display TrueColor images (assuming the image has been appropriately scaled).

The second method uses the optional `channel` keyword accepted by `tv` and `tvscl` to display the individual RGB components in the corresponding channels of the graphics device. Channels 1, 2, and 3 refer to the red, green, and blue channels of the graphics device, respectively. This method allows each of the RGB components to be scaled separately:

```
IDL> red = reform(rose[0, *, *])
IDL> grn = reform(rose[1, *, *])
IDL> blu = reform(rose[2, *, *])
IDL> device, decomposed=1
IDL> tvscl, red, channel=1
IDL> tvscl, grn, channel=2
IDL> tvscl, blu, channel=3
IDL> device, decomposed=0
```

In this example, the RGB components are extracted into separate arrays, with the `reform` function used to remove dimensions that have a size of one. Then each RGB component is scaled and displayed by calling `tvscl`, with the `channel` keyword specifying the display channel. You could also use `bytscl`, `imscale`, or the histogram clipping and equalization methods described previously, in conjunction with `tv`, to scale and display each RGB component. As illustrated in the example, this method also allows more flexibility for displaying TrueColor images created from separate two-dimensional arrays.

Displaying TrueColor Images in 8-Bit Display Mode

To display a TrueColor image when IDL is running in 8-bit display mode, the image must be transformed to PseudoColor format. A color quantization algorithm is applied to convert the 16,777,216 (256^3) potential colors in the TrueColor image to a maximum of 256 colors in the PseudoColor image. While this process does reduce the quality of the image (especially in areas of continuous tones), it usually gives acceptable results.

TrueColor images are quantized by the `color_quan` function, as shown in the following example, where the rose image is displayed in 8-bit mode:

```
IDL> pseudo = color_quan(rose, 1, r, g, b)
IDL> tvlct, r, g, b
IDL> tv, pseudo
```

The `color_quan` argument list includes the TrueColor image array (`rose`), a scalar value (1) that specifies the image dimension containing the RGB components, and color table vectors (`r`, `g`, `b`) that, on output, contain the color table for the quantized image. By default, `color_quan` uses all entries in the color table for the quantized image. The color table vectors are then loaded by calling `tvlct`, and the PseudoColor image is displayed by calling `tv`.

To specify the number of colors in the quantized image, `color_quan` accepts the `colors` keyword:

Note   Recall that when IDL is running in 24-bit display mode, Decomposed Color mode must be de-activated in order to display the quantized PseudoColor image, i.e.,

```
IDL> device, decomposed=0
IDL> tv, pseudo
```

However, there is no need to color quantize a TrueColor image when IDL is running in 24-bit display mode.

```
IDL> bottom = 16
IDL> ncolors = 64
IDL> pseudo = color_quan(image, 1, r, g, b, colors=ncolors) $
IDL>    + byte(bottom)
IDL> tvlct, r, g, b, bottom
IDL> tv, pseudo
```

In this example, 64 entries in the color table starting at entry 16 are used for the quantized image, reserving entries 0 to 15 for graphics overlay colors.

The quality of the quantized image may be improved by using the color_quan keyword dither. Dithering causes neighboring pixels to be assigned colors that approximate a smooth transition from one tone to another, thus helping to avoid sharp color transitions in areas with continuous tones:

```
IDL> pseudo = color_quan(image, 1, r, g, b, /dither)
IDL> tvlct, r, g, b
IDL> tv, pseudo
```

7.6   DISPLAYING IMAGES ON THE POSTSCRIPT AND PRINTER DEVICES

PseudoColor and TrueColor images may be displayed on the PS and PRINTER graphics devices; however, a few extra steps are required to obtain high-quality results. There is necessarily some overlap between this section and the in-depth discussion of the PS and PRINTER devices in Chapter 8. This section provides only very basic information about these devices in order to illustrate how images are displayed.

Displaying PseudoColor Images on the PostScript Device

The PS graphics device allows direct graphics output to be sent to a PostScript output file. When displaying images, the tv and tvscl procedures can automatically attempt to fit an image to the display area, or the size and offset of the image may be set manually.

To demonstrate, an image representing global surface elevation is loaded:

```
IDL> elev = imdata('worldelv.dat', 360, 360)
```

Then the name of the current graphics device is saved, and the PS device is selected and configured for color output:

```
IDL> entry_device = !d.name
IDL> set_plot, 'PS'
IDL> device, /color, bits_per_pixel=8, filename='elev.ps'
```

The default PostScript page is in portrait orientation, with a drawable region 17.78×12.7 centimeters (7×5 inches) in size. Next, the grayscale color table is loaded, and the image is displayed by calling tvscl. To show the extent of the drawable region of the page, a dotted line is plotted by calling plots:

```
IDL> loadct, 0
IDL> tvscl, elev
IDL> x = [0.0, 1.0, 1.0, 0.0, 0.0]
IDL> y = [0.0, 0.0, 1.0, 1.0, 0.0]
IDL> plots, x, y, /normal, linestyle=1, color=0
```

Finally the output file is closed, and the entry graphics device is reselected:

```
IDL> device, /close_file
IDL> set_plot, entry_device
```

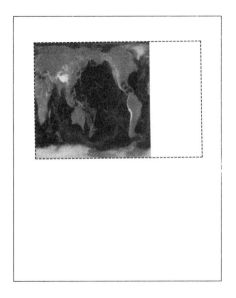

In this example, tvscl sized the image to fit the default drawable region of the page, but did not center the image. To simultaneously center and size the image in the drawable region, the optional tv and tvscl arguments x0 and y0 must be used in conjunction with the optional keywords xsize and ysize described in Table 7.1. The imsize procedure described in Section 7.4 may be used to compute x0, y0, xsize, and ysize in device pixel units as shown in the following example:

```
IDL> entry_device = !d.name
IDL> set_plot, 'PS'
IDL> device, /color, bits_per_pixel=8, filename='elev.ps'
IDL> imsize, elev, x0, y0, xsize, ysize
IDL> loadct, 0
IDL> tvscl, elev, x0, y0, xsize=xsize, ysize=ysize
```

```
IDL> plots, x, y, /normal, linestyle=1, color=0
IDL> device, /close_file
IDL> set_plot, entry_device
```

After selecting and configuring the PS device, imsize is called to compute the image offset and size. The image is displayed by calling tvscl with the x0 and y0 arguments to specify the offset from the lower-left corner of the drawable region, and the keywords xsize and ysize to specify the width and height of the displayed image. Finally, the PostScript output file is closed, and the entry graphics device is reselected.

The values of x0, y0, xsize and ysize computed by imsize are in PS device pixel units:

```
IDL> print, x0, y0, xsize, ysize
      3810        1270       10160       10160
```

The values are relatively large because the native resolution of the PS device is 1,000 pixels per centimeter. When the image is displayed, it is sized to fit the requested width and height on the output page.

Tip   The PS device always has 256 colors available in the color table, regardless of the number of colors available on the screen display in the current IDL session. Thus it is prudent to load the color table and scale the image after the PostScript device has been selected. If necessary, you can obtain and save the current color table by calling `tvlct` with the optional `get` keyword before the `PS` device is selected, and then restore the color table by calling `tvlct` after the entry graphics device is reselected.

Displaying PseudoColor Images on the Printer Device

The `PRINTER` graphics device allows direct graphics output to be sent to the default system printer. The method for displaying PseudoColor images on the `PRINTER` device is very similar to the `PS` device, as shown in the following example:

```
IDL> entry_device = !d.name
IDL> set_plot, 'PRINTER'
IDL> imsize, elev, x0, y0, xsize, ysize
IDL> device, /index_color
IDL> loadct, 0
IDL> tvscl, elev, x0, y0, xsize=xsize, ysize=ysize
IDL> plots, x, y, /normal, linestyle=1, color=0
IDL> device, /close_document
IDL> set_plot, entry_device
```

Like the `PS` device, the default `PRINTER` page is in portrait orientation with a drawable region 17.78×12.7 centimeters (7×5 inches) in size. In this example, after the `PRINTER` device is selected and the image offset and size are computed in pixel units, the `device` procedure is called with the `index_color` keyword set to put the `PRINTER` device in indexed color mode. After the image is displayed and the boundaries of the drawable region are plotted, the `device` procedure is called with the `close_document` keyword set to close the output document, and the entry graphics device is reselected.

Note   IDL version 5.2 or higher is required to support the `tv` and `tvscl` keywords `xsize` and `ysize` when the `PRINTER` device is selected.

Displaying TrueColor Images on the PostScript Device

TrueColor images can be displayed when the PS graphics device is selected. When displaying TrueColor images, the most important difference between the PS device and the WIN, MAC, and X devices is the method by which image intensities are mapped to displayed colors.

When the WIN, MAC, or X device is selected and IDL is running in 24-bit display mode, the color table may be bypassed to allow RGB image intensities to map directly to displayed colors. However, when the PS device is selected, the color table is *always* active. For example, the red component of the image is mapped to shades of red on the output page via the values stored in the red portion of the color table. Thus a color table with linearly increasing red, green, and blue values is required—namely, the grayscale color table:

```
IDL> loadct, 0
IDL> tvlct, r, g, b, /get
IDL> print, r[0:9], g[0:9], b[0:9]
    0   1   2   3   4   5   6   7   8   9
    0   1   2   3   4   5   6   7   8   9
    0   1   2   3   4   5   6   7   8   9
```

The TrueColor image of a rose from Section 7.5 is used as an example:

```
IDL> file = filepath('rose.jpg', subdir='examples/data')
IDL> read_jpeg, file, rose
```

The image is displayed on the PS device using the following method:

```
IDL> entry_device = !d.name
IDL> tvlct, r, g, b, /get
IDL> set_plot, 'PS'
IDL> device, /color, bits_per_pixel=8, filename='rose.ps'
IDL> imsize, reform(rose[0, *, *]), x0, y0, xsize, ysize
IDL> loadct, 0
IDL> tv, rose, x0, y0, xsize=xsize, ysize=ysize, true=1
IDL> device, /close_file
IDL> set_plot, entry_device
IDL> tvlct, r, g, b
```

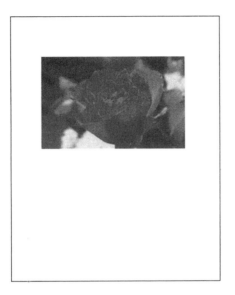

First, the entry graphics device name is saved. Since the color table will be overwritten, the contents of the color table are obtained by calling tvlct. Then the PS device is selected and configured for color output at 8 bits per pixel. The imsize function is called to obtain the offset and size values required to display the image. Then the grayscale color table is loaded by calling loadct, and the image is displayed by calling tv. Finally the output file is closed, and the entry graphics device and color table are restored.

Displaying TrueColor Images on the Printer Device

TrueColor images can also be displayed when the PRINTER graphics device is selected. The color table may be bypassed on the PRINTER device, so there is no need to load the grayscale color table required by the PS device. The following example shows how the TrueColor image of a rose is displayed on the Printer device:

```
IDL> entry_device = !d.name
IDL> set_plot, 'PRINTER'
IDL> device, /true_color
IDL> imsize, reform(rose[0, *, *]), x0, y0, xsize, ysize
IDL> tv, rose, x0, y0, xsize=xsize, ysize=ysize, true=1
IDL> device, /close_document
IDL> set_plot, entry_device
```

In this example, the color table is deactivated by calling device with the true_color keyword set, which puts the PRINTER device into Decomposed Color mode. Once again imsize is called to compute the image offset and size, and the image is displayed by calling tv. Finally the output document is closed, and the entry graphics device is reselected.

7.7   AN IMAGE DISPLAY APPLICATION

The previous sections in this chapter have shown you how to scale, size, and display PseudoColor and TrueColor images. However, there are quite a few rules to remember, such as the following:

1. Decomposed Color must be turned off to display PseudoColor images when IDL is running in 24-bit display mode.
2. TrueColor images must be quantized before they can be displayed when IDL is running in 8-bit display mode.
3. To center and fit an image in a graphics window, the image array must be resized.
4. To center and fit an image in the display area when the PS or PRINTER device is selected, the keywords xsize and ysize must be used in conjunction with tv or tvscl.

Thus, it would be useful to have an image display application that automatically determines the correct method for displaying an image based on the characteristics of the image and the current graphics device.

The following procedure named imdisp.pro allows you to display PseudoColor or TrueColor images on the WIN, MAC, X, PS, and PRINTER graphics devices. Images are automatically byte-scaled, or scaling can be turned off if the image is already scaled. The image is automatically sized to fit the current display while maintaining aspect ratio. Image position can be specified in normal coordinates via a position keyword, and the !p.multi system variable described in Chapter 6 can be used to position multiple images. The range of color table indices may be chosen via the bottom and ncolors keywords, and the display order may be selected via the order keyword. The image aspect ratio is maintained by default, however, the aspect keyword is accepted by imdisp to specify a custom aspect ratio (it is passed to the imsize procedure via the extra keyword mechanism).

```
PRO IMDISP, IMAGE, POSITION=POSITION, OUT_POS=OUT_POS, $
  BOTTOM=BOTTOM, NCOLORS=NCOLORS, NOSCALE=NOSCALE, $
  MARGIN=MARGIN, ORDER=ORDER, _EXTRA=EXTRA_KEYWORDS

;- Check arguments
if (n_params() ne 1) then message, 'Usage: IMDISP, IMAGE'
if (n_elements(image) eq 0) then $
  message, 'Argument IMAGE is undefined'
if (n_elements(margin) eq 0) then begin
  case 1 of
    (max(!p.multi) gt 0)         : margin = 0.025
    (n_elements(position) eq 4)  : margin = 0.0
    else                         : margin = 0.1
  endcase
endif
if (n_elements(order) eq 0) then order = 0

;- Check the image dimensions
result = size(image)
ndims = result[0]
if (ndims lt 2) or (ndims gt 3) then $
  message, 'IMAGE must be a 2D or 3D array'
dims = result[1 : ndims]

;- Check that 3D image array is in valid true color form
true = 0
if (ndims eq 3) then begin
  index = where(dims eq 3L, count)
  if (count lt 1) then $
    message, 'IMAGE must be of the form ' + $
    '[3,NX,NY], [NX,3,NY], or [NX,NY,3]'
  true = 1
  truedim = index[0]
endif

;- Get color table information
if ((!d.flags and 256) ne 0) and $
  (!d.window lt 0) then begin
  window, /free, /pixmap
  wdelete, !d.window
endif
if (n_elements(bottom) eq 0) then bottom = 0
if (n_elements(ncolors) eq 0) then $
  ncolors = !d.table_size - bottom
```

```
;- Check for IDL 5.2 if printer device is selected
version = float(!version.release)
if (version lt 5.2) and (!d.name eq 'PRINTER') then $
  message, 'IDL 5.2 or higher is required ' + $
  'for PRINTER device support'

;- Get red, green, and blue components of true color image
if (true eq 1) then begin
    case truedim of
    0 : begin
          red = image[0, *, *]
          grn = image[1, *, *]
          blu = image[2, *, *]
        end
    1 : begin
          red = image[*, 0, *]
          grn = image[*, 1, *]
          blu = image[*, 2, *]
        end
    2 : begin
          red = image[*, *, 0]
          grn = image[*, *, 1]
          blu = image[*, *, 2]
        end
  endcase
  red = reform(red)
  grn = reform(grn)
  blu = reform(blu)
endif

;- Establish image position
if (n_elements(position) eq 0) then begin
  if (max(!p.multi) eq 0) then begin
    position = [0.0, 0.0, 1.0, 1.0]
  endif else begin
    plot, [0], /nodata, xstyle=4, ystyle=4, $
      xmargin=[0, 0], ymargin=[0, 0]
    position = [!x.window[0], !y.window[0], $
                !x.window[1], !y.window[1]]
  endelse
endif

;- Compute size of displayed image
position_value = position
```

```
case true of
  0 : imsize, image, x0, y0, xsize, ysize, $
        margin=margin, position=position_value, $
        _extra=extra_keywords
  1 : imsize, red, x0, y0, xsize, ysize, $
        margin=margin, position=position_value, $
        _extra=extra_keywords
endcase
out_pos = position_value

;- Choose whether to scale the image or not
if (keyword_set(noscale) eq 1) then begin

  ;- Don't scale the image
  case true of
    0 : scaled = image
    1 : begin
          scaled_dims = (size(red))[1:2]
          scaled = replicate(red[0], $
            scaled_dims[0], scaled_dims[1], 3)
          scaled[*, *, 0] = red
          scaled[*, *, 1] = grn
          scaled[*, *, 2] = blu
        end
  endcase

endif else begin

  ;- Scale the image
  case true of
    0 : scaled = imscale(image, $
          bottom=bottom, ncolors=ncolors)
    1 : begin
          scaled_dims = (size(red))[1:2]
          scaled = bytarr(scaled_dims[0], scaled_dims[1], 3)
          scaled[*, *, 0] = imscale(red, $
            bottom=0, ncolors=256)
          scaled[*, *, 1] = imscale(grn, $
            bottom=0, ncolors=256)
          scaled[*, *, 2] = imscale(blu, $
            bottom=0, ncolors=256)
        end
  endcase
```

```
endelse

;- Display the image on the printer device
if (!d.name eq 'PRINTER') then begin
  case true of
    0 : begin
         device, /index_color
         tv, scaled, x0, y0, $
           xsize=xsize, ysize=ysize, order=order
       end
    1 : begin
         device, /true_color
         tv, scaled, x0, y0, $
           xsize=xsize, ysize=ysize, order=order, true=3
       end
  endcase
  return
endif

;- Display the image on devices with scaleable pixels
;- (including PostScript)
if ((!d.flags and 1) ne 0) then begin
  case true of
    0 : tv, scaled, x0, y0, $
         xsize=xsize, ysize=ysize, order=order
    1 : begin
         tvlct, r, g, b, /get
         loadct, 0, /silent
         tv, scaled, x0, y0, $
           xsize=xsize, ysize=ysize, order=order, true=3
         tvlct, r, g, b
       end
  endcase
  return
endif

;- Get display depth
depth = 8
if (!d.name eq 'WIN') or $
   (!d.name eq 'MAC') or $
   (!d.name eq 'X') then begin
  if (version ge 5.1) then begin
    device, get_visual_depth=depth
  endif else begin
```

```
     if (!d.n_colors gt 256) then depth = 24
   endelse
endif

;- If the display is 8-bit and image is TrueColor,
;- convert image to PseudoColor
if (depth le 8) and (true eq 1) then begin
   scaled = congrid(temporary(scaled), xsize, ysize, 3)
   scaled = color_quan(temporary(scaled), 3, r, g, b, $
     /dither, colors=ncolors) + byte(bottom)
   tvlct, r, g, b, bottom
   true = 0
endif

;- Set decomposed color mode
if (depth gt 8) and (true eq 1) then begin
   device, decomposed=1
endif else begin
   device, decomposed=0
endelse

;- Display the image
case true of
   0 : tv, congrid(scaled, xsize, ysize), x0, y0, $
          order=order
   1 : tv, congrid(scaled, xsize, ysize, 3), x0, y0, $
          order=order, true=3
endcase

;- Turn decomposed color off if required
if (depth gt 8) and (true eq 1) then device, decomposed=0

END
```

The imdisp procedure does the following:

1. The input argument (image) is checked to ensure it exists, and a
   default margin value (margin) is set if the caller did not specify one
   via the margin keyword. Next, the dimensions of the image array
   (dims) are obtained and checked to ensure image is a valid two-
   dimensional or three-dimensional array. If the image is in TrueColor
   form, the dimension (truedim) containing the RGB components is
   obtained.

2. If the current graphics device supports windows and no window has yet been opened, a graphics window is opened and immediately deleted. This has the effect of forcing IDL to set the color table size. Default values are set if necessary for the bottom entry (bottom) and number of colors (ncolors) in the color table to be used for the displayed image.

3. The IDL version number is checked because imdisp requires IDL 5.2 or higher to display images when the Printer device is selected.

4. If the image is in TrueColor form, the RGB components are extracted into separate arrays (red, grn, blu) to simplify image resizing and scaling.

5. If no position vector was specified, a default is computed. If the system variable !p.multi is not set to produce multiple images, the position vector is set to cover the entire display. Otherwise plot is called to determine the position vector for the current image in a multi-image sequence.

6. Next the image is transformed to scaled form. If the caller requested no scaling via the noscale keyword, the image is simply copied to the scaled array (scaled). Otherwise PseudoColor images are scaled by calling imscale with the bottom and ncolors keywords, and TrueColor RGB components are scaled separately. For TrueColor images, bottom and ncolors are set to 0 and 256, respectively, because either the display supports 24-bit color (and the size of the color table is 256), or the display supports 8-bit color and the image will be color-quantized later by calling color_quan.

7. The first graphics device to be handled is the PRINTER device. If the image is PseudoColor, then indexed color output is selected by calling device with the index_color keyword set. Then the image is displayed by calling tv with the offset (x0, y0) and size (xsize, ysize) computed by imsize. If the image is TrueColor, then true color output is selected and the image is displayed by calling tv. The tv keyword true is set to 3 to indicate which dimension of scaled contains the RGB components. Control is then returned to the caller.

8. Graphics devices with scalable pixels are handled next (this includes the PS device). If the image is PseudoColor, it is displayed by calling tv. If the image is TrueColor, the current color table is obtained by calling tvlct, and the grayscale color table is loaded to ensure cor-

rect mapping of RGB intensities. Then the image is displayed by calling tv, and the previous color table is restored. Control is then returned to the caller.

9. The bit depth of the current display is obtained (only the WIN, MAC, and X devices can have bit depths greater than 8). If the current bit depth is 8 or less, and the image is TrueColor, then the image must be converted to PseudoColor form. First the image is resized by calling congrid. Then color quantization is applied by calling color_quan, producing a new image array (scaled), and associated color table vectors (r, g, b). The ncolors and bottom keywords are used to map the quantized image colors into the color table. The color table vectors are loaded by calling tvlct, and the TrueColor flag (true) is set to zero.

10. On displays with bit depths greater than 8, decomposed color is turned off (decomposed=0) if the image is PseudoColor, and turned on (decomposed=1) if the image is TrueColor.

11. The image is resized by calling congrid and displayed by calling tv.

12. Finally, Decomposed Color is turned off, if it was turned on previously.

The following examples show how imdisp is used. First, several example images are loaded:

```
IDL> hurric = imdata('hurric.dat', 440, 340)
IDL> ctscan = imdata('ctscan.dat', 256, 256)
IDL> read_jpeg, filepath('rose.jpg', $
IDL>    subdir='examples/data'), rose
```

- A PseudoColor image, automatically byte-scaled and sized to fit the display:

```
IDL> window, /free
IDL> loadct, 13
IDL> imdisp, hurric
```

- A grayscale image, prescaled via histogram clipping and sized to fill the display (while maintaining aspect ratio):

```
IDL> index = where(ctscan gt 0)
IDL> scaled = imscale(ctscan, range=imclip(ctscan[index]))
IDL> loadct, 0
IDL> imdisp, scaled, /noscale, position=[0.0, 0.0, 1.0, 1.0]
```

■ A PseudoColor and TrueColor image displayed side by side, with a split color table:

```
IDL> !p.multi = [0, 2, 1, 0, 0]
IDL> loadct, 13, bottom=0, ncolors=64
IDL> imdisp, hurric, bottom=0, ncolors=64
IDL> imdisp, rose, bottom=64, ncolors=64
IDL> !p.multi = 0
```

■ On 24-bit displays, a split color table is not necessary:

```
IDL> !p.multi = [0, 2, 1, 0, 0]
IDL> loadct, 13
IDL> imdisp, hurric
IDL> imdisp, rose
IDL> !p.multi = 0
```

■ A TrueColor image with a plot overlay:

```
IDL> imdisp, rose, out_pos=out_pos, bottom=1
IDL> plot, [0], position=out_pos, /nodata, /noerase, $
IDL>   xrange=[0, 226], yrange=[0, 148], xstyle=1, ystyle=1, $
IDL>   charsize=1.5, title='TrueColor Rose'
```

Any of the previous imdisp examples may be executed without modification when the PS or PRINTER graphics device is selected:

```
IDL> entry_device = !d.name
IDL> set_plot, 'PS'
IDL> device, /color, bits_per_pixel=8, file='rose.ps'
IDL> imdisp, rose, out_pos=out_pos
IDL> plot, [0], position=out_pos, /nodata, /noerase, $
IDL>   xrange=[0, 226], yrange=[0, 148], xstyle=1, ystyle=1, $
IDL>   charsize=1.5, title='TrueColor Rose'
IDL> device, /close_file
IDL> set_plot, entry_device
```

8 Creating Graphical Output

This chapter discusses the methods available in IDL for saving and printing graphical output. It begins with the fundamental differences between bitmap and vector output, and then lists the formats of each type supported by IDL. This is followed by a description of the process of capturing the contents of a graphics window to a bitmap output file, with equal treatment given to 8-bit and 24-bit output formats, along with an example program that simplifies the process. Next, the subject of creating publication-quality PostScript output is reviewed in detail, including explanations of the configuration of the PostScript page, along with font and color selection. Example programs are shown that greatly simplify the process and allow true WYSIWYG (what you see is what you get) output. Finally the Printer graphics device is covered in the same level of detail as the PostScript device, along with all the information necessary to produce high-quality printer output on local or networked printers (including those that do not support PostScript).

8.1 BITMAP AND VECTOR OUTPUT

IDL can create graphical output in both bitmap and vector form in a variety of file formats.

Bitmap output is created when the contents of a graphics window or the Z-buffer are saved to an output file. The smallest element that can be represented in a bitmap is a pixel, so the resolution of a bitmap output file

Raster   Vector
(a)   (b)

Figure 8.1   Graphical output: (a) bitmap and (b) vector.

is determined by the width and height of the bitmap in pixels. For example, a typical monitor screen can display about 40 pixels per centimeter, or 100 pixels per inch. When a bitmap file is viewed at high magnification, artifacts such as jagged line edges are visible due to the inherent resolution limits of a bitmap, as shown in Figure 8.1(a). Even with its resolution limitations, the bitmap format is still a versatile and useful method for creating graphical output, especially for images.

Vector output is created when a figure is rendered to a graphics device (such as the PostScript device) that represents lines as vectors at high resolution. For example, the native resolution of the PostScript device is 1,000 pixels per centimeter, or 2,540 pixels per inch. When a vector output file is viewed at high magnification, the edges of curves appear smooth because of the relatively high resolution, as shown in Figure 8.1(b). Vector output is often preferred when graphical output contains sharp lines and curves, such as line graphs.

Apart from resolution differences, there is a fundamental difference in the way bitmap and vector output is created in IDL. Bitmap output is created by saving the contents of a graphics window (or the Z-buffer) to a file. Vector output is created by rendering a figure on a device that supports vector output. The difference can be illustrated by the list of steps involved in creating each kind of output.

For the bitmap method:

1. Create a graphic on-screen.
2. Read the contents of the screen.
3. Save the contents to an output file.

For the vector method:

1. Select a vector output device.
2. Create a graphic.
3. Close the output file.

IDL supports a variety of common bitmap and vector output file formats. Bitmap formats supported include BMP, JPEG, NRIF, PICT, PNG, PPM, SRF, and TIFF. Vector formats supported include PostScript, CGM, HP-GL, PCL, and in IDL 5.4, Windows Enhanced Metafile (on Windows platforms only). In addition, the Printer device supports vector output if the selected printer supports it.

Note The GIF file format is supported in IDL 5.3 and prior versions, but was removed in IDL 5.4 due to licensing issues associated with the LZW compression algorithm. Of the formats supported in IDL 5.4, PNG (Portable Network Graphics) format provides an excellent replacement for GIF, with the added bonus of more efficient compression.

8.2 CREATING BITMAP OUTPUT FILES

This section describes how bitmap output files are created. The first step is to read the contents of an existing graphics window or the Z-buffer into an array. The second step is to write the contents to an output file.

Reading from the Display: tvrd

The tvrd function reads the contents of the current graphics window (or device) into an array. Supported devices include WIN, MAC, X, and Z. The syntax is

```
result = tvrd([x0], [y0], [nx], [ny], [channel], [keywords])
```

The optional arguments x0 and y0 specify the lower-left corner of the window to be read (the default is 0, 0), and the optional arguments nx and ny specify the number of columns and rows to be read from the bottom up (the default is all columns and rows). The optional argument channel specifies the display channel to be read on 24-bit displays only (it is ignored otherwise). Channels 1, 2, and 3 correspond to red, green, and blue, respectively. The most commonly used keywords supported by tvrd are listed in Table 8.1.

Table 8.1   Commonly used tvrd **keywords.**

Keyword	Purpose
order	Set display order for reading* (0 = bottom up, 1 = top down)
true	Set dimension for returning RGB components (1 = first, 2 = second, 3 = third)
channel	Set display channel to read (1 = red, 2 = green, 3 = blue)

* The order keyword overrides the system variable !order.

The form of the array returned by tvrd depends on the IDL display mode:

- If IDL is running in 8-bit display mode on the WIN, MAC, or X device, or the Z device is selected, tvrd returns a two-dimensional PseudoColor byte array containing the contents of the current window or device.
- If IDL is running in 24-bit display mode on the WIN, MAC, or X device, you must turn on Decomposed Color mode and instruct tvrd to return a three-dimensional TrueColor byte array that contains red, green, and blue image components.

Tip The effective resolution of a bitmap output file can be increased by using a graphics device that is larger than the visible screen, such as a scrolling graphics window as described in Section 5.3, or the Z-buffer device as described in Section 5.1.

Reading from an 8-Bit Display

To demonstrate tvrd with an 8-bit display, the Z device is configured to provide a 640 × 512 8-bit display in memory. This example will work on any IDL system, regardless of display mode:

```
IDL> entry_device = !d.name
IDL> set_plot, 'Z'
IDL> xsize = 640
IDL> ysize = 512
IDL> device, z_buffering=0, set_resolution=[xsize, ysize], $
IDL>    set_colors=!d.table_size, set_character_size=[10, 12]
```

A shaded surface is displayed with a color table in shades of red (color table 3). When this color table is loaded, the `color` keyword sets the plotting color to black and the `background` keyword sets the background color to white:

```
IDL> z = dist(64)
IDL> z = shift(z, 32, 32)
IDL> z = exp(-(z * 0.1)^2)
IDL> loadct, 3
IDL> shade_surf, z, xstyle=1, ystyle=1, charsize=2, $
IDL>   color=0, background=(!d.table_size - 1)
```

To read the contents of the display into a two-dimensional `byte` array and obtain the color table vectors:

```
IDL> image = tvrd()
IDL> help, image
IMAGE          BYTE       = Array[640, 512]
IDL> tvlct, red, grn, blu, /get
```

Finally the image is displayed in a graphics window:

```
IDL> set_plot, entry_device
IDL> window, /free, xsize=xsize, ysize=ysize
IDL> device, decomposed=0
IDL> tvlct, red, grn, blu
IDL> tv, image
```

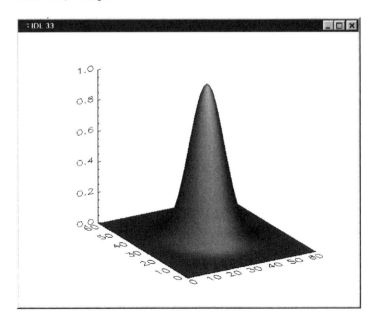

The command device, decomposed=0 is used only to ensure the example works when IDL is running in 24-bit display mode. This command is ignored if IDL is running in 8-bit display mode.

Reading from a 24-Bit Display

When IDL is running in 24-bit display mode on the WIN, MAC, or X device, you must explicitly request (via the true keyword) that tvrd return a TrueColor image containing the RGB components from each display channel. Alternatively, each channel can be obtained individually by tvrd via the channel keyword, or the optional channel argument.

To demonstrate tvrd with a 24-bit display, the shaded surface shown in the previous example is displayed. This example will only work if IDL is running in 24-bit display mode:

```
IDL> window, /free
IDL> device, decomposed=0
IDL> loadct, 3
IDL> shade_surf, z, xstyle=1, ystyle=1, charsize=2, $
IDL>    color=0, background=(!d.table_size - 1)
```

Decomposed Color mode is then activated and the contents of the display are read into a TrueColor byte array:

```
IDL> device, decomposed=1
IDL> image = tvrd(true=1)
IDL> help, image
IMAGE           BYTE      = Array[3, 640, 512]
```

Finally, the image is redisplayed from the array and Decomposed Color mode is turned off:

```
IDL> erase
IDL> tv, image, true=1
IDL> device, decomposed=0
```

Note   It is not possible for tvrd to return a valid PseudoColor image array from a graphics window when IDL is running in 24-bit display mode. If you call tvrd in 24-bit display mode and do not use the true keyword or the optional channel keyword, a two-dimensional byte array containing the maximum RGB value for each pixel is returned. This will almost certainly *not* be what you wanted.

A Wrapper Function for tvrd

The following function named screenread.pro provides a display-independent way to read the contents of a graphics display. It detects whether IDL is running in 8-bit or 24-bit display mode, and calls tvrd with the appropriate keywords. Decomposed Color mode is used when reading from a 24-bit display. The optional depth keyword returns the bit depth of the current display.

```
FUNCTION SCREENREAD, X0, Y0, NX, NY, DEPTH=DEPTH

;- Check arguments
if (n_elements(x0) eq 0) then x0 = 0
if (n_elements(y0) eq 0) then y0 = 0
if (n_elements(nx) eq 0) then nx = !d.x_vsize - x0
if (n_elements(ny) eq 0) then ny = !d.y_vsize - y0

;- Check for TVRD capable device
tvrd_true = !d.flags and 128
if (tvrd_true eq 0) then message, $
  'TVRD is not supported on this device: ' + !d.name

;- On devices which support windows, check for open window
win_true = !d.flags and 256
if (win_true gt 0) and (!d.window lt 0) then message, $
  'No graphics window are open'

;- Get IDL version number
version = float(!version.release)

;- Get display depth
depth = 8
if (win_true gt 0) then begin
  if (version ge 5.1) then begin
    device, get_visual_depth=depth
  endif else begin
    if (!d.n_colors gt 256) then depth = 24
  endelse
endif

;- Set decomposed color mode on 24-bit displays
if (depth gt 8) then begin
  entry_decomposed = 0
  if (version gt 5.1) then $
    device, get_decomposed=entry_decomposed
```

```
    device, decomposed=1
endif

;- Get the contents of the window
if (depth gt 8) then true = 1 else true = 0
image = tvrd(x0, y0, nx, ny, order=0, true=true)

;- Restore decomposed color mode on 24-bit displays
if (depth gt 8) then device, decomposed=entry_decomposed

;- Return result to caller
return, image

END
```

First, default values are set for any optional arguments that are unde-fined. Then !d.flags is checked to ensure tvrd support, and to ensure a window is open on devices that support windows (the Z graphics device does not support windows). The default display depth is then set to 8. If windows are supported, the actual display depth is obtained. If the dis-play depth is greater than 8, the entry Decomposed Color setting is saved, and Decomposed Color mode is turned on (the version-dependent code is required because the device keyword get_decomposed was introduced in IDL 5.2). Then tvrd is called with the appropriate keywords. Finally, the entry Decomposed Color setting is restored if necessary, and the result array (image) is returned to the caller. If the optional output key-word depth is supplied, the display depth is also returned to the caller.

If IDL is running on an 8-bit display, screenread returns a two-dimen-sional array:

```
IDL> image = screenread(depth=depth)
IDL> help, image, depth
IMAGE          BYTE      = Array[640, 512]
DEPTH          LONG      =              8
```

The value returned by the depth keyword tells you whether you need to read the contents of the color table on an 8-bit display:

```
IDL> if (depth le 8) then tvlct, r, g, b, /get
IDL> help, r, g, b
R              BYTE      = Array[236]
G              BYTE      = Array[236]
B              BYTE      = Array[236]
```

If IDL is running on a 24-bit display, `screenread` returns a three-dimensional array with the RGB image components in the first dimension:

```
IDL> image = screenread(depth=depth)
IDL> help, image, depth
IMAGE          BYTE      = Array[3, 640, 512]
DEPTH          LONG      =             24
```

Now that you've read the contents of the screen into an array, you are ready to select an output format and create an output file.

Selecting a Bitmap Output Format

Before you write a bitmap output file, you must select one of the output formats supported by IDL. Your selection of an output format will be guided by the intended application for the file. For example, if you intend to use the file for display on a web page, you could select PNG or JPEG format. If you wish to preserve the full resolution of a 24-bit true color image for high-quality printed output, you could select TIFF format. Table 8.2 lists the bitmap output formats supported by IDL.

You might think that your choice of an output format is determined by whether you read an 8-bit or 24-bit image from the graphics display, as described in the previous section. However, you can select any of the out-

Table 8.2 Bitmap output formats in IDL.

Format	8-bit	24-bit	Default compression	Write procedure
BMP	Yes	Yes	None	`write_bmp`
GIF	Yes	No	Lossless	`write_gif*`
JPEG	No	Yes	Lossy	`write_jpeg`
NRIF	Yes	Yes	None	`write_nrif`
PICT	Yes	No	None	`write_pict`
PNG	Yes	Yes	Lossless	`write_png`
PPM	Yes	Yes	None	`write_ppm`
SRF	Yes	Yes	None	`write_srf`
TIFF	Yes	Yes	None	`write_tiff`

* Supported in IDL 5.3 and earlier versions.

put formats shown in Table 8.2 regardless of the image depth because in IDL, you can convert an 8-bit image to 24-bit form, or you can convert a 24-bit image to 8-bit form. Therefore your choice of an output format should be guided by the intended application for the output file.

Saving an 8-Bit Image to a Bitmap Output File

When IDL is running in 8-bit display mode, the saved contents of a graphics display can be

- written to an 8-bit output format such as BMP or PNG
- converted to 24-bit form and written to a 24-bit output format such as JPEG or TIFF

To demonstrate, the shaded surface described in the previous section of this chapter is displayed and then read from the screen. The output shown below is from a Windows platform running IDL in 8-bit mode:

```
IDL> window, /free, xsize=640, ysize=512
IDL> loadct, 3
IDL> shade_surf, z, xstyle=1, ystyle=1, charsize=2, $
IDL>   color=0, background=(!d.table_size - 1)
IDL> image = screenread(depth=depth)
IDL> tvlct, r, g, b, /get
IDL> help, image, depth, r, g, b
IMAGE          BYTE      = Array[640, 512]
DEPTH          LONG      =               8
R              BYTE      = Array[236]
G              BYTE      = Array[236]
B              BYTE      = Array[236]
```

To write the image in BMP or PNG 8-bit format:

```
IDL> write_bmp, 'surface.bmp', image, r, g, b
IDL> write_png, 'surface.png', reverse(image, 2), r, g, b
```

The write_png procedure writes images in top-down order in IDL 5.3 and earlier versions, hence the call to reverse. In IDL 5.4 and later versions, PNG images are written in bottom-up order, so the second dimension of image need not be reversed.

To write the image in GIF 8-bit format in IDL 5.3 and earlier versions:

```
IDL> write_gif, 'surface.gif', image, r, g, b
```

To write the image in 24-bit format, it must be converted to 24-bit form:

```
IDL> info = size(image)
IDL> nx = info[1]
IDL> ny = info[2]
IDL> true_image = bytarr(3, nx, ny)
IDL> true_image[0, *, *] = r[image]
IDL> true_image[1, *, *] = g[image]
IDL> true_image[2, *, *] = b[image]
```

Now the converted image can be written in JPEG or TIFF 24-bit format:

```
IDL> write_jpeg, 'surface.jpg', true_image, true=1
IDL> write_tiff, 'surface.tif', reverse(true_image, 3), 1
```

The write_jpeg procedure accepts the optional keyword quality to specify the image quality (the default value is 75). Higher values mean higher image quality with less compression. When write_tiff is called, the last dimension of true_image is reversed to conform with the TIFF convention of storing images from the top down.

Note The PNG format supports both 8-bit and 24-bit output. In the examples shown here, the 8-bit form is used.

Saving a 24-Bit Image to a Bitmap Output File

When IDL is running in 24-bit display mode, the saved contents of a graphics display can be

- written directly to a 24-bit output format such as JPEG or TIFF
- converted to 8-bit form and written to an 8-bit output format such as BMP or PNG

Once again, the shaded surface described in the previous section of this chapter is displayed and read from the screen. The output shown is from a Windows platform running IDL in 24-bit mode:

```
IDL> window, /free, xsize=640, ysize=512
IDL> loadct, 3
```

```
IDL> device, decomposed=0
IDL> shade_surf, z, xstyle=1, ystyle=1, charsize=2, $
IDL>   color=0, background=(!d.table_size - 1)
IDL> image = screenread(depth=depth)
IDL> help, image, depth
IMAGE         BYTE      = Array[3, 640, 512]
DEPTH         LONG      =            24
```

To write the image in JPEG or TIFF 24-bit format:

```
IDL> write_jpeg, 'surface.jpg', image, true=1
IDL> write_tiff, 'surface.tif', reverse(image, 3), 1
```

To write the image in 8-bit format, it must be converted to 8-bit form:

```
IDL> pseudo_image = color_quan(image, 1, r, g, b, colors=256)
```

Now the converted image can be written in BMP or PNG 8-bit format:

```
IDL> write_bmp, 'surface.bmp', pseudo_image, r, g, b
IDL> write_png, 'surface.png', reverse(pseudo_image, 2), $
IDL>   r, g, b
```

Reversing the second dimension of the image written to PNG format is necessary only in IDL 5.3 and earlier versions.

To write the converted image in GIF 8-bit format in IDL 5.3 and earlier versions:

```
IDL> write_gif, 'surface.gif', pseudo_image, r, g, b
```

Note   When converting 24-bit screen images that have white backgrounds to 8-bit format, color matching may be improved by using `cube=6` instead of `colors=256` in the call to `color_quan`. See the online help for more information on keywords accepted by `color_quan`.

A Program for Saving the Screen to a Bitmap Output File

The following procedure named `saveimage.pro` reads the contents of the current graphics window and writes it to a bitmap output file (JPEG format by default). An alternative output format (BMP, PNG, GIF, TIFF) may be selected by setting the appropriate optional keyword. IDL 8-bit and

24-bit display modes are handled automatically by the screenread function shown previously. If the output image was read from a 24-bit display
but is saved in an 8-bit format, then dithering or color cube algorithms
may be applied by setting the dither or cube keywords.

```
PRO SAVEIMAGE, FILE, $
  BMP=BMP, PNG=PNG, GIF=GIF, JPEG=JPEG, TIFF=TIFF, $
  QUALITY=QUALITY, DITHER=DITHER, CUBE=CUBE, QUIET=QUIET

;- Check arguments
if (n_params() ne 1) then $
  message, 'Usage: SAVEIMAGE, FILE'
if (n_elements(file) eq 0) then $
  message, 'Argument FILE is undefined'
if (n_elements(quality) eq 0) then quality = 75

;- Get output file type
output = 'JPEG'
if keyword_set(bmp)  then output = 'BMP'
if keyword_set(png)  then output = 'PNG'
if keyword_set(gif)  then output = 'GIF'
if keyword_set(jpeg) then output = 'JPEG'
if keyword_set(tiff) then output = 'TIFF'

;- Check if GIF output is available
version = float(!version.release)
if (version ge 5.4) and (output eq 'GIF') then $
  message, 'GIF output is not available'

;- Get contents of graphics window,
;- and color table if needed
image = screenread(depth=depth)
if (depth le 8) then tvlct, r, g, b, /get

;- Write 8-bit output file
if (output eq 'BMP') or $
   (output eq 'PNG') or $
   (output eq 'GIF') then begin

  ;- If image depth is 24-bit, convert to 8-bit
  if (depth gt 8) then begin
    case keyword_set(cube) of
      0 : image = color_quan(image, 1, r, g, b, $
            colors=256, dither=keyword_set(dither))
```

```
      1 : image = color_quan(image, 1, r, g, b, cube=6)
    endcase
  endif

  ;- Reverse PNG image order if required
  if (output eq 'PNG') and (version le 5.3) then $
    image = reverse(temporary(image), 2)

  ;- Save the image
  case output of
    'BMP'  : write_bmp, file, image, r, g, b
    'PNG'  : write_png, file, image, r, g, b
    'GIF'  : write_gif, file, image, r, g, b
  endcase

endif

;- Write 24-bit output file
if (output eq 'JPEG') or $
   (output eq 'TIFF') then begin

  ;- Convert 8-bit image to 24-bit
  if (depth le 8) then begin
    info = size(image)
    nx = info[1]
    ny = info[2]
    true = bytarr(3, nx, ny)
    true[0, *, *] = r[image]
    true[1, *, *] = g[image]
    true[2, *, *] = b[image]
    image = temporary(true)
  endif

  ;- Reverse TIFF image order
  if (output eq 'TIFF') then $
    image = reverse(temporary(image), 3)

  ;- Write the image
  case output of
    'JPEG' : write_jpeg, file, image, $
                 true=1, quality=quality
    'TIFF' : write_tiff, file, image, 1
  endcase
```

```
endif

;- Report to user
if (keyword_set(quiet) eq 0) then $
  print, file, output, $
    format='("Created ",a," in ",a," format")'

END
```

First, the input arguments are checked, and the output format is set. Then the contents of the screen are read by calling `screenread`, and if the display depth is 8 bits or less, the color table is retrieved. If the caller selected BMP, PNG, or GIF output, the image is written in 8-bit format, with 24-bit images converted by calling `color_quan` if necessary. If the caller selected JPEG or TIFF output, the image is written in 24-bit format, with 8-bit images converted to 24-bit if necessary. Finally the user is notified that the output file was created.

To display the previously shown shaded surface and save it to a bitmap output file:

```
IDL> window, /free, xsize=640, ysize=512
IDL> loadct, 3
IDL> device, decomposed=0
IDL> shade_surf, z, xstyle=1, ystyle=1, charsize=2, $
IDL>   color=0, background=(!d.table_size - 1)
IDL> saveimage, 'surface.jpg'
IDL> saveimage, 'surface.png', /png
```

8.3 CREATING POSTSCRIPT OUTPUT

PostScript is the most commonly used vector output format in IDL because it is compatible with a wide variety of printers, and it can be inserted into many different document preparation applications (e.g., Word, PageMaker). To print a PostScript file, you must have access to a PostScript-capable printer or a software application that allows you to print PostScript files on non-PostScript printers.

The freeware GSview and Ghostview applications are highly recommended for previewing PostScript files (see Appendix A for download details). Versions are available for Windows, MacOS, and a variety of UNIX operating systems. These applications also allow you to print PostScript files on a variety of non-PostScript printers.

Introduction to the PostScript Device

To create Postscript output in IDL, you must first configure the PS device, render the graphic, and then close the device. As a first example, a plot is created with the default page orientation and size:

```
IDL> entry_device = !d.name
IDL> set_plot, 'PS'
IDL> device, filename='plot_example.ps'
IDL> x = findgen(200) * 0.1
IDL> plot, x, sin(x), charsize=1.5
IDL> xc = [0.0, 1.0, 1.0, 0.0, 0.0]
IDL> yc = [0.0, 0.0, 1.0, 1.0, 0.0]
IDL> plots, xc, yc, /normal, linestyle=2
IDL> device, /close_file
IDL> set_plot, entry_device
```

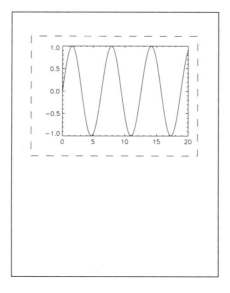

First, the name of the current graphics device is saved (entry_device) so that it can be restored later. Then the PS device is selected by calling set_plot, and the name of the output file is selected by calling device (if a file name is not set, the default file name is idl.ps). A simple plot is then created, and the outlines of the drawable area are plotted with dashed lines. When plotting is complete, device is called with the close_file keyword, which completes and closes the output file (if you forget this step, the output file will be incomplete). Finally, the entry graphics device is reselected by calling set_plot.

Note   It is essential to close the PostScript output file by calling device, /close_file when plotting is complete. Otherwise the printed page may be missing some parts of the plot, or it may be completely blank.

To send a PostScript file to the default printer in Windows (assuming the printer is PostScript-capable):

```
IDL> device, print_file='idl.ps'
```

To send a PostScript file to a printer in MacOS, the freeware Drop*PS utility may be used (see Appendix A for download details). In UNIX simply issue your usual print command from within IDL:

```
IDL> $lpr -Plp2 idl.ps
```

Configuring the PostScript Device

When configuring the PostScript device, the most important options you must set are the following:

- Page orientation (Portrait or Landscape)
- Size of drawable area
- Offset of drawable area origin from page edges
- Color output (enabled or disabled)

To check the configuration of the PostScript device (or any other IDL graphics device), you can call help with the device keyword set, as shown in the following example from IDL 5.4 for Windows:

```
IDL> entry_device = !d.name
IDL> set_plot, 'PS'
IDL> help, /device
Available Graphics Devices: CGM HP METAFILE NULL PCL
  PRINTER PS WIN Z
Current graphics device: PS
    File: <none>
```

```
Mode: Portrait, Non-Encapsulated, EPSI Preview Disabled,
  Color Disabled
Offset (X,Y): (1.905,12.7) cm., (0.75,5) in.
Size (X,Y): (17.78,12.7) cm., (7,5) in.
Scale Factor: 1
Preview Size (X,Y): (4.51556,4.51556) cm.,
  (1.77778,1.77778) in.
Preview Depth: 8 bits per pixel
Font Size: 12
Font Encoding: AdobeStandard
Font: Helvetica    TrueType Font: <default>
# bits per image pixel: 4
```

Note that the "Font Mapping" output section is not shown. From this information, you can see that the default PostScript configuration is as follows:

- Page orientation: Portrait
- Size of drawable area: 7 inches wide, 5 inches high
- Offset of drawable area origin from page edges: 0.75 inch from left, 5 inches from bottom
- Color output: disabled

If you switch to Landscape orientation and check the configuration:

```
IDL> device, /landscape
IDL> help, /device
```

you will see that the default Landscape configuration is as follows:

- Page orientation: Landscape
- Size of drawable area: 9.5 inches wide, 7 inches high
- Offset of drawable area origin from page edges: 0.75 inch from left, 10.25 inches from bottom
- Color output: disabled

To change the PostScript configuration, device is called with the appropriate keyword. For example, to set the drawable area offsets xoffset and yoffset to 2.5 and 3.5 inches, respectively:

```
IDL> device, xoffset=2.5, yoffset=3.5, /inches
```

The most commonly used device keywords for the PS device are shown in Table 8.3.

Table 8.3 **Commonly used** `device` **keywords for the** PS **device.**

Keyword	Purpose
`filename`	Set the output file name (default: `idl.ps`)
`/portrait`	Select portrait orientation (default)
`/landscape`	Select landscape orientation
`/color`	Select color output (default is grayscale)
`bits_per_pixel`	Set number of bits per pixel (default is 4)
`xsize`	Set width of drawable area
`ysize`	Set height of drawable area
`xoffset`	Set offset of drawable area origin from left of page
`yoffset`	Set offset of drawable area origin from bottom of page
`/inches`	Set units of inches for size and offset keywords in this call to `device` only (default is centimeters)
`font_size`	Set font size (points, default is 12)
`/close_file`	Complete and close the output file

Note When you configure the PostScript device using a `device` keyword as shown in Table 8.3, the setting is retained until you subsequently modify the setting, or you exit IDL. For example, if you switch the PostScript device to Landscape orientation:

```
IDL> device, /landscape
```

then it will stay in Landscape orientation until you select Portrait orientation:

```
IDL> device, /portrait
```

This is true for all the keywords shown in Table 8.3 except `/inches`, which sets the default size and offset units to inches for the current call to `device` only (the units are centimeters by default).

Setting Size and Offset Manually

The most difficult part of configuring the PostScript device is setting the size and offset of the drawable area correctly. For example, say you've created a plot in a graphics window that has an aspect ratio of 0.85 (650 pixels wide by 550 pixels high):

```
IDL> set_plot, entry_device
IDL> window, /free, xsize=650, ysize=550
IDL> x = findgen(200) * 0.1
IDL> plot, x, sin(x)
IDL> xc = [0.0, 1.0, 1.0, 0.0, 0.0]
IDL> yc = [0.0, 0.0, 1.0, 1.0, 0.0]
IDL> plots, xc, yc, /normal, linestyle=2
```

Note   The variable `entry_device` contains the name of the default window graphics device (`'WIN'`, `'MAC'`, or `'X'`).

Now you'd like to reproduce the plot in Portrait orientation, on an 8.5-inch × 11-inch page. First, the size and offset of the drawable area of the page are set:

```
IDL> page_width = 8.5
IDL> page_height = 11.0
IDL> xsize = 6.5
IDL> ysize = 5.5
IDL> xoffset = (page_width - xsize) * 0.5
IDL> yoffset = (page_height - ysize) * 0.5
```

Then the PostScript device is selected and configured, and the plot is created:

```
IDL> set_plot, 'PS'
IDL> device, filename='plot_port.ps', /portrait
IDL> device, xsize=xsize, ysize=ysize, $
IDL>   xoffset=xoffset, yoffset=yoffset, /inches
IDL> plot, x, sin(x)
IDL> plots, xc, yc, /normal, linestyle=2
IDL> device, /close_file
```

The result is shown in Figure 8.2(a).

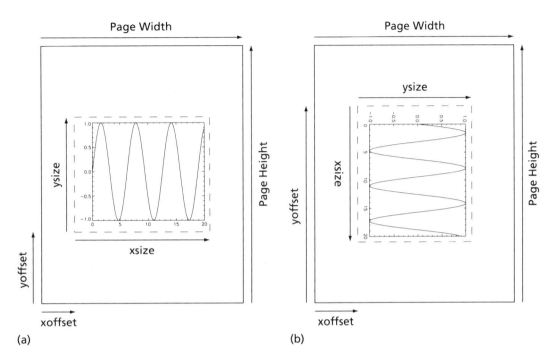

Figure 8.2 PostScript device: (a) Portrait mode and (b) Landscape mode.

To create the same plot in Landscape orientation with the same page size, the offset of the drawable area must be recomputed using a method that takes account of the new orientation:

```
IDL> xoffset = (page_width - ysize) * 0.5
IDL> yoffset = (page_height - xsize) * 0.5 + xsize
```

Then the plot may be created:

```
IDL> device, filename='plot_land.ps', /landscape
IDL> device, xsize=xsize, ysize=ysize, $
IDL>   xoffset=xoffset, yoffset=yoffset, /inches
IDL> plot, x, sin(x)
IDL> plots, xc, yc, /normal, linestyle=2
IDL> device, /close_file
```

The result is shown in Figure 8.2(b). For both the Portrait and Landscape orientations, the size variables xsize and ysize refer to the width and height of the drawable area when the plot is viewed with the x-axis horizontal, and the offset variables xoffset and yoffset refer to the offset of the drawable area origin from the bottom-left corner of the page.

Note   When configuring the PostScript device, you are not actually setting the width and height of the printed page. Rather, you are assuming a certain page size, and then explicitly setting the size and offset of the drawable area on the page. The paper loaded in your printer must match the assumed paper size (e.g., 8.5 × 11 inches) for the plot to be positioned correctly when it is printed.

Setting Size and Offset Automatically

In the previous example, the width and height of the drawable area were manually chosen to fit within the page boundaries, while maintaining the same aspect ratio as the graphics window. Since you will usually design your plot (or any other IDL graphic, including images) in a graphics window first, it would be useful to have IDL configure the PostScript device automatically to match the aspect ratio of the graphics window. In addition, it would be helpful to have a range of paper sizes available to choose from (e.g., Letter, Legal, A4, A3), to have the entry graphics device (e.g., 'WIN') automatically remembered by IDL, and then restored when you are done creating PostScript output.

The following procedure named pson.pro configures the PostScript device to match the aspect ratio of the current graphics window. A default aspect ratio is used if no graphics windows are open, or you can specify an aspect ratio. The drawable area is sized to fit within the default or user-supplied page margin. You can select Portrait or Landscape mode for a range of standard paper sizes or a user-supplied page size. The character size is set to the same relative size and aspect as the current graphics window. The graphics device on entry is remembered and can be restored by the companion procedure psoff.

```
PRO PSON, FILENAME=FILENAME, PAPER=PAPER, MARGIN=MARGIN, $
  PAGE_SIZE=PAGE_SIZE, INCHES=INCHES, ASPECT=ASPECT, $
  LANDSCAPE=LANDSCAPE, QUIET=QUIET

;- Check arguments
if (n_elements(filename) eq 0) then filename='idl.ps'
if (n_elements(paper) eq 0) then paper = 'LETTER'
if (n_elements(margin) eq 0) then begin
  margin = 2.5
```

```
endif else begin
  if keyword_set(inches) then margin = margin * 2.54
endelse

;- Check if Postscript mode is active
if !d.name eq 'PS' then begin
  message, 'POSTSCRIPT output is already active', /continue
  return
endif

;- Get ratio of character width/height to
;- screen width/height
xratio = float(!d.x_ch_size) / float(!d.x_vsize)
yratio = float(!d.y_ch_size) / float(!d.y_vsize)

;- Save current device information in common block
common pson_information, info
info = {device:!d.name, window:!d.window, font:!p.font, $
  filename:filename, xratio:xratio, yratio:yratio}

;- Get size of page (centimeters)
widths  = [[ 8.5,  8.5, 11.0,  7.25] * 2.54, 21.0, 29.7]
heights = [[11.0, 14.0, 17.0, 10.50] * 2.54, 29.7, 42.0]
names   = ['LETTER', 'LEGAL', 'TABLOID', 'EXECUTIVE', $
  'A4', 'A3']
index = where(strupcase(paper) eq names, count)
if (count ne 1) then begin
  message, 'PAPER selection not supported', /continue
  return
endif
page_width  = widths[index[0]]
page_height = heights[index[0]]

;- If page size was supplied, use it
if (n_elements(page_size) eq 2) then begin
  page_width  = page_size[0]
  page_height = page_size[1]
  if keyword_set(inches) then begin
    page_width  = page_width * 2.54
    page_height = page_height * 2.54
  endif
endif

;- Compute aspect ratio of page when margins are subtracted
```

```
page_aspect = float(page_height - 2.0 * margin) / $
              float(page_width  - 2.0 * margin)

;- Get aspect ratio of current graphics window
if (!d.window ge 0) then begin
  win_aspect = float(!d.y_vsize) / float(!d.x_vsize)
endif else begin
  win_aspect = 512.0 / 640.0
endelse

;- If aspect ratio was supplied, use it
if (n_elements(aspect) eq 1) then $
  win_aspect = float(aspect)

;- Compute size of drawable area
;- (method used here is the same as the Printer method)
case keyword_set(landscape) of
  0 : begin
        if (win_aspect ge page_aspect) then begin
          ysize = page_height - 2.0 * margin
          xsize = ysize / win_aspect
        endif else begin
          xsize = page_width - 2.0 * margin
          ysize = xsize * win_aspect
        endelse
      end
  1 : begin
        if (win_aspect ge (1.0 / page_aspect)) then begin
          ysize = page_width - 2.0 * margin
          xsize = ysize / win_aspect
        endif else begin
          xsize = page_height - 2.0 * margin
          ysize = xsize * win_aspect
        endelse
      end
endcase

;- Compute offset of drawable area from page edges
;- (landscape method here is different than
;-  the Printer method)
if (keyword_set(landscape) eq 0) then begin
  xoffset = (page_width  - xsize) * 0.5
  yoffset = (page_height - ysize) * 0.5
endif else begin
```

```
  xoffset = (page_width  - ysize) * 0.5
  yoffset = (page_height - xsize) * 0.5 + xsize
endelse

;- Switch to Postscript device
;- Note (1): Default units are centimeters
set_plot, 'PS'
device, landscape=keyword_set(landscape), scale_factor=1.0
device, xsize=xsize, ysize=ysize, $
  xoffset=xoffset, yoffset=yoffset
device, filename=filename, /color, bits_per_pixel=8

;- Set character size
xcharsize = round(info.xratio * !d.x_vsize)
ycharsize = round(info.yratio * !d.y_vsize)
device, set_character_size=[xcharsize, ycharsize]

;- Report to user
if (keyword_set(quiet) eq 0) then $
  print, filename, $
    format='("Started POSTSCRIPT output to ", a)'

END
```

The pson procedure does the following:

1. First the input keywords are checked, and default values are assigned if necessary. Then it checks to see whether PostScript output is already active, and if true, it returns without taking any action.
2. The relative character size and aspect ratio is obtained, and the current graphics device information is stored via a common block so it can be restored later.
3. The width and height of the page is obtained from the paper keyword, or the default size (Letter, 8.5×11 inches) is used if paper is undefined (pson uses centimeter units internally). If the page_size keyword was passed by the caller and is a two-element array, it is assumed to be a user-supplied page width and height (in default centimeter units). The user-supplied width and height is converted from inches to centimeters if the inches keyword is set.
4. The aspect ratio of the page (page_aspect) is computed. The aspect ratio of the current graphics window (win_aspect) is also computed, or a default value is assigned if no graphics window exists. If

the caller passed an aspect ratio via the aspect keyword, it is used to define win_aspect.

5. The size of the drawable area is computed, with different methods used for Portrait and Landscape orientations. Given the drawable area size, the offsets to the edge of the page are computed.

6. Finally, the PostScript device is selected and configured, the character size is set, and a message is printed to confirm that PostScript output is now active.

The following procedure psoff.pro is designed to work in conjunction with pson. It closes the PostScript output file and switches back to the entry graphics device:

```
PRO PSOFF, QUIET=QUIET

;- Check that PostScript output is active
if (!d.name ne 'PS') then begin
  message, 'POSTSCRIPT output not active: ' + $
    'nothing done', /continue
  return
endif

;- Get entry device information from common block
common pson_information, info
if (n_elements(info) eq 0) then begin
  message, 'PSON was not called prior to PSOFF: ' + $
    'nothing done', /continue
  return
endif

;- Close PostScript device
device, /close_file

;- Switch to entry graphics device
set_plot, info.device

;- Restore window and font
if (info.window ge 0) then wset, info.window
!p.font = info.font

;- Report to user
if (keyword_set(quiet) eq 0) then $
  print, info.filename, $
```

```
      format='("Ended POSTSCRIPT output to ", a)'

END
```

With the aid of `pson` and `psoff`, it is easy to create PostScript output. For example, say you'd like to render the surface described in Section 8.2 to PostScript output. First, render the surface in a graphics window to check its appearance (`entry_device` is the default window graphics device, `'WIN'`, `'MAC'`, or `'X'`):

```
IDL> set_plot, entry_device
IDL> window, /free
IDL> z = dist(64)
IDL> z = shift(z, 32, 32)
IDL> z = exp(-(z * 0.1)^2)
IDL> loadct, 3
IDL> shade_surf, z, xstyle=1, ystyle=1, charsize=2, $
IDL>    pixels=1000, xmargin=[4, 1], ymargin=[1, 0]
```

Then use `pson` to select PostScript output, render the surface, and use `psoff` to close the output file:

```
IDL> pson, file='surface.ps', margin=1.0
IDL> loadct, 3
IDL> shade_surf, z, xstyle=1, ystyle=1, charsize=2, $
IDL>    pixels=1000, xmargin=[4, 1], ymargin=[1, 0]
IDL> psoff
```

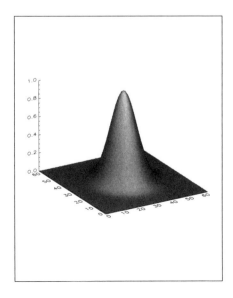

To create a plot on an A4 page in Landscape mode with an aspect ratio of 1.0 and double-size text:

```
IDL> pson, /landscape, paper='A4', aspect=1.0
IDL> x = findgen(200) * 0.1
IDL> plot, x, sin(x), charsize=2
IDL> psoff
```

Color PostScript Output

IDL gives you the option of choosing grayscale or color output in Post-Script mode. In grayscale mode the color table is not used, and intensity values are mapped directly to shades of gray. In color mode, the color table maps intensity values to colors. The default PostScript mode is grayscale output at a depth of 4 bits per pixel. Available depths include 1, 2, 4, and 8 bits per pixel. For example, the shaded surface shown below is rendered in grayscale at 4 bits per pixel:

```
IDL> pson, file='surface.ps', margin=1.0
IDL> device, color=0, bits_per_pixel=4
IDL> z = dist(64)
IDL> z = shift(z, 32, 32)
IDL> z = exp(-(z * 0.1)^2)
IDL> shade_surf, z, xstyle=1, ystyle=1, charsize=2, $
IDL>   pixels=1000, xmargin=[4, 1], ymargin=[1, 0]
IDL> psoff
```

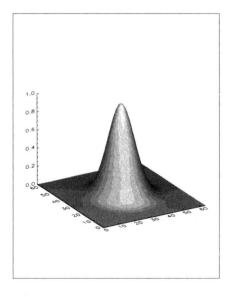

Grayscale output at 4 bits per pixel is selected by calling `device` with the keywords `color=0` and `bits_per_pixel=4`. The main reason to use grayscale mode with reduced color depth is that it generates smaller output files, at the cost of lower-quality color reproduction (note the banding that appears in the surface plot). If your graphical output requires only black and white, then a depth of 1 bit per pixel is sufficient.

However, the use of color mode with 8 bits per pixel is recommended as it supports black and white, grayscale, and color output. To select color output:

```
IDL> device, /color, bits_per_pixel=8
```

This is the default mode used by `pson`. For advice on displaying images when the PostScript device is selected, see Section 7.6. The image display application `imdisp.pro` shown in Section 7.7 is highly recommended for displaying images when the PostScript device is selected.

Using the Color Table in PostScript Mode

When color PostScript output is selected (`device, /color`), the PS device acts as a pseudocolor device, which means the color table is used to map intensity values to colors. Thus you need to know how to work with the color table in PostScript mode.

When you select the PostScript device, the contents of the color table do not change, but its size changes to 256 entries. If IDL is running in 24-bit display mode (where the color table has 256 entries), the switch to PostScript mode does not cause any color table problems. However, if IDL is running in 8-bit display mode where the color table has fewer than 256 entries, you must take appropriate action to ensure that the color table is used correctly. For example, the following output was generated on a Windows PC with IDL running in 8-bit mode:

```
IDL> print, !d.name, !d.table_size
WIN          236
IDL> set_plot, 'PS'
IDL> print, !d.name, !d.table_size
PS           256
```

In this example, the color table has 236 entries in graphics window mode, but has 256 entries in PostScript mode. The safest solution is to load the desired color table just before creating your graphic. This approach is recommended whether IDL is running in 24-bit or 8-bit display mode because it allows you to generate consistent color output regardless of the bit depth of the display. For example, the following code produces identical output on all IDL platforms:

```
IDL> image = dist(256)
IDL> pson
IDL> loadct, 13
IDL> tvscl, image, xsize=5.0, ysize=5.0, /inches
IDL> psoff
```

By loading the rainbow color table with loadct immediately before displaying the image with tvscl, you ensure that red, green, and blue color table vectors of the correct size are loaded no matter what display device is used.

Note   The PS device does not support decomposed colors (e.g., color='00FFFF'XL).

Reversed Background and Drawing Colors

You may have noticed that the default background and drawing colors in PostScript mode are the reverse of what you see in a graphics window. By default, IDL uses a black background color and a white drawing color in graphics windows, corresponding to the lowest and highest entries in the color table. Most of the predefined color tables in IDL have black at the lowest color table entry and white at the highest color table entry. However, when creating PostScript output, you probably don't want a black background, so IDL does not set a background color, and the default plotting color is set to the lowest index in the color table (which is usually black). You can use a specific color table index for the plotting color by passing the color keyword to the relevant IDL plotting command (e.g., plot, surface).

To set the background to a specific color when the PostScript device is selected, you can call the polyfill procedure to fill the drawable area with the selected color. For example, to create a white plot on a blue background.

```
IDL> pson
IDL> tvlct, [0B, 255B], [0B, 255B], [127B, 255B]
IDL> polyfill, [0, 1, 1, 0, 0], [0, 0, 1, 1, 0], $
IDL>    /normal, color=0
IDL> plot, x, sin(x), color=1, /noerase
IDL> psoff
```

In this example, blue is loaded at color index 0, and white is loaded at color index 1. First, the entire drawing area is filled with color index 0; then, the plot is created with color index 1. Note the use of the noerase keyword when plot is called.

Fonts Overview

The PostScript device supports vector, device, and TrueType fonts, as shown in the following example:

```
IDL> pson
IDL> xyouts, 0.0, 0.75, 'Vector Font (-1) ', $
IDL>    /normal, charsize=3.5, font=-1
IDL> xyouts, 0.0, 0.50, 'Device Font (0)',   $
IDL>    /normal, charsize=3.5, font=0
IDL> xyouts, 0.0, 0.25, 'TrueType Font (1)', $
IDL>    /normal, charsize=3.5, font=1
IDL> psoff
```

Vector Font (−1)

Device Font (0)

TrueType Font (1)

The xyouts keyword font is used to specify the font index (vector fonts are the default if font is not specified). The font keyword is accepted by the following procedures: axis, contour, plot, shade_surf, surface, xyouts. For more information on vector fonts, see the online help.

The TeXtoIDL package described in Section 6.5 supports both vector and device fonts when the PostScript graphics device is selected. TeXtoIDL allows complex mathematical equations to be expressed using a simple TeX-like syntax and is highly recommended.

Tip   The pson procedure described earlier in this chapter automatically sizes vector and TrueType fonts in PostScript mode to match the font proportions in the graphics window.

PostScript Device Fonts

A total of 35 different device fonts are available in PostScript mode. To use device fonts, set the font keyword to zero when calling a plot command (axis, contour, plot, shade_surf, surface, or xyouts). To select a specific device font, PostScript-specific keywords are passed to device:

```
IDL> pson
IDL> device, /helvetica, font_size=16
IDL> xyouts, 0.0, 0.75, 'Helvetica', $
IDL>   /normal, charsize=3.5, font=0
IDL> device, /times, /bold
IDL> xyouts, 0.0, 0.50, 'Times Bold', $
IDL>   /normal, charsize=3.5, font=0
IDL> device, /palatino, /italic
IDL> xyouts, 0.0, 0.25, 'Palatino Italic', $
IDL>   /normal, charsize=3.5, font=0
IDL> psoff
```

Helvetica

Times Bold

Palatino Italic

You may need to adjust the font size using the device keyword font_size to obtain a reasonable match between fonts in the graphics window and fonts in PostScript output. If you are creating multiple-panel plots via the !p.multi system variable, you may need to adjust the font magnification via the charsize keyword, which is accepted by the axis, contour, plot, shade_surf, surface, and xyouts procedures. For more information on device fonts, see the online help.

Tip	To obtain comparable font sizes in window graphics and PostScript modes, set the window graphics character size with the command `device, set_character_size=[10, 12]` (the default units are pixels).

TrueType Fonts

Device fonts in PostScript mode have one drawback: they cannot be rendered in three dimensions (e.g., `shade_surf` axis labels), even though they can be rotated in two dimensions (e.g., a `plot` *y*-axis title). To obtain good font quality, and to allow three-dimensional font scaling, TrueType fonts may be used in PostScript mode. When `axis`, `contour`, `plot`, `shade_surf`, `surface`, or `xyouts` is called with the keyword `font=1`, TrueType fonts are used. To select a specific TrueType font, TrueType-specific keywords are passed to `device`:

```
IDL> pson
IDL> device, set_font='Helvetica', /tt_font
IDL> xyouts, 0.0, 0.75, 'Helvetica', $
IDL>    /normal, charsize=3.5, font=1
IDL> device, set_font='Times Bold', /tt_font
IDL> xyouts, 0.0, 0.50, 'Times Bold', $
IDL>    /normal, charsize=3.5, font=1
IDL> device, set_font='Times Italic', /tt_font
IDL> xyouts, 0.0, 0.25, 'Times Italic', $
IDL>    /normal, charsize=3.5, font=1
IDL> psoff
```

Helvetica

Times Bold

Times Italic

To render a surface in PostScript mode with TrueType fonts:

```
IDL> pson, file='surface.ps', margin=1.0
IDL> device, set_font='Times Italic', /tt_font
```

```
IDL> z = dist(64)
IDL> z = shift(z, 32, 32)
IDL> z = exp(-(z * 0.1)^2)
IDL> loadct, 3
IDL> shade_surf, z, xstyle=1, ystyle=1, charsize=2, font=1, $
IDL>    pixels=1000, xmargin=[4, 1], ymargin=[1, 0]
IDL> psoff
```

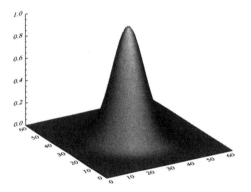

For more information on TrueType fonts, see the online help.

Note While TrueType fonts can be used in both PostScript mode and within a graphics window, the font rendering in graphics windows is unspectacular. The rendering of TrueType fonts in PostScript mode is, however, quite acceptable.

Positioning Graphics in the Drawable Area

To successfully position graphics in the drawable area regardless of the selected device, you should use normal coordinates rather than data or device coordinates. This is because no matter which output device is selected, the bottom-left corner of the drawable area is (0.0, 0.0), and the top-right corner of the drawable area is (1.0, 1.0) in normal coordinates.

For example, the following technique for positioning a plot title should be avoided:

```
IDL> window, /free
IDL> shade_surf, dist(256), charsize=2.0
IDL> xyouts, 300, 450, 'Test Plot', charsize=2.0, /device
```

Here the xyouts keyword device was set to specify the title position at (300, 450) in device coordinates (a location arrived at by trial-and-error). However, if this same technique is used in PostScript mode, the title will be positioned in the lower left of the drawable area because in PostScript mode there are 1,000 pixels per centimeter (2,540 pixels per inch).

Instead, you should use normal coordinates to position the title:

```
IDL> shade_surf, dist(256), charsize=2.0
IDL> xyouts, 0.5, 0.9, 'Test Plot', charsize=2.0, $
IDL>    /normal, align=0.5
```

By using normal coordinates, you ensure that the title will be positioned correctly regardless of which output device is selected. Data coordinates should be used sparingly for position titles or labels. One case where data coordinates are recommended is when you wish to label a specific feature on a plot (say, a local minimum of a curve). However, the use of data coordinates for other text annotations, symbols, or legends is discouraged.

Adding an EPS Preview

Many word processing and page layout applications (e.g., Word, Page-Maker) can import encapsulated PostScript (EPS) files. An EPS file is a special kind of PostScript file that can be embedded in a document as a figure, while retaining full print resolution. If the EPS file contains a preview image (a rasterized version of the figure), the preview image is displayed while the document is edited. When the document is subsequently printed on a PostScript printer, the full-resolution vector figure is printed. If the document is printed on a non-PostScript printer, the rasterized preview image is printed.

IDL can create EPS files by using the device keywords encapsulated and preview, as shown in the following example:

```
IDL> x = findgen(200) * 0.1
IDL> pson, filename='idl_preview.eps'
IDL> device, /encapsulated, preview=2
IDL> plot, x, sin(x)
IDL> psoff
```

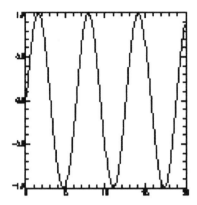

Figure 8.3 Example of a low-quality EPS preview image.

The resulting EPS preview image is shown in Figure 8.3. While the preview image is of low quality, the EPS file can be imported into a word processing or page layout application.

Note IDL version 5.2.1 or higher is required to generate an EPS preview that can be viewed in Word 97 (or later versions of Word). Earlier versions of IDL will create an EPS file that can be imported into Word 97; however, a preview image will not be seen while the document is edited.

To create EPS files with high-quality color previews that can be imported into a wide range of applications, the freeware GSview application mentioned previously in this section can be used. The following instructions apply to the Windows version of GSview. First, create a standard PostScript output file in IDL in Portrait mode without a preview (not an EPS file). Then launch GSview, and do the following:

1. File/Open, to open your PostScript file (e.g., `idl.ps`).
2. File/PS to EPS, check "Automatically calculate Bounding Box," and select Yes.
3. File/Save, and save the EPS file as `temp.eps`.

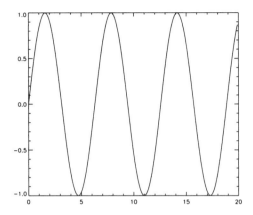

Figure 8.4 Example of a high-quality EPS preview image.

4. File/Close, to close the PostScript file.
5. File/Open, to open the EPS file.
6. Options/EPS Clip, to select EPS clipping.
7. Edit/Add EPS Preview/TIFF 6 packbits, to add a compressed color preview image.
8. File/Save, to save the EPS file (e.g., idl.eps).

The resulting preview image is shown in Figure 8.4.

On UNIX platforms, the freeware epstool application can be used to convert IDL PostScript output to EPS format with a preview image. (See Appendix A for download details.) For example, to create an EPS file with a TIFF 6 packed preview:

```
% epstool -b -t6p -oidl.eps idl.ps
```

Note   EPS files created via the method shown above cannot be sent directly to a printer; they can only be included in a document. When EPS files of this type are transferred via FTP, the transfer mode should be set to binary, because the preview image contains binary data.

8.4   CREATING PRINTER OUTPUT

The PRINTER graphics device in IDL allows you to send graphical output directly to a printer. The printer need not understand PostScript. IDL interfaces with the operating system to send output to the printer in a format that the printer understands, assuming that a driver for the printer has been installed. On UNIX systems, IDL supplies drivers for a range of printers. Because PostScript is not used, you can select from a wider range of printers for creating graphical output. In fact, even relatively inexpensive color inkjet printers can be used to generate high-quality printed output (many inkjet printers support 1,440 dpi resolution, rivaling laser printers for vector plots).

Note   In the following discussion, IDL version 5.2 or higher is assumed. Although the PRINTER graphics device was introduced in IDL 5.0, the device keywords xsize, ysize, xoffset, and yoffset were not supported by the Printer device until IDL 5.2.

The Printer device and the PostScript device are used in a similar fashion. That is, you configure the device, render the graphic, then close the device. As an example, the first plot shown in Section 8.3 is recreated on the Printer device:

```
IDL> entry_device = !d.name
IDL> set_plot, 'PRINTER'
IDL> x = findgen(200) * 0.1
IDL> plot, x, sin(x), charsize=1.5
IDL> xc = [0.0, 1.0, 1.0, 0.0, 0.0]
IDL> yc = [0.0, 0.0, 1.0, 1.0, 0.0]
IDL> plots, xc, yc, /normal, linestyle=2
IDL> device, /close_document
IDL> set_plot, entry_device
```

On Windows and MacOS platforms, the output is sent directly to the default system printer. On UNIX systems, the output is sent to an encapsulated PostScript file named xprinter.eps by default.

Selecting a Printer

In some cases, you may wish to select a printer other than the default system printer. For example, the default printer might be a black-and-white laser printer, and you wish to select a color laser printer for your output. On a UNIX system, rather than sending output to `xprinter.eps` by default, you may wish to send output directly to a printer (which requires selecting a print command, e.g., `lpr -Plp4`).

To select a printer, the `dialog_printersetup` function is called:

```
IDL> result = dialog_printersetup()
```

On a Windows or MacOS system, calling `dialog_printersetup` invokes the system printer dialog, where you can select a different printer or change printer settings such as output resolution, as shown in Figure 8.5.

On a UNIX system, calling `dialog_printersetup` invokes a dialog box that can be used to select or install a printer, as shown in Figure 8.6. To select an installed printer on a UNIX system, click on "Printer Specific", then select "Options". To install a new printer, select "Install/Add Printer". Here you must select a specific printer model (on the left), and also specify the print command, such as `lpr -Plp4` (on the right). Once these options are configured correctly, subsequent output will be sent

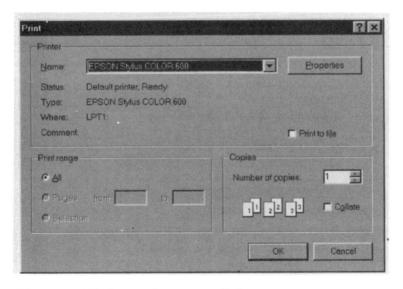

Figure 8.5 Windows printer setup dialog.

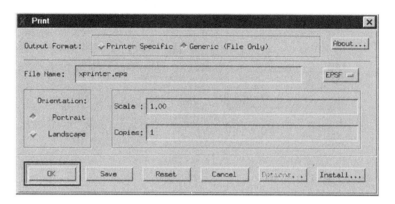

Figure 8.6 UNIX printer setup dialog.

directly to this printer when the `PRINTER` graphics device is selected. This printer will be the default for the remainder of the IDL session, or until `dialog_printersetup` is called again.

Tip   If you use `dialog_printersetup` to change the page size (e.g., Letter, A4, etc.) or orientation (Portrait or Landscape), make sure you use the same page width, height, and orientation when you subsequently select and configure the Printer device. The `printon` procedure described later in this chapter shows one way to configure the size and orientation of the page.

Configuring the Printer Device

Just like the PostScript device, the most important options you must set with the Printer device are the following:

- Page orientation (Portrait or Landscape)
- Size of drawable area
- Offset of drawable area origin from page edges
- Color output (enabled or disabled)

You can check the configuration of the Printer device by calling `help` with the `device` keyword set. The default settings for the Printer device are the same as for the PostScript device, except that indexed color output is enabled by default. If you switch to Landscape orientation, you will find that the configuration is once again very similar to the PostScript device, except that the yoffset value is 0.75 inch, rather than 10.25 inches (more on this in the next section).

To change any of the Printer device settings, call device with the appropriate keyword. The keywords most commonly used with the Printer device are shown in Table 8.4.

Setting Size and Offset Manually

Setting the size and offset of the drawable area correctly is just as important with the Printer device as with the PostScript device. Ideally, you'd like to create a drawable area with the same aspect ratio as the current window, where you've already checked the layout of your IDL graphics.

The device procedure in IDL 5.2 and higher versions accepts the xsize, ysize, xoffset, and yoffset keywords when the PRINTER device is selected. For example, say you require Portrait orientation output with an aspect ratio of 0.85 (550/650):

```
IDL> set_plot, entry_device
IDL> window, /free, xsize=650, ysize=550
IDL> x = findgen(200) * 0.1
IDL> plot, x, sin(x)
```

Table 8.4   Commonly used device **keywords for the** PRINTER **device.**

Keyword	Purpose
/portrait	Select portrait orientation (default)
/landscape	Select landscape orientation
/index_color	Select indexed color output (default)
/true_color	Select true color output
xsize	Set width of drawable area
ysize	Set height of drawable area
xoffset	Set offset of drawable area origin from left of page
yoffset	Set offset of drawable area origin from bottom of page
/inches	Set size and offset units (default is centimeters)
scale_factor	Set scaling factor (default is 1.0)
/close_document	Send output to default system printer

```
IDL> xc = [0.0, 1.0, 1.0, 0.0, 0.0]
IDL> yc = [0.0, 0.0, 1.0, 1.0, 0.0]
IDL> plots, xc, yc, /normal, linestyle=2
```

Note   The variable `entry_device` contains the name of the default window graphics device (`'WIN'`, `'MAC'`, or `'X'`).

To reproduce the plot in Portrait orientation on an 8.5×11-inch page, the size and offset of the drawable area of the page are set:

```
IDL> page_width = 8.5
IDL> page_height = 11.0
IDL> xsize = 6.5
IDL> ysize = 5.5
IDL> xoffset = (page_width - xsize) * 0.5
IDL> yoffset = (page_height - ysize) * 0.5
```

Then the Printer device is selected and configured, and the plot is created:

```
IDL> set_plot, 'PRINTER'
IDL> device, /portrait
IDL> device, xsize=xsize, ysize=ysize, $
IDL>   xoffset=xoffset, yoffset=yoffset, /inches
IDL> plot, x, sin(x)
IDL> plots, xc, yc, /normal, linestyle=2
IDL> device, /close_document
```

The result is shown in Figure 8.7(a). To recreate the plot in Landscape orientation, the offset of the drawable area must be recomputed. This method is different than the method used for computing offsets on the PostScript device:

```
IDL> xoffset = (page_height - xsize) * 0.5
IDL> yoffset = (page_width  - ysize) * 0.5
```

Finally the plot is created:

```
IDL> device, /landscape
IDL> device, xsize=xsize, ysize=ysize, $
IDL>   xoffset=xoffset, yoffset=yoffset, /inches
IDL> plot, x, sin(x)
IDL> plots, xc, yc, /normal, linestyle=2
IDL> device, /close_document
```

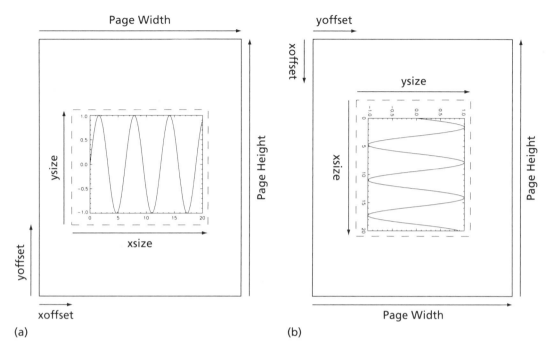

Figure 8.7   Printer device: (a) Portrait and (b) Landscape mode.

The result is shown in Figure 8.7(b).

In Portrait orientation, the Printer device definitions of page width, page height, and drawable area size and offset are exactly the same as for the PostScript device. In Landscape orientation, the Printer device definitions of page width, page height, and drawable area size are the same as for the PostScript device, but the definitions of drawable area offsets are different. This must be taken into account when configuring the Printer device using the device keywords xoffset and yoffset.

Note   As of IDL 5.3, the page orientation (e.g., landscape) must be set in a separate device command before the size and offset values. If the orientation is set in the same device command as the size and offset values, the size and offset values are ignored. Thus, it is safest to separate the orientation and size/offset device commands.

Setting Size and Offset Automatically

Rather than configuring the Printer device manually, it would be useful to have a procedure that automatically configures it to match the aspect ratio of the current graphics window, such as the pson procedure for the PostScript device shown in Section 8.3.

The following procedure named printon.pro is essentially a Printer device version of pson. Just like pson, printon offers a selection of page sizes (e.g., Letter, Legal, A4, A3) in Portrait or Landscape orientation, and automatically configures the Printer device to match the aspect ratio of the current graphics window (or a default aspect ratio if no graphics window is present). The drawable area is sized to fit within the default or user-supplied page margin. The character size is set to the same relative size and aspect as the current graphics window. The graphics device on entry is remembered and is restored by the companion procedure printoff.pro.

```
PRO PRINTON, PAPER=PAPER, MARGIN=MARGIN, $
  PAGE_SIZE=PAGE_SIZE, INCHES=INCHES, ASPECT=ASPECT, $
  LANDSCAPE=LANDSCAPE, QUIET=QUIET

;- Check arguments
if (n_elements(paper) eq 0) then paper = 'LETTER'
if (n_elements(margin) eq 0) then begin
  margin = 2.5
endif else begin
  if keyword_set(inches) then margin = margin * 2.54
endelse

;- Check for IDL 5.2 or higher
if (float(!version.release) lt 5.2) then $
  message, 'IDL 5.2 or higher is required'

;- Check if Printer mode is active
if !d.name eq 'PRINTER' then begin
  message, 'PRINTER output is already active', /continue
  return
endif

;- Get ratio of character width/height to
;- screen width/height
xratio = float(!d.x_ch_size) / float(!d.x_vsize)
yratio = float(!d.y_ch_size) / float(!d.y_vsize)
```

```
;- Save current device information in common block
common printon_information, info
info = {device:!d.name, window:!d.window, font:!p.font, $
  xratio:xratio, yratio:yratio}

;- Get size of page (centimeters)
widths  = [[ 8.5,  8.5, 11.0,  7.25] * 2.54, 21.0, 29.7]
heights = [[11.0, 14.0, 17.0, 10.50] * 2.54, 29.7, 42.0]
names   = ['LETTER', 'LEGAL', 'TABLOID', 'EXECUTIVE', $
  'A4', 'A3']
index = where(strupcase(paper) eq names, count)
if (count ne 1) then begin
  message, 'PAPER selection not supported', /continue
  return
endif
page_width  = widths[index[0]]
page_height = heights[index[0]]

;- If page size was supplied, use it
if (n_elements(page_size) eq 2) then begin
  page_width  = page_size[0]
  page_height = page_size[1]
  if keyword_set(inches) then begin
    page_width  = page_width * 2.54
    page_height = page_height * 2.54
  endif
endif

;- Compute aspect ratio of page when margins are subtracted
page_aspect = float(page_height - 2.0 * margin) / $
              float(page_width  - 2.0 * margin)

;- Get aspect ratio of current graphics window
if (!d.window ge 0) then begin
  win_aspect = float(!d.y_vsize) / float(!d.x_vsize)
endif else begin
  win_aspect = 512.0 / 640.0
endelse

;- If aspect ratio was supplied, use it
if (n_elements(aspect) eq 1) then $
  win_aspect = float(aspect)

;- Compute size of drawable area
;- (method used here is the same as PostScript method)
```

```
case keyword_set(landscape) of
  0 : begin
        if (win_aspect ge page_aspect) then begin
          ysize = page_height - 2.0 * margin
          xsize = ysize / win_aspect
        endif else begin
          xsize = page_width - 2.0 * margin
          ysize = xsize * win_aspect
        endelse
      end
  1 : begin
        if (win_aspect ge (1.0 / page_aspect)) then begin
          ysize = page_width - 2.0 * margin
          xsize = ysize / win_aspect
        endif else begin
          xsize = page_height - 2.0 * margin
          ysize = xsize * win_aspect
        endelse
      end
endcase

;- Compute offset of drawable area from page edges
;- (landscape method here is different
;-  than the PostScript method)
if (keyword_set(landscape) eq 0) then begin
  xoffset = (page_width  - xsize) * 0.5
  yoffset = (page_height - ysize) * 0.5
endif else begin
  xoffset = (page_height - xsize) * 0.5
  yoffset = (page_width  - ysize) * 0.5
endelse

;- Switch to Printer device
;- Note (1): Default units are centimeters
;- Note (2): Separate device commands are required!
set_plot, 'PRINTER'
device, landscape=keyword_set(landscape), scale_factor=1.0
device, xsize=xsize, ysize=ysize, $
  xoffset=xoffset, yoffset=yoffset
device, /index_color

;- Set character size
xcharsize = round(info.xratio * !d.x_vsize)
ycharsize = round(info.yratio * !d.y_vsize)
```

```
device, set_character_size=[xcharsize, ycharsize]

;- Report to user
if (keyword_set(quiet) eq 0) then $
  print, 'Started PRINTER output'

END
```

Much of the code in printon is borrowed directly from pson. The main differences are the following:

1. No filename keyword (not applicable for the Printer device).
2. IDL 5.2 is required.
3. The common block is named printon_information instead of pson_information.
4. The method used to compute drawable area offsets is different than the PostScript method.
5. The device keyword index_color is used instead of color and bits_per_pixel.

The printon procedure is designed to work in conjunction with the following procedure named printoff.pro, which terminates output to the printer (causing printing to begin) and switches back to the entry graphics device.

```
PRO PRINTOFF, QUIET=QUIET

;- Check that Printer output is active
if (!d.name ne 'PRINTER') then begin
  message, 'PRINTER output not active: ' + $
    'nothing done', /continue
  return
endif

;- Get entry device information from common block
common printon_information, info
if (n_elements(info) eq 0) then begin
  message, 'PRINTON was not called prior to PRINTOFF: ' + $
    'nothing done', /continue
  return
endif

;- Close Printer device
```

```
device, /close_document

;- Switch to entry graphics device
set_plot, info.device

;- Restore window and font
if (info.window ge 0) then wset, info.window
!p.font = info.font

;- Report to user
if (keyword_set(quiet) eq 0) then $
  print, 'Ended PRINTER output'

END
```

The `printon` and `printoff` procedures make it easy to create Printer output. To print the surface plot described at the beginning of Section 8.2, you would first render the surface in a graphics window to check its appearance (`entry_device` is the default window graphics device, `'WIN'`, `'MAC'`, or `'X'`):

```
IDL> set_plot, entry_device
IDL> window, /free, retain=2
IDL> z = dist(64)
IDL> z = shift(z, 32, 32)
IDL> z = exp(-(z * 0.1)^2)
IDL> loadct, 3
IDL> shade_surf, z, xstyle=1, ystyle=1, charsize=2, $
IDL>   pixels=1000, xmargin=[4, 1], ymargin=[1, 0]
```

Then select Printer output by calling `printon`, render the surface plot, and call `printoff` to end output to the printer and start printing:

```
IDL> printon, margin=1.0
IDL> loadct, 3
IDL> shade_surf, z, xstyle=1, ystyle=1, charsize=2, $
IDL>   pixels=1000, xmargin=[4, 1], ymargin=[1, 0]
IDL> printoff
```

To create a plot on an A4 page in Landscape mode with an aspect ratio of 1.0 and double-size text:

```
IDL> printon, /landscape, paper='A4', aspect=1.0
IDL> x = findgen(200) * 0.1
IDL> plot, x, sin(x), charsize=2
IDL> printoff
```

Tip Most printers do not allow printing to the edge of the page, and therefore impose a small default margin around the edge of the page (usually about 0.5 cm). The width and height of the *printable* area of the page in centimeters can be obtained when the Printer device is selected using the following method:

```
IDL> device, get_page_size=page_size
IDL> width = page_size[0] / !d.x_px_cm
IDL> height = page_size[1] / !d.y_px_cm
```

The default margin can be found by comparing the page size (e.g., 21.0 by 29.7 cm for A4) to the values of width and height. The default page margin is not accounted for in the printon procedure: this is left as an exercise for the reader (Hint: before the page aspect ratio is computed, briefly select the Printer device to get the width and height).

Color Printer Output

Color output is enabled by default on the PRINTER device, assuming your printer supports color. The Printer device is configured for 8-bit Indexed Color by default, which means the color table is used to map intensity values to colors. To force this behavior, use the device keyword index_color:

```
IDL> device, /index_color
```

The color table always has 256 entries when the Printer device is selected (like the PostScript device). Therefore the comments in "Using the Color Table in PostScript Mode" in Section 8.3 apply to the Printer device as well as the PostScript device. The Printer device background and drawing colors are reversed by default (like the PostScript device), so the comments in "Reversed Background and Drawing Colors" in Section 8.3 apply to the Printer device as well as the PostScript device.

In addition to 8-bit Indexed Color, the Printer device supports 24-bit Decomposed Color, where the color table is bypassed and colors are determined purely by combinations of red, green, and blue intensities as described in Section 5.4. To select Decomposed Color on the PRINTER device, use the device keyword true_color:

```
IDL> device, /true_color
```

For advice on displaying images when the Printer device is selected, see Section 7.6. The image display application imdisp.pro shown in Section 7.7 is highly recommended for displaying images when the Printer device is selected.

Note The Printer device supports decomposed plotting colors (e.g., color= '00FFFF'XL) when in 24-bit Decomposed Color mode.

Fonts and Positioning

The Printer device supports the same vector and TrueType fonts as the PostScript device; see "Fonts Overview" in Section 8.3 for details. The character-sizing code in printon ensures that the relative size and aspect ratio of vector and TrueType fonts on the Printer device will be identical to those in the graphics window.

Device fonts on the Printer device cannot be resized via the device procedure; only the PostScript device has resizable device fonts. To obtain WYSIWYG font output on the Printer device, vector or TrueType fonts are recommended.

Normal coordinates are recommended for positioning graphics on the Printer device. For more information, see "Positioning Graphics in the Drawable Area" in Section 8.3.

9

Graphical User Interfaces

This chapter introduces you to the concepts necessary to create IDL applications with graphical user interfaces (GUIs). The chapter begins with a review of the reasons for creating a GUI application, and an overview of the GUI components (widgets) available in IDL. This is followed by a discussion of the differences between GUI programming and procedural programming, and a brief philosophy of GUI design. The chapter continues with an in-depth explanation of the functions used to create widgets. Examples of good and bad widget layouts are given, along with guidelines for naming widget buttons. This is followed by a discussion of events and event handling, and example programs demonstrating event management. Finally, a complete GUI application for displaying images is built from scratch, with code examples for widget creation, event handling, and application management.

9.1   INTRODUCTION TO GUI PROGRAMMING

GUIs provide a point-and-click way to run applications in a windowed environment. Complex and repetitive tasks can often be simplified by an interactive GUI that hides the implementation details and allows the user to focus on completing the task. IDL provides a built-in GUI development toolkit that allows you to create interactive applications on any IDL platform.

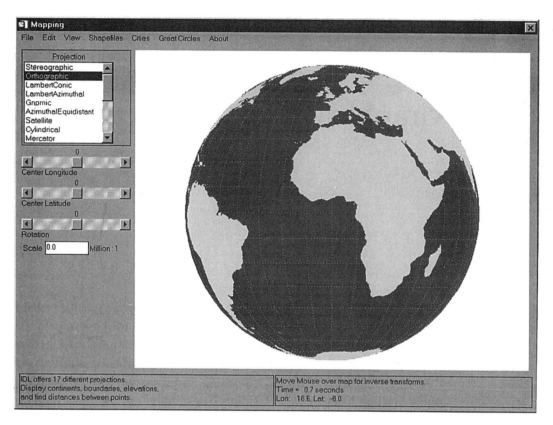

Figure 9.1 GUI mapping demonstration.

For example, the demo procedure includes an application built entirely with the GUI toolkit that demonstrates IDL mapping capabilities. To start the application, call the demo procedure:

```
IDL> demo
```

Select "Earth Sciences", then "Mapping", and a GUI similar to the one shown in Figure 9.1 should appear (the screenshot is from IDL for Windows).

This GUI offers a variety of ways to discover the mapping capabilities of IDL. The user can examine the available map projections by selecting a projection type from the list shown at the upper left, without having to learn the syntax of the map_set procedure. Likewise, by roaming the cursor over the image, the user discovers that screen coordinates can be converted to map coordinates, without having to know anything about coordinate systems in IDL. The user can learn about mapping features in IDL quickly and interactively without needing to know how map projections are implemented. This is one of the most important benefits of a GUI application: it can be designed for users who may not be familiar with IDL.

For the experienced user, a GUI can streamline complex data analysis, allowing you to focus your attention on the characteristics of your data, rather than the mechanics of entering IDL commands. This is especially true when many commands must be entered in sequence at the command line and executed repeatedly. A GUI also allows you to implement interactive features that are simply not possible at the command line, such as dragging a slider to adjust a parameter and automatically updating a plot. For example, when the Orthographic projection is selected in the mapping GUI, clicking and dragging on the map causes the projection to be recentered. It is difficult to achieve such a close relationship between interactive input and on-screen visualization in IDL unless the GUI toolkit is used.

The GUI toolkit also allows cross-platform interactive applications to be developed. For example, the appearance of the mapping GUI remains fundamentally the same regardless of which platform is used to run IDL. Thus it is possible to use a UNIX platform to design a GUI application that executes in IDL on a Windows or MacOS platform.

Note Most of the screenshots in this chapter were created in IDL for Windows. GUI applications on other IDL platforms will have a slightly different appearance.

GUI Components (Widgets)

A GUI application typically contains a variety of components known as *widgets*. Each widget has a particular appearance, and the application responds in a certain way when you interact with the widget. Inspection of the mapping GUI reveals the following widgets:

- A menu bar at the top allows configuration of application properties.

- A scrolling list allows a map projection to be chosen.
- Three horizontal sliders allow the projection center and rotation to be changed.
- A text entry field allows a map scale factor to be entered.
- A graphics window displays the name of the currently selected map projection.
- Labels at the bottom of the GUI display text information, including the current cursor location.
- A system menu button at top left and a Close button at top right (depending on platform) allow the GUI to be closed.

The application responds to interaction with each widget in different ways. For example, when a new projection is selected, the map is redrawn. When the cursor is moved over the map, the position display is updated. Thus the GUI application includes code not only to create widgets, but also to take action when the user interacts with each widget (i.e., an event handler). To create a GUI application, you need to arrange appropriate widgets in a sensible way, and then provide code that handles user interaction. These two aspects of a GUI—the appearance and layout of widgets, and their response to user interaction—reflect the essence of GUI programming.

GUI Programming versus Procedural Programming

The flow of control in a GUI program is fundamentally different than in a procedural program. A comparison of these types of programs illustrates some of the fundamental concepts involved in GUI programming. In Figure 9.2, a typical procedural program is described on the left, while a typical GUI program is described on the right.

In the procedural program, the bulk of the effort is expended in processing the input data. The procedural program keeps working busily until it reaches the end of the input data, at which time it cleans up and exits. The execution of the procedural program is driven by the size of the input data file.

The GUI program, however, is driven not by input data, but by user interaction. After it creates the GUI layout on-screen, it begins waiting for user interaction. When user interaction is detected, the program takes a particular course of action depending on the widget that received

Typical procedural program	Typical GUI program
Check arguments.	Check arguments.
Open input and output files.	Create GUI.
Begin processing:	Wait for user to interact with GUI:
Read data from input file.	Take required action.
Process data.	Repeat until GUI is closed by user.
Write data to output file.	Return to caller.
Repeat until end of input data.	
Return to caller.	

Figure 9.2 Flow of control in a procedural versus GUI program.

input from the user. When the GUI program finishes processing the user request, it waits for the next interaction from the user, and keeps doing so until the user either interacts with another component, or closes the GUI.

GUI Design

Many people assume that just because an application has a GUI, it must be easy to use. However, you've probably had to use GUI applications that were confusing, nonintuitive, or clumsily laid out. GUI applications that are well laid out and easy to use don't happen by accident; they happen because someone took the time to design an interface that met the needs of humans who wish to perform a particular task. Therefore, the following planning and design steps are recommended before coding begins:

1. Write a succinct statement of the task.
2. Decide who the users will be.
3. Write down the essential functions that are required.
4. Sketch a layout on paper that includes all the GUI elements (buttons, menus, etc.).
5. On paper, simulate the interactions the user will have with the GUI.

At any point in this cycle, you might need to go back a step as your concept of the GUI evolves. When this process is complete, you should have a

fairly clear description on paper of how the GUI will look and behave. A
few minutes spent in this planning stage can save hours of coding.

One major design decision that must be made early on is to determine the modality of the GUI in question. For example, the file selector
`dialog_pickfile` only appears on-screen long enough for the user to
select a file, which might take less than 10 seconds:

```
IDL> file = dialog_pickfile()
```

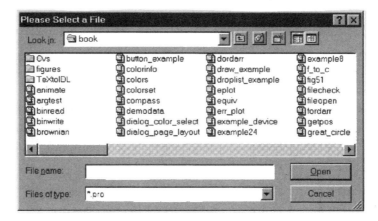

On Windows and MacOS platforms (or if you are running `idlde` on a
UNIX platform), you will notice that while `dialog_pickfile` is on the
screen, the window behind it no longer accepts input. This is an example
of a short-lived GUI application that occupies your entire attention while
it is active.

On the other hand, the color table selector `xloadct` can stay resident
on the screen for an extended period of time, while you continue to enter
commands at the command line:

```
IDL> xloadct
```

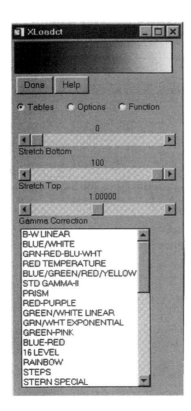

You can switch your attention to the xloadct dialog for a few seconds to select a different color table, and then switch your attention back to another task (say, redisplaying an image).

Another type of GUI application is one that occupies your attention for an extended period of time. An example is the mapping demonstration shown earlier in this chapter. The mapping application stays resident on the screen as long as required while you select different projections and map configuration properties.

Thus, it is possible to identify at least three different classes of GUI application:

1. An application that appears on-screen for a short time, and during this time occupies the user's attention completely (e.g., dialog_ pickfile). While the application is active, input to all other IDL applications is blocked.

2. An application that appears on-screen for a short time or an extended time, and occupies the user's attention only when the user

is interacting directly with the application (e.g., `xloadct`). The rest of the time, the user is free to focus attention on other tasks. While the application is active, other IDL applications still accept input.

3. An application that appears on-screen for an extended time and occupies most of the user's attention while it is active (e.g., the mapping demonstration). This application allows commands to be entered at the IDL command line while it is running.

Early in the design of a GUI application, you should start thinking about which elements of the application fall into the classes mentioned above or some other class. Keep in mind that an application may have elements that only appear at certain times, such as when the user selects "File/Save". Beware of GUI applications that show every possible control on-screen all the time. Such applications show a failure to classify the application into elements that should always be visible, and elements that should only be visible when the user requires them.

9.2   CREATING WIDGETS

The on-screen components of a GUI, such as buttons and sliders, are known collectively as *widgets*. The GUI development toolkit in IDL supports nine fundamental widget types. These basic widgets are used individually or in hierarchical combination to construct all GUI applications in IDL. Examples of each of the fundamental widget types are shown in Figure 9.3.

While there are minor differences in appearance between the Windows and UNIX widget layouts, the functionality is identical. A base widget contains all the other widgets in this example, and in this case also contains the system menu buttons for minimizing, maximizing, and closing the window. A menu widget allows the familiar drop-and-select style of menus to be implemented. A draw widget is a special kind of graphics window that can only exist inside a base widget, but which in most other respects acts like a normal graphics window. On the right side of the draw widget are examples of list, droplist, button, exclusive button, text entry field, and slider widgets. The labels below the menu bar level that describe the widget types are label widgets (with the exception of the label in the draw widget). At the bottom of the GUI is a table widget.

The nine fundamental widget types available in IDL are listed in Table 9.1, along with the name of the function used to create each widget.

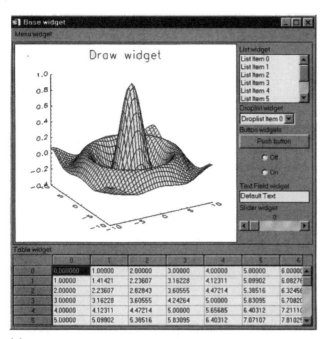

(a)

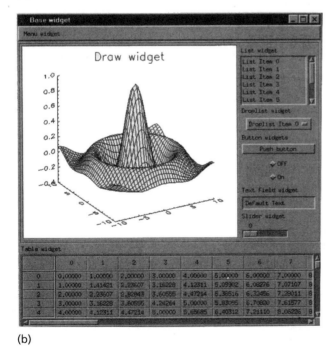

(b)

Figure 9.3 Fundamental widget types: (a) Windows and (b) UNIX.

Table 9.1   Fundamental widget types.

Widget	Description	Create function
Base	Container for other widgets*	`widget_base()`
Button	Clickable button[†]	`widget_button()`
Draw	Graphics window	`widget_draw()`
Droplist	Button that drops to reveal a selectable list	`widget_droplist()`
Label	Noneditable label	`widget_label()`
List	List of selectable items, often with scrollbars	`widget_list()`
Slider	Horizontal or vertical slider	`widget_slider()`
Table	Editable table	`widget_table()`
Text	Editable text field	`widget_text()`

* Menu bars are special cases of base widgets.

[†] Exclusive buttons (also known as radio buttons) are special cases of button widgets.

The first widget created in a GUI must be a base because a base is required to contain all the widgets subsequently created inside the GUI. A base of this type is known as a *top-level base.* A top-level base is thus a parent to all the widgets contained within it. Base widgets or any other widgets that have offspring are known as *parent widgets,* and the offspring are known as *child widgets.* Child widgets can in turn be parents and have widget children. The widget parent/child relationship is useful because it allows actions to be applied to a "family" of widgets as a whole. For example, when a top-level base is destroyed, all child widgets within the base are destroyed as well. Families of related widgets that can be traced back to a common top-level base are known as *widget hierarchies.*

Here is a simple example that creates a base widget and a label widget:

```
IDL> base = widget_base()
IDL> label = widget_label(base, $
IDL>   value='Welcome to the world of widgets')
IDL> widget_control, base, /realize
```

The base widget is created by calling `widget_base`, returning the widget identifier `base`. Then, a label widget is created by calling `widget_label`, returning the widget identifier `label`. The widget identifier `base` is passed to `widget_label` to identify the parent of the new label widget. Finally the `widget_control` procedure is called to `realize` (i.e., render on-screen) the widget hierarchy headed by `base`. Until a widget is realized, it is just a construct in memory.

Note   Widgets are supported on the following IDL graphics devices: `WIN`, `MAC`, `X`.

Widget Attributes

Widgets have common attributes that may be set when they are created and modified during their lifetime. Two of the most important attributes are the widget value and the widget user value:

- The value of a widget defines the visible "setting" of the widget. For example, the value of a label widget is the text that appears in the label, while the value of a list widget is a string array of list items. Widget values are usually defined at the time the widget is created; however, the value may also be modified during the lifetime of the widget. Base widgets are the only widgets that do not have values.
- The user value of a widget is reserved for the GUI developer and may be used to store any IDL variable or data type. Widget user values are often set to a string variable that contains a unique name for the widget, and may also be used to store information about the state of a GUI application.

Another characteristic of widgets is that they generate events. An event occurs when the user interacts with a widget, such as pressing a button, moving a slider, or selecting an item from a menu. Events allow the GUI developer to identify the widget that the user selected, and to take the appropriate action. Some widgets, such as button widgets, generate events by default, while others, such as base widgets, do not. A widget can be configured at the time it is created to generate events, or at some later point in the lifetime of the widget.

Table 9.2   Commonly used widget creation keywords.

Keyword	Purpose
value	Set value for this widget*
uvalue	Set user value for this widget
group_leader	Identifier of widget that is the leader of this group[†]
frame	Draw a frame around this widget (value sets frame width)[‡]
sensitive	Make this widget sensitive (sensitive=1) or insensitive (sensitive=0)[§]
map	Make this widget visible (map=1) or invisible (map=0)

* Base widgets do not have values, and therefore do not support the value keyword. Draw widget values may be read, but not set.

[†] When the group leader dies, all other widgets in the group die. This keyword is often used to identify top-level bases that should be destroyed when another top-level base dies.

[‡] Some IDL platforms may ignore this keyword or refuse to create a frame width larger than one.

[§] Insensitive widgets do not respond to user interaction and appear "grayed out" on most platforms. Desensitizing a base widget causes all widgets within the base to become desensitized.

The keywords listed in Table 9.2 are commonly used in conjunction with the widget creation functions listed in Table 9.1 to customize the behavior and appearance of widgets.

widget_base *function*

The widget_base function is used to create base widgets. The syntax is

id = widget_base([*parent*], [*keywords*])

where id is the identifier returned for the new base, *parent* is an optional argument that specifies the parent of the new base, and *keywords* are optional keywords. To create a new top-level base, omit the optional *parent* argument. Base widgets do not have a value, and therefore do not support the value keyword. The keywords listed in Table 9.3 are commonly used when calling widget_base. See the online help for the full list of supported keywords.

widget_button *function*

The widget_button function is used to create button widgets. Buttons can have four forms: rectangular push buttons with text labels (the

Table 9.3 **Commonly used** `widget_base` **keywords.**

Keyword	Purpose
`title`	Set title for a top-level base
`mbar`	Return the identifier of a menu bar in a top-level base
`tlb_frame_attr`	Set frame attributes for a top-level base*
`column`	Create base with column layout (value sets number of columns)
`row`	Create base with row layout (value sets number of rows)
`xoffset`	Set horizontal offset from top left of screen for a top-level base (pixels)
`yoffset`	Set vertical offset from top left of screen for a top-level base (pixels)
`/tlb_size_events`	Generate resize events for this base
`/exclusive`	Create a base to hold exclusive radio buttons only
`/nonexclusive`	Create a base to hold nonexclusive radio buttons only
`/grid_layout`	Create a base with grid layout (equally sized rows and columns)†
`/align_bottom`	Align this base with bottom of parent row base
`/align_top`	Align this base with top of parent row base
`/align_center`	Align this base with center of parent row or column base
`/align_left`	Align this base with left side of parent column base
`/align_right`	Align this base with right side of parent column base
`/base_align_bottom`	Align future children with bottom of this row base
`/base_align_center`	Align future children with center of this row or column base
`/base_align_left`	Align future children with left of this column base
`/base_align_right`	Align future children with right of this column base
`/base_align_top`	Align future children with top of this row base

* A common setting for this keyword is `tlb_frame_attr=1`, which means the top-level base cannot be resized, minimized, or maximized. This setting is often used when there is no reason to resize the base. See the online help for other settings for this keyword.
† The size of each row and column in the grid layout is determined by the size of the largest child widget in the base.

default); rectangular push buttons with bitmap labels; pulldown menu buttons; and exclusive or nonexclusive radio buttons. The value of a button widget determines either the label for the button or the bitmap used for the button.

The syntax for `widget_button` is

id = widget_button(parent, [*keywords*])

where id is the identifier returned for the button widget, parent specifies the parent of the button widget, and *keywords* are optional keywords. The keywords listed in Table 9.4 are commonly used when calling widget_button. See the online help for the full list of supported keywords.

To demonstrate the different types of buttons available in IDL, the following sample procedure named button_example.pro creates the GUI shown below.

Table 9.4   Commonly used widget_button **keywords.**

Keyword	Purpose
value	Set value of button*
xsize	Set width of button (default units: pixels)[†]
/bitmap	Create a bitmap button
/menu	Create a pulldown menu button[‡]
/separator	Add a separator line above this pulldown menu entry
/no_release	Generate only "press" events for exclusive or nonexclusive buttons[§]

* If value is a text string, the button will have a text label. In IDL 5.2 and higher versions, value may be set to the name of a 16-color bitmap (.bmp) file to create a bitmap button label (the bitmap keyword must be set in this case). Predefined bitmaps are available in the IDL installation directory under resource/bitmaps. See the online help for widget_button for more information on creating and editing bitmap labels.

[†] The size of a text button is normally determined by the length of the label string. To create buttons with consistent sizes, the xsize keyword may be used. This is one of the few cases when the xsize keyword is advised for sizing a widget; it should normally be avoided.

[‡] Buttons created as pulldown menus can have button children that become menu selections. Button menus can be created anywhere inside a parent base; buttons created in a menu bar automatically become pulldown menus.

[§] Exclusive or nonexclusive radio buttons can only be created inside parent bases that are configured for radio buttons (see widget_base).

```
PRO BUTTON_EXAMPLE

;- Create column-aligned non-resizeable top level base
;- with menu bar
tlb = widget_base(column=1, mbar=mbar, $
  title='Button Example', tlb_frame_attr=1)

;- Create menu buttons in menu bar base
filemenu = widget_button(mbar, value='File')
fileopt1 = widget_button(filemenu, value='Open')
fileopt2 = widget_button(filemenu, value='Save')
fileopt3 = widget_button(filemenu, value='Exit', /separator)
editmenu = widget_button(mbar, value='Edit')
helpmenu = widget_button(mbar, value='Help')

;- Create bitmap buttons in row-aligned base
iconbase = widget_base(tlb, row=1, /frame)
subdir   = 'resource/bitmaps'
mapfile  = filepath('open.bmp', subdir=subdir)
iconopt1 = widget_button(iconbase, value=mapfile, /bitmap)
mapfile  = filepath('save.bmp', subdir=subdir)
iconopt2 = widget_button(iconbase, value=mapfile, /bitmap)
mapfile  = filepath('print1.bmp', subdir=subdir)
iconopt3 = widget_button(iconbase, value=mapfile, /bitmap)

;- Create text buttons
buttbase = widget_base(tlb, row=1)
buttsize = 60
buttopt1 = widget_button(buttbase, value='OK', $
  xsize=buttsize)
buttopt2 = widget_button(buttbase, value='Cancel', $
  xsize=buttsize)
buttopt3 = widget_button(buttbase, value='Help', $
  xsize=buttsize)

;- Create exclusive and non-exclusive radio buttons
buttbase = widget_base(tlb, row=1, /exclusive)
buttopt1 = widget_button(buttbase, value='On')
buttopt2 = widget_button(buttbase, value='Off')
buttbase = widget_base(tlb, row=1, /nonexclusive)
buttopt1 = widget_button(buttbase, value='Lettuce')
buttopt2 = widget_button(buttbase, value='Tomato')
buttopt3 = widget_button(buttbase, value='Mustard')
```

```
;- Realize widgets
widget_control, tlb, /realize

END
```

One notable feature of this example is that separate bases are used to organize each collection of buttons.

Tip   There is often no need to come up with unique variable names to hold the identifier for each newly created widget. In the previous example, the variable name `buttbase` is used several times for the return value of `widget_base`. Normally this practice is discouraged, but when creating many widgets in succession it can be difficult to keep inventing new and unique widget identifier variable names.

`widget_draw` *function*

The `widget_draw` function is used to create draw widgets. Draw widgets are the containers for on-screen graphics in GUI applications, and they function in many respects just like direct graphics windows. The value of a draw widget is the graphics window index, as described in Section 5.3. The value of a draw widget may be read but not written and is valid only after the widget has been realized.

The syntax for `widget_draw` is

```
id = widget_draw(parent, [keywords])
```

where `id` is the identifier returned for the draw widget, `parent` specifies the parent base, and *keywords* are optional keywords. The keywords listed in Table 9.5 are commonly used when calling `widget_draw`. See the online help for the full list of supported keywords.

The following example program demonstrates how to create non-scrolling and scrolling draw widgets:

Table 9.5   Commonly used `widget_draw` **keywords.**

Keyword	Purpose
`xsize`	Set width of draw widget (default units: pixels)
`ysize`	Set height of draw widget (default units: pixels)
`x_scroll_size`	Set visible width of scrolling draw widget (default units: pixels)
`y_scroll_size`	Set visible height of scrolling draw widget (default units: pixels)
`/button_events`	Generate mouse button events inside the draw widget*
`/motion_events`	Generate cursor motion events inside the draw widget[†]

* When `/button_events` is set, an event is generated when a mouse button is pressed or released while the cursor is within the draw widget.
[†] When `/motion_events` is set, an event is generated when cursor motion is detected within the draw widget.

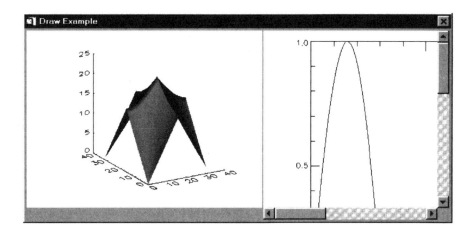

```
PRO DRAW_EXAMPLE

;- Create row-aligned non-resizeable top level base
base = widget_base(row=1, title='Draw Example', $
  tlb_frame_attr=1)

;- Create non-scrolling draw widget
draw1 = widget_draw(base, xsize=400, ysize=300)

;- Create scrolling draw widget
draw2 = widget_draw(base, xsize=900, ysize=900, $
```

```
   x_scroll_size=300, y_scroll_size=300)

;- Realize widgets
widget_control, base, /realize

;- Get draw window indices
widget_control, draw1, get_value=winid1
widget_control, draw2, get_value=winid2

;- Create a plot in each draw widget
wset, winid1
shade_surf, dist(32), charsize=1.5
wset, winid2
plot, sin(findgen(200) * 0.1)

END
```

widget_droplist *function*

The `widget_droplist` function is used to create droplist widgets. Droplist widgets allow the user to select a single value from a list that appears when the user clicks on the widget. The value of a droplist widget is an array of strings containing the list of selectable items.

The syntax for `widget_droplist` is

```
id = widget_droplist(parent, [keywords])
```

where `id` is the identifier returned for the droplist widget, `parent` specifies the parent base, and *keywords* are optional keywords. The keywords listed in Table 9.6 are commonly used when calling `widget_droplist`. See the online help for the full list of supported keywords.

Table 9.6   Commonly used `widget_droplist` **keywords.**

Keyword	Purpose
`value`	Set droplist value*
`title`	Set droplist title
`/dynamic_resize`	Create a dynamically resizing droplist[†]

* The width of a droplist widget is determined by the number of characters in the largest element of the value array (unless the optional `xsize` keyword is set).
[†] If the `dynamic_resize` keyword is set, the widget will automatically resize itself whenever a new value is set for the list.

The following example program demonstrates how a droplist widget may be created:

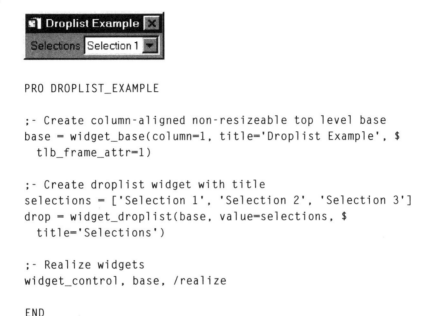

```
PRO DROPLIST_EXAMPLE

;- Create column-aligned non-resizeable top level base
base = widget_base(column=1, title='Droplist Example', $
  tlb_frame_attr=1)

;- Create droplist widget with title
selections = ['Selection 1', 'Selection 2', 'Selection 3']
drop = widget_droplist(base, value=selections, $
  title='Selections')

;- Realize widgets
widget_control, base, /realize

END
```

widget_label *function*

The widget_label function is used to create label widgets. Label widgets display a noneditable text string inside a parent base. The value of a label widget is a string containing the label text.

The syntax for widget_label is

```
id = widget_label(parent, [keywords])
```

where id is the identifier returned for the label widget, parent specifies the parent base, and *keywords* are optional keywords. The keywords listed in Table 9.7 are commonly used when calling widget_label. See the online help for the full list of supported keywords.

The following example program demonstrates how label widgets may be created:

Table 9.7   **Commonly used** `widget_label` **keywords.**

Keyword	Purpose
`value`	Set label value*
`/align_left`	Left-justify the label
`/align_center`	Center-justify the label
`/align_right`	Right-justify the label
`/dynamic_resize`	Create a dynamically resizing label[†]

* The width of a label widget is determined by the number of characters in the value string (unless the optional `xsize` keyword is set).
[†] If the `dynamic_resize` keyword is set, the widget will automatically resize itself whenever a new value is set for the label.

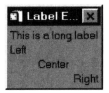

```
PRO LABEL_EXAMPLE

;- Create column aligned non-resizable top level base
tlb = widget_base(column=1, title='Label Example', $
  tlb_frame_attr=1)

;- Create label widgets
label1 = widget_label(tlb, value='This is a long label')
label2 = widget_label(tlb, value='Left', /align_left)
label3 = widget_label(tlb, value='Center', /align_center)
label4 = widget_label(tlb, value='Right', /align_right)

;- Realize widgets
widget_control, tlb, /realize

END
```

widget_list *function*

The `widget_list` function is used to create list widgets. List widgets display a list from which the user may select one or more items. The value of a list widget is a string array containing the list of selectable items.

The syntax for `widget_list` is

```
id = widget_list(parent, [keywords])
```

where `id` is the identifier returned for the list widget, `parent` specifies the parent base, and *keywords* are optional keywords. The keywords listed in Table 9.8 are commonly used when calling `widget_list`. See the online help for the full list of supported keywords.

The following example program demonstrates how list widgets with single and multiple selections may be created:

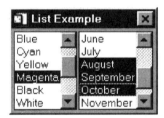

Table 9.8   Commonly used `widget_list` keywords.

Keyword	Purpose
value	Set list value*
xsize	Set list width (in characters)
ysize	Set list height (in items)[†]
multiple	Allow multiple selections[‡]

* The width of the list widget is determined by the length of the largest string in the value array. The value of a list widget can only be set; it cannot be retrieved.

[†] If the list height is less than the number of items in the list, a vertical scrollbar will be added to the list widget.

[‡] If the `multiple` keyword is set, multiple items may be selected from the list. This feature is available in IDL 5.1 and higher.

```
PRO LIST_EXAMPLE

;- Create row-aligned non-resizeable top level base
tlb = widget_base(row=1, title='List Example', $
  tlb_frame_attr=1)

;- Create single selection list widget
colors = ['Red', 'Green', 'Blue', 'Cyan', $
  'Yellow', 'Magenta', 'Black', 'White', $
  'Gray', 'Navy', 'Brown', 'Gold']
list1 = widget_list(tlb, value=colors, ysize=6)

;- Create multiple selection list widget
months = ['January', 'February', 'March', 'April', $
  'May', 'June', 'July', 'August', $
  'September', 'October', 'November', 'December']
list2 = widget_list(tlb, value=months, ysize=6, /multiple)

;- Realize widgets
widget_control, tlb, /realize

END
```

widget_slider *function*

The widget_slider function is used to create slider widgets. Slider widgets provide a horizontal or vertical sliding control that allows the user to adjust an integer value. The value of a slider widget is the current slider value.

The syntax for widget_slider is

```
id = widget_slider(parent, [keywords])
```

where id is the identifier returned for the slider widget, parent specifies the parent base, and *keywords* are optional keywords. The keywords listed in Table 9.9 are commonly used when calling widget_slider. See the online help for the full list of supported keywords.

The following example program demonstrates how horizontal slider widgets may be created:

Table 9.9 **Commonly used** `widget_slider` **keywords.**

Keyword	Purpose
`value`	Set slider value
`title`	Set slider title
`minimum`	Set minimum slider value
`maximum`	Set maximum slider value
`xsize`	Set slider width (default units: pixels)*
`ysize`	Set slider height (default units: pixels)[†]
`/vertical`	Create a vertical slider (default: horizontal)
`/suppress_value`	Suppress display of slider value

* The `xsize` keyword is often used to set the width of horizontal sliders.

[†] The `ysize` keyword is often used to set the height of vertical sliders.

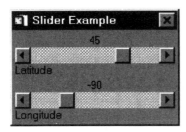

```
PRO SLIDER_EXAMPLE

;- Create column-aligned non-resizeable top level base
tlb = widget_base(column=1, title='Slider Example', $
  tlb_frame_attr=1)

;- Create slider widgets
width = 200
slider1 = widget_slider(tlb, value=45, min=-90, max=90, $
  title='Latitude', xsize=width)
slider2 = widget_slider(tlb, value=-90, min=-180, max=180, $
  title='Longitude', xsize=width)

;- Realize widgets
widget_control, tlb, /realize

END
```

widget_table *function*

The `widget_table` function is used to create table widgets. Table widgets display a two-dimensional array or a vector of structures in a table format with one value per cell, with the option of editing table cells. The value of a table widget can be a two-dimensional array of any numeric or string type, or a vector of structures.

The syntax for `widget_table` is

```
id = widget_table(parent, [keywords])
```

where `id` is the identifier returned for the slider widget, `parent` specifies the parent base, and *keywords* are optional keywords. The keywords listed in Table 9.10 are commonly used when calling `widget_table`. See the online help for the full list of supported keywords.

Table 9.10   Commonly used `widget_table` keywords.

Keyword	Purpose
value	Set table value*
x_scroll_size	Set visible width of table in columns
y_scroll_size	Set visible height of table in rows
column_widths	Set column width (default units: pixels)[†]
/editable	Create an editable table[‡]
/no_headers	Do not display column or row labels
column_labels	Set array of column labels
row_labels	Set array of row labels

* By default, the number of rows and columns in the table is determined by the size of the value array or vector, unless the `scr_xsize`, `scr_ysize`, `xsize`, or `ysize` keywords are used.

[†] If the `column_widths` keyword is not set, all columns are set to a default platform-dependent width. If `column_widths` is set to a scalar value, all columns are set to the specified width. If `columns_widths` is set to an array, the width of each column is determined by the width of the corresponding array element.

[‡] If the `editable` keyword is set, cells in the table may be edited. When a cell is edited, the value entered by the user is automatically converted to the cell data type. If the value entered by the user cannot be converted to the cell data type, the cell value is unchanged. On Windows platforms, cells must be double-clicked to be edited.

The following example program demonstrates how table widgets may be created:

```
PRO TABLE_EXAMPLE

;- Create column-aligned non-resizeable top level base
tlb = widget_base(column=1, title='Table Example', $
  tlb_frame_attr=1)

;- Create label widget
label = widget_label(tlb, value='2D array')

;- Create table widget for a 2D array
data = dist(32)
table1 = widget_table(tlb, value=data, $
  x_scroll_size=4, y_scroll_size=4, /editable)

;- Create label widget
label = widget_label(tlb, value='Vector of structures')

;- Create table widget for a vector of structures
record = {lat:45.0, lon:-89.0, $
  altitude:20500.0, heading:245.0}
data = replicate(record, 100)
```

```
names = tag_names(data)
table2 = widget_table(tlb, value=data, $
  x_scroll_size=4, y_scroll_size=4, $
  column_labels=names, /editable)

;- Realize widgets
widget_control, tlb, /realize

END
```

widget_text *function*

The widget_text function is used to create text widgets. Text widgets display one or more lines of text information, with the option of editing the text contained in the widget. The value of a text widget is a scalar string or an array of strings.

The syntax for widget_text is

id = widget_text(parent, [*keywords*])

where id is the identifier returned for the text widget, parent specifies the parent base, and *keywords* are optional keywords. The keywords listed in Table 9.11 are commonly used when calling widget_text. See the online help for the full list of supported keywords.

Table 9.11   Commonly used widget_text **keywords.**

Keyword	Purpose
value	Set text value
xsize	Set width of text widget* (characters)
ysize	Set height of text widget (text lines)
/editable	Create an editable text widget
/scroll	Create a scrolling text widget
/wrap	Wrap long text lines

* The default width is system dependent. On Windows and MacOS platforms, the width is around 20 characters. On UNIX platforms, the default size depends on the length of the text field(s).

The following example program demonstrates how text widgets may be created:

```
PRO TEXT_EXAMPLE

;- Create column-aligned non-resizeable top level base
tlb = widget_base(column=1, title='Text Example', $
  tlb_frame_attr=1)

;- Create label widget
label1 = widget_label(tlb, value='Single line text widget')

;- Create single line editable text widget
text1 = widget_text(tlb, value='Default text', /editable)

;- Create label widget
label2 = widget_label(tlb, value='Multi line text widget')

;- Create multi line text widget
value = ['Text line 1', 'Text line 2', 'Text line 3']
text2 = widget_text(tlb, value=value, ysize=3)

;- Realize widgets
widget_control, tlb, /realize

END
```

Widget Layout

When you create more complex GUI applications with a greater number and variety of widgets, the layout of the widgets becomes an important issue. If you throw the widgets together as they occur to you, it is possible to end up with a GUI which is nonintuitive, visually unappealing, and occupies too much screen space. Think carefully about exactly which widgets should be visible at any given time while the application is active. If the user only needs to use a particular function every now and then, such as a drawing color selector, make sure the relevant widgets are only visible when the user needs them. Remember that the widgets are not the star of the show—your *data* is. You should endeavor to have on-screen only the widgets that are absolutely necessary at any given time.

The `widget_base` keywords `column` and `row` are recommended to specify the layout of widgets in a base, because this allows the host window manager to shuffle the widgets around to their final positions. This method produces GUIs that have a relatively consistent appearance on all IDL platforms. Avoid using the size and position keywords `xsize`, `ysize`, `xoffset`, and `yoffset`. Using these keywords is a bit like positioning the elements of a plot using device coordinates. You might spend hours making the widgets look perfect on your system, but the first time you try running the application on another system, the layout looks terrible because of different font sizes, screen resolution, or widget appearance. Also, the `xsize`, `ysize`, `xoffset`, and `yoffset` keywords are only suggestions to the window manager, which is free to ignore them.

As an example of what *not* to do, Figure 9.4 shows an example of a badly designed layout for a GUI that allows the user to read an image from a binary file:

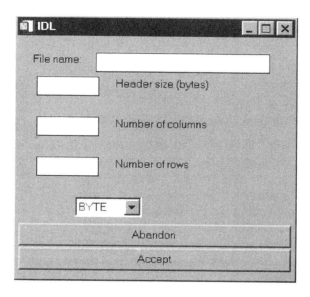

Figure 9.4 A badly designed layout.

```
PRO WBADLAYOUT

;- Create widgets
tlb = widget_base(xsize=350, ysize=300, $
  xoffset=400, yoffset=300)

label = widget_label(tlb, value='File name:', $
  xoffset=20, yoffset=20)
text = widget_text(tlb, xsize=30, $
  xoffset=100, yoffset=20, /editable)

text = widget_text(tlb, xsize=10, $
  xoffset=25, yoffset=50, /editable)
label = widget_label(tlb, value='Header size (bytes)', $
  xoffset=125, yoffset=50)

text = widget_text(tlb, xsize=10, $
  xoffset=25, yoffset=100, /editable)
label = widget_label(tlb, value='Number of columns', $
  xoffset=125, yoffset=100)

text = widget_text(tlb, xsize=10, $
  xoffset=25, yoffset=150, /editable)
label = widget_label(tlb, value='Number of rows', $
  xoffset=125, yoffset=150)

drop = widget_droplist(tlb, xoffset=75, yoffset=200, $
  value=['BYTE', 'INT', 'LONG', 'FLOAT', 'DOUBLE'])

bbase = widget_base(tlb, xsize=350, yoffset=230, column=1)
buttb = widget_button(bbase, value='Abandon')
butta = widget_button(bbase, value='Accept')

;- Realize widgets
widget_control, tlb, /realize

END
```

Problems with this widget layout are the following:

- *System menu bar allows resizing.* There is no need to resize this GUI, so resizing should be disabled when the top-level base is created by including the keyword tlb_frame_attr=1 in the call to widget_base.

- *Excessive gray space.* If an excessive fraction of the area occupied by the GUI contains gray "dead" pixels, it's a good indication the GUI was poorly conceived and executed.
- *Widgets not column or row aligned.* The code that creates the GUI uses `xsize`, `ysize`, `xoffset`, and `yoffset` keywords for widget placement. Instead, use the `widget_base` keywords `column` and `row` to align widgets within a base. If you need a new row or column, simply create a new base. The `xoffset` and `yoffset` keywords are only appropriate for positioning a top-level base on the screen.
- *Inconsistent widget alignment.* Some widgets are right-aligned, some are left-aligned, and some are centered. This creates unnecessary visual confusion.
- *Extra large buttons.* If a GUI contains a stack of buttons that look more like horizontal bars, the GUI designer was not thinking hard enough about widget layout. Instead of stacking buttons vertically, smaller buttons can be laid out horizontally in a row-oriented base. Also, avoid the temptation to place buttons such as "OK" and "Cancel" in a new position in every GUI. Decide on a convention (e.g., centered at the bottom of the GUI) and stick to it.
- *Nonstandard button names.* Buttons with nonstandard names for standard functions are a common cause of user confusion; see the following section on naming buttons.

Figure 9.5 shows the same GUI redesigned to use a more visually pleasing and platform-independent layout:

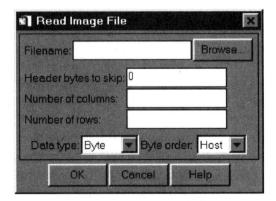

Figure 9.5 A well-designed layout.

```
PRO WGOODLAYOUT

;- Create top level base
tlb = widget_base(column=1, title='Read Image File', $
  tlb_frame_attr=1)

;- Create base to hold everything except buttons
main = widget_base(tlb, column=1, frame=1)

;- Create file widgets
fbase = widget_base(main, row=1, /base_align_center)
label = widget_label(fbase, value='Filename:')
text  = widget_text(fbase, /editable, xsize=20)
butt  = widget_button(fbase, value='Browse...')

;- Create array size widgets
abase = widget_base(main, row=3, $
  /grid_layout, /base_align_center)
label = widget_label(abase, value='Header bytes to skip:')
text  = widget_text(abase, value='0', /editable, xsize=8)
label = widget_label(abase, value='Number of columns:')
text  = widget_text(abase, /editable, xsize=8)
label = widget_label(abase, value='Number of rows:')
text  = widget_text(abase, /editable, xsize=8)

;- Create data type and order droplists
dbase = widget_base(main, row=1, /align_center)
label = widget_label(dbase, value='Data type:')
drop  = widget_droplist(dbase, value=['Byte', 'Integer', $
  'Long', 'Float', 'Double'])
label = widget_label(dbase, value='Byte order: ')
drop  = widget_droplist(dbase, value=['Host', 'Swap', 'XDR'])

;- Create ok and cancel buttons
buttsize = 75
bbase = widget_base(tlb, row=1, /align_center)
butt  = widget_button(bbase, value='OK', xsize=buttsize)
butt  = widget_button(bbase, value='Cancel', xsize=buttsize)
butt  = widget_button(bbase, value='Help', xsize=buttsize)

;- Realize widgets
widget_control, tlb, /realize

END
```

Now gray dead space is reduced, and the GUI is more compact. It cannot be resized, which is appropriate for this type of dialog box. The text widgets are all left-aligned, and a file browse button has been added for the user to browse other files (clicking the "Browse . . ." button would invoke the file selector `dialog_pickfile`). The droplist widgets are now centered in a row-aligned base; the "Byte order" droplist allows the user to select Host, Swap, or XDR byte ordering. Notice the frame around the file information widgets. This helps to visually separate them from the action buttons at the bottom. The action buttons (OK, Cancel, Help) are now centered in a row-aligned base, and they are named and ordered in a familiar way. Note how the `xsize` keyword was used only to specify a common button size. This is an acceptable use of the `xsize` keyword, particularly when a single variable (`buttsize`) is clearly identified.

Tip   It may seem obvious, but if you are designing a GUI application that is intended to run on more than one IDL platform, make sure you test the application on each target platform.

Naming Buttons

If you are careless with defining button names, you can make the application confusing. For example, consider the dialog in Figure 9.6 from a Windows application, which appears when you attempt to close an image that has been modified.

The chances are that you intended to close the window, and you would have already saved the changes if you wanted them saved. However, the application asks if you wish to save the modified image. The possible answers are "Save", "Abandon", and "Cancel". Does it mean abandon the

Figure 9.6 A poorly designed dialog.

image, or abandon the close request? Does it mean cancel the image, or cancel the close request? This dialog is guaranteed to make most users stop and think, which is a sure sign that it is badly designed. A more sensible design is shown in Figure 9.7.

Now, the text label tells the user the reason for the dialog and asks a simple question. The possible answers are "Yes" or "No", with the default answer "No". This dialog was created in IDL using the `dialog_message` function:

```
IDL> result = dialog_message('Image was changed: Save it?', $
IDL>   /question, $
IDL>    title='Save Image?', /default_no)
IDL> print, result
No
```

The message here is that you should think very carefully about how button widgets are named; otherwise you run the risk of creating a confusing and unfriendly GUI. Try to stick with simple and familiar words. If the buttons exist to allow the user to answer a question, try to make the answers "Yes" or "No". If the buttons exist to allow the user to select an action, then choose from the button names shown in Table 9.12.

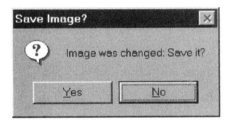

Figure 9.7 A sensible dialog design.

Table 9.12   Button name/action conventions.

Name	Action
OK	Accept changes, apply them, and close the dialog.
Cancel	Cancel changes, revert to entry configuration, and close the dialog.
Apply	Apply changes, but don't close the dialog.
Help	Create a new dialog box containing help text.
Close	Close the dialog (use when OK and Cancel are not appropriate).

Compound Widgets

In IDL it is possible to create widget applications that act as though they are fundamental widgets. Such applications are known as *compound widgets* because they have many of the properties of fundamental widgets, but they usually combine several different widget types into one functional unit. Writing compound widgets is a task best undertaken once you have a solid grasp of the fundamentals of GUI programming. For the purposes of this book, it is sufficient to list the name and purpose of some compound widgets available in IDL in Table 9.13. You may wish to use these compound widgets in your own GUI applications, or they could serve as templates for creating your own compound widgets. The source code for each compound widget is contained in the IDL installation `lib` subdirectory. In the IDL Development Environment, simply compile the procedure to open it in the editor:

```
IDL> .compile cw_bgroup
```

Tip   Sometimes it is easier to create your own widgets for a particular task, rather than trying to fit your task to the capabilities of a compound widget.

Table 9.13   Selected compound widget applications.

Name	Purpose
cw_bgroup	Button menu group
cw_defroi	Define region of interest
cw_field	Data entry field(s)
cw_filesel	File selection dialog
cw_fslider	Floating-point slider
cw_pdmenu	Pulldown menu(s)
cw_rgbslider	RGB color value sliders
cw_tmpl	Template for a compound widget application

9.3   WORKING WITH EXISTING WIDGETS

After a widget has been created, it is often necessary to set various properties of the widget, or to retrieve information about its status. For this purpose, IDL provides the `widget_control` procedure and the `widget_info` function. The `widget_control` procedure allows modification of existing widgets, while the `widget_info` function returns information about existing widgets.

Setting Widget Properties: `widget_control`

The `widget_control` procedure is used to perform several important functions for existing widgets, including

- realizing widget hierarchies
- setting and getting widget user values
- modifying widget properties
- destroying widget hierarchies

The syntax for `widget_control` is

`widget_control, id, [keywords]`

where `id` is the identifier of the widget, and *keywords* are optional keywords that modify the properties of the widget. The most commonly used keywords applicable to all widget types are listed in Table 9.14.

In addition, many of the keywords supported by `widget_control` are widget-specific. The most commonly used `widget_control` keywords for each type of widget are listed in Appendix D.

Table 9.14   Commonly used `widget_control` keywords applicable to all widgets.

Keyword	Purpose
`get_uvalue`	Get user value of a widget
`set_uvalue`	Set user value of a widget
`/no_copy`	Transfer user values in set or get operations (default: copy)
`hourglass`	Display (1) or destroy (0) an hourglass cursor
`scr_xsize`	Set screen width of a widget (default units: pixels)
`scr_ysize`	Set screen height of a widget (default units: pixels)
`default_font`	Set the default font for widgets

Getting Widget Information: widget_info

The widget_info function returns information about an existing widget. The syntax is

info = widget_info(id, [*keyword*])

where id is the identifier of the widget from which information is to be obtained, *keyword* is a keyword that specifies the information to be returned, and info is the result. Only one keyword at a time should be passed. If an array of widget identifiers is passed, an array of results will be returned. Table 9.15 lists the keywords commonly used in conjunction with widget_info.

9.4　EVENTS AND EVENT HANDLING

In the previous section on widgets and GUI layout, the example programs for each widget type are static. That is, they do not respond to user inter-

Table 9.15　Commonly used widget_info **keywords.**

Keyword	Return value
/valid_id	1 if this is a valid widget, 0 otherwise
/geometry	Size and offset information for this widget*
/parent	Identifier of the parent of this widget (0 if no parent)
/child	Identifier of the first child of this widget (0 if no children)
/name	Name of this widget type[†]
/droplist_number	Number of items in a droplist widget
/droplist_select	Index of currently selected item in a droplist widget
/list_number	Number of items in a list widget
/list_select	Indices of currently selected items in a list widget
/slider_min_max	Minimum and maximum values of a slider widget
/table_select	Indices of currently selected cells in a table widget[‡]
/text_number	Number of characters in a text widget
/text_select	Location of currently selected text in a text widget[§]

* The returned value is a structure; see the online help for the fields contained in the structure.
[†] Possible type names are BASE, BUTTON, DRAW, DROPLIST, LABEL, LIST, SLIDER, TABLE, TEXT.
[‡] The selected indices are returned in a four-element vector of the form [*left, top, right, bottom*].
[§] The character locations are returned in a two-element vector of the form [*start, number*].

action, other than automatic responses such as destroying a GUI when the window manager "Close" is selected. The next step in constructing a GUI application is to add code that takes action when the user interacts with the widgets that form the GUI.

When the user interacts with a widget, such as clicking a button or selecting an item from a list, it causes an *event* to be generated. An event is a signal to the application that identifies both the widget causing the event, and the type of event. For example, if a draw widget is configured to detect both cursor motion and button presses, then each case would generate a separate event. An application must therefore be able to wait for events, intercept them when they occur, and take appropriate action depending on the widget that caused the event. This is known as *event handling.*

Event handling is done by procedures or functions known as *event handlers.* An event handler obtains information about the widget that generated the event, retrieves any required information about the state of the application, and then takes the appropriate course of action. For example, in a draw widget configured to detect cursor motion, the event handler would identify the cursor motion event, retrieve the pixel coordinates of the new cursor location, and then perhaps update a pixel coordinate display.

Event Structures

Event information is packaged in a named structure known as an *event structure,* which is passed to the event handler when an event occurs. The structure contains the identifier of the widget that caused the event, the identifier of the top-level base containing the widget, and other type-specific information about the widget that caused the event.

To examine the characteristics of widget events, consider the following two procedures named wsimple_event and wsimple. These procedures should be stored in a source file named wsimple.pro in the order shown. In this example, wsimple creates the widgets and starts the built-in event manager (xmanager), and wsimple_event is the user-written event handler:

```
PRO WSIMPLE_EVENT, EVENT

print, 'Event detected'
```

```
;- Display event structure
help, event, /structure

END

PRO WSIMPLE

print, 'Creating widgets'

;- Create top level base
device, get_screen_size=screen_size
xoffset = screen_size[0] / 3
yoffset = screen_size[1] / 3
tlb = widget_base(column=1, tlb_frame_attr=1, $
  xoffset=xoffset, yoffset=yoffset)

;- Create widgets
text = widget_text(tlb, value='Edit this text', /editable)
base = widget_base(tlb, row=1, /align_center)
button = widget_button(base, value='Click here')
widget_control, base, /realize

;- Start managing events
xmanager, 'wsimple', tlb, /no_block

END
```

When wsimple.pro is compiled and executed, a dialog box containing a text widget and a button widget is created:

```
IDL> .compile wsimple
IDL> wsimple
Creating widgets
```

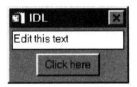

If you edit the text shown in the text widget and hit the Enter key, information similar to the following will be printed:

```
Event detected
** Structure WIDGET_TEXT_CH, 6 tags, length=24:
   ID              LONG                8
   TOP             LONG                7
   HANDLER         LONG                7
   TYPE            INT           0
   OFFSET          LONG                8
   CH              BYTE         10
```

If you click on the button widget, information similar to the following will be printed:

```
Event detected
** Structure WIDGET_BUTTON, 4 tags, length=16:
   ID              LONG               10
   TOP             LONG                7
   HANDLER         LONG                7
   SELECT          LONG                1
```

The wsimple procedure creates a top-level base that is offset from the top-left corner of the screen. Then the text field and button widgets are created and realized. Finally the built-in IDL event manager (xmanager) is called to start managing events. The purpose of the event manager is to intercept widget events and forward information about the event to the user-written event handler, which in this case is wsimple_event (more on xmanager in a moment).

The wsimple_event procedure accepts a single argument: a named structure of information about the widget that caused the event (i.e., an event structure). In this example, the only action taken by wsimple_event is to print a message indicating that an event was detected, and then print the contents of the event structure. Each event structure has a name indicating the type of widget that caused the event (in this case, WIDGET_TEXT_CH or WIDGET_BUTTON), and each structure contains the fields ID, TOP, and HANDLER. Every event structure contains these three fields, which are defined as follows:

- ID: The identifier of the widget that generated the event
- TOP: The identifier of the top-level base widget that contains ID
- HANDLER: The identifier of the widget associated with the event handler

In addition to these three fields, the event structure contains type-specific information about the widget that caused the event. For example, the button widget event structure contains the field SELECT, which is set to 1 if the button was pressed, or 0 if the button was released (only radio buttons generate release events). For widgets that generate more than one type of event, the widget-specific information in the event structure notifies the application what type of event occurred. For a complete description of the event structures for each of the nine fundamental widget types, see Appendix C.

Event Management

In the previous example program, the wsimple procedure calls the xmanager procedure in order to start event handling. The purpose of xmanager is to route event information to the appropriate event handler(s), and to keep track of which GUI applications are active at any given time. The syntax for xmanager is

xmanager, name, id, [*keywords*]

where name is a string variable containing the name of the procedure or function that created the widgets to be managed, id is the identifier of the top-level base widget hierarchy to be managed, and *keywords* are optional keywords. By default, _event is appended to name to obtain the name of the event handler procedure to be notified when events occur in the widget hierarchy specified by id. For example, in the previous program the name of the procedure that created the widgets is wsimple; therefore the default name of the event handler procedure is wsimple_event.

The xmanager procedure accepts a number of keywords that may be used to modify its default behavior. The most commonly used keywords are listed in Table 9.16.

Tip   In the previous example program, the event handler procedure (wsimple_event) appears in the source file before the procedure that creates the widgets (wsimple). This is because when xmanager is called, the event handler must be compiled and ready to run. By placing the event handler first in the source file, the event handler will always be compiled before xmanager is called. Alternatively, place the event handler in a separate source file.

Table 9.16 **Commonly used** `xmanager` **keywords.**

Keyword	Purpose
`event_handler`	Set name of event handler to call when an event occurs*
`/no_block`	Do not block command line[†]
`cleanup`	Set name of procedure to call when `id` is destroyed[‡]

* Setting the `event_handler` keyword overrides the default event handler name.
[†] By default the command line is blocked (i.e., it does not respond) when `xmanager` is managing events. Setting this keyword allows the command line to remain active while a widget application is running.
[‡] A `cleanup` procedure accepts only one argument: the identifier of the dying widget. This is different from a normal event handler, which accepts one argument in the form of an event structure.

Event Handlers and Application State Information

It is now appropriate to discuss a GUI application that actually handles widget events, rather than just printing the identity of each widget that causes an event. In addition, it is now necessary to provide a mechanism that allows information about the application to be shared by the components of the application. For example, if you constructed a GUI to display an image, it might be necessary to store the image array as a variable that could be passed around within the application. Alternatively, it might be necessary to return information that the user entered in a text widget. Such information is known as *application state information,* and in IDL it often takes the form of a structure.

As an example, figure 9.8 shows a dialog box that prompts the user to enter his or her name and returns the name as a string variable. The following procedures should be stored in a source file named `wgetname.pro` in the order shown:

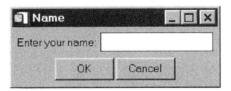

Figure 9.8 A dialog box for entering a name.

```
PRO WGETNAME_EVENT, EVENT

print, 'Event detected'

;- Get state information
widget_control, event.top, get_uvalue=infoptr
info = *infoptr

;- Identify widget which caused the event
widget_control, event.id, get_uvalue=widget
help, widget

;- Handle events
if (widget eq 'Text') or (widget eq 'OK') then begin
  widget_control, info.text, get_value=name
  info.name = name
  info.status = 'OK'
endif else begin
  info.name = ''
  info.status = 'Cancel'
endelse

;- Save state information
*infoptr = info

;- Destroy the widget hierarchy
widget_control, event.top, /destroy

END

PRO WGETNAME_CLEANUP, ID

print, 'Cleaning up'

;- Get state information
widget_control, id, get_uvalue=infoptr
info = *infoptr

;- Save result
result = {name:info.name, status:info.status}
*infoptr = result

END
```

```
PRO WGETNAME, NAME, STATUS

print, 'Creating widgets'

;- Create top level base
device, get_screen_size=screen_size
xoffset = screen_size[0] / 3
yoffset = screen_size[1] / 3
tlb = widget_base(column=1, title='Name', $
  xoffset=xoffset, yoffset=yoffset, tlb_frame_attr=1)

;- Create text entry widgets
tbase = widget_base(tlb, row=1)
label = widget_label(tbase, value='Enter your name: ')
text  = widget_text(tbase, uvalue='Text', /editable)

;- Create button widgets
bbase = widget_base(tlb, row=1, /align_center)
bsize = 75
butta = widget_button(bbase, value='OK', $
  uvalue='OK', xsize=bsize)
buttb = widget_button(bbase, value='Cancel', $
  uvalue='Cancel', xsize=bsize)

;- Realize widgets
widget_control, tlb, /realize

;- Create and store state information
info = {text:text, name:'', status:'Cancel'}
infoptr = ptr_new(info)
widget_control, tlb, set_uvalue=infoptr

;- Manage events
xmanager, 'wgetname', tlb, cleanup='wgetname_cleanup'

;- Get result
result = *infoptr
ptr_free, infoptr
name = result.name
status = result.status

END
```

If you type your name and then hit the Enter key, output similar to the following will be displayed:

```
IDL> .compile wgetname
IDL> wgetname, name, status
Creating widgets
Event detected
WIDGET          STRING      = 'Text'
Cleaning up
IDL> help, name, status
NAME            STRING      = 'Liam Gumley'
STATUS          STRING      = 'OK'
```

You can also try typing your name and then pressing the OK or Cancel buttons, or closing the dialog using the system menu. Note how the application blocks the command line while it is running, which, in this case, is appropriate behavior for a dialog box that requests the user to enter a name. An application of this type is known as a *modal application*. This example has three important features that are worthy of further examination.

First, you will notice that information about the state of the application is contained in an anonymous structure. The structure in this example contains the identifier of the text field widget (text), a string variable containing the name entered by the user (name), and a string variable containing the final status of the application (status). The structure is stored via a pointer (infoptr), and the pointer itself is stored in the user value of the top-level base (tlb). Recall that when an event occurs, an event structure containing the field TOP is passed to the event handler (TOP is the identifier of the top-level base containing the widget that caused the event). Thus an event handler can easily retrieve the user value (infoptr) of the top-level base, and therefore the contents of the application state information structure. In this example, the application state information structure is used to share information between the main procedure (wgetname) and the event handler (wgetname_event), and also to package the return values in the cleanup procedure (wgetname_cleanup).

Second, the event handler in this example (wgetname_event) utilizes widget user values to identify the widget that caused the event. After obtaining the application state information (info) from the top-level base (event.top), the event handler obtains the user value of the widget that caused the event. If the user value obtained matches the user value of the text widget or OK button widgets, the name is extracted from the text field by calling `widget_control`, and the status string is set to `'OK'`. If any other widget generates the event, the name is set to the null string and the status string is set to `'Cancel'`. The application exits after it processes one event.

Third, this application uses a cleanup procedure (`wgetname_cleanup`) to package the information to be returned to the main procedure. The cleanup procedure is called when the top-level base is destroyed, either by the event handler (`wgetname_event`), or by the user clicking on the system menu close button. The cleanup procedure is a convenient place to clean up anything that is no longer required, such as any pointers contained in the state information structure, and to package results for return to the main procedure.

Tip Avoid using `common` blocks to store application state information for GUI applications. In particular, do not store widget identifiers in a common block to enable an event handler to determine which widget caused an event. This technique should be avoided because it is difficult to keep inventing unique variable names for widget identifiers, and the use of a common block implies that only one instance of the application can be active at any time.

Multiple Instances of an Application

The previous example program only allowed one instance of itself to be active at any time and blocked input from the command line while it was running. However, there may be occasions when it makes sense for multiple instances of an application to run in the same IDL session, while still allowing input from the command line. Figure 9.9 shows a draw widget where the user may sketch a pattern as long as a mouse button is pressed. As an example, the following procedures should be stored in a source file named `wpaint.pro` in the order shown:

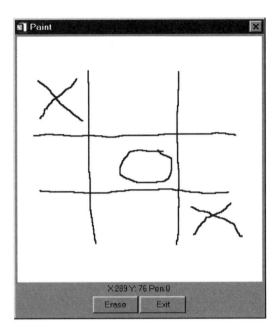

Figure 9.9 A sketching application.

```
PRO WPAINT_EVENT, EVENT

;- Get information structure
widget_control, event.top, get_uvalue=infoptr
info = *infoptr

;- Get widget identity
widget_control, event.id, get_uvalue=widget

if (info.pen eq 0) then $
  print, 'Event detected in top level base ', event.top

;- Handle events
case widget of

  'Draw' : begin

    ;- Handle button press events (start drawing)
    if (event.press gt 0) then begin
      print, 'Pen down'
      widget_control, event.id, draw_motion_events=1
      info.pen = 1
      info.x = event.x
```

```
          info.y = event.y
      endif

      ;- Handle button release events (stop drawing)
      if (event.release gt 0) then begin
        print, 'Pen up'
        widget_control, event.id, draw_motion_events=0
        info.pen = 0
      endif

      ;- If pen is down, draw from old location
      ;- to new location
      if (info.pen eq 1) then begin
        wset, info.winid
        plots, [info.x, event.x], [info.y, event.y], $
          /device, thick=2
        info.x = event.x
        info.y = event.y
      endif

      ;- Update the label widget
      label_text = string(info.x, info.y, info.pen, $
        format='("X:", i3, 1x, "Y:", i3, 1x, "Pen:", i1)')
      widget_control, info.label, set_value=label_text

    end

    'Erase' : begin
      print, 'Erasing'
      wset, info.winid
      erase
    end

    else : print, 'Unrecognized event: ', widget

  endcase

  ;- Update state information
  *infoptr = info

END

PRO WPAINT_EXIT, EVENT
```

```
widget_control, event.top, /destroy

END

PRO WPAINT_CLEANUP, ID

print, 'Cleaning up'
widget_control, id, get_uvalue=infoptr
ptr_free, infoptr

END

PRO WPAINT

print, 'Creating widgets'

;- Create base widget
device, get_screen_size=screen_size
xoffset = screen_size[0] / 5
yoffset = screen_size[1] / 5
tlb = widget_base(column=1, title='Paint', $
  xoffset=xoffset, yoffset=yoffset, tlb_frame_attr=1)

;- Create draw and button widgets
draw = widget_draw(tlb, xsize=400, ysize=400, $
  uvalue='Draw', /button_events)
label = widget_label(tlb, value='X: Y: Pen:', $
  /align_center, /dynamic_resize)
base = widget_base(tlb, row=1, /align_center)
buttsize = 75
butt = widget_button(base, value='Erase', $
  uvalue='Erase', xsize=buttsize)
butt = widget_button(base, value='Exit', $
  uvalue='Exit', xsize=buttsize, $
  event_pro='wpaint_exit')

;- Realize widgets and get draw window index
widget_control, tlb, /realize
widget_control, draw, get_value=winid
wset, winid
erase

;- Create and store information structure
info = {winid:winid, label:label, pen:0, x:-1L, y:-1L}
```

```
infoptr = ptr_new(info)
widget_control, tlb, set_uvalue=infoptr

;- Start managing events
xmanager, 'wpaint', tlb, $
  cleanup='wpaint_cleanup', /no_block

print, 'Done creating widgets'

END
```

Features of this application that enable multiple instances to run include the following:

- The graphics window index is stored for each instance, and is used to explicitly set the current graphics window before plotting occurs.
- Application state information is stored in a pointer, rather than a global variable.
- The no_block keyword is set when xmanager is called.

The application creates a nonresizable top-level base containing a draw widget, along with Erase and Exit buttons. Button press/release events are enabled in the draw widget when it is created. The graphics window index for the draw widget is obtained after the widgets are realized, and the information structure contains the window index, the "pen" status (0 = up, 1 = down), and the coordinates of the last event. The call to xmanager includes the no_block keyword, which tells IDL to return to the command line after starting the event manager. When the application is compiled and executed, the following output will be seen:

```
IDL> .compile wpaint
IDL> wpaint
Creating widgets
Done creating widgets
```

At this point, the widget creation procedure wpaint has finished. However, the event manager xmanager is now ready to intercept events from the GUI and route them to the event handlers wpaint_event or wpaint_exit. When an event is routed to wpaint_event, the application state information structure is obtained, and the widget causing the event is identified from its user value. A case statement is used to test for each widget. For the draw widget, an if statement checks if the event was a button press or release. If a button press occurs, the "pen" status is set to down, and the event location is saved. If a button release occurs, the "pen" status is set to up. If the pen is down, the graphics window index for this instance of the application is made the current window by calling wset, and a line is plotted from the previous event location to the current event location. When a mouse button is pressed and held down inside the draw widget and the cursor is moved, output similar to the following will be seen:

```
Event detected in top level base          78
Pen down
Pen up
```

When the Exit button is pressed, the wpaint_exit event handler is called. Its only function is to destroy the top-level base of the widget hierarchy, which in turn causes the cleanup procedure wpaint_cleanup to be called. The cleanup procedure is also called if the application is closed via the system menu.

Try starting two or three instances of wpaint from the command line. From the printed output, you will see that xmanager automatically determines which instance of the application is being manipulated, without requiring any special user-written code to check for switches between instances. Each instance of the application becomes a separate entity that remains independent until it is terminated.

Note   If you press the mouse button inside the draw widget, and then drag the cursor outside the draw widget, the draw widget still generates motion events.

9.5   A GUI APPLICATION

As a final example, a GUI application for displaying images is designed and constructed. Following the suggestion of Section 9.1, the first job is to define the task, identify the users, and list the requirements.

Task: Provide an interactive viewer for PseudoColor and TrueColor image arrays.

Users: This GUI will be suitable for users who would otherwise use `tv` or `tvscl` to display an image. The users of this GUI will understand how an image is represented in IDL (e.g., as a two- or three-dimensional array), but may not wish to understand all the subtleties of image display (e.g., 8-bit versus 24-bit display mode).

Requirements: The application must do the following:

1. Display a PseudoColor or TrueColor image supplied by the caller
2. Run in 8-bit or 24-bit display mode
3. Support IDL 5.0 and higher on Windows, MacOS, and UNIX
4. Allow multiple instances of itself to run at the same time while leaving the command line available
5. Allow itself to be resized, minimized, maximized, and closed
6. Maintain image aspect ratio
7. Automatically byte-scale the image from minimum to maximum data value
8. Allow the user to save the image to a JPEG, TIFF, or PostScript file
9. Allow the user to select or modify the color table
10. Provide a live display of the image data value underneath the cursor

The application will have a menu bar at the top where the user can select application options from pulldown menus. The focal point of the application will be a graphics window where the image is displayed. A text display of the image data value(s) under the cursor will complete the GUI.

Design Implications

Requirements 1, 2, 6, and 7 call for an application that displays Pseudo-Color or TrueColor images reliably in 8-bit or 24-bit mode with automatic image scaling while maintaining image aspect ratio. The `imdisp` procedure described in Chapter 7 is designed for just this task. Thus `imdisp` is required for this application.

Requirements 1, 2, 4, and 9 imply the user can modify the color table for the current instance of the application, regardless of how many instances exist on the screen. Thus, the application must handle color table changes intelligently and allow the user to specify which portion of the color table is to be used for the current instance of the application.

Requirement 5 means that a system menu must exist on the GUI to allow minimize and maximize functions. This requirement also implies that the GUI must support a system menu "Close".

Requirement 8 means that a "Save Image" capability must be available. The saveimage and screenread procedures described in Chapter 8 are designed for this purpose. In addition, PostScript output is required. The pson and psoff procedures described in Chapter 8 meet this requirement. Thus saveimage, screenread, pson, and psoff are required for this application.

Startup Procedure

The startup procedure for this application is named imgui, and the application will be called with the following syntax:

```
imgui, image
```

For example, an image of New York City may be displayed as follows, using the imdata function from Chapter 7 to load the example data file (the debug keyword causes diagnostic information to be printed while imgui is running):

```
IDL> image = imdata('nyny.dat', 768, 512)
IDL> imgui, image, /debug
IMGUI_GETCOLORS
IMGUI_DISPLAY
IMGUI startup is done
```

The startup procedure named imgui is responsible for checking the input arguments, verifying that the input array is a valid PseudoColor or TrueColor image, creating widgets, saving state information, and starting the event manager. The event-handler routines and service routines described in the next two sections must be available for the imgui to execute successfully. As in the previous example, you should store all the imgui procedures in one source file named imgui.pro, with the imgui procedure appearing last in the file.

```
PRO IMGUI, IMAGE, BOTTOM=BOTTOM, NCOLORS=NCOLORS, $
  XSIZE=XSIZE, YSIZE=YSIZE, TITLE=TITLE, TABLE=TABLE, $
  DEBUG=DEBUG

;- Display an image in a GUI window
```

```
;- Check arguments
if (n_elements(image) eq 0) then $
  message, 'Argument IMAGE is undefined'
if (n_elements(xsize) eq 0) then xsize = 640
if (n_elements(ysize) eq 0) then ysize = 512
if (n_elements(title) eq 0) then title = 'IMGUI Window'
if (n_elements(table) eq 0) then table = 0
if (n_elements(debug) eq 0) then debug = 0

;- Check image dimensions
imageinfo = size(image)
ndim = imageinfo[0]
if (ndim ne 2) and (ndim ne 3) then $
  message, 'IMAGE must be a 2D or 3D array'
dims = imageinfo[1 : ndim]
if (ndim eq 3) then begin
  index = where(dims eq 3, count)
  if (count eq 0) then $
    message, 'RGB images must have one dimension of size 3'
  truedim = index[0]
endif else begin
  truedim = -1
endelse

;- Check for widget support
if ((!d.flags and 65536) eq 0) then $
  message, 'Widgets are not supported on this device'

;- Limit draw widget size to 90% of screen size
device, get_screen_size=screen_size
draw_xsize = xsize < (0.9 * screen_size[0])
draw_ysize = ysize < (0.9 * screen_size[1])

;- Create widgets
tlb = widget_base(column=1, mbar=mbar, title=title, $
  /tlb_size_events)
fmenu = widget_button(mbar, value='File')
butt1 = widget_button(fmenu, value='Save JPEG...', $
  uvalue='JPEG', event_pro='imgui_saveimage')
butt2 = widget_button(fmenu, value='Save TIFF...', $
  uvalue='TIFF', event_pro='imgui_saveimage')
butt3 = widget_button(fmenu, value='Save PostScript...', $
  uvalue='PostScript', event_pro='imgui_postscript')
butt4 = widget_button(fmenu, value='Exit', $
```

```
  /separator, event_pro='imgui_exit')
imenu = widget_button(mbar, value='Image')
butt5 = widget_button(imenu, value='Refresh', $
  uvalue='Refresh', event_pro='imgui_refresh')
butt6 = widget_button(imenu, value='Colors...', $
  uvalue='Colors', event_pro='imgui_colors')
if (ndim eq 3) then widget_control, butt6, sensitive=0
draw_id = widget_draw(tlb, $
  xsize=draw_xsize, ysize=draw_ysize, $
  uvalue='Draw', event_pro='imgui_draw', /motion_events)
base = widget_base(tlb, row=1, /align_center)
label_id = widget_label(base, value=' ', $
  /align_left, /dynamic_resize)
widget_control, tlb, /realize

;- Get window id, device name, and top level base size
widget_control, draw_id, get_value=draw_window
wset, draw_window
device = !d.name
widget_control, tlb, tlb_get_size=base_size

;- Get color information
version = float(!version.release)
if (version ge 5.1) then begin
  device, get_visual_depth=depth
endif else begin
  if (!d.n_colors le 256) then depth = 8 else depth = 24
endelse
if (n_elements(bottom) eq 0) then bottom = 0
if (n_elements(ncolors) eq 0) then $
  ncolors = !d.table_size - bottom

;- Create state information structure
info = {image:image, truedim:truedim, $
  bottom:bottom, ncolors:ncolors, debug:debug, $
  draw_xsize:draw_xsize, draw_ysize:draw_ysize, $
  tlb:tlb, draw_id:draw_id, draw_window:draw_window, $
  label_id:label_id, device:device, base_size:base_size, $
  version:version, depth:depth, $
  red:bytarr(ncolors), $
  grn:bytarr(ncolors), $
  blu:bytarr(ncolors), $
  out_pos:fltarr(4)}
```

```
;- Load entry color table and display image
loadct, table, bottom=bottom, ncolors=ncolors, /silent
imgui_getcolors, info
imgui_display, info

;- Store state information
infoptr = ptr_new(info)
widget_control, tlb, set_uvalue=infoptr

;- Start event manager
xmanager, 'imgui', tlb, $
  event_handler='imgui_tlb', cleanup='imgui_cleanup', $
  /no_block
if debug then print, 'IMGUI startup is done'

END
```

The imgui procedure does the following:

1. First, the input arguments are checked, and any undefined key-words have values assigned. Then, the input array dimensions are checked to ensure the input array is a valid PseudoColor or True-Color image. The system variable !d.flags is checked to ensure widgets are supported on the current graphics device. The size of the initial graphics window is limited to no more than 90 percent of the total screen size.

2. The top-level base (tlb) is created by calling widget_base, base resize events are enabled, a menu bar widget (mbar) is created, and a title is assigned. Normally bases do not generate events; however, setting the widget_base keyword tlb_size_events causes the base to generate an event when the base is resized, minimized, or maximized.

3. The menu bar entries are created by calling widget_button. The names of menu selections that invoke another GUI (e.g., Save JPEG) are followed by three periods by convention. The Exit button has an event handler explicitly named via the event_pro keyword, which will be called when the button generates an event. The /separator keyword causes a horizontal line to appear above the Exit button in the menu list. The "Colors..." entry in the Image menu is always created, but is desensitized (grayed out) if the image is TrueColor because color table modifications are not required in this case.

4. The draw widget (`draw_id`) is created by calling `widget_draw` with cursor motion events enabled to allow a live display of the image value under the cursor.

5. The application state information is assembled, including the draw widget identifier (`draw_id`), and the graphics window identifier (`draw_window`). The current graphics device name (`device`) and the top-level base size (`base_size`) are obtained. Color information about the current IDL session is then obtained, including the graphics display depth (`depth`), and default values for `bottom` and `ncolors` if necessary. The color information is obtained after the draw widget is realized because the size of the color table is not set until a graphics window is created in the current IDL session (and this might be the first window).

6. The state information structure (`info`) is created to hold all the information needed by the event-handling routines. The initial color table is loaded by calling `loadct`, and the color table values are obtained by calling `imgui_getcolors` (which is explained in the next section). The `bottom` and `ncolors` keywords identify a specific part of the color table to be used. The entire color table is used if the caller of `imgui` specifies neither the `bottom` nor `ncolors` keyword.

7. The initial image is displayed by calling `imgui_display` (which is explained in the next section).

8. The state information structure is stored via a pointer (`infoptr`) in the user value of the top-level base (`tlb`), and the event manager (`xmanager`) is invoked.

After `xmanager` is called, the startup procedure exits, and control is returned to the command line. In the background, `xmanager` begins processing events from this instance of the application. Rather than using one large event handler for all `imgui` widgets, separate event handlers are identified for each widget via the `event_pro` keyword when the widgets are created. This technique helps reduce the complexity of event handling in larger GUI applications.

Event-Handler Procedures

The event-handler procedures listed in Table 9.17 are responsible for taking action when events are generated by the widgets in the `imgui` application.

Table 9.17   `imgui` **event handlers.**

Procedure	Events handled
`imgui_tlb`	Resize events from top-level base
`imgui_saveimage`	Select events from "Save JPEG…" and "Save TIFF…" buttons
`imgui_postscript`	Select events from "Save PostScript…" button
`imgui_refresh`	Select events from "Refresh" button
`imgui_colors`	Select events from "Colors…" button
`imgui_draw`	Cursor motion events from draw widget
`imgui_exit`	Select events from Exit button*
`imgui_cleanup`	Destruction of top-level base†

* The `imgui_exit` procedure destroys the top-level base, causing `imgui_cleanup` to be called.
† The top-level base can be destroyed by selecting the Exit button, or by selecting the system menu "Close".

The event-handler procedures are now listed and described in the order shown in Table 9.17. The first procedure is `imgui_tlb`, whose purpose is to resize the draw widget when the top-level base is resized:

```
PRO IMGUI_TLB, EVENT

;- Get state information
imgui_get_state, event, info

if info.debug then print, 'IMGUI_TLB'

;- Get change in size of top level base
if (info.version lt 5.4) then begin
  xchange = event.x - info.base_size[0]
  ychange = event.y - info.base_size[1]
endif else begin
  widget_control, event.id, tlb_get_size=base_size
  xchange = base_size[0] - info.base_size[0]
  ychange = base_size[1] - info.base_size[1]
endelse

;- Set new size of draw window
info.draw_xsize = (info.draw_xsize + xchange) > 200
info.draw_ysize = (info.draw_ysize + ychange) > 200
widget_control, info.draw_id, $
  xsize=info.draw_xsize, ysize=info.draw_ysize
```

```
;- Store new top level base size and display image
widget_control, event.top, tlb_get_size=base_size
info.base_size = base_size
imgui_display, info

;- Set state information
imgui_set_state, event, info

END
```

The first step is to get the application state information by calling imgui_get_state (which is described in the next section). Next, the change in the size of the top-level base is obtained (xchange and ychange). The method used is version dependent because prior to IDL 5.4, the top-level base size obtained by calling widget_control with the tlb_get_size keyword returned a base height that did not include the height of the menu bar. The new size of the draw widget is then computed (info.draw_xsize, info.draw_ysize), and the draw widget is resized by calling widget_control. The updated base size is confirmed by calling widget_control, and then saved in the state information structure (info.base_size). Finally the image is displayed in the resized window by calling imgui_display, and the application state information is updated.

The next procedure is imgui_saveimage, whose purpose is to save a copy of the displayed image in a bitmap output file:

```
PRO IMGUI_SAVEIMAGE, EVENT

;- Get state information
imgui_get_state, event, info

if info.debug then print, 'IMGUI_SAVEIMAGE'

;- Save a bitmap image
filename = dialog_pickfile(/write, group=event.top)
if (filename ne '') then begin
  widget_control, event.top, hourglass=1
  widget_control, event.id, get_uvalue=widget
  wset, info.draw_window
  case widget of
    'JPEG' : saveimage, filename, /quiet, /jpeg
    'TIFF' : saveimage, filename, /quiet, /tiff
  endcase
  widget_control, event.top, hourglass=0
```

```
endif

END
```

After obtaining the application state information (info), the user is prompted for an output file name by calling dialog_pickfile. If a valid filename is entered, an hourglass cursor is displayed, and the user value of the widget causing the event is obtained. The draw widget becomes the current graphics window by calling wset with the window identifier (info.draw_window). The image is saved in the appropriate format by calling saveimage (from Chapter 8). Finally the hourglass cursor is deactivated.

The next procedure is imgui_postscript, whose purpose is to render the image to a PostScript output file:

```
PRO IMGUI_POSTSCRIPT, EVENT

;- Get state information
imgui_get_state, event, info

if info.debug then print, 'IMGUI_POSTSCRIPT'

;- Save a PostScript rendering of the image
filename = dialog_pickfile(/write, group=event.top)
if (filename ne '') then begin
  widget_control, event.top, hourglass=1
  pson, filename=filename, margin=1.0, /quiet
  imgui_display, info
  psoff, /quiet
  widget_control, event.top, hourglass=0
endif

END
```

After obtaining the application state information (info), the user is prompted for an output file name by calling dialog_pickfile. If a valid filename is entered, an hourglass cursor is displayed. Then PostScript output is selected by calling pson, the image is displayed by calling imgui_display, and the PostScript output file is closed by calling psoff (pson and psoff are from Chapter 8). Finally the hourglass cursor is deactivated.

The next procedure is imgui_refresh, whose purpose is to redisplay the image when the Refresh button is selected:

```
PRO IMGUI_REFRESH, EVENT

;- Get state information
imgui_get_state, event, info

if info.debug then print, 'IMGUI_REFRESH'

;- Refresh image
imgui_display, info

END
```

This procedure simply obtains the application state information and
then calls imgui_display. The display procedure imgui_display is kept
separate so it can be called as a service procedure by other event handlers
(e.g., by imgui_tlb).

The next procedure is imgui_colors, whose purpose is to invoke the
xloadct color table GUI when the Colors button is selected:

```
PRO IMGUI_COLORS, EVENT

;- Get state information
imgui_get_state, event, info

if info.debug then print, 'IMGUI_COLORS'

;- Start color table widget
if (info.version ge 5.2) then begin
  tvlct, info.red, info.grn, info.blu, info.bottom
  xloadct, bottom=info.bottom, ncolors=info.ncolors, $
    group=event.top, updatecallback='imgui_xloadct', $
    updatecbdata=event
endif else begin
  result = dialog_message('IDL 5.2 or higher required', $
    dialog_parent=event.id)
endelse

END
```

First the application state information is obtained. Then if the IDL version is 5.2 or greater, the color table for this image is loaded, and xloadct
is invoked. The name of the service procedure (imgui_xloadct) to be
called by xloadct when it modifies the color table is passed by the

updatecallback keyword. The event structure (event) is passed via the updatecbdata keyword so that xloadct can update the color table stored in the application state information structure. If the IDL version if less than 5.2, a dialog is displayed to notifiy the user that color table changes are not supported.

The next procedure is imgui_draw, whose purpose is to provide a live display of the image value at the cursor location when motion is detected inside the draw widget:

```
PRO IMGUI_DRAW, EVENT

;- Get state information
imgui_get_state, event, info, /no_copy

;- Convert event device coordinates to normal coordinates
xn = float(event.x) / float(info.draw_xsize)
yn = float(event.y) / float(info.draw_ysize)
xn = (xn > 0.0) < 1.0
yn = (yn > 0.0) < 1.0

;- Convert to fraction of image size
xf = (xn - info.out_pos[0]) / $
  (info.out_pos[2] - info.out_pos[0])
yf = (yn - info.out_pos[1]) / $
  (info.out_pos[3] - info.out_pos[1])

;- Update image value
if (xf gt 0.0) and (xf lt 1.0) and $
  (yf gt 0.0) and (yf lt 1.0) then begin

  ;- Get image size
  dims = size(info.image, /dimensions)
  case info.truedim of
    -1 : dims = dims
     0 : dims = [dims[1], dims[2]]
     1 : dims = [dims[0], dims[2]]
     2 : dims = [dims[0], dims[1]]
  endcase

  ;- Convert fractional image size to array indices
  xi = floor(xf * dims[0])
  yi = floor(yf * dims[1])
  xi = (xi > 0L) < (dims[0] - 1L)
```

```
yi = (yi > 0L) < (dims[1] - 1L)

;- Get image data
case info.truedim of
  -1 : data = info.image[xi, yi]
   0 : data = info.image[*, xi, yi]
   1 : data = info.image[xi, *, yi]
   2 : data = info.image[xi, yi, *]
endcase

;- Update label widget
if (size(data, /tname) eq 'BYTE') then data = fix(data)
label = string('X:', strcompress(xi), $
  ', Y:', strcompress(yi), ', Data:')
for index = 0L, n_elements(data) - 1L do $
  label = label + strcompress(data[index])
widget_control, info.label_id, set_value=label

endif

;- Restore state information
imgui_set_state, event, info, /no_copy

END
```

After obtaining application state information, the normal coordinates (xn, yn) of the motion event are computed. Since motion events continue to occur when a mouse button is clicked inside the draw widget and then dragged outside the draw widget, the normal coordinates of the motion event are limited to the range 0.0 to 1.0. Next, the normal coordinates are converted to fractions of the image width and height (xf, yf). If the coordinates lie within the image boundaries, the procedure prepares to obtain the image value. First the image width and height (dims) are found. Then the array indices (xi, yi) corresponding to the event coordinates are computed, and the image value (data) is obtained from the image array. The event location (in array index units) along with the data value are then displayed in the label widget by calling widget_control. Finally, the state information structure (info) is restored (see the description of imgui_get_state and imgui_set_state in the next section for more details on the no_copy keyword).

The next procedure is imgui_exit, whose purpose is to destroy the top-level base (and therefore the entire widget hierarchy) when the Exit button is selected. Note that this procedure is *not* called when a system menu "Close" occurs:

```
PRO IMGUI_EXIT, EVENT

;- Get state information
imgui_get_state, event, info

if info.debug then print, 'IMGUI_EXIT'

;- Destroy the top level base
widget_control, event.top, /destroy

END
```

After obtaining the application state information, the top-level base is destroyed by calling widget_control. This causes the cleanup procedure (imgui_cleanup) to be called.

The next procedure is imgui_cleanup, which is called when the top-level base is destroyed either when imgui_exit is called, or a system menu "Close" occurs. In this example, the purpose of imgui_cleanup is to free any pointers used by the application; however, the cleanup procedure may also be used to package result values.

```
PRO IMGUI_CLEANUP, ID

;- Get information structure
widget_control, id, get_uvalue=infoptr
info = *infoptr

if info.debug then print, 'IMGUI_CLEANUP'

;- Free the information pointer
ptr_free, infoptr

END
```

The application state information is obtained from the single argument (id), which is the identifier of the widget that is dying (note that id is *not* an event structure). The pointer (infoptr) containing the state information is freed, and the procedure ends, at which point the GUI application exits.

Table 9.18 imgui **service procedures.**

Procedure	Purpose
imgui_get_state	Get application state information
imgui_set_state	Set application state information
imgui_getcolors	Get current color table
imgui_display	Load current color table, and display image
imgui_xloadct	Update color table, and display image when color table is modified

Service Procedures

The service procedures listed in Table 9.18 are used to manage application state information and the color table, and to display the image.

The event handler procedures are now listed and described in the order shown in Table 9.18. The first procedures shown are imgui_get_state and imgui_set_state, which are used to retrieve and store the application state information structure:

```
PRO IMGUI_GET_STATE, EVENT, INFO, NO_COPY=NO_COPY

;- Get pointer
widget_control, event.top, get_uvalue=infoptr
if (ptr_valid(infoptr) eq 0) then $
  message, 'State information pointer is invalid'

;- Get state information structure
if (n_elements(*infoptr) eq 0) then $
  message, 'State information structure is undefined'
if keyword_set(no_copy) then begin
  info = temporary(*infoptr)
endif else begin
  info = *infoptr
endelse

END

PRO IMGUI_SET_STATE, EVENT, INFO, NO_COPY=NO_COPY

;- Get pointer
widget_control, event.top, get_uvalue=infoptr
if (ptr_valid(infoptr) eq 0) then $
```

```
      message, 'State information pointer is invalid'

;- Set state information structure
if (n_elements(info) eq 0) then $
  message, 'State information structure is undefined'
if keyword_set(no_copy) then begin
  *infoptr = temporary(info)
endif else begin
  *infoptr = info
endelse

END
```

In both procedures, the information pointer is obtained from the top-level base (event.top) and checked for validity. Then the state information structure (info) is either obtained (imgui_get_state) or set (imgui_set_state). If the no_copy keyword is set, the structure is transferred directly between the pointer (infoptr) and the variable (info). This is more efficient than copying the structure, especially for events that are likely to occur many times, such as cursor motion events in this example. However, a side effect is that when the state information is obtained by calling imgui_get_state with the no_copy keyword set, the state information stored in the pointer becomes undefined, and it must therefore be restored at the end of the event-handler procedure (see the imgui_draw procedure for an example). The error checking built into these procedures makes it easier to track down cases where you may have forgotten to restore the information structure at the end of an event handler.

The next procedure is imgui_getcolors, whose purpose is to get the current color table for this instance of imgui, and store it in the application state information structure:

```
PRO IMGUI_GETCOLORS, INFO

if info.debug then print, 'IMGUI_GETCOLORS'

;- Get the current color table
tvlct, red, grn, blu, info.bottom, /get
info.red = red[0 : (info.ncolors - 1)]
info.grn = grn[0 : (info.ncolors - 1)]
info.blu = blu[0 : (info.ncolors - 1)]

END
```

The red, green, and blue color table vectors (info.red, info.grn, info.blu) are obtained by calling tvlct and are stored in the information structure (info). Maintaining a color table for each instance of imgui allows multiple instances to run simultaneously, each with its own color table.

The next procedure is imgui_display, whose purpose is to display the image:

```
PRO IMGUI_DISPLAY, INFO

if info.debug then print, 'IMGUI_DISPLAY'

;- Load color table and display image
widget_control, info.tlb, hourglass=1
tvlct, info.red, info.grn, info.blu, info.bottom
if (!d.name eq info.device) then begin
  wset, info.draw_window
  erase, info.bottom
endif
imdisp, info.image, bottom=info.bottom, $
  ncolors=info.ncolors, out_pos=out_pos, margin=0.0
info.out_pos = out_pos
widget_control, info.tlb, hourglass=0

END
```

First, an hourglass cursor is displayed; then the color table for this instance of imgui is loaded by calling tvlct. If the current graphics device (!d.name) is the same as the graphics device that was active when imgui started (info.device), the draw widget is made the current graphics window by calling wset, and the screen is erased (this check is necessary in case the PostScript graphics device is selected). Then the image is displayed by calling imdisp (from Chapter 7) with the out_pos keyword returning the position of the displayed image (which is required by imgui_draw). Finally the output position is stored in the information structure (info), and the hourglass cursor is deactivated.

The next procedure is imgui_xloadct, which is called internally by the xloadct procedure whenever the user modifies the color table via the xloadct GUI. The purpose of imgui_xloadct is to update the color table values stored by imgui, and redisplay the image if necessary.

```
PRO IMGUI_XLOADCT, DATA=EVENT

;- Get state information
imgui_get_state, event, info

if info.debug then print, 'IMGUI_XLOADCT'

;- Get color table and display image
imgui_getcolors, info
if (info.depth gt 8) then imgui_display, info

;- Set state information
imgui_set_state, event, info

END
```

The updated color table is stored in the information structure (info) by calling imgui_getcolors. If IDL is running in 24-bit mode, the image is redisplayed by calling imgui_display. If IDL is running in 8-bit mode, the color table changes are seen immediately in the image and no redisplay is necessary.

Compiling and Running imgui

To compile and run the imgui application successfully, the following procedures should now be contained in one source file named imgui.pro, with the imgui procedure last:

```
imgui_tlb
imgui_saveimage
imgui_postscript
imgui_refresh
imgui_colors
imgui_draw
imgui_exit
imgui_cleanup
imgui_get_state
imgui_set_state
imgui_getcolors
imgui_display
imgui_xloadct
imgui
```

To verify that the application compiles and runs successfully:

```
IDL> .compile imgui
IDL> imgui, dist(32), /debug
```

Setting the `debug` keyword causes diagnostic information to be printed while the application is running.

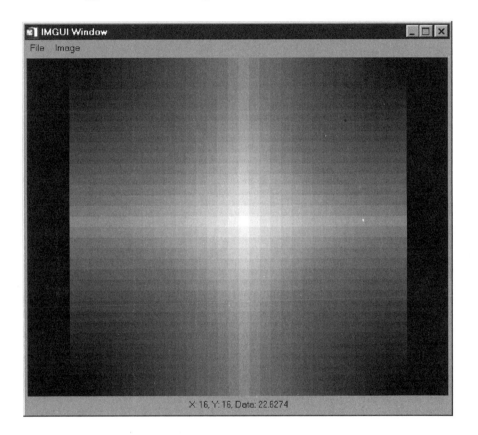

When you resize the window, the image will resize itself accordingly while maintaining aspect ratio. Try the menu options as well to see what imgui can do. To further demonstrate the capabilities of imgui, load these example images (the imdata function is shown in Chapter 7):

```
IDL> ctscan = imdata('ctscan.dat', 256, 256)
IDL> hurric = imdata('hurric.dat', 440, 340)
IDL> read_jpeg, filepath('rose.jpg', subdir='examples/data'), $
IDL> rose
```

Each image may be displayed in a separate imgui window:

```
IDL> imgui, ctscan
IDL> imgui, hurric
IDL> imgui, rose
```

If IDL is running in 24-bit mode, each image will maintain its own color table automatically. If you select "Colors..." for either of the first two images, only the color table for that image will be modified (remember that only one instance of xloadct can run at a time). The "Colors..." option is grayed out in the TrueColor (rose) image window because this image does not use the color table.

If IDL is running in 8-bit mode, the color table of the last image displayed takes precedence. However, selecting Refresh for any of the images redraws that image with the correct color table. If you wish to have separate color tables when IDL is running in 8-bit graphics mode, then use the bottom and ncolors keywords. For example, close any existing imgui windows and try the following:

```
IDL> ncolors = !d.table_size / 2
IDL> print, ncolors
IDL> imgui, ctscan, ncolors=ncolors, bottom=0
IDL> imgui, hurric, ncolors=ncolors, bottom=ncolors
```

Now when you select "Colors..." and modify the color table of either image, the color tables stay separate.

If you are using an IDL version prior to 5.2, you can still specify a color table for each image via the imgui keyword table:

```
IDL> imgui, ctscan, ncolors=ncolors, bottom=0, table=3
IDL> imgui, hurric, ncolors=ncolors, bottom=ncolors, table=13
```

IDL on the Internet

The Internet provides a rich source of information about IDL. The online community of IDL programmers is more than willing to share source code and advice, and it is often possible to find a procedure or function for a specific task, or to have a question answered in a short time. This appendix lists some of the most useful IDL resources on the Internet.

A.1 RESOURCES BY THE AUTHOR

The author's website includes the source code for all the example programs shown in the book, as well as samples of netCDF and HDF data files. Additional material is also available, including more IDL utility programs, specialized topics not covered in the book (such as resampling satellite images to maps), and a more extensive list of links to other IDL resources on the Internet. The author's website is at

```
http://www.gumley.com/
```

A.2 RSI INFORMATION

Product information about IDL (e.g., current supported platforms) and other products developed in IDL (e.g. ENVI, RiverTools) is available at

```
http://www.researchsystems.com/
```

Installable versions of IDL for all supported platforms may be downloaded from

```
ftp://ftp.researchsystems.com/pub
```

A searchable database of technical tips about IDL from the RSI support staff is available at

```
http://www.researchsystems.com/services/
```

A.3   NEWSGROUP

The IDL Usenet newsgroup is an active discussion forum for IDL programming issues. It is frequented by many expert IDL programmers who are willing to answer questions, often within a couple of hours:

```
comp.lang.idl-pvwave
```

A.4   LIBRARIES

The IDL Astronomy Library includes thousands of IDL procedures and functions developed by the astronomical community. This site also offers a searchable index, and a comprehensive list of links to other IDL-related websites and project-specific IDL libraries, including a library for reading and writing data in the Flexible Image Transport System (FITS) format:

```
http://idlastro.gsfc.nasa.gov/
```

The Applied Physics Laboratory at Johns Hopkins University has compiled a comprehensive general-purpose IDL library containing over 600 procedures and functions:

```
http://fermi.jhuapl.edu/s1r/idl/s1rlib/local_idl.html
```

A.5   SEARCHABLE LIBRARY DATABASE

This site at the University of Washington (maintained by Eric Deutsch) provides a searchable index of just about every publicly available IDL procedure or function. Type a routine name or a topic keyword and a list of all matching procedures and functions will be returned, along with a link to the source code for each routine:

```
http://www.astro.washington.edu/deutsch/idl/htmlhelp/
```

A.6 EDITORS

Nedit is a freely available point-and-click text editor for all major UNIX platforms (including Linux):

```
http://www.nedit.org/
```

The IDL Emacs mode provides a customized environment for editing and running IDL applications:

```
http://www.strw.leidenuniv.nl/~dominik/Tools/idlwave/
```

BBEdit is a point-and-click text editor for MacOS platforms. A free version is available at:

```
http://www.barebones.com/
```

A.7 POSTSCRIPT VIEWERS

On Windows and UNIX platforms the Ghostview and GSView applications may be used to view PostScript files created in IDL. In addition, the epstool application may be used to create Encapsulated PostScript files with preview images :

```
http://www.cs.wisc.edu/~ghost/
```

On MacOS platforms, the MacGhostView application may be used to view PostScript files:

```
http://www.kiffe.com/macghostview.html
```

To print PostScript files on MacOS platforms, the Drop*PS application may be used:

```
http://www.barebones.com/
```

A.8 PEOPLE

Many of the best IDL programmers maintain websites that provide high-quality IDL source code relevant to a range of disciplines.

Marc Buie provides a library of astronomy-specific and general-purpose routines:

```
http://www.lowell.edu/users/buie/idl/idl.html
```

Matthew Craig developed the TeXtoIDL package, which allows equation formatting in IDL using a TeX-like syntax:

`http://physweb.mnstate.edu/mcraig/TeXtoIDL/`

Eric Deutsch maintains the IDL Library Searchable Database, and also offers a collection of his own astronomy-related IDL routines:

`http://www.astro.washington.edu/deutsch/idl/`

David Fanning maintains a comprehensive IDL website that includes a collection of illustrative and useful IDL programs, a valuable list of IDL programming tips, information about his book *IDL Programming Techniques*, and many other useful resources:

`http://www.dfanning.com/`

Struan Gray has written an excellent tutorial on creating complex shaded surfaces in IDL:

`http://www.sljus.lu.se/stm/IDL/Surf_Tips/`

Mark Hadfield provides a collection of procedures and functions with an emphasis on objects:

`http://www.dfanning.com/hadfield/README.html`

Eric Korpela has developed a memory-mapped extension for IDL on UNIX platforms that allows the use of very large arrays:

`http://sag-www.ssl.berkeley.edu/~korpela/mmap/`

Craig Markwardt has implemented a robust set of generalized curve-fitting routines in IDL, and also provides a useful set of array and graphics utilities:

`http://cow.physics.wisc.edu/~craigm/idl/idl.html`

Martin Schultz provides a collection of general-purpose IDL utilities, along with specialized applications for the analysis of geophysical data:

`http://www.mpimet.mpg.de/en/misc/software/idl/`

J. D. Smith maintains the IDL Mode for Emacs:

`http://www.idlwave.org`

David Windt maintains a library of specialized optics routines along with a set of general-purpose routines:

`http://cletus.phys.columbia.edu/~windt/idl/`

Mathematical Routines

IDL includes a comprehensive built-in set of mathematical routines. The following tables list by problem category the name and a brief functional summary for each of the mathematical routines included in IDL version 5.4 (reproduced with permission from Research Systems, Inc.).

Table B.1 Complex numbers.

Name	Purpose
complex	Converts argument to complex type.
conj	Returns the complex conjugate of the argument.
dcomplex	Converts argument to double-precision complex type.
imaginary	Returns the imaginary part of a complex value.

Table B.2 Correlation analysis.

Name	Purpose
a_correlate	Computes autocorrelation.
c_correlate	Computes cross-correlation.
correlate	Computes the linear Pearson correlation.
m_correlate	Computes multiple correlation coefficient.
p_correlate	Computes partial correlation coefficient.
r_correlate	Computes rank correlation.

Table B.3   Curve and surface fitting.

Name	Purpose
comfit	Fits paired data using one of six common filtering functions.
crvlength	Computes the length of a curve.
curvefit	Fits multivariate data with a user-supplied function.
gauss2dfit	Fits a two-dimensional elliptical Gaussian equation to rectilinearly gridded data.
gaussfit	Fits the sum of a Gaussian and a quadratic.
grid_tps	Uses thin plate splines to interpolate a set of values over a regular two-dimensional grid, from irregularly sampled data values.
krig2d	Interpolates set of points using kriging.
ladfit	Fits paired data using least absolute deviation method.
linfit	Fits by minimizing the chi-square error statistic.
lmfit	Performs a nonlinear least-squares fit.
min_curve_surf	Interpolates over either a plane or a sphere with a minimum curvature surface or a thin-plate-spline surface.
poly_fit	Performs a least-squares polynomial fit.
regress	Computes fit using multiple linear regression.
sfit	Performs polynomial fit to a surface.
svdfit	Multivariate least-squares fit using SVD method.
trigrid	Interpolates irregularly gridded data to a regular grid from a triangulation.

Table B.4   Differentiation and integration.

Name	Purpose
crvlength	Computes the length of a curve.
deriv	Performs differentiation using three-point Langrangian interpolation.
derivsig	Computes standard deviation of derivative found by deriv.
int_2d	Computes the double integral of a bivariate function.
int_3d	Computes the triple integral of a trivariate function.
int_tabulated	Integrates a tabulated set of data.
lsode	Advances a solution to a system of ordinary differential equations one time-step H.
qromb	Evaluates integral over a closed interval.
qromo	Evaluates integral over an open interval.
qsimp	Evaluates integral using Simpson's rule.
rk4	Solves differential equations using fourth-order Runge-Kutta method.

Table B.5   Eigenvalues and eigenvectors.

Name	Purpose
eigenql	Computes eigenvalues and eigenvectors of a real, symmetric array.
eigenvec	Computes eigenvectors of a real, nonsymmetric array.
elmhes	Reduces nonsymmetric array to upper Hessenberg form.
hqr	Returns all eigenvalues of an upper Hessenberg array.
triql	Determines eigenvalues and eigenvectors of tridiagonal array.
trired	Reduces a real, symmetric array to tridiagonal form.

Table B.6   Gridding and interpolation.

Name	Purpose
bilinear	Computes array using bilinear interpolation.
grid_tps	Uses thin plate splines to interpolate a set of values over a regular two-dimensional grid, from irregularly sampled data values.
grid3	Creates a regularly gridded three-dimensional dataset from a set of scattered three-dimensional nodes.
interpol	Performs linear interpolation on vectors.
interpolate	Returns an array of interpolates.
krig2d	Interpolates set of points using kriging.
min_curve_surf	Interpolates points with a minimum curvature surface or a thin-plate-spline surface. Useful with contour.
polar_surface	Interpolates a surface from polar coordinates to rectangular coordinates.
sph_scat	Performs spherical gridding.
spl_init	Establishes the type of interpolating spline.
spl_interp	Performs cubic spline interpolation.
spline	Performs cubic spline interpolation.
spline_p	Performs parametric cubic spline interpolation.
tri_surf	Interpolates gridded set of points with a smooth quintic surface.
triangulate	Constructs Delaunay triangulation of a planar set of points.
trigrid	Interpolates irregularly gridded data to a regular grid from a triangulation.
value_locate	Finds the intervals within a given monotonic vector that brackets a given set of one or more search values.
voronoi	Computes Voronoi polygon given Delaunay triangulation.

Table B.7   Hypothesis testing.

Name	Purpose
cti_test	Performs chi-square goodness-of-fit test.
fv_test	Performs the F-variance test.
kw_test	Performs Kruskal-Wallis H-test.
lnp_test	Computes the Lomb Normalized Periodogram.
md_test	Performs the Median Delta test.
r_test	Runs test for randomness.
rs_test	Performs the Wilcoxon Rank-Sum test.
s_test	Performs the Sign test.
tm_test	Performs t-means test.
xsq_test	Computes chi-square goodness-of-fit test.

Table B.8   Linear systems.

Name	Purpose
choldc	Constructs Cholesky decomposition of a matrix.
cholsol	Solves set of linear equations (use with choldc).
cond	Computes the condition number of a square matrix.
cramer	Solves system of linear equations using Cramer's rule.
crossp	Computes vector cross-product.
determ	Computes the determinant of a square matrix.
gs_iter	Solves linear system using Gauss-Seidel iteration.
identity	Returns an identity array.
invert	Computes the inverse of a square array.
linbcg	Solves a set of sparse linear equations using the iterative biconjugate gradient method.
lu_complex	Solves complex linear system using LU decomposition.
ludc	Replaces array with the LU decomposition.
lumprove	Uses LU decomposition to iteratively improve an approximate solution.
lusol	Solves a set of linear equations. Use with ludc.
norm	Computes Euclidean norm of vector or Infinity norm of array.
svdc	Computes Singular Value Decomposition of an array.
svsol	Solves set of linear equations using back-substitution.
trace	Computes the trace of an array.
trisol	Solves tridiagonal systems of linear equations.

Table B.9   Mathematical error assessment.

Name	Purpose
check_math	Returns and clears accumulated math error status.
finite	Returns true if its argument is finite.
machar	Determines and returns machine-specific parameters affecting floating-point arithmetic.

Table B.10   Miscellaneous math routines.

Name	Purpose
abs	Returns the absolute value of argument.
ceil	Returns the closest integer greater than or equal to argument.
cir_3pnt	Returns radius and center of circle, given three points.
complexround	Rounds a complex array.
dist	Creates array with each element proportional to its frequency.
exp	Returns the natural exponential function of given expression.
floor	Returns closest integer less than or equal to argument.
imaginary	Returns the imaginary part of a complex value.
isnft	Performs integer bit shift.
leefilt	Performs the Lee filter algorithm on an image array.
matrix_multiply	Calculates the IDL matrix-multiply operator (#) of two (possibly transposed) arrays.
pnt_line	Returns the perpendicular distance between a point and a line.
poly_area	Returns the area of a polygon given the coordinates of its vertices.
primes	Computes prime numbers.
round	Returns the integer closest to its argument.
sph_4pnt	Returns center and radius of a sphere given four points.
sqrt	Returns the square root of argument.
total	Sums the elements of an array.
voigt	Calculates intensity of atomic absorption line (Voight) profile.

Table B.11   Multivariate analysis.

Name	Purpose
clust_wts	Computes the cluster weights of an array for cluster analysis.
cluster	Performs cluster analysis.
cti_test	Performs chi-square goodness-of-fit test.
kw_test	Performs Kruskal-Wallis H-test.
m_correlate	Computes multiple correlation coefficient.
p_correlate	Computes partial correlation coefficient.
pcomp	Computes principal components/derived variables.
standardize	Computes standardized variables.

Table B.12   Nonlinear equations.

Name	Purpose
broyden	Solves nonlinear equations using Broyden's method.
fx_root	Computes real and complex roots of a univariate nonlinear function using an optimal Müller's method.
fz_roots	Finds the roots of a complex polynomial using Laguerre's method.
newton	Solves nonlinear equations using Newton's method.

Table B.13   Optimization.

Name	Purpose
amoeba	Minimizes a function using downhill simplex method.
constrained_min	Minimizes a function using Generalized Reduced Gradient method.
dfpmin	Minimizes a function using Davidon-Fletcher-Powell method.
powell	Minimizes a function using the Powell method.

Table B.14   Probability.

Name	Purpose
binomial	Computes binomial distribution function.
chisqr_cvf	Computes cutoff value in a chi-square distribution.
chisqr_pdf	Computes chi-square distribution function.
f_cvf	Computes the cutoff value in an F distribution.
f_pdf	Computes the F distribution function.

gauss_cvf	Computes cutoff value in Gaussian distribution.
gauss_pdf	Computes Gaussian distribution function.
gaussint	Returns integral of Gaussian probability function.
t_cvf	Computes the cutoff value in a Student's t distribution.
t_pdf	Computes Student's t distribution.

Table B.15   Signal processing.

Name	Purpose
a_correlate	Computes autocorrelation.
blk_con	Convolves input signal with impulse-response sequence.
c_correlate	Computes cross-correlation.
convol	Convolves two vectors or arrays.
correlate	Computes the linear Pearson correlation.
digital_filter	Calculates coefficients of a nonrecursive, digital filter.
fft	Returns the Fast Fourier Transform of an array.
hanning	Creates Hanning and Hamming windows.
hilbert	Constructs a Hilbert transform.
interpol	Performs linear interpolation on vectors.
leefilt	Performs the Lee filter algorithm on an image array.
m_correlate	Computes multiple correlation coefficient.
median	Returns the median value of an array or applies a median filter.
p_correlate	Computes partial correlation coefficient.
r_correlate	Computes rank correlation.
savgol	Returns coefficients of Savitzky-Golay smoothing filter.
smooth	Smooths with a boxcar average.
ts_coef	Computes the coefficients for autoregressive time-series.
ts_diff	Computes the forward differences of a time-series.
ts_fcast	Computes future or past values of a stationary time-series.
ts_smooth	Computes moving averages of a time-series.
wtn	Returns wavelet transform of the input array.

Table B.16   Sparse arrays.

Name	Purpose
fulstr	Restores a sparse matrix to full storage mode.
linbcg	Solves a set of sparse linear equations using the iterative biconjugate gradient method.
read_spr	Reads a row-indexed sparse matrix from a file.
sprsab	Performs matrix multiplication on sparse matrices.
sprsax	Multiplies sparse matrix by a vector.
sprsin	Converts matrix to row-index sparse matrix.
sprstp	Constructs the transpose of a sparse matrix.
write_spr	Writes row-indexed sparse array structure to a file.

Table B.17   Special math functions.

Name	Purpose
beseli	Returns the I Bessel function of order N.
beselj	Returns the J Bessel function of order N.
beselk	Returns the K Bessel function of order N.
besely	Returns the Y Bessel function of order N.
beta	Returns the value of the beta function.
errorf	Returns the value of an error function.
expint	Returns the value of the exponential integral.
gamma	Returns the gamma function.
ibeta	Computes the incomplete beta function.
igamma	Computes the incomplete gamma function.
laguerre	Returns the value of the associated Laguerre polynomial.
legendre	Returns the value of the associated Legendre polynomial.
lngamma	Returns logarithm of the gamma function.
poly	Evaluates polynomial function of a variable.
spher_harm	Returns the value of the spherical harmonic function.

Table B.18   Statistical fitting.

Name	Purpose
comfit	Fits paired data using one of six common filtering functions.
curvefit	Fits multivariate data with a user-supplied function.
funct	Evaluates the sum of a Gaussian and a second-order polynomial and optionally returns the value of its partial derivatives.
ladfit	Fits paired data using least absolute deviation method.
linfit	Fits by minimizing the chi-square error statistic.
regress	Multiple linear regression.
svdfit	Multivariate least-squares fit using SVD method.

Table B.19   Statistical tools.

Name	Purpose
factorial	Computes the factorial $N!$.
hist_2d	Returns histogram of two variables.
histogram	Computes the density function of an array.
kurtosis	Computes statistical kurtosis of n-element vector.
max	Returns the value of the largest element of an array.
mean	Computes the mean of a numeric vector.
meanabsdev	Computes the mean absolute deviation of a vector.
median	Returns the median value of an array or applies a median filter.
min	Returns the value of the smallest element of an array.
moment	Computes mean, variance, skewness, and kurtosis.
randomn	Returns normally distributed pseudorandom numbers.
randomu	Returns uniformly distributed pseudorandom numbers.
ranks	Computes magnitude-based ranks.
skewness	Computes statistical skewness of an n-element vector.
sort	Returns the indices of an array sorted in ascending order.
stddev	Computes the standard deviation of an n-element vector.
total	Sums the elements of an array.
variance	Computes the statistical variance of an n-element vector.

Table B.20   Time-series analysis.

Name	Purpose
a_correlate	Computes autocorrelation.
c_correlate	Computes cross-correlation.
smooth	Smooths with a boxcar average.
ts_coef	Computes the coefficients for autoregressive time-series.
ts_diff	Computes the forward differences of a time-series.
ts_fcast	Computes future or past values of a stationary time-series.
ts_smooth	Computes moving averages of a time-series.

Table B.21   Transcendental functions.

Name	Purpose
acos	Returns the arc-cosine.
alog	Returns the natural logarithm.
alog10	Returns the logarithm to the base 10.
asin	Returns the arc-sine.
atan	Returns the arc-tangent.
cos	Returns the cosine.
cosh	Returns the hyperbolic cosine.
exp	Returns the natural exponential function of a given expression.
sin	Returns the trigonometric sine.
sinh	Returns the hyperbolic sine.
tan	Returns the tangent.
tanh	Returns the hyperbolic tangent.

Table B.22   Transforms.

Name	Purpose
blk_con	Convolves input signal with impulse-response sequence.
chebyshev	Returns the forward or reverse Chebyshev polynomial expansion.
convol	Convolves two vectors or arrays.
fft	Returns the Fast Fourier Transform of an array.
hilbert	Constructs a Hilbert transform.
hough	Returns the Hough transform of a two-dimensional image.
radon	Returns the Radon transform of a two-dimensional image.
wtn	Returns the wavelet transform of the input array.

Widget Event Structures

The event structures returned by the fundamental widgets in IDL are described in this appendix. Each event structure contains the fields ID, TOP, and HANDLER, as described in Chapter 9. This appendix defines the meaning of the widget-specific fields in each event structure.

It is possible for a given widget to generate more than one type of event. For example, base widgets can generate resize, kill request, and keyboard focus events. One way to distinguish between different event types is to examine the name of the event structure:

```
event_name = tag_names(event, /structure_name)
```

For example, the event structure generated by a base widget as a result of a resize event would have the name WIDGET_BASE.

BASE WIDGETS

Resize

```
{WIDGET_BASE, ID:0L, TOP:0L, HANDLER:0L, X:0L, Y:0L}
```

    X: New width of the base

    Y: New height of the base

Resize events are generated only by top-level bases that are created with the `tlb_size_events` keyword set. In IDL 5.3 and earlier versions, the height of the base does not include the height of a menubar, if one exists inside the base. This problem was fixed in IDL 5.4.

Kill Request

`{WIDGET_KILL_REQUEST, ID:0L, TOP:0L, HANDLER:0L}`

Kill request events are generated only by top-level bases that are created with the `tlb_kill_request_events` keyword set.

Keyboard Focus

`{WIDGET_KBRD_FOCUS, ID:0L, TOP:0L, HANDLER:0L, ENTER:0}`

`ENTER`: 1 if the base is gaining keyboard focus, or 0 if the base is losing keyboard focus.

BUTTON WIDGETS

Press, Release

`{WIDGET_BUTTON, ID:0L, TOP:0L, HANDLER:0L, SELECT:0}`

`SELECT`: 1 if the button was pressed, or 0 if the button was released.

Buttons normally do not generate events when released. However, exclusive and nonexclusive radio buttons generate events when pressed or released.

DRAW WIDGETS

Button Press, Button Release, Cursor Motion, Expose

`{WIDGET_DRAW, ID:0L, TOP:0L, HANDLER:0L, TYPE: 0, X:0L, Y:0L, PRESS:0B, RELEASE:0B, CLICKS:0}`

`TYPE`: Event type code (0: Button Press, 1: Button Release, 2: Cursor Motion, 3: Viewport Scroll, 4: Visibility Changed).

X: X device coordinate where event occurred.

Y: Y device coordinate where event occurred.

PRESS: Bitmask where the least significant bit represents the leftmost mouse button. A bit is set when the corresponding mouse button is pressed.

RELEASE: Bitmask where the least significant bit represents the leftmost mouse button. A bit is set when the corresponding mouse button is released.

CLICKS: 1 if the interval between double-clicks is greater than the time interval for a double-click event, and 2 if the interval between double-clicks is less than the time interval for a double-click.

Draw widgets normally do not generate events. If the draw widget is created with the button_events keyword set, events are generated when a mouse button is pressed or released over the draw widget. If the draw widget is created with the motion_events keyword set, events are generated when the cursor moves over the widget. Double-clicks in draw widgets generate two events: the CLICKS field returns a 1 on the first click and a 2 on the second click.

DROPLIST WIDGETS

Select

{WIDGET_DROPLIST, ID:OL, TOP:OL, HANDLER:OL, INDEX:OL}

INDEX: The zero-based index of the selected item.

LABEL WIDGETS

Label widgets do not return events.

LIST WIDGETS

Select Single or Multiple Items

{WIDGET_LIST, ID:OL, TOP:OL, HANDLER:OL, INDEX:OL, CLICKS:OL}

INDEX: The zero-based index or indices of the selected item(s).

CLICKS: 1 if the interval between double-clicks is greater than the time interval for a double-click event, and 2 if the interval between double-clicks is less than the time interval for a double-click.

Double-clicks in list widgets generate two events: the CLICKS field returns a 1 on the first click, and a 2 on the second click.

SLIDER WIDGETS

Release, Drag

{WIDGET_SLIDER, ID:OL, TOP:OL, HANDLER:OL, VALUE:OL, DRAG:0}

VALUE: The new value of the slider.

DRAG: 1 if event was generated during a slider drag, and 0 if the event was generated at the end of a slider drag.

Slider widgets generate drag events when the DRAG keyword is set on UNIX and OpenVMS platforms only.

TABLE WIDGETS

Insert Single Character

{WIDGET_TABLE_CH, ID:OL, TOP:OL, HANDLER:OL,
 TYPE:0, OFFSET:OL, CH:OB, X:OL, Y:OL }

OFFSET: Position of character after insertion (zero-based).

CH: ASCII value of the inserted character.

X: Column address of cell within the table (zero-based).

Y: Row address of cell within the table (zero-based).

Insert Multiple Characters

```
{WIDGET_TABLE_STR, ID:0L, TOP:0L, HANDLER:0L,
  TYPE:1, OFFSET:0L, STR:'', X:0L, Y:0L}
```

OFFSET: Position of text after insertion (zero-based).

STR: The text that was inserted.

X: Column address of cell within the table (zero-based).

Y: Row address of cell within the table (zero-based).

Delete Text

```
{WIDGET_TABLE_DEL, ID:0L, TOP:0L, HANDLER:0L,
  TYPE:2, OFFSET:0L, LENGTH:0L, X:0L, Y:0L}
```

OFFSET: Position of the first deleted character (zero-based).

LENGTH: Number of characters deleted.

X: Column address of cell within the table (zero-based).

Y: Row address of cell within the table (zero-based).

Select Text

```
{WIDGET_TABLE_TEXT_SEL, ID:0L, TOP:0L, HANDLER:0L,
  TYPE:3, OFFSET:0L, LENGTH:0L, X:0L, Y:0L}
```

OFFSET: Position of the first character selected (zero-based).

LENGTH: Number of characters selected (zero means no selection; i.e., cursor movement only).

X: Column address of cell within the table (zero-based).

Y: Row address of cell within the table (zero-based).

Select Cell

```
{WIDGET_TABLE_CELL_SEL, ID:0L, TOP:0L, HANDLER:0L,
  TYPE:4, SEL_LEFT:0L, SEL_TOP:0L, SEL_RIGHT:0L, SEL_BOTTOM:0L}
```

SEL_LEFT: Column index of leftmost selected cell (zero-based).

SEL_TOP: Row index of top selected cell (zero-based).

SEL_RIGHT: Column index of rightmost selected cell (zero-based).

SEL_BOTTOM: Row index of bottom selected cell (zero-based).

Cell selection events are generated when a range of cells are selected or deselected. When cells are deselected, the SEL_LEFT, SEL_TOP, SEL_RIGHT, and SEL_BOTTOM fields are set to −1.

Change Row Height

```
{WIDGET_TABLE_ROW_HEIGHT, ID:0L, TOP:0L, HANDLER:0L,
  TYPE:6, ROW:0L, HEIGHT:0L}
```

ROW: Row index (zero-based).

HEIGHT: Row height.

Note that there is no table event type 5.

Change Column Width

```
{WIDGET_TABLE_COLUMN_WIDTH, ID:0L, TOP:0L, HANDLER:0L,
  TYPE:7, COLUMN:0L, WIDTH:0L}
```

COLUMN: Column index (zero-based).

WIDTH: Column width.

Invalid Data

```
{WIDGET_TABLE_INVALID_ENTRY, ID:0L, TOP:0L, HANDLER:0L,
  TYPE:8, STR:'', X:0L, Y:0L}
```

STR: Invalid cell data converted to a text string (cell contents are unchanged).

X: Column address of cell within the table (zero-based).

Y: Row address of cell within the table (zero-based).

Keyboard Focus

```
{WIDGET_KBRD_FOCUS, ID:0L, TOP:0L, HANDLER:0L, ENTER:0}
```

ENTER: 1 if the table is gaining keyboard focus, or 0 if the table is losing keyboard focus.

TEXT FIELD WIDGETS

Insert Single Character

```
{WIDGET_TEXT_CH, ID:0L, TOP:0L, HANDLER:0L,
  TYPE:0, OFFSET:0L, CH:0B}
```

OFFSET: Position of character after insertion (zero-based).

CH: ASCII value of the inserted character.

Insert Multiple Characters

```
{WIDGET_TEXT_STR, ID:0L, TOP:0L, HANDLER:0L,
  TYPE:1, OFFSET:0L, STR:''}
```

OFFSET: Position of text after insertion (zero-based).

STR: The text that was inserted.

Delete Text

```
{WIDGET_TEXT_DEL, ID:0L, TOP:0L, HANDLER:0L,
  TYPE:2, OFFSET:0L, LENGTH:0L}
```

OFFSET: Position of the first deleted character (zero-based).

LENGTH: Number of characters deleted.

Select Text

```
{WIDGET_TEXT_SEL, ID:0L, TOP:0L, HANDLER:0L,
  TYPE:3, OFFSET:0L, LENGTH:0L}
```

OFFSET: Position of the first character selected (zero-based).

LENGTH: Number of characters selected (zero means no selection; i.e., cursor movement only).

Keyboard Focus

```
{WIDGET_KBRD_FOCUS, ID:0L, TOP:0L, HANDLER:0L, ENTER:0}
```

ENTER: 1 if the text field is gaining keyboard focus, or 0 if the text field is losing keyboard focus.

Widget Properties

The widget_control procedure described in Section 9.3 accepts many keywords for modifying widget properties, some of which are applicable only to certain widget types. The syntax for widget_control is

widget_control, id, [*keywords*]

where id is the identifier of the widget, and *keywords* are optional keywords that modify the properties of the widget.

The tables in this appendix show commonly used widget_control keywords for each type of widget. See the online help for widget_control for more information on each keyword. For definitions of the value of each widget, refer to Section 9.2.

Table D.1   `widget_control` **Keywords for Base widgets.**

Keyword	Purpose
/realize	Realize a widget hierarchy
/destroy	Destroy a widget hierarchy
map	Display (1) or hide (0) a widget hierarchy
iconify	Iconify (1) or display (0) a widget hierarchy
tlb_get_size	Return width and height of a top-level base*
tlb_set_title	Set title of a top-level base
tlb_get_offset	Get horizontal and vertical offset of a top-level base
tlb_set_xoffset	Set horizontal offset of a top-level base (default units: pixels)
tlb_set_yoffset	Set vertical offset of a top-level base (default units: pixels)

* Keywords with a tlb prefix accept any widget identifier as an argument. If the specified widget is not a base, the operation refers to the top-level base of the hierarchy containing the widget.

Table D.2   `widget_control` **Keywords for Button widgets.**

Keyword	Purpose
get_value	Get value of the widget
set_value	Set value of the widget
/input_focus	Give the button input focus
set_button	Set (1) or unset (0) a radio button

Table D.3   `widget_control` **Keywords for Draw widgets.**

Keyword	Purpose
get_value	Get value of the widget*
draw_xsize	Set the width of the widget
draw_ysize	Set the height of the widget
get_draw_view	Get the current location of the widget viewport[†]
set_draw_view	Set the current location of widget viewport

* The value of a draw widget is the graphics window index. The value is valid only after the draw widget has been realized, and cannot be set by the user.

[†] Used for scrolling draw widgets. The value returned is the X and Y position of the lower left pixel in the viewport.

Table D.4 `widget_control` **Keywords for Droplist widgets.**

Keyword	Purpose
set_value	Set value of the widget*
set_droplist_select	Set the index of the currently selected item[†]

* To get the value of a droplist widget (i.e., the array of list items), you must store the current setting of the droplist in a separate location, such as a program state information structure.

[†] To get the index of the currently selected list item, you must examine the `index` field returned in the droplist event structure.

Table D.5 `widget_control` **Keywords for Label widgets.**

Keyword	Purpose
get_value	Get value of the widget
set_value	Set value of the widget

Table D.6 `widget_control` **Keywords for List widgets.**

Keyword	Purpose
set_value	Set value of the widget*
set_list_select	Set index of the item to be highlighted
set_list_top	Set index of the item to be displayed at the top

* To get the value of a list widget (i.e., the array of list items), you must store the current setting of the list in a separate location, such as an application state information structure.

Table D.7 `widget_control` **Keywords for Slider widgets.**

Keyword	Purpose
get_value	Get value of the widget
set_value	Set value of the widget
set_slider_min	Set slider minimum value
set_slider_max	Set slider maximum value

Table D.8   widget_control **Keywords for Table widgets.**

Keyword	Purpose
get_value	Get value of the widget
set_value	Set value of the widget
table_xsize	Set number of columns in table
table_ysize	Set number of rows in table
format	Set table-formatting string
edit_cell	Put a cell into edit mode*
set_table_select	Select a range of table cells[†]
set_table_view	Set cell to be viewed at top left[‡]

* The cell is specified by a two-element vector of the form [*column, row*].

[†] The range of cells is specified by a four-element vector of the form [*left, top, right, bottom*].

[‡] The cell is specified by a two-element vector of the form [*column, row*].

Table D.9   widget_control **Keywords for Text widgets.**

Keyword	Purpose
get_value	Get value of the widget
set_value	Set value of the widget
/input_focus	Give the widget input focus
set_text_select	Select text within the widget*

* The characters to be selected are specified by a two-element vector of the form [*start, number*].

Graphics Device Properties

The system variable !d.flags is a long scalar that contains information about the current graphics device. Bits are set in !d.flags depending on whether the current graphics device has certain properties, as shown in Table E.1.

To determine whether the current graphics device has a certain property, apply a bit-wise and to the bit in question. For example, to test whether the device supports widgets:

```
IDL> if ((!d.flags and 65536) ne 0) then $
IDL>    print, 'Widgets are supported'
```

Table E.1   **Meanings of bits in** `!d.flags`.

Bit	Value	Device property
0	1	Has scalable pixels
1	2	Can output text at an arbitrary angle using hardware
2	4	Can control line thickness using hardware
3	8	Can display images
4	16	Supports color
5	32	Supports polygon filling with hardware
6	64	Hardware characters are monospace
7	128	Supports the `tvrd` function
8	256	Supports graphics windows
9	512	Prints black on a white background
10	1,024	Has no hardware characters
11	2,048	Does line-fill style polygon filling in hardware
12	4,096	Applies Hershey-style embedded formatting commands to device fonts
13	8,192	Is a pen plotter
14	16,384	Can transfer 16-bit pixels
15	32,768	Supports Kanji characters
16	65,536	Supports widgets
17	131,072	Has a Z-buffer
18	262,144	Supports TrueType fonts

Index